The Heavener Sub:
History Through the Miles

Barton Jennings

The Heavener Sub: History Through the Miles

The Heavener Sub: History Through the Miles
Copyright © 2022 by Barton Jennings

All rights reserved. This book may not be duplicated or transmitted in any way, or stored in an information retrieval system, without the express written consent of the publisher, except in the form of brief excerpts or quotations for the purpose of review. Making copies of this book, or any portion, for any purpose other than your own, is a violation of United States copyright laws.

Publisher's Cataloging-in-Publication Data
Jennings, Barton

The Heavener Sub: History Through the Miles
598p.; 21cm.
ISBN: 978-1-7327888-8-6

Library of Congress Control Number: 2022946388

Front cover photo by Barton Jennings
Back cover photo by Sarah Jennings
All interior photos by Barton Jennings unless otherwise noted.

Please send comments or corrections to sarah@techscribes.com

TechScribes, Inc.
PO Box 2199
Alma, AR 72921
www.techscribes.com

Printed in the United States of America

Dedication

To Mike Haverty,
who never hesitated to answer my questions.

Other books by Barton Jennings

History Through the Miles

Arkansas & Missouri Railroad: History Through the Miles
Alaska Railroad: History Through the Miles
Iowa Interstate Railroad: History Through the Miles
Everett Railroad: History Through the Miles
Tennessee Central Railway: History Through the Miles
Whitewater Valley Railroad: History Through the Miles
Oregon's Joseph Branch: History Through the Miles
Missouri & North Arkansas Railroad: History Through the Miles
Hennepin Canal Parkway: History Through the Miles
Idaho's Payette River Railroads: History Through the Miles
Delta Heritage Trail (Missouri Pacific's Wynne Subdivision): History Through the Miles
The Choctaw Route: History Through the Miles
The Railroads of U.S. Sugar: History Through the Miles

Textbook

The Basics of Transportation: Policies, Practices and Pricing – An Applied Perspective

Contents

What Is the Heavener Subdivision? 9
Development of the Heavener Subdivision 19
Passenger Service Over the Heavener Subdivision 35
Creating a Heavener Subdivision Route Guide 43
Route Guide for the Heavener Subdivision 47
Route Guide for the Fort Smith Branch 475
Route Guide for the Waldron Branch 523
About the Author 597

Acknowledgments

The author has been fortunate enough to know some of the employees who worked for the railroad over the last several decades. Additionally, he has had the pleasure to get to know a number of the people who have researched the railroad. These all deserve a thanks for their help.

A number of documents were also used in writing this book. It is amazing what can be found on the internet these days. Copies of the *Official Guide*, the annual reports of various state railroad and corporation commissions, Interstate Commerce Commission reports, and other such documents were great resources.

The Kansas City Southern itself produced numerous documents that are still available. These include timetables, track charts, lists of stations, contracts, and even its own magazine, which changed its name several times over the years. Related sources such as the *Arkansas Marketing and Industrial Guide*, *The Coal Dealers Blue Book*, local histories published by the Goodspeed Publishing Company, Sanborn Insurance Maps, and others were a great aid. Newspapers also reported heavily on the construction and operations of the Choctaw Route.

David Hoge is a master of newspaper research, and his collection of more than 3000 pages of railroad-related newspaper articles from Arkansas is a masterful source of information. He deserves thanks for sharing this resource. Books written by Boyd, Goen and others provided a good start, and the writings of Fred Frailey have provided good histories of the railroad over multiple decades.

Introduction

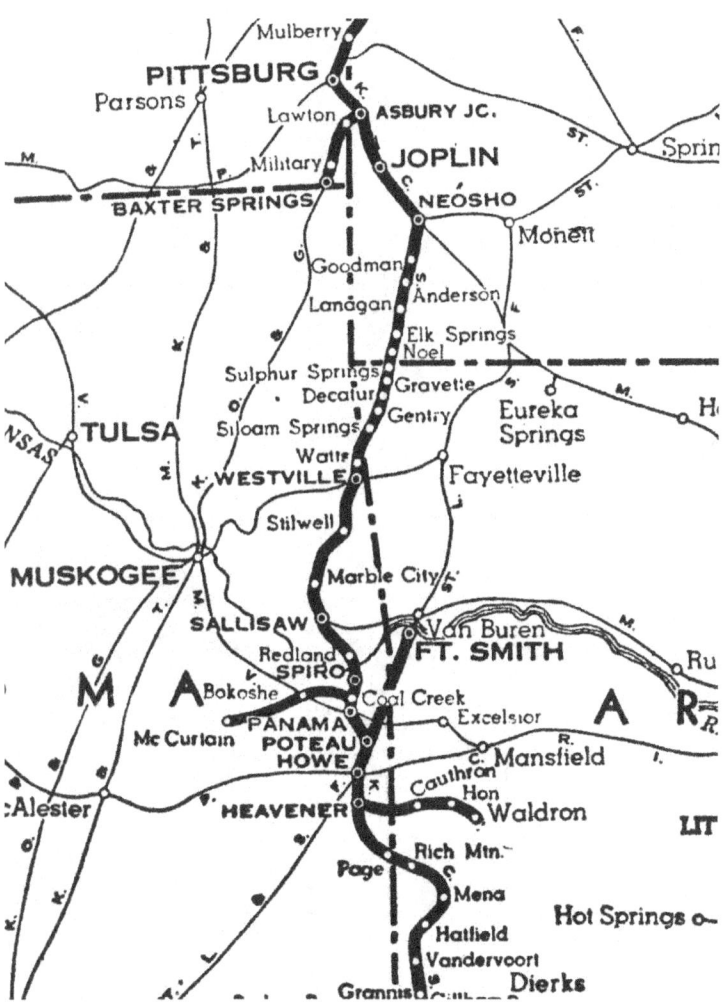

Map of the Second and Third Subdivisions from the *Kansas City Southern Lines Time Table No. 2*, effective January 5, 1964. Employee timetable from the author's collection.

The Heavener Sub: History Through the Miles

What Is the Heavener Subdivision?

The 209.8-mile-long Heavener Subdivision of the Kansas City Southern Railroad is one of the best known parts of the railway that stretches from Illinois to Mexico. Located between Pittsburg, Kansas, and Heavener, Oklahoma, this territory features numerous grades and curves thanks to the Ozark and Boston Mountains. It also features large shippers due to the region's poultry industry and several on-line power plants, but the route generally passes through small, rural communities. While the region is booming, few know the details about the railroad and the territory that it serves.

For the Kansas City Southern Railroad, the Heavener Subdivision connects the former shops and yard at Pittsburg, Kansas, with the yard and fueling complex at Heavener, Oklahoma. This route was once the Second Subdivision (Pittsburg to Watts, Oklahoma) and the Third Subdivision (Watts to Heavener). These two subdivisions were merged to create the Heavener Subdivision in 1985, a part of a number of operational changes across the railroad at the time.

Building what became the Heavener Subdivision required overcoming a number of challenges. The first was money, a typical challenge for most railroads. Much of this funding came from a group of east coast investors, plus investors from Europe. The second challenge was determining a route, and the donations and influence of cities like Pittsburg, plus the routes of several existing railroads, helped to solve this problem.

The third major challenge was building through Indian Territory, later eastern Oklahoma. The route from near Siloam Springs, Arkansas, all the way to Heavener, Oklahoma, required the permission of the United States Congress, as well as the Secretary of the Interior, since it was through the lands of the Cherokee Nation. This permission was received on February 27, 1893.

The final challenge was the Ozark and Boston Mountains along much of the Arkansas and Oklahoma route. One of the first questions most visitors have is about the name Boston Mountains, which covers northwest Arkansas and northeast Oklahoma. These mountains create a rugged terrain and have limited growth in the area. The word Boston was a slang word for a difficult task, and some sources state that it is the corruption of a French phrase for "rough road." Much of the area is part of the Ozark National Forest.

The Ozark Mountains actually include the Boston and St. Francois Mountains, plus the Boston, Springfield and Salem Plateaus. The source of the name Ozark is not clear, but it is often credited to the French term aux arcs which referred to the northernmost arc in the whole of the lower Arkansas River. Other sources state that the term means land of the arches for a number of natural bridges, or even "toward the rainbows" (French term arcs-en-ciel). No matter the sources of the names, the mountains are rugged. The phrase "its not how high the mountains are but how low the river valleys are" really explains the many grades on the railroad.

The Kansas City Southern (notice that in its home territory, it is nearly always *the* KCS, not just a generic NS, UP or CSX) is a unique north-south railroad operation that through hard work and high risks has connected the grain fields of the Midwest with the markets and manufacturing of Central Mexico. It has also become the favored route between the southeast and the booming Dallas-Fort Worth area with its Meridian Speedway. This service made it an

What Is the Heavener Subdivision?

acquisition target of railroads like Canadian National and Canadian Pacific during the early 2020s. As this is being written, the railroad is in its last days as an independent operation and will soon be part of the larger Canadian Pacific Kansas City (CPKC). With the plans of the merger, the Heavener Subdivision will only see more traffic and investment.

During early 2022, several company and contractor crews were busy replacing bridges across the railroad. These old beams at Marble City, Oklahoma, show just some of the line improvements underway at the time.

The Kansas City Southern

From the very beginning, the KCS was a maverick, building after all of the "great" railroads had been built and building in the wrong direction – north/south instead of east/west. Similar railroads such as the Clinchfield and Florida East Coast somehow captured the country's attention while the KCS just worked on. Like the others, it took one very powerful and determined individual to make the arrangements work. In the case of the KCS, that individual was former insurance salesman Arthur E. Stilwell.

With the experience he had gained building the Kansas City Suburban Belt Railroad just a few years earlier, he began laying the tracks of the Kansas City, Pittsburg & Gulf (KCP&G) in 1890. Even during the financial panic of 1893, when most Europeans pulled their funds from American ventures, Stilwell was able to raise $3 million by selling securities to the Dutch. This Dutch influence explains many of the names along the KCS such as the Queen Wilhelmina lodge, originally built by the railroad.

The route south out of Kansas City was designed to provide Gulf port access to farmers who were suffering from what they thought were extraordinarily high freight rates. The general route chosen was typically flat except for the Ozark and Ouachita Mountains in the Arkansas area. By buying and connecting lines already built to the south, Stilwell occasionally altered his intended route to the Gulf but was able to speed up the construction until the rails to Port Arthur, Texas, were completed on September 11, 1897. Stilwell's celebrations lasted only for a short while, however, as the KCP&G entered receivership before the turn of the century. On April 1, 1900, the Kansas City Southern Railway emerged from these financial difficulties. However, as often happened in those days, the founder Stilwell was no longer part of the scene. Instead, for the next dozen years, he would be president of the then-building Kansas City, Mexico & Orient Railway trying to link Kansas with a Pacific port in Mexico.

While the railway was built to give farmers in the Midwest a cheaper route to export markets, 1901 introduced the product which would make the KCS healthy through today. On the 9th of January in that year, oil was found near Beaumont, Texas, triggering a boom in refining and chemical production. Throughout much of this century, nearly 40 percent of the railroad's operating revenue has come from petrochemical movements.

What Is the Heavener Subdivision?

Because of the wealth provided by the grain export and oil businesses, the KCS looked to grow further. During the 1920s, the railway acquired control of the Missouri, Kansas & Texas Railway (Katy, later the Missouri–Kansas–Texas Railway) and the St. Louis Southwestern Railway Company (Cotton Belt) but was forced to sell them (at a good profit) by the Interstate Commerce Committee. These profits and the steady oil and grain revenues allowed the railroad to stay solvent throughout the Depression of the 1930s. Also because of this wealth, the railroad could afford to look around for other ways to expand.

Along the midsection of the line, there were numerous other opportunities to grow. Near Stamps, Arkansas, a logging railroad was developing around the connection with the aforementioned Cotton Belt. Started by William Buchanan in 1896, the railroad had grown to stretch from Alexandria, Louisiana, northward to Hope, Arkansas. Named the Louisiana & Arkansas Railway (L&A), a line was built into Shreveport, Louisiana, in 1910 to provide a connection to the KCS. Other railroads were also building in the area. To the south, the Louisiana Railway & Navigation Company (LR&NC) had been constructed at about the same time as the KCS. This railway connected Shreveport and New Orleans with the aid of some Mississippi River ferry service. The railroad had been built by William Edenborn, who had made his fortune by holding nail and barbed wire patents. The LR&NC also operated a former Katy line from west of Shreveport to near Dallas, Texas. This cluster of railroads in northern Louisiana and southern Arkansas attracted Arkansas utility giant Harvey C. Couch, who acquired and merged the railroads as the Louisiana & Arkansas. With Couch's business and political connections, the railroad prospered and certain key routes were finished or expanded.

The KCS and the L&A eyed each other, each knowing that a merger would extend their territories and provide numerous benefits. In May of 1939, Harvey Couch became KCS chairman, starting a strong relationship between the railroad and area electric utility companies. The two lines merged later that year and the name Kansas City Southern Lines was commonly used to signify this operation. Although merged, the L&A maintained some separation and it wasn't until 1995 that the railroad was fully acquired and merged by the KCS.

The merged railways produced a very profitable system. Under the tenure of William N. Deramus, just about the entire railroad received new rail, ties, and ballast. It was often bragged that no derailment or delay would be caused by the track. At the same time, dieselization was completed on the line in 1953. However, the prosperity of the KCS may have hurt it as heavy expenditures on track and equipment during the 1940-50s were followed by a decade or more of profit-taking. Beginning in the late 1950s, investment in the railroad almost stopped and a new management team acted as if the improvements would last forever. Thus, the 1970s were hard on the railroad as coal and grain traffic volumes exploded on an infrastructure which was near failure. Several years of almost total system collapse, especially on the curvy and hilly Heavener Subdivision, required the KCS to basically rebuild the railroad, resulting in what is today described as a top-class railroad. Heavy rail, new ties, and tons of ballast are the norm today.

The 1990s saw a sudden change in personality as the railroad was involved in a number of acquisitions. In 1994, KCS acquired the MidSouth Rail Corporation, taking the railroad into Mississippi, Alabama and Tennessee. The next year, the railroad bought into MexRail Inc., owner of the Texas-Mexican Railway Company (Tex Mex). Tex Mex operated between Laredo and Corpus Christi, Texas, and

What Is the Heavener Subdivision?

provided a link between the United States and Mexico via the International Bridge at Laredo. This was an important move as KCS began efforts to acquire the rights to operate a series of lines in northeast and central Mexico. Trackage rights were obtained to connect the Texas lines to the rest of the Kansas City Southern. In another year (1996), the railroad acquired the Gateway Western Railway Company. The Panama Canal Railway Company became the next part of the system in 1998.

Even with all of these changes, the KCS main trunk still runs along the Missouri/Kansas and Arkansas/Oklahoma borders from Kansas City to Shreveport, where the roots set out for New Orleans/Baton Rouge, Dallas, and Port Arthur. Traffic is an even mix of coal, chemicals, and grain with general merchandise making up only a small part of the shipments. The territory between Pittsburg, Kansas, and Heavener, Oklahoma, is known for the heavy freights that fight the steep mountain grades, making the Heavener Subdivision one of the most popular parts of the railroad for enthusiasts. This book and route guide is designed to provide a history of the Heavener Subdivision as well as a description of the railroad's operations.

The Heavener Sub: History Through the Miles

SECOND SUBDIVISION—Pittsburg to Watts

TIME TABLE No. 2 — Effective SUNDAY, JAN. 5, 1964

SOUTHWARD							NORTHWARD			
SECOND CLASS		FIRST CLASS		Capy, Other Tracks, S, T, PH, O, W, Y	Capacity of Siding	STATIONS	Mile-Post Location	FIRST CLASS		SECOND CLASS	
77 Merchandise Special	41 Manifest Freight	1 Southern Belle	15 Passenger				Office Calls	16 Passenger	2 Southern Belle	42 Manifest Freight	82 Manifest Freight
Daily	Daily	Daily	Daily					Daily	Daily	Daily	Daily
Lv 11.50ᴬᴹ	Lv 1.50ᴬᴹ	Lv 11.33ᴬᴹ / 11.35 / Lv 11.45ᴬᴹ	12.36ᴬᴹ / 12.40 / 12.55ᴬᴹ	Yard OWST		NORTH YARD	128.2	NY	Ar 4.32ᴬᴹ / 4.36 / Ar 4.15ᴬᴹ	5.27ᴬᴹ / 5.25 / 5.15ᴬᴹ	Ar 1.15ᴬᴹ	Ar 2.40ᴬᴹ
				Yard		PITTSBURG	129.2					
				Connection		A. T. & S. F. Crossing	129.4					
						St. L. & S. F. Rty. Crossing	129.5					
						St. L. & S. F. Crossing	129.6					
				Connection		St. L. & S. F. Crossing	129.7					
						K. O. G. JCT.	139.0					
12.13ᴬᴹ	2.20	11.55 / 11.58ᴬᴹ	1.08 / 1.10	Branch / 10	143	ASBURY ★	140.3		3.56	5.01	12.45	2.05
		12.04ᴬᴹ	1.17	11		GULFTON / St. L. & S. F. Crossing	147.2					
12.40	2.55	12.25	1.45	S Yard Connection	110	JOPLIN Union Depot	154.2	JO	3.40	4.45	12.25ᴬᴹ	1.45
						St. L. & S. F. Crossing	154.8					
						St. L. & S. F. Crossing	154.9					
1.03	3.25	12.46	2.06		134	DALBY	170.1		3.00	4.15	11.30ᴬᴹ	1.03
				Connection		St. L. & S. F. Crossing	172.7					
1.12	4.10	1.00	2.25	OYW Yard	76	NEOSHO	174.1	ON	2.55	4.10	11.20	12.50
1.28	4.28	1.09	2.37	17	111	McELHANY	180.8		2.37	3.53	11.03	12.36
1.34	4.35	1.13	2.42	75	62	GOODMAN ★	184.6		2.31	3.49	10.55	12.27
1.46	4.49	1.22	2.52	75	66	ANDERSON ★	191.7	RS	2.20	3.38	10.38	12.08ᴬᴹ
		1.27	2.57	20		LANAGAN	195.5		2.15	3.33		
2.06	5.10	1.38	3.08	41	135	NOEL ★	200.7	NE	2.06	3.24	10.15	11.45ᴬᴹ
		1.42	3.16			SULPHUR SPRGS. ★	205.3		1.58	3.16		
2.42	5.35	1.50	3.26	39	133	GRAVETTE ★	209.9	BO	1.52	3.10	9.50	11.25
2.53	5.48	1.58	3.35	25	36	DECATUR ★	217.0	DE	1.42	3.00	9.35	11.09
3.05	6.01	2.05	3.43	47	154	GENTRY	222.5		1.36	2.53	9.25	10.59
3.15	6.12	2.20	4.03	Yard	163	SILOAM	229.3	SX	1.27	2.45	9.10	10.45
Ar 3.30ᴬᴹ	Ar 6.30ᴬᴹ	Lv 2.30ᴬᴹ	Lv f 4.13ᴬᴹ	W Yard	251	WATTS ★	236.0	WS	Lv f 1.10ᴬᴹ	2.30ᴬᴹ	Lv 8.50ᴬᴹ	Lv 10.25ᴬᴹ
Daily	Daily	Daily	Daily			106.8			Daily	Daily	Daily	Daily
3.46	4.40	2.45	3.18			Time on Subdivision			3.05	2.45	4.28	4.18

Timetables from *Kansas City Southern Lines Time Table No. 2*, effective January 5, 1964. Second Division – Pittsburg to Watts, Third Division – Watts to Heavener. Employee timetable from the author's collection.

THIRD SUBDIVISION—Watts to Heavener

TIME TABLE No. 2 — Effective SUNDAY, JAN. 5, 1964

SOUTHWARD							NORTHWARD			
SECOND CLASS		FIRST CLASS		Capy, Other Tracks, S, T, PH, O, W, Y	Capacity of Siding	STATIONS	Mile-Post Location	FIRST CLASS		SECOND CLASS	
41 Manifest Freight	77 Merchandise Special	1 Southern Belle	15 Passenger				Office Calls	2 Southern Belle	16 Passenger	42 Manifest Freight	82 Manifest Freight
Daily	Daily	Daily	Daily					Daily	Daily	Daily	Daily
Lv 6.40ᴬᴹ	Lv 3.35ᴬᴹ	Lv 2.30ᴬᴹ	Lv f 4.13ᴬᴹ	W Yard	251	WATTS ★	236.0	WS	Ar 2.30ᴬᴹ	f 1.10ᴬᴹ	8.40ᴬᴹ	Ar 10.15ᴬᴹ
		2.41	4.23	46	168	WESTVILLE ★	244.4	VI	2.16	f 12.58		
		2.58	4.41	Yard	168	STILWELL ★	258.2	Z	1.59	f 12.41		
		3.06	4.50	8	153	LYONS	265.7		1.49	12.31		
		3.13	4.57	78		BUNCH	271.7		1.42	12.23		
		3.24	5.08	49	165	MARBLE CITY ★	281.4		1.31	12.12ᴬᴹ		
				Connection		Mo. Pac. Crossing	290.4					
		3.40	5.35	S160	116	SALLISAW ★	291.1	CK	1.20	11.59ᴬᴹ		
		3.49	5.44	6	164	GANS	299.2		1.04	11.41		
		4.03	5.59	Yard V	160	SPIRO	311.7		12.51	11.27		
				F.S.&V.B.Br. / 33 / Connection		COAL CREEK ★	315.7					
		4.09	6.05		62	PANAMA ★	317.3	JA	12.45	11.20		
						Mid. Valley Crossing						
		4.12	6.08		150	SHADY POINT	320.0		12.42	11.16		
						St. L. & S. F. Crossing	325.6					
		4.23	6.23	Y Yard Connection	56	POTEAU ★	326.4	AU	12.35	11.09		
						C. R. I. & P. Crossing						
		4.31	6.33	Connection Yard T	150	HOWE ★	333.0	BX	12.27	10.58		
Ar 9.50ᴬᴹ	Ar 6.30ᴬᴹ	4.40ᴬᴹ	6.40ᴬᴹ	Yard T OWS	Yard	HEAVENER	338.0	HV	Lv 12.20ᴬᴹ	10.50ᴬᴹ	Lv 5.00ᴬᴹ	Lv 6.40ᴬᴹ
Daily	Daily	Daily	Daily			102.0			Daily	Daily	Daily	Daily
3.10	2.55	2.10	2.27			Time on Subdivision			2.10	2.20	3.40	3.30

No. 1 is superior to No. 16
No. 77 is superior to No. 42 and No. 82

Hours of Telegraph Service
Watts, Howe, Heavener, Continuous.
Stilwell—7A-5P, Except Sat., Sun., Hol.
Sun., Hol.
Spiro, 7:30A-4:30P, Except Sat.,
Sallisaw, 8:30A-5:30P, Daily
Panama, 8:30A-5:30P, Except Sat., Sun., Hol.
Poteau, 8A-5P, Except Sun., Hol.

CONDITIONAL FLAG STOPS
Nos. 1 and 2 stop on flag at Westville, Stilwell, Spiro and Howe for revenue passengers to or from regular stops.
Nos. 15 and 16 stop on flag at Bunch, Marble City, and Panama for revenue passengers to and from regular stops.

Tracks not shown on face of time table.

	Mile No.	Car Capcy.
Baron	249	21
Marble City Qry. Spur	282	189
Okla. Creosoting Co.	290	Conn.
Redland	306	15

What Is the Heavener Subdivision?

Change has been constant on the Heavener Subdivision, as shown by KCS 4006, the railroad's SD70ACE "Veterans Day Salute" locomotive, sitting next to an old telephone box abandoned on the right-of-way of the Heavener Subdivision.

Kansas City Southern rail pass, front and back, circa 1916. From the author's collection.

Development of the Heavener Subdivision

The Heavener Subdivision of today consists of the historic Second and Third districts, known as subdivisions by the 1950s. The Second District covered North Yard at Pittsburg, Kansas, to Watts, Oklahoma. Meanwhile, the Third District covered Watts to Heavener, Oklahoma. Much of the early construction of these two districts seems confusing to many due to the number of companies involved, often with names of communities where the railroad never ran. Detailed reports from the Interstate Commerce Commission (ICC) attempted to clarify the construction history and to place a valuation on the route, and much of the detailed history is available due to this work.

The ICC stated that the track in this territory dates to the **Kansas City, Nevada & Fort Smith Railroad Company**, incorporated in Missouri on November 6, 1889. The company was organized by Arthur E. Stilwell, Edward L. Martin, and William S. Taylor, who were the officers and directors of the Missouri, Kansas & Texas Trust Company of Kansas City, Missouri. The goal of the railroad was to build a standard-gauge railroad from Kansas City "to the southern boundary of that State."

The three organizers of the company each played a major role in the organization, and the creation of the initial KCS mainline that included the Heavener Subdivision. William S. Taylor of Philadelphia represented many of the eastern bond holders, and was a known bond salesman and investor. Taylor was a director and trustee of the Guardian Trust Company, which financed the Kansas City, Pittsburg & Gulf Railroad Company. Besides being a director of the trust company, he held several titles among the railroads that eventually became the Kansas City Southern. This included being the president of the Texarkana & Fort Smith Railway in 1895, when Stilwell was listed as the first vice president.

Edward Lowe Martin was a businessman and politician. Based in Kansas City, Martin managed a number of businesses and owned the Kansas City Distilling Company. He also served as mayor (1873-1874) and then on the Board of Education (1875-1896) where he is credited with saving the city and school system when he personally paid off a series of municipal bonds in danger of default. Somehow Martin gained control of a franchise for building a belt railroad around Kansas City, but he lacked the funding required. His connections with Arthur E. Stilwell led to the creation of the companies needed to build The Kansas City Suburban Belt Railroad Company, and then the Kansas City, Pittsburg & Gulf Railroad. Edward Lowe Martin also developed area real estate, including the Kansas City neighborhood still known as Martin City.

Arthur Edward Stilwell was an insurance salesman who developed a coupon annuity life-insurance policy which paid the policy holder an income after a certain age. This guarantee return led to greater sales, and Stilwell used the cash to invest in real estate, businesses and railroads around Kansas City. Along with Martin and a few other local businessmen, he built The Kansas City Suburban Belt Railroad Company, and then the Kansas City, Pittsburg & Gulf Railroad. His promotion of the railroad as a low-cost ocean outlet for Midwest farmers won him fame and local support, but it was his European connections that allowed him to continue building the railroad in the 1890s when most Europeans had pulled their funds from American ventures following the Panic of 1893. In particular, he found a number of Dutch investors and named a series of stations along the line after them. Despite this, an unpaid

Development of the Heavener Subdivision

printing bill started a series of complaints which led the railroad into receivership in 1899, and the creation of the Kansas City Southern, but without Stilwell, who went on to build the Kansas City, Mexico & Orient Railway.

The first big change in the plans of the railroad dealt with the "Nevada" in the company's name. During the early 1890s, Franklin Playter, one of the leaders of the development of Pittsburg, Kansas, went to Kansas City to convince Arthur Stilwell to build his railroad through Playter's new city. Playter offered a right-of-way, financial help, and connections to the growing coal fields in the area. His efforts to partner with Stilwell were so successful that the railroad changed its name to **Kansas City, Pittsburg & Gulf Railroad Company** (KCP&G) on January 26, 1893. The KCP&G then located their primary shops at Pittsburg, bypassing Nevada, Missouri, completely. Additionally, the company's charter was amended "so as to permit the extension of the line by construction, purchase, or lease to the Gulf of Mexico, through the states of Missouri, Kansas, Arkansas, Texas, and Louisiana."

As with many railroads, a number of companies were created to handle the construction. One of these was the **Kansas City, Pittsburg & Western Railroad Company**, which was incorporated on July 22, 1892, to "build, construct, maintain, and operate a standard-gauge line of railroad, and telegraph lines" southward from Kansas City for an estimated 250 miles. By 1893, the railroad had built 9.5 miles of track from "a point at Seventh Street and Michigan Avenue in the city of Pittsburg" to "the boundary line between Kansas and Missouri." The railroad company was at first simply operated by the KCP&G, but was then sold to the Gulf on September 25, 1894.

A major issue was the ability to build through parts of Indian Territory to avoid the worst of the Ozark and Ouachita mountains. However, on February 27, 1893, the

United States Congress granted the Kansas City, Pittsburg & Gulf the authority to build a railroad and construct telegraph and telephone lines in the Indian Territory. In return for a $50 per mile fee, plus $15 per mile, per year, to the Secretary of the Interior to benefit the Indian tribes on whose land the railroad was constructed, the railroad obtained a 100-foot-wide right-of-way, with the right-of-way for depots and stations measuring 200 feet wide by 3000 feet long. With this issue solved, the Kansas City, Pittsburg & Gulf was incorporated in Arkansas on April 26, 1893, and construction went quickly. More than 25 miles of track from Pittsburg, Kansas, to Joplin, Missouri, were completed by Summer 1893.

Stilwell was said to have at times a lucky streak, and in this case it was the existence of the **Kansas City, Fort Smith & Southern Railway Company**. This company had been incorporated in Missouri on March 7, 1887, by Mathias Splitlog, often described as being "a wealthy Indian Chief." Splitlog had owned land near the mouth of the Kaw River, property that later became the location of the Kansas City stockyards and packing houses. He sold the land and moved to southwest Missouri, based upon the promise of great wealth in the area. Splitlog built his railroad in 1890-1891 south from Joplin, Missouri, with the goal of building all the way to the Gulf of Mexico. The line reached the Goodman, Missouri, area (thirty miles) and then turned west four miles to Splitlog City, where Mathias was developing a town. The 1890 census (June 30, 1890) reported that the railroad had 34.10 miles of track in Missouri, all using steel rails. The railroad operated using one passenger and two freight locomotives, and the company only owned two passenger coaches, two combination cars, and four coal cars.

Development of the Heavener Subdivision

Mathias Splitlog grew tired of his businesses and sold the railroad, which was acquired by the **Missouri Coal & Construction Company** in January 1893. The railroad was bought as part of the Missouri Coal & Construction contract with the Kansas City, Pittsburg & Gulf to build the railroad south from Joplin. At this time, there was still a great deal of uncertainty about the route that the railroad would take. For example, an article in the May 25, 1893, issue of the *Arkansas Gazette* reported that the Kansas City, Pittsburg & Gulf had asked Fort Smith, Arkansas, to raise $80,000-$90,000 to donate for right-of-way and depot grounds. In return, the KCP&G would make Fort Smith a division point with shops and a roundhouse, and trains would be running into Fort Smith by December 31, 1894.

			SPLITLOG DIVISION.			
	2	4	Mls	December 18, 1892.	1	3
Daily hack line between Pineville and Lanagan, carrying passengers, U. S. Mail and Adams Express, connecting with all trains. A daily hack line (except Sunday) runs between South West City, Mo., and Noel, carrying passengers and Adams Express.	P. M. 8 20			LEAVE] [ARRIVE ....St. Louis.......		A.M. 7 15
	A M. 9 50	P. M 9 15		LEAVE] [ARRIVE .....Kansas City....	P. M. 5 35	P. M. 11 55
	P. M. *5 25 5 42 6 08 6 24 6 43 6 59	A.M. †6 55 .... 7 18 7 45 8 35 9 02 9 18	.0 6.3 14.6 19.6 26.2 30.8	LEAVE] [ARRIVE .Joplin⁶ (*Broadway*)⚭ .Joplin⁶ (*Gulf Depot*)⚭ ....Saginaw........ ....Boyden....... ......Neosho⁷....⚭ ......McElhany...... ari......Wade....⚭ lve.	A.M. 9 35 9 12 8 50 8 35 8 15 8 04	P. M. 4 50 .. 4 15 3 45 3 25 2 55 2 40
		9 42 9 50	34.1 34.1	arr.....Splitlog. ⚭ lve. lve....Spiltlog....arr.	9 42	9 50
	6 59 7 23 7 37 7 45 7 58 8 15 P. M.	10 11 10 40 10 59 11 05 11 18 11 45 A.M.	30.8 37 2 41.5 43.0 46.2 51.1	lve ....Wade......arr. ....Anderson........⚭ ....Lanagan......... ....Rutledge....⚭ ....Noel.......⚭ ..Sulphur Springs.⚭ ARRIVE] [LEAVE	8 04 7 41 7 28 7 24 7 14 *7 00 A M.	2 40 2 00 1 35 1 28 1 13 †1245 NO'N

CONNECTIONS.—¹ With railroads diverging. ² With Atchison, Topeka & Santa Fé R.R.; Missouri Pacific; Chicago, Milwaukee & St. Paul, and Kansas City. Oscola & Southern Rys. ³ With Kansas City, Osceola & Southern Ry. ⁴ With Kansas City, Ft. Scott & Memphis Ry. ⁵ With Missouri Pacific Ry. ⁶ With Kansas City, Ft. Scott & Memphis: Missouri Pacific, and St. Louis & San Francisco Rys. ⁷ With St. Louis & San Francisco Ry.

The December 18, 1892, schedule for the Kansas City, Pittsburg & Gulf Railroad includes this listing for the Splitlog Division. From *Travelers' Official Guide of the Railway and Steam Navigation Lines in the United States and Canada*, June 1893, page 614.

By May 1, 1893, the line was completed from Joplin to Sulphur Springs, Arkansas, a total of 50.6 miles. Despite the proposal to Fort Smith, construction continued southward, with the line completed to Siloam Springs, Arkansas, on January 12, 1894 (24.0 miles); Stilwell, Oklahoma, on November 1, 1895 (24.0 miles); Sallisaw, Oklahoma, on February 9, 1896 (37.8 miles); Poteau, Oklahoma, on May 3, 1896 (35.2 miles); and through Heavener, Oklahoma, to Mena, Arkansas, on October 6, 1896 (53.5 miles). According to the Interstate Commerce Commission, these various sections of construction were accomplished "by construction companies organized for that specific purpose by the **Missouri, Kansas & Texas Trust Company**."

On October 30, 1897, all of these properties were sold to the Kansas City, Pittsburg & Gulf Railroad Company. Soon the railroad was faced with large payments on various bonds and was unable to make them. Because of the default in the payment of interest on these bonds, the KCP&G was placed in the hands of receivers on April 1, 1899. The property was sold on March 22, 1900, to **The Kansas City Southern Railway Company**, which began operating the property on April 1, 1900.

The creation of the new company provided the opportunity to make a number of improvements along the line. Among these were projects to reduce the many grades and to strengthen the bridges to handle heavier trains. Much of this work came about starting in 1911 when a series of bonds were issued to pay for the improvements. Throughout the next few years, various contractors with their steam shovels worked to raise sags and cut down the tops of grades. Bridges were also replaced. The Arkansas Bridge Company was awarded a contract to supply steel and erect "21 new steel bridges to replace lighter structures now in use on its main line between Kansas City and Port Arthur,

Texas." More work continued, and in 1923, the railroad extended 54 passing tracks and built 2 new ones.

Operations of the Kansas City Southern

During the first part of the twentieth century, both state and federal governmental agencies investigated the details of the railroad industry and produced substantial reports. *The Report of the Corporation Commission of the State of Oklahoma for the Year 1908* included a number of these details. For example, it reported that Wells Fargo & Company handled the express business on the Kansas City Southern and paid "50 per cent of its gross earnings on express matter handled over the line of this company." At the time, payments for moving the mail were based upon a yearly contract. For the Kansas City to Siloam Springs Route No. 155,054, KCS was paid $38,144.95 yearly. For Siloam Springs to Port Arthur, Texas, on Route No. 153,011, the payment was $78,454.49. The mail was moved between Fort Smith and Spiro (Route No. 147,019) for $1,162.04.

Other activities were also reported on, including sleeping cars, freight cars, and telegraph services. Pullman provided the sleeping cars and paid the railroad "2 cents per mile for each mile made over its lines by sleeping cars of the Pullman Company, fuel for heating oil and gas for illumination, and all lubricants furnished by the Railway Company, which company also cleans outside of cars and trucks." It was noted that the Pullman Company received all of the revenue from the cars.

Kansas City Southern also had an agreement with Armour Car Lines. Armour furnished "refrigerator cars for the movement of berries, fruits, vegetables in carloads, under Tariff I.C.C. No. 2197. The Railway Company shall also pay the car lines as rental charge for the use of the cars, three-fourths of one cent per mile run, both loaded and empty."

A final area that was researched was the telegraph service, provided in partnership with the Western Union Telegraph Company. At the time, the contract provided KCS "shall furnish labor and Telegraph Company shall furnish material for maintenance. Railway Company to have free use of wires at all times – railway business to take precedence over commercial business, except upon such wires as are used exclusively by the Telegraph Company – Telegraph Company receives revenue from all commercial business."

The Changing of the Districts

The two districts saw several changes over the years. Watts was not the first, or even the second division point between the Second District and the Third District. Both districts saw their end points changed several times over the years. For the Second District, the north end has traditionally been at North Yard at Pittsburg, Kansas, thanks to the large shop complex that was built there during the first years of the railroad. The south end has been a very different matter, with a number of locations claiming that title.

Initially, the south end was the end of track, and included Sulphur Springs, Arkansas. However, as the railroad was built southward, Gentry, Arkansas, was made a division point. This title moved to Stilwell, Oklahoma, in 1895. In 1912, the division point between the Second District and the Third District was moved to the new town of Watts, Oklahoma, where it remained until the two districts were combined. The south end division point for the Third District was once at Mena, Arkansas. In 1910, it was moved to Heavener, Oklahoma, where it remained for decades.

Development of the Heavener Subdivision

In January 1985, KCS announced plans to operate interdivisionally between Pittsburg and Heavener, eliminating Watts as a crew change point. This plan was possible due to a combination of improved signaling and more powerful locomotives. By 1989, the Second and Third subdivisions were consolidated into the Heavener Subdivision, and the last of the crew change facilities at Watts were removed within a few years.

Fighting the Grades

The Heavener Subdivision can basically be broken down into several territories, each with its own physical characteristics. North of Joplin, the railroad passes over the Ozark Plateau, a mix of interior plains and woods. This part of the route features rolling hills, gentle grades and moderate curves.

South of Joplin, the railroad enters the interior highlands. This area is what the former Second District was known for best. There are many steep grades, often required to cross the ridges between streams. The design of the line led to a general rule: "as the railroad heads east it climbs, as it heads west it drops." The reason for these grades are the Ozark and Boston Mountains, and trains face a series of 1.5% grades as they approach almost every major station along the line. While the line gets a bit straighter and flatter south of Watts, the line still descends almost 800 feet from Stilwell to Poteau, where it begins a climb to Heavener.

During the first decade of the twentieth century, there were a number of studies and surveys made to deal with these grades. Larger steam locomotives were ordered, but the big news was multiple plans to build a new mainline with maximum grades of 0.5%, instead of the 1.5% that existed in many places. During 1906, the railroad had five "corps of engineers" making surveys to find ways to lower the grades. One of these surveys was along the original route which would have been to the east of the route built. Known as the Noble Survey, the route would have headed south from Siloam Springs, Arkansas, through Van Buren and Fort Smith, and on to the Gulf. If built, the Noble Line would have been 65 miles shorter than the existing route, but would have required the construction of several tunnels and a number of extensive fills and cuts. One problem was the Arkansas River, where KCS would either build a new bridge or obtain trackage rights over the existing Missouri Pacific bridge.

News about the Noble Survey continued through at least 1907. One description stated that the new mainline would run through the "Illinois valley, Cove Creek gap and by Prairie Grove." Despite the potential improvements, no new construction took place. However, a series of smaller projects did occur, often resulting in lowered summits and raised sags with lessened grades. A few short realignments were completed, such as the three miles that were built between Howe and Heavener in 1908. A few more news reports came out in 1909 that more surveys were being made, especially south of Fort Smith through the Ouachita Mountains. However, like the ones to the north of Fort Smith, little ever became of them.

Even with all of the work conducted along the line, the Heavener Subdivision still features six heavy grades that are specifically mentioned in the employee timetable. Heading south, these grades are:

Development of the Heavener Subdivision

Milepost 174.3 to 177.7
    1.31% Uphill Neosho to near McElhany
Milepost 184.5 to 188.3
    1.32% Downhill Goodman to near Anderson
Milepost 206.2 to 209.8
    1.42% Uphill near Butler Creek to Gravette
Milepost 209.9 to 212.6
    1.29% Downhill Gravette to Spavinaw Creek
Milepost 215.3 to 219.1
    1.43% Uphill Dorsey to near Gentry
Milepost 230.3 to 233.6
    1.36% Downhill Siloam Springs to Illinois River

Historically, pushers or helpers were used to help the trains up and down these grades. These pushers were based at Watts and Neosho for decades. Today, higher horsepower locomotives and distributed power (DPU) take care of these needs. The fuel racks at Heavener are designed for these trains, with the head end power being fueled on one side of Industrial Road, and then the train can pull forward to fuel the DPU locomotives on the other side without blocking the street for long periods of time. Even with all of the progress made to reduce the grades and increase the horsepower, trains are still often required to crawl their way up these grades, and use all of the braking available to keep the trains under control as they drop down them.

The Heavener Subdivision Today

The Heavener Subdivision is now shown to be 209.8 miles long between Pittsburg and Heavener. The line features a long siding about every 15 miles, and serves small clusters of shippers at several points along the route. It still features several power plants where coal trains are delivered, plus several large feed mills where grain trains are handled. However, the Heavener Subdivision is probably best known as simply being the middle of the Kansas City Southern mainline between Kansas City, Missouri, and Shreveport, Louisiana.

Train speeds are not fast, with a maximum speed of 40 miles per hour from north of Neosho, Missouri, to near the Arkansas River crossing. Many sharp curves are even slower than that. However, the trains seem to keep moving, thanks to the good track, regularly spaced sidings, and fine dispatching. Secondary roads often follow the tracks, especially through the towns along the line.

The Heavener Subdivision passes through a series of small towns with easy access for the photographer, but please heed the signs like this one found at Pittsburg, Kansas.

Development of the Heavener Subdivision

Unfortunately, with the modernization of the railroad, only a few station buildings remain beside the tracks, all used as city office space or museums. Plenty of signs can be seen at the various control points and shipper tracks, and the traditional concrete mileposts can still be found along the line. Locomotive paint schemes have also changed, going through white to gray to the historic "Southern Belle" red, yellow and black schemes. However, locomotive power on the Heavener Subdivision can be almost anything, with lots of Union Pacific, BNSF, Canadian Pacific and other units working trains.

Concrete mileposts can be found all along the Kansas City Southern, such as this Milepost 139 at the old KO&G Junction near Asbury, Missouri.

The Heavener Sub: History Through the Miles

Concrete signs were popular on the Kansas City Southern. This whistle board for an upcoming grade crossing can be found at Heavener, Oklahoma.

The Heavener Subdivision keeps changing, and with the plans of the new Canadian Pacific Kansas City (CPKC), new and extended sidings, additional trains, and many other changes will certainly take place.

Development of the Heavener Subdivision

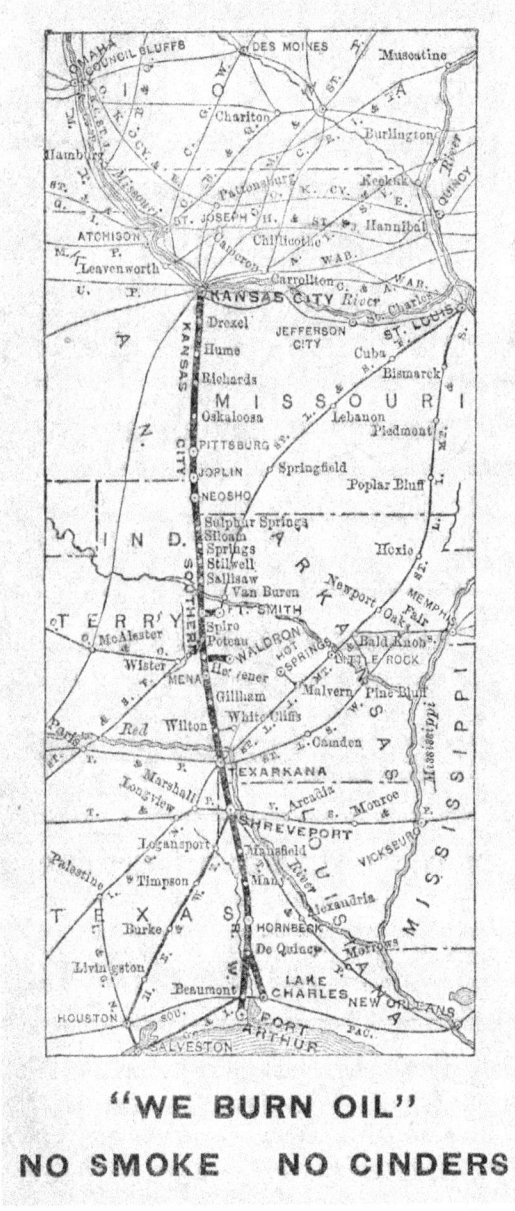

Map of the Port Arthur Route of the Kansas City Southern Railway / Texarkana & Fort Smith Railway / Arkansas Western Railway, "Straight as the Crow Flies." From *Travelers Railway Guide, Western Section*, March 1913, page 398.

The Heavener Sub: History Through the Miles

Schedule for the Port Arthur Route of the Kansas City Southern Railway / Texarkana & Fort Smith Railway / Arkansas Western Railway, "Straight as the Crow Flies." From *Travelers Railway Guide, Western Section,* March 1913, page 399.

Passenger Service Over the Heavener Subdivision

Being the result of a merger of the historic Second and Third districts, known as subdivisions by the 1950s, there has never been any scheduled passenger service over the Heavener Subdivision. However, the earlier Second and Third districts were once the home of limited passenger service. The Kansas City Southern was never a major operator of passenger trains, but it generally operated a mix of local services plus several Kansas City-Gulf Coast premium trains. The passenger service seldom required more than three pages (one for the map, one for the listing of officers and a listing of the sleeping car services, and then one page for the train schedules) for the Kansas City Southern listing in the *Official Guide of the Railways*.

As was custom, passenger trains were added to the line as it was expanded. In 1892, the route between Joplin and Sulphur Springs was known as the "Splitlog Division" and featured two trains in each direction daily. Each morning (except Sunday) at 6:55am, train No. 4 departed the Broadway Station in Joplin and headed south to Sulphur Springs, 51.1 miles away. This train made a 3.3-mile side trip to and from Splitlog before arriving at Sulphur Springs at 11:45am. The second southbound train was No. 2, which departed the Gulf Depot daily at 5:25pm and arrived at Sulphur Springs at 8:15pm. Northbound, train No. 1 left Sulphur Springs at 7:00am, while No. 3 left at 12:45pm. Both trains headed straight to Joplin, arriving at 9:35am (Gulf Depot) and 4:50pm (Broadway Station) respectively.

Once the track was completed between Kansas City, Missouri, and Port Arthur, Texas, the railroad began to develop a passenger strategy that would be used for decades. During June 1897, the Kansas City, Pittsburg & Gulf announced that it would begin operating sleeping cars between Kansas City, Missouri, and Port Arthur, Texas, via Lake Charles, Louisiana. Since the tracks weren't completed between DeQuincy and Beaumont, it would use the Southern Pacific's tracks between Lake Charles and Beaumont, Texas. Another interesting announcement was made in January 1901 that a Kansas City, Missouri – Hot Springs, Arkansas, sleeping car would be operated jointly with the Choctaw, Oklahoma & Gulf through the connection at Howe, Oklahoma.

In 1908, the railroad operated train Nos. 1 and 2, described as "Solid Vestibuled Trains with Pullman Buffet Sleepers between Kansas City and Port Arthur." These trains were basically long-distance locals which made all of the stops along the route. At the time, No. 1 departed the Second and Wyandotte Station in Kansas City at 12:30pm, Pittsburg at 5:35pm, Spiro (where it made a connection with a Fort Smith train) at 12:40am, and Heavener at 1:43am. It eventually arrived at Port Arthur at 9:25pm late that evening. Train No. 2 departed Port Arthur at 7:00am, Heavener at 3:04am the next morning, Spiro at 4:13am, Pittsburg at 11:45am, and then it arrived at Kansas City at 4:55pm.

Train Nos. 3 and 4 were a bit fancier and skipped a number of stops. The trains were described by KCS as "Solid Vestibuled Trains with Pullman Buffet Observation Sleepers between Kansas City and Port Arthur; also Through Pullman Sleepers between Kansas City and Joplin; between Kansas City and Fort Smith and between Lake Charles and Shreveport without change." Southbound No. 3 left the Second and Wyandotte Station at Kansas City at 11:55pm daily, passed through Heavener at 1:34pm, and arrived at Port Arthur at 10:00am the next day. No. 4 headed north,

Passenger Service

leaving Port Arthur at 9:25pm, passing through Heavener at 5:47pm, and arriving at Kansas City at 7:00am.

There were also a number of connecting trains that filled in the system's schedule. All of these trains had connecting service to and from Fort Smith from the junction at Spiro. There were also three daily trains between Heavener and Waldron, including Nos. 7 and 8 which operated between Fort Smith and Waldron. No. 8 would head north in the morning, departing Waldron at 7:00am. It would pass through Heavener at 8:50am and Spiro at 9:50am before arriving at Fort Smith at 10:40am. Later that day, No. 7 would leave Fort Smith at 4:20pm, Spiro at 5:05pm, and Heavener at 6:20pm before arriving at Waldron at 7:50pm to end the day.

By the late 1910s, a basic schedule was set that was followed for decades, even though the train names, numbers, services and equipment changed. This schedule had two trains covering the line daily between Kansas City and Port Arthur, typically leaving midday and close to midnight, putting them about twelve hours apart over the line. One set of trains typically made more stops, but at times, the daytime train through an area made the stops while the train passing through at night skipped the smaller stations.

Descriptions of the trains (Nos. 1 and 2, and Nos. 3 and 4) varied over the years as services and connections were added and subtracted. For example, in 1917, southbound passenger train No. 1 typically consisted of one baggage car, one coach, one chair car, and one Pullman sleeping car. An Interstate Commerce Commission report from 1919 stated that southbound passenger train No. 3 was "a through mail and express train running between Kansas City, Mo., and Port Arthur, Texas." It consisted of a "combination mail and express car, one baggage car, one coach, two chair cars and two Pullman sleeping cars."

In late 1925, the train numbers still existed, but the trains had been assigned names and a series of connections and services. Train Nos. 1 and 2, known as the *Texas Special*, featured coaches, a drawing room sleeper Kansas City-Shreveport, a drawing room sleeper Fort Smith-Shreveport, drawing room sleepers St. Louis-Port Arthur and St. Louis-Shreveport off Missouri Pacific's *Sunshine Special*, and a Kansas City-Houston drawing room sleeper using the *Sunshine Special*. Train Nos. 3 and 4 were the *Gulf Coast Express* and they handled cars exclusively operating on the Kansas City Southern. The trains handled coaches and drawing room sleepers between Kansas City and Port Arthur. There were also drawing room sleepers between Kansas City-Joplin, Kansas City-Fort Smith, and Shreveport-Lake Charles. The Arkansas Western Railway operated a daily except Sunday roundtrip between Heavener and Waldron.

Passenger Trains of the Heavener Subdivision (1925)

#3	#1	Station	#2	#4
4:20am	6:05pm	Pittsburg	11:40am	3:00am
5:20am	7:15pm	Joplin	10:50am	2:00am
8:57am	10:00pm	Watts	7:35am	11:05pm
11:40am	12:45am	Spiro	5:12am	8:20pm
1:05pm	1:45am	Heavener	4:15am	7:15pm

As the 1920s ended, KCS lost its through services on Missouri Pacific, but it began operating train Nos. 15 and 16 – *The Flying Crow* – on July 15, 1928. This became the premier train between Kansas City and Port Arthur, Texas. As the Great Depression hit the economy, much of the passenger service ended. By 1933, *The Flying Crow* was the only train covering the mainline, and it was shown to have chair cars and coaches, plus a drawing-room sleeper between Kansas City and Port Arthur. The trains covered this territory early in the morning, with southbound No. 15 entering the Second Subdivision at Pittsburg at 1:20am, crossed between the Second and Third Subdivisions at Watts at 5:10am, and left Heavener at 10:00am. Northbound No. 16 left Heavener at 1:50am, Watts at 6:30am, and Pittsburg at 10:05am.

One interesting route detail at the time was that *The Flying Crow* actually served Fort Smith by looping up and back on the Spiro-Fort Smith branch, taking about 90 minutes to provide the service. Each morning, No. 15 would depart Spiro at 7:25am, be at Fort Smith 8:00am-8:15am, and return to Spiro at 9:00am. Northbound No. 16 would leave Spiro at 2:45am, be at Fort Smith 3:20am-3:30am, and be back at Spiro at 4:15am. On the Waldron line, a tri-weekly mixed train provided service between Heavener and Forester.

One note about *The Flying Crow* deserves to be mentioned. This train was the first regular use of KCS mainline diesel-electric locomotives when several E3 locomotives, built by the Electro-Motive Corporation, started covering the service. One of these locomotives was EMC demonstrator 822, while the other was built for the KCS. Both were delivered in late July 1939 and put to work on *The Flying Crow*.

As the Great Depression ended, Kansas City Southern announced on July 13, 1940, that the railroad had purchased three new streamlined passenger trains to operate as the *Southern Belle* between Kansas City and New Orleans. The *Southern Belle* began operating on September 2, 1940, as Nos. 1 and 2. This left *The Flying Crow* as the main train to Port Arthur. With the post-war boom, a third train was added to the route in 1949. This train never had a name, but it served as secondary service on the Kansas

City-New Orleans route, using the older 1940 consist of the *Southern Belle*.

Passenger Trains of the Heavener Subdivision (1952)

#15	#9	#1	Station	#2	#10	#16
12:30am	12:10pm	6:15pm	Pittsburg	7:55am	5:15pm	4:55am
1:20am	12:55pm	6:46pm	Joplin	7:17am	4:30pm	4:10am
3:35am	2:50pm	8:22pm	Siloam Springs	5:42am	2:32pm	1:50am
5:45am	4:45pm	9:56pm	Spiro	4:08am	12:48pm	11:45pm
6:40am	5:25pm	10:30pm	Heavener	3:37am	12:10pm	10:55pm

The three-train schedule lasted until 1957 when train Nos. 9 and 10 became Shreveport-New Orleans connecting trains for *The Flying Crow*. With this, they became day trains without sleepers, and were soon down to a baggage car, several coaches, and an observation-lounge. On November 27, 1967, KCS announced plans to seek permission to end the *Southern Belle* and its connecting service to Port Arthur. Much of this was due to the end of the mail contract which was set to expire on January 12, 1968. The application was made with the Interstate Commerce Commission (ICC) on December 4, 1967, and also included train Nos. 9 and 10 operating between Kansas City and New Orleans, and train Nos. 15 and 16 operating between Kansas City and Port Arthur. On May 6, 1968, the ICC granted authority to abolish passenger train Nos. 9, 10, 15 and 16, but required that the *Southern Belle* operate for at least another six months. After just two months short of sixty years of operations, *The Flying Crow* was discontinued May 10, 1968.

On October 14, 1968, KCS again applied to end the *Southern Belle*, claiming losses of more than one million dollars in the previous year of operating the train. While

Passenger Service

the application was eventually withdrawn, another request was made in August 1969. This time permission was received and the Kansas City Southern ended the *Southern Belle* passenger service on November 2, 1969, the last passenger trains over what became the Heavener Subdivision.

Flying Crow departure board in Kansas City's Union Station.

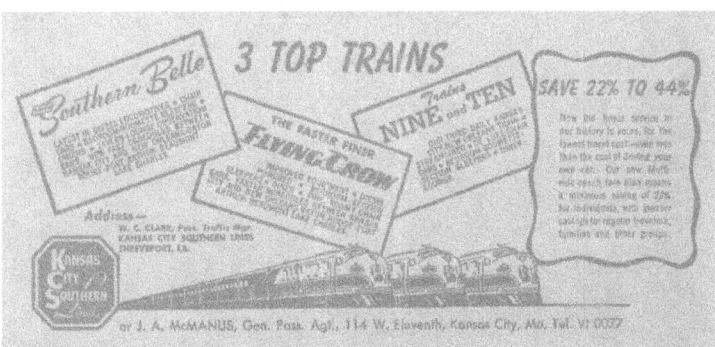

Photo of brochure displayed at the Union Station Kansas City Model Train Gallery advertising Kansas City Southern's passenger trains.

The Heavener Sub: History Through the Miles

```
┌─────────┐
│  PORT   │   THE KANSAS CITY SOUTHERN
│ ARTHUR  │        RAILWAY COMPANY
│  ROUTE  │
└─────────┘  1921      DUPLICATE      B 9386

 Pass          --Mr R W Hunt-Chanute Kans-
  ACCOUNT       Fuel Supvr A T & S F Ry
  BETWEEN      Kansas City and Joplin
          UNTIL  December 31st  UNLESS OTHERWISE ORDERED
          DATE ISSUED  3-30-21   REQUESTED BY   FCF
                  SUBJECT TO CONDITIONS ON BACK
          VALID WHEN COUNTERSIGNED BY A.M. CALHOUN OR J.M. PRICKETT

 COUNTERSIGNED
      [signature]                    [signature] JA Edson
                                                  PRESIDENT
```

```
        UNLESS LIMITED ON OPPOSITE SIDE, THIS PASS IS GOOD
                       ALSO ON TRAINS OF
              TEXARKANA & FT. SMITH RAILWAY CO.
              THE ARKANSAS WESTERN RAILWAY CO.

       THE PERSON ACCEPTING AND USING THIS PASS THEREBY
       ASSUMES ALL RISK OF ACCIDENT AND INJURY TO PERSON
       AND ALL DAMAGE TO OR LOSS OF PROPERTY.

       IF PRESENTED BY ANY OTHER THAN THE INDIVIDUAL
       NAMED HEREON CONDUCTOR WILL TAKE UP PASS AND
       COLLECT FARE.

       AS A CONDITION PRECEDENT TO THE ISSUE AND USE OF
       THIS PASS, THE RECIPIENT REPRESENTS AND DECLARES BY
       SIGNATURE HEREUNDER THAT HE OR SHE IS NOT PROHIBITED
       BY FEDERAL OR STATE LAWS FROM RECEIVING FREE TRANS-
       PORTATION, AND THAT THIS PASS WILL BE LAWFULLY USED.

                      [signature] R W Hunt
```

Kansas City Southern rail pass, front and back, circa 1921. From the author's collection.

Creating a Heavener Subdivision Route Guide

This book is designed to provide a guide to the Heavener Subdivision. The rail line has been rebuilt and improved numerous times over its 130 years. Hills have been cut down and bridges strengthened, stations and agents have been replaced by modern signals, and sidings have been installed and lengthened to handle the trains that pound across the line. Even with these changes, much of the line's history can still be found along its route. There are several museums along the line, a number of stations and bridges, and lots of trains that can still be photographed.

Some of the history of the Heavener Subdivision can be found along the railroad with each concrete milepost, such as this one just south of the Dalby siding near Neosho, Missouri.

This work is based upon several earlier research projects on the railroad that led to articles in magazines such as *Railfan & Railroad* (April 1998) and *Pacific Rail News* (September 1990). This research has led to a collection of thousands of photographs and drawers full of railroad documents and company history. There is always the question about how much detail to provide in a book like this. One reader told the author that in a previous book, if someone once tied a mule to a she-shed along the line, it was reported. While that is not quite the goal, there is an effort to explain the history of each community along the line, what shippers were located there, and what facilities the railroad had. Obviously, all of these changed over the more than one hundred years of the railroad's history, so the challenge is how much information to report. In writing this book, the author attempted to include information about the first few years of the railroad's existence, the peak of a community's activity, and what remains today. Not everything is reported, but enough history is provided to give the reader an idea of what happened at each location.

The railroad historically used north-south as the line's description, although in some areas it curves greatly from these directions. The route description will use the north-south railroad directions, but will often use the real directions when describing certain features along the route. Additionally, the tracks were often described by their car-lengths. These car-lengths varied over the years, but were generally around 45 feet per car. Therefore a track listed as being 20 cars in length could hold about 900 feet of train. Many of the bridges have also been replaced or improved, so where timber trestles once stood, ballast-deck concrete spans can now be found.

Another help in following the railroad and knowing what was at many of the locations are the many maps available on the internet. County road maps, topographic

Creating a Route Guide

(topo) maps, and many other maps from the era can be found. Comparing these older maps with newer maps can often make finding the railroad easier. The U.S. Geological Survey has been very active making their Historical Topographic Map Collection available through TopoView. These maps are highly recommended.

A final issue deals with all of the names that were used to represent parts of the railroad over its one-hundred-plus years. To simplify the issue, the term Kansus City Southern or KCS will generally be used, even when another railroad originally built the line. Additionally, an ampersand (&) will be used in railroad company names to make them easier to identify. Especially with companies like the Kansas City, Nevada & Fort Smith, mixing the railroad name and the cities that it served can get very confusing. Therefore, even if the firm did not use or always use an ampersand, one will be used in this book. Please forgive these simplifications.

The Heavener Sub: History Through the Miles

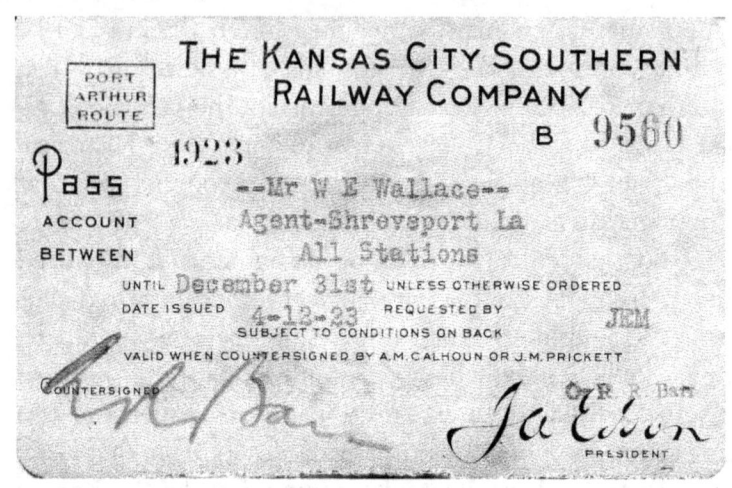

Kansas City Southern rail pass, front and back, circa 1923. From the author's collection.

Route Guide for the Heavener Subdivision

This route guide covers the former Second and Third Districts of KCS, now the Heavener Subdivision. It follows the line from north (Pittsburg, Kansas) to south (Heavener, Oklahoma), passing through four different states. The route guide provides information about each current and former station location, junctions and crossings, and major bridges. To explain some of the operations, it includes the mileposts, office calls (telegraph station code) from 1936, and the schedule for KCS passenger train No. 1, the *Southern Belle*.

128.2 PITTSBURG NORTH YARD (NY) – The designated milepost for North Yard at Pittsburg was the Yard Office. There were crossover switches just north and south of the Yard Office, used to exchange locomotives and to switch trains as necessary. Today, this location is officially known as Pittsburg, but it was once a mile north of the Pittsburg passenger station and divisional office building, located north and south of East 7th Street & Michigan Avenue.

North Yard at Pittsburg was a major facility on the Kansas City Southern Railway Company, and the earlier Kansas City, Pittsburg & Gulf Railroad Company. The facility began when the railroad arrived in 1893, and eventually a large yard, many shop buildings, and numerous offices were located here.

In 1906, major improvements were made at North Yard. According to the August 31, 1906, issue of *The Railroad Gazette*, the Arnold Company of Chicago was awarded a contract for the designing and construction of the new shops and facilities. These improvements would double the capacity of the shops at North Yard, and add additional work that could be conducted there. The plans at the time included keeping the current "car shed and planing mill, 203 x 117 ft.; coach and paint shop, 144 x 107 ft.; and storehouse, 173 x 55 ft."

The July 1923 issue of The Kansas City Southern Railway's *Agricultural and Industrial Bulletin* had a large article about the "P&G" shops at Pittsburg.

> Twenty-two years ago the machine, boiler, blacksmith, coach, paint and pattern shops, as well as the power room, storeroom and mill room were all located in a building 120 ft. by 290 ft., having a floor space of 8,700 square feet. The 8-stall round house equipped with a 60-foot turn table, the cinder pit and 100-ton coal tipple were near by. Since then, improvements, enlargements have been constantly made. In 1906 there were added a machine shop 153 ft. by 357 ft., a fifteen-stall round house with 90-foot stalls, an oil house 37 ft. by 56 ft.; extension to coach shop 67 ft. by 100 ft., power house 99 ft. by 102 ft., outside traveling crane over casting and material storage. The old round house was removed and the original main building is now used for boiler and blacksmith work. A thirty-ton traveling crane was installed in the boiler shop in 1911, and a water treating plant of 300,000 gallons capacity per day was installed in 1921. The machine shop

was enlarged to 153 ft. by 604 ft. in 1922. In addition to the 120-ton crane formerly used a 250-ton twin bridge crane and two smaller traveling cranes were installed. A railsaw plant was built in 1923 by which 300 eighty-five pound rails can be sawed and drilled at both ends in eight hours. The power plant was greatly enlarged in capacity by new installations. The existing round house will now be enlarged. An eight-stall addition, each stall 110 feet long to accommodate the large Mallet locomotives, which are 97 feet long over all and weigh 528,000 pounds, will soon be built. When the buildings now under construction are completed the total floor area will amount to 250,000 square feet as compared to an area of 23,000 square feet twenty-two years ago.

The December 1927 issue reported on the completion of the work, and stated that the shops covered 172 acres and included a 55,000-barrel fuel oil storage tank, a steel freight car repair shop, and several divisional terminal buildings. In total, 1307 local citizens were employed by the railroad at Pittsburg. Later, diesel repair and servicing facilities were completed at Pittsburg in 1949 at a cost of more than $350,000.

Nearby were other train services, including a regular icing station used to restock ice in refrigerator cars that moved fruits and berries. The railroad iced their own cars as well as those of other car owners. One of these was the American Refrigerator Transit

Company, which had a contract with KCS to carry perishable freight.

At its peak, North Yard covered some three hundred acres. It was the headquarters of the Northern Division, as well as the entire mechanical and store departments for the railroad. In 1964, North Yard had continuous telegraph service, and general order books were based here. It was also a register station. Passenger train No. 1, the southbound *Southern Belle*, at the time was scheduled to arrive here at 11:33am and depart at 11:35am after a quick crew change, resupply, and inspection. For years, there were also instructions that the "conductors of first-class trains will leave a register ticket with operator at Yard Office, North Yard."

This is how the KCS shop complex at Pittsburg, Kansas, looked in 1997.

Heavener Sub Route Guide

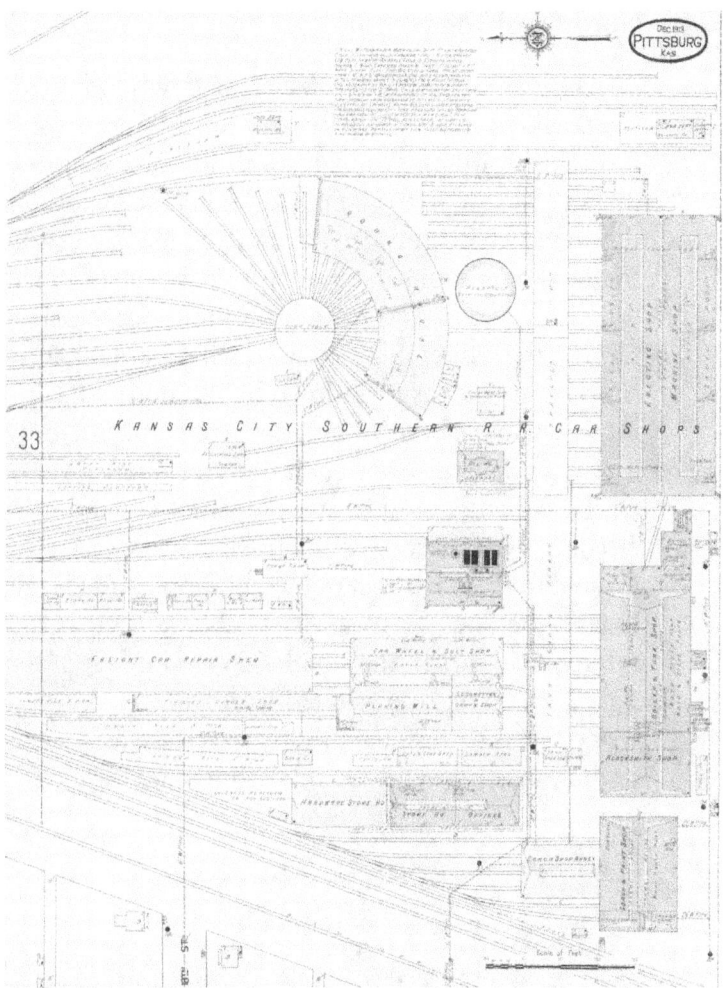

This map by Sanborn, while titled "Kansas City Southern R. R. Car Shops," showed the entire roundhouse and shop complex that was located north of downtown Pittsburg, Kansas. *Sanborn Fire Insurance Map from Pittsburg, Crawford County, Kansas.* Sanborn Map Company, Dec 1913. Map. Retrieved from the Library of Congress, https://www.loc.gov/item/sanborn03060_006/.

North Yard Today

As the railroad modernized and grew southward, the facilities at Pittsburg became less important and more awkward in their location. In particular, the massive steam shops were no longer needed after the Kansas City Southern completed its conversion to diesel operations in 1953. After being abandoned for many years, several of the buildings burned. During the winter of 2010-2011, what was left of the shop complex was torn down by the railroad. Currently, many of the foundations remain, but only a few tracks still exist at the former shops. These tracks are often used to store locomotives and other equipment. A connecting track and wye are now located to the northeast of the old shop complex, allowing the South Kansas & Oklahoma Railroad to interchange cars in the small KCS yard north of the East 23rd Street overpass (Milepost 128.3). A walkway on the north side of the overpass provides views of the yard office and the small four-track yard.

While North Yard can be viewed from several highway overpasses, the KCS yard is private property. This sign warns that security is enforced 24 hours a day, so please don't trespass and ruin it for others.

Heavener Sub Route Guide

All of the KCS facilities that once stood at Pittsburg, Kansas, are now represented by this small metal building, almost surrounded by the automobiles of train crews and other employees.

East of the yard, a spur track serves the distribution yard of the Baldwin Pole & Piling Company. Baldwin Pole is privately owned and was founded in 1945 to produce poles and pilings. In 1958, the company began operating its first creosote treatment facility at Bay Minette, Alabama, producing 40,000 poles per year. The firm now produces about 200,000 poles per year, using chromated copper arsenate (CCA) or pentachlorophenol. The company has its own trucks, and also uses contract haulers, to deliver their products from its plants and distribution centers.

This sign identifies the Baldwin Pole & Piling Company facility, located just east of Pittsburg North Yard.

128.8 SEK CONNECTION – Once known as Mo. Pac. Crossing, the former connection with the Southeast Kansas Railroad (SEKR) marks the south end of two main tracks through the North Yard area. About Milepost 127.0, located north of the Rouse Street overpass, is the north switch.

For many years, there was a connection with the Southeast Kansas Railroad (SEKR), earlier Missouri Pacific, in the northwest quadrant of the diamond that once stood south of here. This connection has been removed as the Southeast Kansas Railroad track to the west has been abandoned, and a new connection has been built for the track to the east.

128.9 AT&SF CROSSING – When the Santa Fe built their line into Pittsburg, it crossed the KCS at this location. North of here, the ATSF line, which ran north-south through Pittsburg, was to the west of the KCS mainline; to the south, it was to the east. It followed the KCS closely through the east side of Pittsburg before crossing back over to the west near Fourth Street.

The Atchison, Topeka & Santa Fe Railroad (ATSF or Santa Fe) connected to the Pittsburg area to reach coal mines. The ATSF first bought the Southern Kansas Railway Company, which had built a line from Chanute to Girard, both in Kansas. The line was extended through Frontenac to Pittsburg, with service beginning on June 12, 1887. Reportedly, the Santa Fe leased a train depot from the Frisco Railroad on the southeast corner of Fourth and Locust, and later built their own station between Second and Third Streets. The former Frisco freight house still stands on the south side of East Fourth.

One of the primary reasons for the ATSF interest in Pittsburg was coal. At the time, the Santa Fe burned enormous volumes of coal each year in its steam locomotives. In 1886, the Cherokee & Pittsburg Coal Company opened Santa Fe Mine No. 1 at what became the town of Frontenac in 1887. The Cherokee & Pittsburg Coal & Mining Company was owned by the Santa Fe and operated mines here and as far west as New Mexico, and several spur lines connected to a number of mines in the area.

The line to Pittsburg passed just west of KCS' North Yard. By the 1950s, this was the Girard District of the ATSF's Eastern Division. It actually extended on south to Joplin, Missouri, using "KCS main track and sidings between Pittsburg KCS and Joplin and tracks of Joplin Union Depot Company at Joplin." An early report by the Interstate Commerce Commission stated that the ATSF had trackage rights over 24.39 miles of Kansas City Southern Railway Company tracks between Pittsburg and Joplin. The agreement had started on April 1, 1911, and the fee was "2½ per cent per annum on valuation of property, plus a proportion on a car and engine basis of maintenance, operation, taxes, etc.; includes certain station and yard facilities at both points."

128.9 SEK RRX – Known as the Southeast Kansas Railroad Crossing, and earlier the Missouri Pacific Crossing (Mo. Pac. Crossing shown as being at Milepost 129.0), this diamond has been removed and the crossing track is now abandoned. There was a Mo. Pac. Connection not far to the south.

While the tracks are gone and a paved trail has replaced the line to the west, the old Missouri Pacific Crossing was once located to the east of the intersection of 12th Street and Michigan Street.

Heavener Sub Route Guide

Although gone, signs of the old Missouri Pacific Crossing at Milepost 128.9 can still be found throughout the area, like this old signal foundation that now sits west of the tracks.

This route dates back to the Nevada & Girard Railway, incorporated in September 1882. While no track was built, it had a goal of connecting Nevada, Missouri, with the expanding coal fields around Pittsburg and to the west. The company was backed by Jay Gould and the Missouri Pacific Railroad, and was reorganized as The Nevada & Minden Railway Company on April 17, 1885. Plans for the newly named railroad included building 32 miles of track west from Nassau Junction to the Missouri-Kansas border. Then, the Nevada & Minden Railway Company of Kansas (incorporated December 14, 1885) would build 41 miles of track west from the border to Chetopa, Kansas. Both projects were organized, funded, and later operated by Missouri Pacific.

The first Missouri Pacific Railroad train pulled into Pittsburg on July 3, 1886, and The Nevada & Minden Railway Company line was completed on August 11, 1886. The railroad built a passenger station and freight house on the south side of their mainline and on the north side of 11th Street, where the Pittsburg Farmers Market parking lot and an athletic field are now located. The small brick passenger station (1102 North Broadway) was later replaced by an even smaller pre-fab metal building. The freight house (1111 North Elm) was located south of the mainline and a four-track yard.

On August 9, 1909, the two Nevada & Minden railroads were part of a general consolidation of lines that created The Missouri Pacific Railway Company. By the 1960s, much of the coal traffic had dried up and the line from Cornell Junction to Fort Scott was abandoned in 1964. Next, the line was operated as the Pittsburg Subdivision between Nassau Junction and Coffeyville.

On January 8, 1980, the Union Pacific Corporation announced an agreement to buy the Missouri Pacific Railroad. Approval was finally received on September 13, 1982, after a series of hearings and lawsuits. It finally took a Supreme Court ruling to allow the merger on December 22, 1982. A unique detail not known by many was that the Missouri Pacific had a number of outstanding bonds that prevented a full merger of the two companies. The bonds were finally closed during the mid-1990s, and the merger became final on January 1, 1997.

With the larger railroad, lightly-used branch lines like the Pittsburg Subdivision were looked at as candidates for sale or abandonment. In 1987, the rail line was sold to Charles R. Webb and his Watco Companies. This was the first shortline sale, and Watco's first shortline purchase. On April 13, 1987, the Southeast Kansas Railroad (SEKR) began operating the Coffeyville, Kansas, to Nassau Junction, Missouri, line that passed through Pittsburg. In 1994, the shortline grew when it added the Bartlesville, Oklahoma, to Coffeyville line. At the time, the railroad moved about 5000 carloads a year. During July 2000, Watco merged the SEKR into the South Kansas & Oklahoma Railroad (SKOL). The SKOL operates former Missouri Pacific, Frisco and Santa Fe lines in Kansas, Oklahoma and Missouri, moving primarily grain and grain products, cement, coal, chemicals, steel, and plastics. The combined railroad has almost 400 miles of track and interchanges with the Kansas City Southern here at Pittsburg, Kansas.

In 1989, these two locomotives, CF-7 locomotives that had been assembled by the Atchison, Topeka & Santa Fe years earlier, were at Pittsburg, Kansas, just two years after the Southeast Kansas Railroad was created.

As Watco acquired more lines, the Pittsburg Subdivision route duplicated other routes. On September 29, 2000, the Surface Transportation Board approved the abandonment of the six miles of track west from Pittsburg to Cherokee. Much of the grade through Pittsburg became the Watco Trail by 2011. Other changes have also taken place, such as Watco moving its headquarters from Coffeyville, Kansas, to 315 West 3rd Street in Pittsburg, Kansas.

To the east of the KCS mainline are the remains of the Missouri Pacific's Pittsburg Subdivision. The track is used as a stub for the newly built wye track that serves as the new connection between the KCS and South Kansas & Oklahoma Railroad. The KCS diamond was Milepost 357.6 on the SKOL line, and the line still exists to near U.S. Highway 160 at Milepost 352.0. The new connecting track is at Milepost 356.9, and further to the northeast is an industrial park with several shippers. At Milepost 352.8, location of the former Cornell siding, is a Watco Companies carshop.

This Watco sign is located at a warehouse in the industrial park just east of North Yard in Pittsburg, Kansas.

Heavener Sub Route Guide

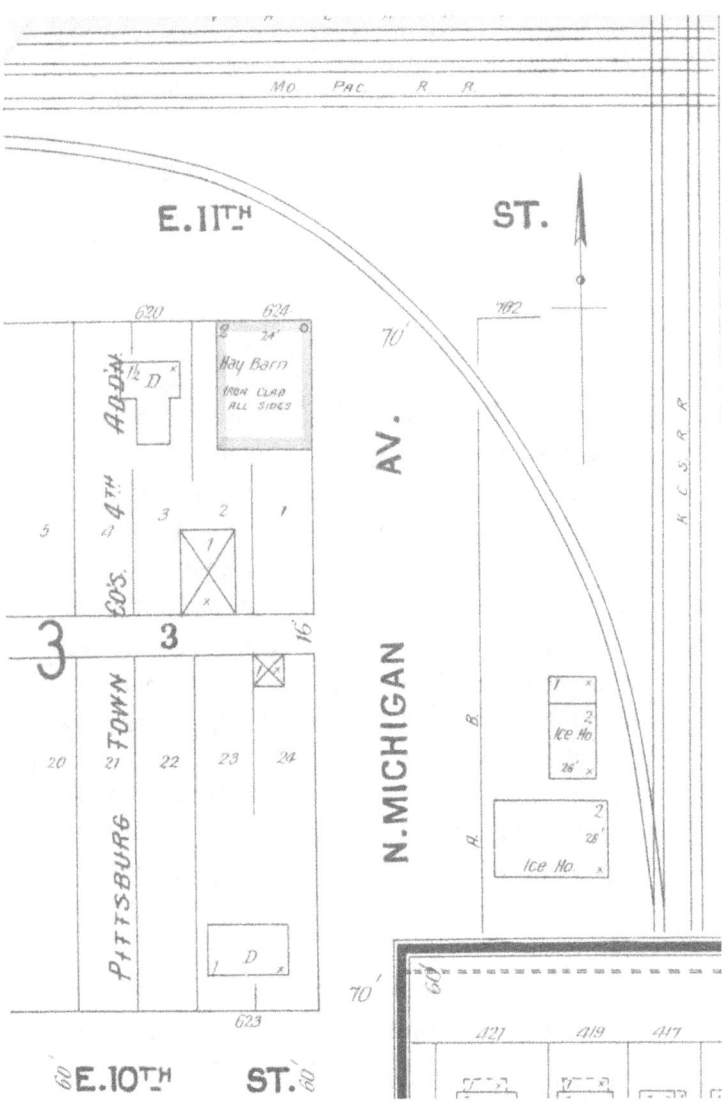

This Sanborn map from March 1902 shows the busy crossing area just north of East 11th Street where three Missouri Pacific tracks headed east-west across the tracks of Kansas City Southern. A connecting track was located in the southwest quadrant, where several ice houses were also located. *Sanborn Fire Insurance Map from Pittsburg, Crawford County, Kansas.* Sanborn Map Company, March 1902. Map. Retrieved from the Library of Congress, https://www.loc.gov/item/sanborn03060_004/.

Heading south, KCS' Heavener Subdivision passes around the east side of downtown Pittsburg. Doing so, it crosses East Tenth Street (Milepost 129.1) and East Seventh Street (Milepost 129.3) at grade. It then passes under East Fourth Street at Milepost 129.5. This area was once busy with warehouses, lumberyards, and other shippers. Today, Kansas City Southern trains simply pass right through this part of town.

129.2 PITTSBURG (DO) – This was where the KCS passenger station once stood (shown as Pittsburg Passenger in some documents), now an open area west of the KCS mainline where a few foundations can still be found. The station was a nice yellow-painted brick building with a baggage room on the north end, located just north of Seventh Street. Over the years, it generally housed a standard clock and bulletin books at the telegraph office, and maintained copies of the general orders. By the 1950s, the station had been modernized with larger windows, a covered platform, and a much simpler look. In 1964, the *Southern Belle* (train No. 1) was scheduled to depart Pittsburg at 11:45am, with the next stop being Joplin.

Just south of Seventh Street was the two-story divisional office building. This building had the look of a typical freight house with the two-story section fronting Seventh Street, and a one-story section to the south. In fact, during the 1910s, there were two tracks immediately to the east of the building, typical of a freight house. However, a new and larger freight house was built several blocks to the west nearer downtown Pittsburg at Locust and 6th Street. Both the passenger station and office building have been torn down, and only a few signs of their foundations mark their former locations.

The Pittsburg passenger station used to be located north of 7th Street, while the divisional office building was to the south.

Some of the foundations from the KCS passenger station can still be seen on the west side of the tracks at Pittsburg, Kansas.

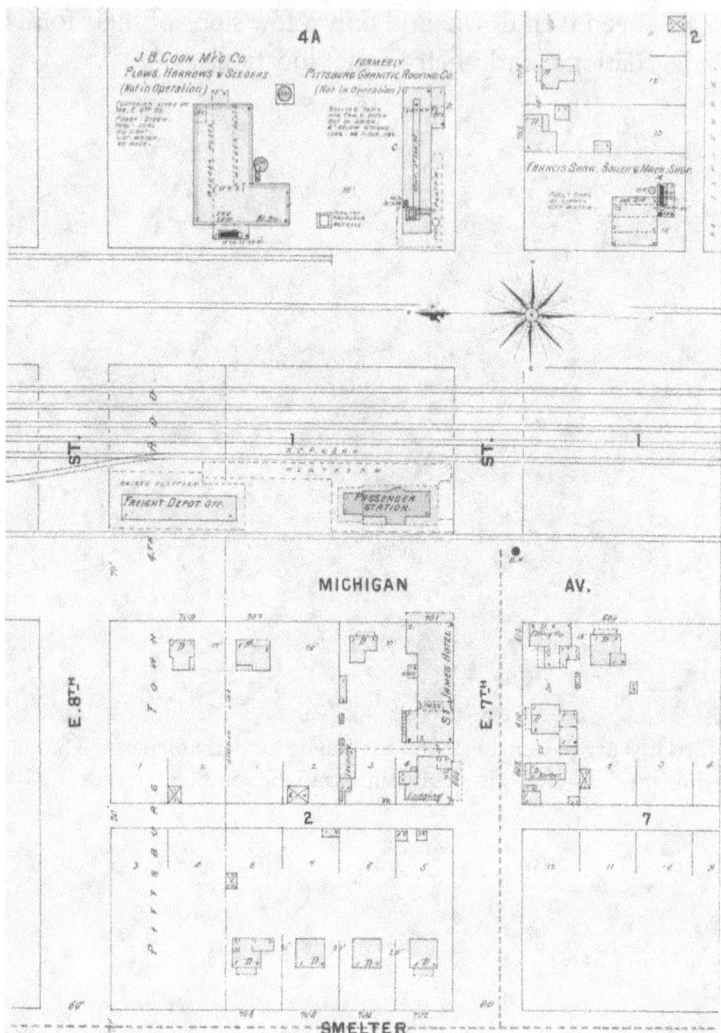

This Sanborn map from 1897 shows that the Kansas City, Pittsburg & Gulf had their freight depot north of the passenger depot soon after the railroad was built. *Sanborn Fire Insurance Map from Pittsburg, Crawford County, Kansas.* Sanborn Map Company, August 1897. Map. Retrieved from the Library of Congress, https://www.loc.gov/item/sanborn03060_003/.

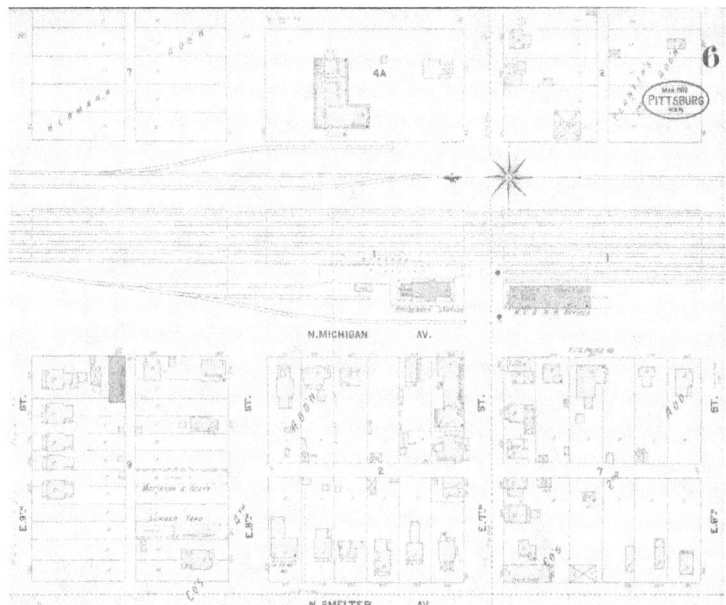

By 1902, a new freight house was located south of East 7th Street. It was shown to include freight and division offices in its north end. *Sanborn Fire Insurance Map from Pittsburg, Crawford County, Kansas.* Sanborn Map Company, March 1902. Map. Retrieved from the Library of Congress, https://www.loc.gov/item/sanborn03060_004/.

The Heavener Sub: History Through the Miles

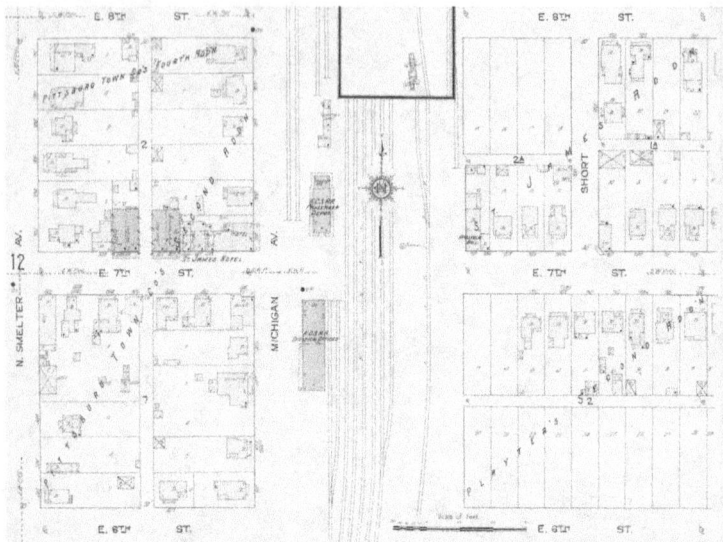

This Sanborn map from 1913 showed the KCS passenger station and divisional office buildings, located north and south of East 7th Street and Michigan Avenue. Note that the freight building just showed it housing division offices. By this time, a new freight house had been built on the southeast corner of East 6th Street and North Locust. *Sanborn Fire Insurance Map from Pittsburg, Crawford County, Kansas.* Sanborn Map Company, Dec 1913. Map. Retrieved from the Library of Congress, https://www.loc.gov/item/sanborn03060_006/.

For decades, the Kansas City Southern actually had two main tracks through downtown Pittsburg. This short section required a number of special rules in the employee timetables. These include the following from Timetable No. 24, dated Sunday, May 31, 1936.

Rule 17. The current of traffic for all except Kansas City Southern first-class trains, using double track between Santa Fe crossing south of dispatchers' office Pittsburg and Mile Post 128.1 will be on the right; Kansas City Southern first-

class trains will use the track on the west for movement in either direction. The normal position of main line switches at each end of this double track is lined and locked for the southward or track on the west.

Rule 18. *Locomotives moving light between Seventh Street, Pittsburg, and North Yard may, under the protection of the yard limit rule, use the southward or track on the west to reach the cross-over at Fourteenth Street.*

Rule 19. *The northward or track on the east will be used as a passing track between Fourth and Twenty-third Streets, Pittsburg; but when first-class trains are to meet at Pittsburg on special orders, the order will designate which train shall take siding and at what point.*

These rules came about because the KCS passenger station was located on the west side of the right-of-way, just north of East 7th Street. At least five tracks were east of the mainline tracks before World War II, and a small flagman shanty once stood nearby to protect vehicles using the Seventh Street grade crossing. Several tracks were located near the depot where the business cars of the division management were maintained. An oil house, ice house, and inspectors office were located just north of the depot to handle these cars, and any services that passenger trains required during their short stops.

Just south of the Division Office Building was a track that curved west to reach the KCS freight house. Located on the southeast corner of East Sixth Street and North Locust, the 18' x 90' building had a long shipping shed to the east. Two tracks served the freight building, and a third track was farther to the south and was used for direct transfer between railcars and trucks. Farther south a fourth track served the Long-Bell Lumber Company. Along the line were also several spur tracks which served the Pittsburg Grocery Company warehouse and the Standard Ice & Fuel Company artificial ice plant. None of these buildings, except for a few parts of the Long-Bell Lumber Company, remain today.

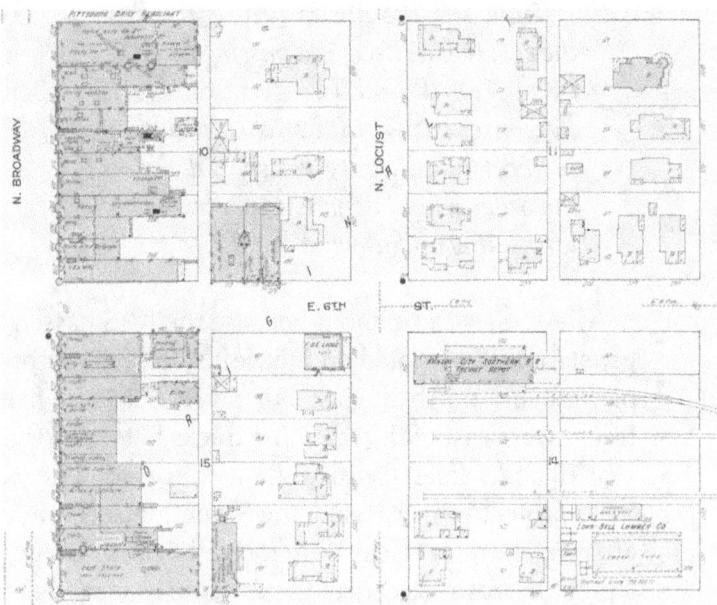

The Kansas City Southern Freight Depot was located west of the passenger station and general office building on the southeast corner of East 6th Street and North Locust. *Sanborn Fire Insurance Map from Pittsburg, Crawford County, Kansas.* Sanborn Map Company, Dec 1913. Map. Retrieved from the Library of Congress, https://www.loc.gov/item/sanborn03060_006/.

The City of Pittsburg

Long before Pittsburg was founded, this was simply open prairie. While several trails and roads passed through the area, little development took place here. One of the first recorded events near here was on October 23, 1864, when Confederate Major Andrew Jackson Piercy and his 1st Indian Brigade attacked a Union wagon train commanded by Colonel William Campbell. The wagon train contained refugees fleeing combat near Fort Smith, Arkansas, as well as troops heading home at their end of their enlistments. The "Cow Creek Skirmish" resulted in almost twenty Union deaths and the burning of a number of wagons. Little happened again in the area until coal was discovered and railroads began to build in this direction.

With speculators seeing the potential of railroads and coal, a town was platted here on May 20, 1876. The town came about when Franklin Playter, a Girard banker, was approached by several individuals involved in the lead and zinc business at Joplin. They wanted to build a railroad to create new markets for their ores. Playter knew about the coal in the area, and agreed to help finance the railroad if it went along a route of his choosing.

Playter envisioned the town booming with coal and ores, much like Pittsburgh, Pennsylvania. He selected the name of Pittsburgh for the community, which was eight blocks long and eight blocks wide. However, W. A. Pitt had already created a Pittsburg, Kansas, in 1872, and Playter was forced to use the name New Pittsburgh for his growing town. New Pittsburgh was incorporated in 1879, and the following year Playter was finally able to buy the Pittsburg name from W. A. Pitt, who agreed to change the name of his town to Tipton. The City of Pittsburgh (third class city) was incorporated on June 1, 1881, and became Pittsburg in 1894. In 1905, Pittsburg became a first class city.

Different sources credit different people as working with Playter to create Pittsburg. Among these others were Elliot Raines Moffett and John B. Sergeant, the men who dug the first mine shaft in what became Joplin, striking lead ore. Moffett and Sergeant built the first lead smelter and opened the first bank at Joplin. Moffett was also the first mayor of Joplin. More importantly to this story, Moffett and Sergeant founded the Joplin Railroad Company that led Playter to create the Pittsburg townsite. Another important figure was Colonel E. H. Brown, who conducted the actual survey of the property.

Each of these four men took a quarter section of Pittsburg. Each man was to erect a building at the corner of what became Fourth and Broadway, but only Playter and Sergeant actually did so. Playter built his on the southwest corner, and his brother-in-law, W. G. Seabury, operated a general store there. Sergeant built his building on the northwest corner. This building was used as a drugstore by George F. Richey, but whiskey seemed to be his main business. Within a few years the building was replaced by the brick Lindberg Pharmacy, which lasted until the 1980s.

While this was going on, J. T. Roach built the first dwelling in 1876 and has that claim to fame. Another person, George Hobson, can also be credited with helping to form the community. In 1865, George and Mary Hobson left Iowa and moved to southeast Kansas, homesteading 160 acres nearby. The family, using the name Iowa City, opened the first post office, school, store, saloon and dance hall in the area. Hobson was involved with the first city government of New Pittsburgh, and was a community leader until he died in April 1891. Hobson was buried in the family cemetery, which is now part of the Highland Park Cemetery at the south end of town.

A post office using the name New Pittsburgh opened in 1876, and became Pittsburgh in 1881. It finally became Pittsburg in 1894 after action by the U. S. Board of Geographic Names recommended "burg" instead of "burgh." Commercial coal mining started by 1879 with the help of Moffett and Sergeant. The Pittsburg & Midway Coal Company was founded in 1885, and remained in business for almost a century in Kansas. Other coal companies opened, including the Ellsworth and Klaner Company, Mackie Clements Coal Mine, Meyer Coal Company, Mount Carmel Coal Mining Company, and the Sheridan Coal Company. Throughout the late 1800s, the coal industry in the Cherokee-Crawford Coal Field developed, and the population was 6,697 in 1890 and 10,112 in 1900. As more coal mines opened, the population reached 14,755 by the 1910 census.

Many of the mines were located right in Pittsburg, and the number of miners peaked about 1915 when Pittsburg was reportedly the most heavily unionized city in Kansas. Many of these workers were from Southern and Eastern Europe, and more than fifty nationalities came to mine coal and work the smelters at Pittsburg. About a dozen smelters had also been built around Pittsburg to work the lead and zinc ores, and a number of manufacturers had located here to take advantage of the smelting.

Smelters such as the Lanyon Zinc Works; W. and J. Lanyon Company; Robert Lanyon Zinc Works; S. H. Lanyon & Brother's Zinc Works; and the Granby Mining and Smelting Company all once stood here, attracting businesses like the United Iron Works Company.

Supporting the mine workers were almost every business imaginable, including grocery and drug stores, meat markets, billiard halls and barbershops, hotels and restaurants, clothing, banking, saloons (although prohibition was the law of Kansas), gambling houses, and houses of prostitution. The heavy use of mine labor started to end when the first steam shovel arrived at Pittsburg in 1911. The arrival of every large shovel seemed to have been the subject of an article in a local newspaper or a national magazine. For example, the March 1917 issue of *the Excavating Engineer* reported on the arrival of a Model 250 Marion steam shovel at the Pittsburg-Oskaloosa Coal Company, located "on a 320-acre field at Oskaloosa on the Kansas City Southern."

Another business that supported Pittsburg was the railroad industry. Leaders of Pittsburg worked to bring as many railroads as possible to town, and eventually four major railroads operated in and out of Pittsburg. There are several good examples of the efforts involved. In 1889, the Pittsburg Town Company gave seven lots to the Nevada & Minden Railway Company to assist in locating new rail facilities. During the early 1890s, Franklin Playter went to Kansas City to convince Arthur Stilwell to build his railroad through town, offering a right-of-way and even financial help. His efforts to partner with Stilwell were so successful that the railroad took on the name of the Kansas City, Pittsburg & Gulf and located their primary shops here.

Another railroad heavily involved in the development of Pittsburg was the St. Louis & San Francisco Railroad Company, and their Pittsburg Town Company, which acquired the land owned by Moffett & Sargent. The land company added several 40-acre additions to the town, helping the community to grow. The KCS passenger station and office building were both located in the Pittsburg Town Company's Second Addition.

The 1920s were the peak of the coal mining and smelting activities, and the population exceeded 18,000 residents, a number that Pittsburg has maintained to today. The *Agricultural and Industrial Bulletin* of the Kansas City Southern Railway (October 1923) had an article about Pittsburg.

> There are in the city seventy-four manufacturing industries with a capital investment of $4,000,000, 2,400 employees, and a payroll of $260,000. The combined payroll of all institutions is $2,000,000. The largest shops of the Kansas Southern Railway are located here, the same now in process of enlargement. Among the greater industrial enterprises are a large clay working and tile plant, three large brick plants and a large pottery plant. In this coal district are seventy-two strip coal mines operated with some of the largest steam shovels in the world, in addition to which there are operated one hundred and fifty deep shaft mines. Pittsburg is well favored in the matter of fuel, lying

in the center of a great coal field, having natural gas and cheap electric power, all available for manufactures. Not far from the city are great deposits of lead and zinc ores, in the immediate vicinity of great beds of valuable clays and shales, suitable for the manufacture of clay products of all kinds, hardwoods are within reasonable distance and agricultural products of many kinds in Crawford and adjacent counties. Good pure water is abundant and the climate leaves nothing to be desired.

One thing that wasn't noted in the article was that William Neal Deramus III was born here on December 10, 1915. Deramus was a noted railroad executive after World War II, serving as president of the Chicago Great Western Railway (1949-1957), Missouri-Kansas-Texas Railroad (1957-1961), and Kansas City Southern Railway (1961-1973).

Pittsburg continues to be a regional trade and business center, and currently has a population of about 20,000. The city has grown northward and it and Frontenac have essentially become one community. It is the home of Pittsburg State University, and the annual Little Balkans Days every Labor Day. Some coal is still mined in the region, and farming and ranching play important roles in the local economy. U.S. Highway 160 serves as the primary north-south road, and most of the rail lines that once served Pittsburg are now simply grades, with only the Kansas City Southern having a through mainline.

For those wanting to know more about the history of Pittsburg, Kansas, and especially its transportation history, check out the website *Pittsburg, Kansas Memories*.

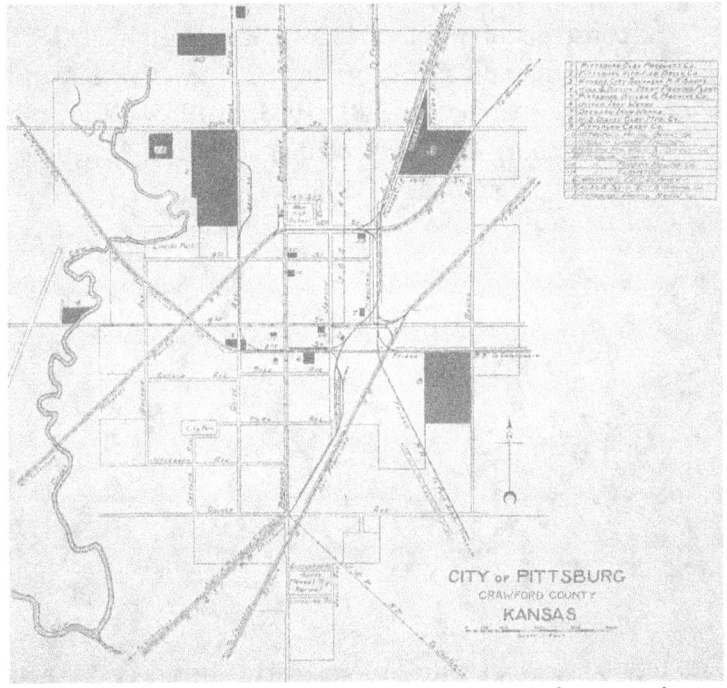

This map of Pittsburg was published in 1922 as part of a series of maps of Kansas. It shows the many railroads that served Pittsburg at the time. Note the error having the Kansas City Southern (Kansas City, Pittsburg & Gulf) line shown as "Frisco R. R. To Port Arthur, Texas." Walker, Perley F. *Industrial development of Kansas*. Topeka: Kansas state printing plant, B. P. Walker, printer, 1922. Pdf. Retrieved from the Library of Congress, https://www.loc.gov/item/22027281/.

Kansas City Southern Locomotive #1023

For years, KCS #1023 was a fixture in Schlanger Park at Pittsburg. The park is located east of the KCS mainline and north of Fourth Street. The steam locomotive was built in July 1906 by Alco-Pittsburg (construction number 40166). It was originally KCS #488 and built as a 2-8-0. In 1925, it was rebuilt and became switcher (0-8-0) #1023. In 1955, it was sold to Pittsburg for $1.00 and installed in Schlanger Park on September 17, 1955.

KCS 1023, a steam locomotive that was sold to Pittsburg in 1955, was on display in Schlanger Park until 2012. This photo shows the locomotive in 1989.

After more than a half-century, the City of Pittsburg grew tired of the steam locomotive and gave it to the Heart of the Heartlands organization at Carona, Kansas. On Wednesday, February 21, 2012, the locomotive was moved to Carona where efforts have continued to preserve one of the last steam locomotives owned by Kansas City Southern.

129.5 AT&SF CROSSING – Depending upon the timetable, this crossing is either at Milepost 129.4 or 129.5. Here, the Santa Fe line from Chanute, the Girard District, crossed back to the west side of the Kansas City Southern. This line curved further west to reach the Santa Fe station and freight house. In the 1970 timetable, this location is shown to be the AT&SF South Connection.

For the Kansas City Southern, the mainline curves to the south and once crossed a number of other railroads.

129.6 AT&SF CROSSING – The KCS once had a diamond here with a Santa Fe line that headed east to provide a connection with the Frisco. There was also a connection between the Santa Fe and the KCS that allowed ATSF trains to head south to Joplin. This is another crossing that was shown to be in a slightly different place in different timetables. This one was generally shown to be at Milepost 129.5 or 129.6.

Heading south, the KCS passed between properties shown to be the Arkansas Real Estate & Investment Company (to the west) and the Central Coal & Coke Company (to the east). The Central Coal & Coke Company was once the largest coal firm in the West. It had mines in many of the producing regions, including here and the Rock Springs, Wyoming, area. It had more than a dozen mines in Missouri alone. At Pittsburg, Central Coal & Coke was one of the largest producers, and also cleaned and processed coal from other smaller mines. The company was also the largest producer of semi-anthracite coal in western Arkansas, and worked with the KCS in those fields. The firm was much more than a coal company. It operated several lumber mills along the Kansas City, Pittsburg & Gulf in Louisiana and southwest Arkansas, and provided most of the bridge timbers for the Frisco extension across Indian Territory.

Recent employee timetables show this area to be Kelso, likely named for the Kelso Grain Company and Kelso Milling Company. A short 370-foot spur track curves west just south of Fourth Street, once the connecting track to the ATSF and their passenger station.

KCS 609 pulls a train southward in October of 1989. It is crossing the AT&SF just south of 4th Street at Pittsburg, Kansas.

Heavener Sub Route Guide

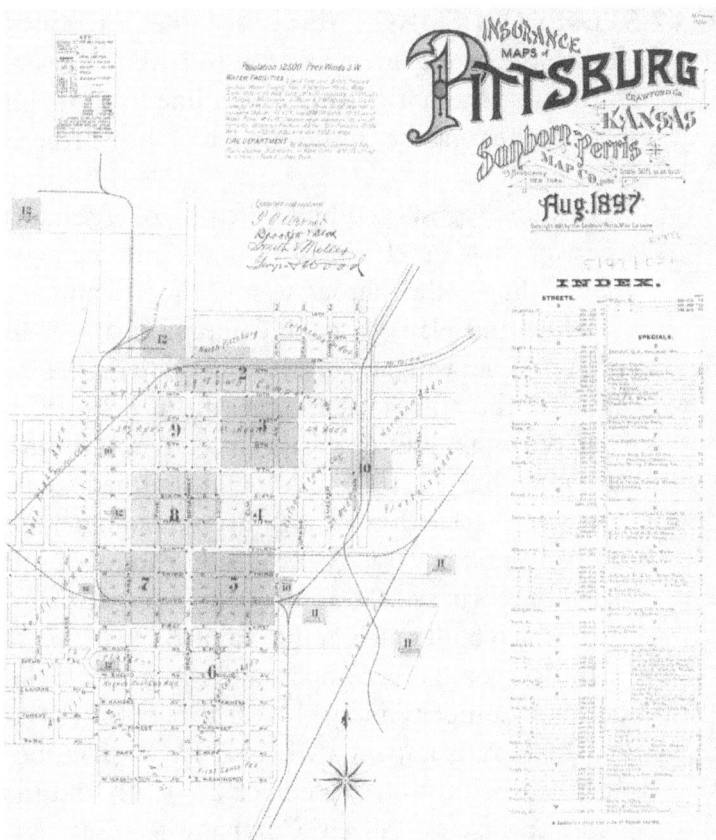

This 1897 Sanborn map shows the many at-grade crossings that the Kansas City, Pittsburg & Gulf had to deal with between Fourth Street and just south of Second Street. *Sanborn Fire Insurance Map from Pittsburg, Crawford County, Kansas*. Sanborn Map Company, Aug, 1897. Map. Retrieved from the Library of Congress, https://www.loc.gov/item/sanborn03060_003/.

129.6 STL&SF CONNECTION - This location was shown during the mid-twentieth century, and was the interchange track associated with the crossing to the south.

129.7 STL&SF CROSSING – This Frisco line was located along East Second Street and ran east-west. However, this was the northern end of a line from Joplin that later became the Girard Branch of the Northern Division.

This line was started by Moffett and Sergeant as a part of their development of mining in the area. The building of the railroad went through a number of names and plans, but the common goal was to connect Joplin with an outside railroad to reach new markets. The railroad dates back to July 25, 1874, when the Joplin Railroad was chartered in Missouri. On December 22, 1875, the Joplin Railroad Company was chartered in Kansas. Even though neither company built any track or grade, they were consolidated in February 1876 as the Joplin Railroad Company, which built much of the planned line.

Things got more complicated when the Joplin Railroad Company merged with the Joplin & Galena Railway Company (Missouri J&G – incorporated in Missouri on September 28, 1880) and the Joplin & Galena Railway Company (Kansas J&G – incorporated in Kansas on September 28, 1880). The Missouri J&G owned about six miles of track from Joplin to a point on the Missouri-Kansas state line, while the Kansas J&G owned about two miles of track from the state line southwesterly towards Galena, Kansas. The new Joplin Railway Company was formed in February 1882, and almost immediately was sold to the St. Louis & San Francisco Railway Company during March. The railroad became the St. Louis & San Francisco Railroad Company on June 30, 1896, and then the St. Louis-San Francisco Railway on August 24, 1916. The Frisco became part

Heavener Sub Route Guide

of the Burlington Northern Railroad on November 21, 1980.

At the time of the 1882 sale to the Frisco, the Joplin Railway Company had about 45 miles of mainline track from Girard (KS) through Pittsburg to Joplin (MO), and then west to Galena (KS). For a number of years, traffic on what was called the Girard Branch was heavy, with four passenger trains each way a day in 1899. A report by the Public Service Commission of the State of Missouri at the end of 1914 provided the following information about the line.

> *The Girard Branch (Northern Division) extends from Pittsburg, Kansas, to Carl Junction, Missouri. This branch enters Missouri from Kansas just north of Asbury, Missouri, crosses the main line of the Frisco running west from Carthage at Carl Junction, also connects with the Tuckahoe Branch at this point. 11.3 miles of the line is in Missouri. The track is laid with 75 pound rail from the Illinois Steel Company rolled in 1900 and relaid on this branch in 1907. Cinders and chat ballast are used and additional application to round out the ballast section is suggested. The right of way is clean, but the fences should have attention, and a few of the embankments should be widened. There are 3 pile trestles and one 45-foot deck plate girder on this branch, all in good condition.*

In 1936, there was both a diamond and an interchange track here. As the Frisco absorbed other lines in the area, the Girard Branch became less important. In 1959, the Frisco abandoned the line between Girard and Pittsburg, and Opolis and Carl Junction. By 1961, the line simply connected Pittsburg to Opolis, 7.2 miles in total length. In 1984, the line south of Pittsburg was abandoned and the Frisco obtained trackage rights over the KCS between here and Empire to serve a power plant. The short piece of track just west of the diamond was leased to the South Kansas & Oklahoma. After 2002, the route was fully abandoned and the railroad crossing no longer exists.

129.8 STL&SF CROSSING – This route once headed east from Cherryvale, running through Parsons, Cherokee, Pittsburg, and Minden Mines. There, the line turned north to pass through Mulberry, before connecting to the Fort Scott-Springfield mainline at Arcadia.

The route was built over a few years, and some of the history is confusing and even conflicts with itself since some of the location names changed and moved, and the railroads were commonly owned and funded. The first part was built by the Memphis, Kansas & Colorado Railway (MK&C), which built a narrow-gauge line from Cherokee to Parsons, Kansas, in 1878. The line was soon extended eastward to Weir City and Kramer. In 1880, the MK&C was purchased by the Missouri River, Fort Scott & Gulf Railroad, which extended the line from Parsons to Cherryvale, and then standard-gauged the line in one day.

Heavener Sub Route Guide

In 1881, construction from the north began when the Ft. Scott & Carthage Railroad built from Arcadia to Alston, with the Ft. Scott, South Eastern & Memphis Railway building between Mulberry and Minden Mines. The next year, the line was completed through Pittsburg and on to Kramer by the Kansas & Missouri Railroad. All of these railroad companies were related, and in 1888, the Ft. Scott, South Eastern & Memphis and Kansas & Missouri were consolidated into the Kansas City, Ft. Scott, & Gulf (KCFS&G). The KCFS&G was then consolidated into the Kansas City, Ft. Scott & Memphis. In 1901, the Frisco leased the Kansas City, Ft. Scott & Memphis, and then acquired it in 1928.

Kansas City Southern documents from 1936 show that there was a connection at this crossing, often listed as a separate station just to the south. The documents also showed that the crossing was gated. In 1961, the crossing was still gated and the Frisco route was the Parsons Subdivision of the Northern Division. The subdivision covered Dennis (east of Cherryvale, the route between Dennis and Cherryvale was abandoned in 1960) and Arcadia, and handled a great deal of coal. In 1976, the route west of Parsons to Dennis was abandoned. During the same year, the Frisco obtained trackage rights over KCS between Pittsburg and Mulberry, allowing the end of service over the nearly parallel route.

The Frisco became part of the Burlington Northern Railroad on November 21, 1980. In 1987, BN abandoned the rest of the route from Arcadia to Minden Mines. BN then abandoned the Parsons-Cherokee route in 1990. This left the Cherokee-Pittsburg tracks as the only remaining part of the line. About 2002, work was underway to sell the line to the

South Kansas & Oklahoma Railroad (SKOL). The SKOL was formed by Watco in 1990, and acquired 287 miles of rail lines from the ATSF on December 28, 1990. By the 2002 purchase of the remains of the Parsons Subdivision, the Southeast Kansas Railroad had been merged into the SKOL, and the tracks of the two railroads were consolidated in the Pittsburg area. According to the *Kansas Statewide Rail Plan* (2017), the line is operated as part of the SKOL Coffeyville Subdivision which extends from Sherman to Cherokee to Pittsburg. The report also stated that the SKOL handled 68,800 carloads of corn, wheat, fertilizers, lumber, cement and sand in 2016, the most of any short line railroad in Kansas.

With the abandonment of the former Missouri Pacific line west of Pittsburg, operated at the time by the Southeast Kansas Railroad, a new connection was necessary to tie the former Frisco and former Missouri Pacific lines operated by the SKOL together. Both Frisco crossings here are now gone, and a connection was built northward onto the KCS mainline. The new junction has been shown to be the SEK Junction for years in various KCS timetables, and allows South Kansas & Oklahoma trains to head north over KCS to North Yard, where a connection is made with the old Southeast Kansas line.

Today, this former crossing is in a wooded area east of an older residential area, and the KCS turns to the southeast as it leaves town. During the early days of Pittsburg, the land was owned by the Central Coal & Coke Company.

Heavener Sub Route Guide

130.3 INTERNATIONAL PAPER – As late as the early 2000s, there was a spur track to the west at Jefferson Street to serve an International Paper warehouse. A short distance south of here was once the Alphons Custodis Chimney Construction Company. A spur track cut west to the company, which was located south of Quincy Avenue. The firm specialized in curved brick that was used in tall smokestacks and factory chimneys, and the company built chimneys across the country. In 1869, Alphons Custodis developed perforated radial brick in Germany, which made the construction of very tall chimneys practical. His firm was incorporated in New York City in 1902 and later manufactured brick at a number of facilities across the country. During the early 1900s tall brick chimneys became important as they allowed factories to discharge smoke at greater heights, reducing ground level pollution. Taller chimneys also increased draft allowing for hotter fires and more energy production. The company continues to operate to this day as Hamon Custodis. Don't look for many remains of the industry as it was not operated after 1908.

132.4 EAST COW CREEK BRIDGE – This is a three-span plate girder bridge. Also known as Little Cow Creek, East Cow Creek forms northeast of Pittsburg and flows south and then west around town. It flows into Cow Creek several miles southwest of here.

132.6 JOPLIN & PITTSBURG RAILWAY COMPANY CONNECTION – From near Pittsburg to KOG Junction near Asbury, the Joplin & Pittsburg Railway Company line followed closely to the west of the KCS mainline. This was part of the series of electric railroad passenger lines that served the Pittsburg, Kansas, region. During their last years of operations, many relied more upon freight movements and interchanged freight with the steam railroads to pay their bills.

On March 20, 1890, the Pittsburg Railway Company received a franchise to build an electric railroad at Pittsburg, with all of the shops and offices located there. The railway was owned by B. F. Hobart, the president of the Pittsburg Town Company. Service began over three miles of track on October 30, 1890, heading north and south along Broadway.

The Forest Park Electric Railway received a franchise on January 25, 1891, to build east-west along Fourth Street. On September 5, 1894, the Pittsburg, Frontenac & Suburban Railway Company (PF&S) also received a franchise, and eventually owned the Forest Park Electric Railway. The PF&S soon built to the town of Chopee, and after several management changes, became the Pittsburg Railroad Company on July 12, 1901. A few more management changes took place and more lines were built over the next few years, including to Weir City and further to the southwest. Meanwhile, a number of other proposals were made to build electric lines throughout southeast Kansas and southwest Missouri.

The Joplin & Pittsburg Railway Company was one of these new organizations, receiving a Kansas charter on July 16, 1907. The firm acquired the former operations of the Pittsburg, Frontenac & Suburban Railway and its new owner, the Pittsburg Railroad Company. This included the large car barn and repair complex at East 20th Street and North Michigan Avenue, not far west of the Kansas City Southern's North Yard and shops. Work started quickly on a planned 150-mile route that would connect Pittsburg, Joplin and Neosho, plus many smaller communities. The Joplin-Pittsburg Line (Air Line Division) was completed on March 19, 1908, despite the Financial Panic of 1907.

On March 1, 1910, a number of the lines were reorganized and consolidated, with the Joplin & Pittsburg Railway Company and J. J. Heim leading the way. This company operated 110 miles of track, handling both passengers and freight with their electric trolleys and interurban trains. The routes served Mulberry, Girard and many other coal mining and trade towns north of Pittsburg. To the southwest, a series of lines served Weir City, Columbus, and Mineral. Finally, there was this route between Pittsburg and Joplin.

The next few years saw financial troubles, a long strike in 1914, political problems, and even pauses in rail service. Services changed as mines moved, and it seemed that every union held a strike against the electric rail service. At the same time, new public roads were being built and private automobiles began to appear, an issue common with all electric railroads. By 1918, the Joplin & Pittsburg Railway Company was in financial trouble again, but there were still pressures to increase employee pay, lower fares, and add services. Numerous studies by the Kansas and Missouri public utility commissions failed to find solutions. Several strikes, sometimes violent, continued. Freight movements seemed to be the answer as passenger volumes decreased, and interchange tracks were built in several locations. Despite this, on February 29, 1924, the Joplin & Pittsburg Railway entered receivership.

The first receivership was temporary, but a second one was announced on September 18, 1924. The railroad was sold to its bondholders on March 14, 1925. Some physical improvements were made, but taxes remained unpaid. Passenger service was reduced, and even halted on some lines. The Joplin-Pittsburg service ended on the last day of March, 1929. On May 14th, a sale of the property took place, with most lines sold for scrap. The Joplin & Pittsburg Railway officially ended on June 15, 1929. For those wanting more details, check out *A History of the Joplin & Pittsburg Electric Railway Company, 1890-1929* by Robert Eastman Hickman, available from Pittsburg State University.

133.9 CONTROL POINT EMPIRE – A junction was here with a line heading about six miles to the east to serve the Asbury Generating Station of the Empire District Electric Company. The Empire District was organized as a Kansas corporation in 1909. Like many electric utilities, Empire District has a bit of a complex ownership. The Algonquin Power & Utilities Corporation is the main company, and uses Liberty Utilities to manage and operate their electricity, water, and natural gas utility services. A subsidiary is Empire District Electric, which serves about 215,000 customers in Missouri, Kansas, Oklahoma and Arkansas.

Heavener Sub Route Guide

This is part of the Ashbury Power Plant complex. The tall brick building supports the coal conveyors once used to move coal around the plant, while the building to the left is where coal was unloaded from KCS trains.

Control Point Empire was for years a busy junction with the line to the Asbury Generating Station. However, the plant is now closed and coal trains no longer head east from this switch.

This sign stands just outside of the Ashbury Power Plant at the end of the Empire Coal Spur.

Unit 1 of the Asbury plant was commissioned in 1970 and produced 213 megawatts. A smaller 19 megawatt Unit 2 was commissioned in 1986. For years, the plant was fueled primarily by coal, with oil being used as start-up fuel. The plant's coal was a blend of approximately 92% Powder River Basin coal and 8% local blend coal. For years, the Wyoming coal came from the Rochelle/North Antelope mines owned by Peabody. The coal was moved by Union Pacific and Kansas City Southern, and the plant featured the typical loop track to turn the trains – C-KCEM (earlier train No. 61, operating as a coal load from Kansas City to Empire Electric) and C-EMKC (earlier train No. 62, operating as a coal empty from Empire Electric to Kansas City). At the mainline, the switch was a control point, operated by the KCS dispatcher.

Heavener Sub Route Guide

Until very recently, this plant was still active, producing electrical power for the region, However, during October 2017, Empire District filed an application with the Missouri Public Service Commission to start replacing the Asbury plant with a wind and solar farm. After several years of planning, the plant closed in March 2020.

Control Point Empire was located just north of East 510th Avenue. Located between the switch and the road crossing is a tall communications tower.

Near Control Point Empire is Milepost 134, which is a measured mile for northbound trains.

135.3 KNIVETON – Look for the location where the tracks pass under Kansas Highway 171, also known as County Line Road. The railroad once had a long siding here, 96 cars long in 1936. The name Kniveton comes from a small unincorporated community in the area. Kniveton started in Crawford County, and then moved to the railroad about 1895 when a post office opened in the new community. The community didn't grow and the post office closed in 1902. The name Kniveton likely came from the Kniveton family who lived in this part of Kansas.

Kniveton was actually located at an important crossroads, the intersection of the old Fort Leavenworth-Fort Scott-Fort Gibson military road with Kansas Highway 57. On July 2, 1836, President Andrew Jackson signed a bill to provide for better protection of the Western frontier. Among the plans was a new military road that would run just west of the states of Missouri and Arkansas and that would connect a series of military outposts. U. S. Army officers Colonel Zachary Taylor (later 12th president of the United States from 1849 until his death in 1850), Major W. G. McNeil, and Major T. F. Smith were made commissioners to lay out the road and locate sites for the military posts.

The road was surveyed in 1837, and by the early 1840s the military road connected South Dakota with the Red River in Texas. The route is currently the U.S. Highway 69 corridor. To mark the importance of the military road, a Daughters of the American Revolution (DAR) granite marker was placed on the north side of the road, a short distance east of the railroad tracks at Kniveton, on June 19, 1935. Because the roads have moved, the marker was later moved to the west at the intersection of U.S. Highway 69/160.

County Line

Kansas Highway 171 also marks the county line between **Crawford County** to the north, and **Cherokee County** to the south. **Crawford County** was created from parts of Bourbon and Cherokee counties in 1867. It was named for Samuel J. Crawford, who was the governor of Kansas at the time. The county's economy has long been based upon coal mining (Pittsburg-Weir Coalfield) and its population peaked at 61,800 in the 1920 census when mining was also at its peak. Today, the county's population is less than 40,000. While Pittsburg is the most populous city, Girard is the county seat.

Cherokee County is located in the southeastern corner of Kansas. When Indian Territory was created west of the Mississippi River, this area was included in the Cherokee Neutral Lands. The Kansas Territory was created in 1854, and in 1861 Kansas was admitted as the 34th state. The county was created in 1855 and named for E. McGee of Missouri, a member of the Territorial Legislature. It was renamed in 1866 to recognize the previous owners of much of the land. The county seat is Columbus and the biggest town is Baxter Springs. The county's population peaked in 1920 with 42,694 residents, but has dropped to about 20,000 today.

The railroad is in Cherokee County, Kansas, for only 3.2 miles before it enters Jasper County, Missouri.

136.3 COAL VALLEY ROAD – This was not a station on the railroad, but it does use the name of a small coal mining community to the west. This area was part of the Cherokee-Crawford Coal Field, a large development that once included both shaft and strip mines.

The railroad spends a great deal of time and money maintaining the Heavener Subdivision. During February 2022, Loram rail grinder RG401 was found working in the Coal Valley area at Milepost 137.0.

This road sign is one of the few reminders of the Coal Valley community, once a part of the Cherokee-Crawford Coal Field.

Heavener Sub Route Guide

The abandoned grade of the Joplin & Pittsburg Railway Company follows the KCS mainline through this area. At the Weir Road grade crossing at Milepost 137.7, the old grade is easy to find as it passes through the woods on the west side of the KCS.

138.5 KANSAS/MISSOURI STATE LINE – Look for State Line Avenue (NE 118th Street), a typical area farm road. To the west is Cherokee County, Kansas, while to the east is Jasper County, Missouri. **Kansas** was a part of the Louisiana Purchase, but it wasn't until 1827 that settlement began with the establishment of Fort Leavenworth. The Kansas-Nebraska Act of 1854 officially opened the state and created the Kansas Territory on May 30, 1854. It became a state on January 29, 1861, making it the 34th state. The area was named for the Kansas River, which took the name from the Kansa Native Americans who lived along the river's banks. The state is the 15th largest and the 34th most populous, and Topeka is the state capital. The state is officially The Sunflower State, but it is also known as The Wheat State, The Jayhawker State, and The Free State. Its state anthem is *Home on the Range*.

KCS only has 3.2 miles of mainline across **Cherokee County**, located in the southeastern corner of Kansas. When Indian Territory was created west of the Mississippi River, this area was included in the Cherokee Neutral Lands. The county was created in 1855 and named for E. McGee of Missouri, a member of the Territorial Legislature. It was renamed in 1866 to recognize the previous owners of much of the land. The county seat is Columbus and the biggest town is Baxter Springs. The county's population peaked in 1920 with 42,694 residents, but has dropped to about 20,000 today.

Missouri borders eight different states. No state borders on more. Missouri became the 24th state on August 10, 1821. Today, Missouri is the 21st largest and the 18th most populated of the states. Known as the "Gateway to the West," Missouri was the starting point and the return destination of the Lewis and Clark Expedition, as well as the starting points of the Pony Express Trail and Oregon Trail. Its capital is Jefferson City, one of the smaller cities in the state and named for Thomas Jefferson, the third President of the United States. There is actually no official state nickname, but the "Show Me State" has appeared on its license plates. The phrase "The Lead State" has been used, and is explained by the lead mining history in this part of Missouri.

Jasper County was created on January 29, 1841, with the first government organized on February 25, 1841. A new town, Carthage, was created as the county seat on March 28, 1842. At the time, Jasper County also included what eventually became Barton County. Like many area counties, it was mostly abandoned during the guerrilla wars of the Civil War. Later, the county boomed due to lead and zinc mining.

The county honors Sergeant William Jasper, a Revolutionary War hero. During the battle of Sullivan's Island in June 1776, the British pounded the American fort, eventually shooting down the flagpole bearing the Fort Moultrie Flag – a blue flag with a white crescent used by South Carolina forces. William Jasper, a member of the Second South Carolina Regiment, jumped out of the fort, walked the entire length in full view of the British, and then cut the flag from its pole. Climbing the wall, he fastened the flag to a cannon sponge-staff and planted it in the wall, all while in the face of deadly fire. For this feat, South Carolina President John Rutledge presented Jasper with his dress sword at a review held soon after the battle and offered him a commission. Jasper turned the commission down, instead preferring to serve as a scout for the American forces. Jasper was also recognized later for his scouting efforts against the British until he was killed at Savannah in 1779 while planting the colors of the Second South Carolina Regiment on the British lines. He was buried somewhere near the scene of the battle in a mass grave with many of his comrades.

1914 Public Service Commission Report

A very detailed report about the Kansas City Southern mainline was produced by the Public Service Commission of the State of Missouri in their *Report of Miscellaneous Orders, Authorities, Accidents, Inspections, and Conference Rulings – April 15, 1913, to December 31, 1914*. The report covered everything from rail size to the number of track workers, as well as the condition of the cuspidors, drinking fountains, and outhouses at each of the KCS stations.

The report showed that the railroad was replacing the existing rail with larger rail sizes from north to south. Mileposts 23 to 172.8, the railroad had installed 85-pound rail in 1906. From Milepost 172.8 to Milepost 178.6, the rail dated from 1905 and weighed 80 pounds per yard. The track on south to the Arkansas border had 75-pound rail from 1899. To maintain the track between this Kansas line and the Arkansas line 65 miles to the south, the railroad had 11 section foremen and 66 section laborers. The Public Service Commission report made some specific observations about the track structure, including that from "milepost 164 to milepost 173 the track is subject to overflow from Shoal Creek."

A major part of the report dealt with an inspection of each Missouri passenger station on the line. Their observations provide an interesting idea of what a station from that era was like, so some of the comments are included here.

Westline – No cuspidors; no water cooler; no water supply; no sanitary drinking cups for sale.

Gulfton – No cuspidors; no water cooler; no sanitary drinking cups for sale.

Joplin New Union Depot – Just completed at a cost of approximately $115,000. Condition excellent.

Neosho – No cuspidors; no water cooler; drinking fountain suggested and agreed to.

Goodman – No cuspidors; no water cooler; no sanitary drinking cups for sale; outhouses not stenciled to denote sex compartment.

Anderson – No cuspidors; condition of outhouses very bad. This depot to be rebuilt on new location.

139.0 KO&G JUNCTION – While KO&G or KOG Junction was the common name used for this location, some documents show it to also be Asbury Junction. In 1964, the Southern Belle passenger train No. 1 was scheduled to pass here heading southbound at 11:55am. While it had a scheduled time here, KO&G Junction was not a stop for the train.

So why was there a schedule for this location? The main answer is that this was the junction with the Baxter Springs Branch, a line that once headed southwest 20.4 miles to Baxter Springs, Kansas. Baxter Springs is known as the first "Kansas Cow Town." About 1850, Mr. A. Baxter claimed land in the area and opened an inn and tavern. During the Civil War, a military post opened there to protect the area and to serve as a supply post. After the war, a surplus of cattle in Texas and a shortage of beef in the north led to efforts to connect the two. Baxter Springs had rail access and the Stockyards and Drovers Association was created to buy and sell cattle. At times, the Association handled 20,000 cows scattered across grazing land and in a series of corrals. By the mid-1870s, railroads were reaching Texas and the boom at Baxter Springs was over.

However, Baxter Springs took on a new role as a railroad junction town. This line's history dates back to the creation of the Muskogee Union Railway on May 26, 1903. This railroad built 8.3 miles of track between Wagoner and Okay, Oklahoma, before being sold to the Missouri, Oklahoma & Gulf Railway Company (MO&G) on October 29, 1904. The MO&G extended the line to the south and then looked northward for a connection to the northern markets. The Missouri, Oklahoma & Gulf Railroad Company was incorporated on December 12, 1911, to extend the line. It built 2.524 miles of track from the Oklahoma-Kansas state line to Baxter Springs. The relationship between the two MO&G companies was explained by the Interstate Commerce Commission.

> *The property of the Missouri, Oklahoma and Gulf Railroad was operated by its own organization from the date of acquisition thereof to September 21, 1912; by the Missouri, Oklahoma and Gulf Railway, under lease, from September 21, 1912, to December 12, 1913; and from the latter date to December 31, 1918, by receivers. From January 1, 1919, to date of valuation, it was operated by the United States Railroad Administration as a part of the operating unit of the Missouri, Oklahoma and Gulf Railway.*

To solve the financial problems, the Kansas, Oklahoma & Gulf Railway (KO&G) was incorporated on July 31, 1919, to take over the assets of the Missouri, Oklahoma & Gulf Railway, giving it a line from Baxter Springs, Kansas, to Denison, Texas. The KO&G entered receivership in 1924 and was acquired by those involved with the Midland Valley Railroad. The partnership created a connecting route between the Texas & Pacific Railway to the south, and its owner Missouri Pacific Railroad to the north. The line was eventually sold to the Texas & Pacific about the time the railroad abandoned the track between Baxter Springs and North Muskogee.

The Missouri, Oklahoma & Gulf Railroad Company had petitioned the ICC for permission to build a line northward from Baxter Springs to a junction with the Kansas City Southern. From there, the MO&G would use trackage rights to reach Kansas City. Construction reportedly started in 1918, but the nationalization of the railroads during WWI and then the receivership of the KO&G delayed progress on the route. The KO&G slowly continued with the plans, but on June 8, 1925, Kansas City Southern applied to lease the work started and complete the line at their own cost since the receivers of the KO&G were "unable to operate the extension and the receivers have not the available funds for that purpose." At Baxter Springs, KCS would use the facilities of the Kansas, Oklahoma & Gulf. In return, KCS agreed...

> *to pay monthly one-twelfth of an amount equal to 5 per cent per annum on a valuation thereof to be hereafter agreed upon. The applicant will also pay all taxes assessed against the leased line and all ex-*

> *penses of maintenance and operation. As rental for the joint facilities at Baxter Springs, the applicant is to pay monthly one-twelfth of an amount equal to 2.5 per cent per annum on a valuation of such facilities to be hereafter agreed upon. The applicant will bear a proportionate part of the expenses of maintenance and operation and a proportionate part of the taxes assessed against the joint facilities.*

There was a very interesting statement in the Interstate Commerce Commission report about possible additional trackage rights. Apparently, Kansas City Southern stated that "the extension will enable it to enter into negotiations for trackage rights over the line of the Oklahoma Company between Baxter Springs and Wagoner, Okla., and over the Missouri Pacific Railroad between Wagoner and Sallisaw, Okla., by means of which trackage rights it can run its trains from Asbury, Mo., to Sallisaw over lines of railroad with a maximum grade of 1 per cent, whereas the maximum grade is now 1.62 per cent on parts of its existing line between Asbury and Sallisaw."

The Interstate Commerce Commission had earlier examined the use of the Kansas, Oklahoma & Gulf by the Kansas City Southern. In *Decisions of the Interstate Commerce Commission of the United States – July 1921 to September 1921*, research on combining various railroads into larger systems looked at merging KCS and KO&G with Missouri Pacific. It also examined the use of trackage owned by the KO&G and Missouri Pacific to improve the KCS. At the time, there were a number of reports about survey crews looking for a better route through the Ozarks for the KCS.

> An improvement now being developed by the Kansas City Southern in order to make it a low-grade line to the Gulf is under way. At present the main line south of Joplin has some grades as high as 1.4 per cent, through the western foothills of the Ozarks. Swinging the road farther to the west, out into the flat country, would make it possible to eliminate this handicap. Negotiations are now in hand for trackage rights over the Kansas, Oklahoma & Gulf from Joplin, through Baxter Springs down to Muskogee, Okla. Thence trackage is to be taken over the Missouri Pacific back to the main line of the Kansas City Southern at Sallisaw, Okla. This detour would give a low grade line with a maximum of 0.5 per cent grade to be utilized for through freight only. The old main line, still tapping important territory, would be utilized for passenger and lighter business.

The July-August 1925 issue of *Agricultural and Industrial Bulletin* reported on the new line to Baxter Springs. It stated that the line was completed on July 31, 1925, and that it provided a connection to the Kansas, Oklahoma & Gulf Railroad and the markets of Texas and the Southwest. While no passenger service was planned, one or more freight trains were to be part of the operation. The article reported that the manifest train from Kansas City "arrives at Pittsburg at 4:40 in the morning. The train for Baxter Springs will leave at 5:30 a.m., transferring freight at Baxter to the K.O. & G. Railroad."

The October issue included more information about the Baxter Springs Branch. "The new Baxter Springs Branch of the Kansas City Southern Railway, connecting with the Kansas, Oklahoma & Gulf Ry., is reported to be doing business on a satisfactory scale. There is a good south bound business from Kansas City and large northbound shipments of cattle, ores, oil. Daily trains of fifty or more cars are reported to pass over this branch."

Business held steady for a few years, but the consolidation of the railroads in the region and the changing markets slowly made the branch line less important. By the late 1980s, the line was cut in half with less than ten miles remaining between here and the Frisco at Crestline (once known as Military Junction). An application to abandon this line was made in 1995, and in 1997, KCS received permission to abandon the branch line, but with a notice of interim trail use/rail banking. The Rails to Trails Conservancy pushed the idea of the interim trail use and several efforts were made to turn the branch into a trail. However, on June 22, 2015, the plans were terminated and on July 22, 2015, the Surface Transportation Board officially stated that "KCS may fully abandon the Baxter Springs Branch line from milepost 139.01 L at the connection with the KCS main line to the end of the line at milepost 148.51 L near Crestline, Kan."

A few signs of the old Baxter Springs Branch can still be found. The switch for KO&G Junction was once located just south of Pine Road, where an Automatic Equipment Identification, or AEI reader, is

Heavener Sub Route Guide

now located. The grade of the Baxter Springs Branch stayed on the west side of the mainline before turning south and passing west of Asbury. A few signs of the old grade remain where it crosses Oak Road on the northwest side of Asbury. The old grade turns to the southwest near Waco.

The location of KO&G Junction can still be found thanks to the AEI reader and the concrete Milepost 139 marker.

139.9 STL&SF CROSSING – This crossing was with the Girard Branch of the Northern Division of the Frisco, the former Joplin Railroad. This line connected Pittsburg and Joplin and was opened about 1876. The Joplin Railroad, built by local mine owners, has the claim of being the first railroad to serve Joplin. The history of this line is included with information about the crossing at Pittsburg at Milepost 129.7.

In 1936, this crossing was shown to be interlocked. In 1959, the Frisco abandoned the line between Opolis (to the north) and Carl Junction (to the south), ending the need for this crossing. When the Frisco abandoned the line, a few miles of track was sold to KCS to maintain service to a grain elevator at Waco, Missouri. Waco was laid out in 1875 as the Joplin Railroad built northward from Joplin to Pittsburg. A post office opened at Waco in 1878, and the population peaked at 368 in the 1920 census. The original townsite included six blocks east of the tracks with the Frisco depot to the east between Collins and Main streets. Depot Street ran north-south on the east side of the tracks. The post office closed during the early 2000s and the population was 87 in 2010. Valley Grain still has a small elevator at Waco.

Waco Spur

After the line to Waco was acquired, a new connecting switch and track was installed to allow KCS trains to serve Waco. This led to the station of Waco Spur at Milepost 139.8. The Waco Spur was shown to be from Milepost W 139.80 at the connection with the KCS main line, to the end of the line at Milepost W 142.9, a distance of 2.69 miles. Like the Baxter Springs Branch, the Waco Spur, also known as the Waco Branch, was first involved in an abandonment application in 1995. Also like the Baxter Branch, permission was received to end service on the line in 1997, with the provision that interim trail use/rail banking be included in the plan. The Ozark Regional Land Trust was assigned the right to develop the rail to trail project. In 2015, a request was made to assign another party to the Waco Spur project.

Heavener Sub Route Guide

Several old foundations of grain elevators and warehouses can still be found along the abandoned Waco Spur at Asbury, Missouri.

Little exists of the former Waco Spur, but at Waco, this street sign still reminds folks that there was once a depot here.

140.3 ASBURY – The community of Asbury started here in the late 1800s, and a post office opened using that name in 1894. According to the 1930 masters thesis of Robert Lee Meyers ("Place Names In The Southwest Counties Of Missouri"), there were many Asburys in the vicinity and it was very likely named for the family.

With a town already forming, Asbury was platted in 1896 and promoted by the Kansas City, Pittsburg & Gulf. The *Agricultural and Industrial Bulletin* (March 1924) reported that Asbury had about 300 inhabitants, seven or more mercantile houses, a lumber yard, two churches, one grammar and one high school, electric lights, a lodge building, several minor businesses, and the Bank of Asbury. It also reported that the principal commodities shipped from Asbury were "grain, hay, poultry, cream, eggs, hogs, and pedigreed cattle." The population has stayed between 200 and 250 since that time.

Asbury is a small community, and this sign marks the City of Asbury Municipal Building.

Heavener Sub Route Guide

The Asbury post office, located a block west of the tracks, uses the old Bank of Asbury building.

The importance of Arthur E. Stilwell and his railroad to Asbury is demonstrated by this street – Stilwell Avenue.

A map from 1895 showed the plans for Asbury. At the time, there were 16 blocks to the east of the Kansas City, Pittsburg & Gulf, which had a depot on the west side of their mainline with a siding around its west side. Stock yards were further to the south and for years a mail crane also stood near the station. An 84-car siding has historically been located on the west side of the mainline, but is located on the east side today. In 2002, the siding was shown to be 6963 feet long, and then 9724 feet by 2012. In 1964, the *Southern Belle* (No. 1 southbound) was shown to pass here at 11:58am, but no stops were shown in the timetable.

At the very northwest corner of the town was the crossing of the KCP&G and the St. Louis & San Francisco. The SL&SF was not far west of the KCP&G, and there were three industrial blocks between the two railroads. The KCS showed that in 1917, there were interchange tracks with Joplin & Pittsburg and the Missouri Pacific.

The siding at Asbury is a popular place for the dispatcher to meet trains. On May 18, 2021, KCS 5010 pulls southward through Asbury's siding, while a northbound train sits on the mainline.

Heavener Sub Route Guide

Heading south, Missouri Highway 171 closely follows the KCS mainline to near Joplin, Missouri.

143.3 SPRING RIVER BRIDGE – This bridge crosses the Spring River. It includes a long Pratt through truss over the main channel, and two deck plate girder spans on the south approach. The north approach is much longer and requires 25 concrete ballast deck spans. The Pratt through truss was built in 1905 and was designed by Waddell & Hedrick of Kansas City, Missouri. The entire structure is easily visible from the adjacent Missouri Highway 171.

This plate on the south end of the through truss span shows that Waddell & Hedrick designed the bridge in 1905.

During May of 2021, KCS 4707 and a number of other locomotives were photographed heading north across the Spring River bridge.

The Spring River is about 130 miles long and starts at a spring near Verona, Missouri, and flows southwest into the Grand Lake O' the Cherokees (Neosho River in Oklahoma). The river took its name from the many springs which feed water into the river. It was an important water source for Native Americans and settlers, and was also used by a number of grist and other mills.

147.2 GULFTON – Gulfton is essentially an eastern suburb of the larger Carl Junction. The first settlement in the area was about three miles southwest of Carl Junction, founded in 1848 by Daniel Hunt. Hunt's trading post was a regional supply center, and he traded with Native Americans for horses and pelts.

With the discovery of lead ore, railroads began to be built throughout the area. During April 1877, Charles L. Skinner platted Carl Junction with 81 lots, seven streets and four alleys. Skinner was a German

Heavener Sub Route Guide

immigrant whose real name was Charles Carl, thus the name of Carl Junction. A post office opened in 1878 as the community grew. Located at an elevation of 896 feet, the new community was located at a planned railroad junction between the Joplin & Girard Railway and the Kansas City, Fort Scott & Gulf route. The history of Carl Junction states that the first train arrived at the new depot on July 20, 1879. Because of the junction, a number of facilities were located here, including a switching yard, interchange tracks, section houses, and a coal chute and water tower. Today, the junction area is used by the new Carl Junction Community Center complex.

Carl Junction became famous in August of 1892 when the remains of four American elephants (Elephas Americanus) were found. The fossilized bones of the two adult and two infant elephants were sold and then displayed at the Columbian Exposition of the Chicago World's Fair in 1893. Carl Junction was a railroad and mining town, but today benefits from being a suburb of nearby Joplin, Missouri. Today's population is at its highest ever of about 8300.

Just east of Carl Junction is Gulfton, where the KCS crossed the former Frisco Carthage Subdivision at what was shown as STL&SF Crossing. The track between Carthage and Carl Junction was built in 1872-1873 by the Memphis, Carthage & Northwestern Railroad Company (MC&N). In 1877, the MC&N became part of the Missouri & Western and the line was extended west to Oswego. In 1879, all of the line went to the Frisco. The route was extended by several other companies, which also became part of the St. Louis-San Francisco. Burlington Northern abandoned the line from Carthage through Carl Junction to Columbus in 2002. The grade through the Carl Junction area is now a walking and biking trail, known as the Ruby Jack Trail. The trail is 16 miles long, running from the Kansas state line eastward to Carthage, Missouri.

About 1900, the Gulfton area was busy with a number of tracks. There was an 84-car siding to the east, located north of the diamond. There was an interchange track off the south end of the siding that curved to the east to connect with the Frisco. A small station owned by the KCS was located in the northeast corner of the interlocked diamond. The small community of Gulfton was located to the east between the KCS and Ivy Road to the north (McFerran Road in 1895), and Missouri Highway 270 (Texas Avenue in 1895) to the east.

While the Kansas City Southern track still exists, the former Frisco line at Gulfton is now the Ruby Jack Trail.

For a number of years, Gulfton was a regular stop, and even a transfer location, for passengers between the Frisco and the KCS. However, by 1964, the southbound *Southern Belle* (No. 1) wasn't scheduled to stop here, although a time of 12:04pm was shown in the schedule.

Railway Signaling

During the early 1900s, the Interstate Commerce Commission (ICC) obtained the authority to research railroad block-signal systems and to require them where they would add significant safety. The use of block-signal systems became a common recommendation of accident investigators. From August 18, 1941, to May 25, 1942, KCS experienced four serious collisions between trains that resulted in this recommendation.

On April 13, 1939, the ICC had ordered the Kansas City Southern to install an automatic block signal system on several sections of the railroad, including between Joplin and McElhany, both in Missouri. The reason that Joplin-McElhany was one of the areas chosen for the signals was that it had some of the heaviest traffic density on the entire railroad. Additionally, the track between Joplin and Neosho was also used by the Missouri & Arkansas Railway.

This installation was delayed by World War II, and on December 30, 1943, the ICC again ordered the installation of the signals, with installations to be completed on or before July 1, 1944. This second order included the provision that if a centralized traffic control system was installed, that all hand-operated main track switches within the installation would be equipped with electric switch locks.

In 1945, the railroad installed 33.5 miles of Automatic Block Signaling south from Gulfton to McElhany. During this work, the semaphore signals at the automatic interlocking at Gulfton were replaced with color-light signals, described as being General Railway Signal Company searchlights. KCS cited that the route between Neosho and Joplin was also used by the Missouri & Arkansas, but those operations ended within a year. The track north of Joplin was signaled because of the many industries in the area, as was the track Neosho south past Camp Crowder to McElhany. The following is from the August 1945 issue of *Railway Signaling*.

> In this territory, the Kansas City Southern operates two passenger trains. One of these, the "Flying Crow," including standard equipment and steam locomotives, is operated between Kansas City, Mo., and Port Arthur, Tex. The other, the "Southern Belle," is made up of streamlined lightweight equipment with Diesel-electric locomotives, and is operated between Kansas City and New Orleans, La. The schedules include two fast through freight trains each way daily for the Kansas City Southern, and one freight train each way daily for the Missouri & Arkansas. Extra trains are operated as required so that a total of 14 to 16 trains are operated daily over this territory, in addition to 6 to 8 switching moves between Neosho and Camp Crowder.

Heavener Sub Route Guide

149.0 CENTER CREEK BRIDGE – Look for the five-span deck plate girder bridge with various length spans. The stream forms to the east near Monett, Missouri, and flows west to enter the Spring River. In total, it is almost thirty miles long. Center Creek is a fast and narrow creek, and floating and fishing reports describe it as having many sharp turns and obstacles. The name of the stream came from its location near the center of old Barry County.

KCS train No. 91 was photographed heading south in 1997. This photo of grey KCS 663 on the Center Creek bridge was one of the results of that chase.

Several miles to the east was once Lakeside Park, operated by the Southwest Missouri Electric Railway. The park was built to get people to ride the interurban line, and was free for those who rode the electric trains. It featured a large lake built with a dam on Center Creek, and a number of amusement rides. The park began a quick decline when Route 66 passed nearby, and then closed for good when the electric rail line shut down.

150.4 CHAT JUNCTION – Chat Junction was once located near where the railroad now bridges over Fir Road. This was the junction with the 3.8-mile-long Webb City Branch, which headed to the northeast to serve several lead and zinc mines, and later a number of chat facilities. Timetables from the 1930s showed that there was a 26-car siding here on the branch.

Chat Junction was listed as a KCS station served by Wells Fargo & Company in the *ABC Pathfinder Shipping and Mailing Guide* of 1915. The line looped around the northwest side of Webb City, where there were once a number of mines. Later, many of the mine tailings were processed into chat that was used in road construction around the country. Webb City chat was also used by area railroads to ballast their lines. Some of the Webb City companies that specialized in chat included the Webb City-Joplin Ballast Company (formed 1902) and the Independent Gravel Company of Webb City (formed 1905).

The 1906 KCS annual report covered the efforts of the railroad to improve its track, and the topic of ballast was covered in great detail. It stated that chat was being used on much of the railroad. The report further stated that chat was "a waste product from

Heavener Sub Route Guide

the zinc works, near Joplin (MP 154), which costs 16 cents loaded on cars. This is a fine, gravelly substance, which, if enough is put under the ties, seems to answer fairly well. The supply is limited, however, to about 10 cars per day."

On October 7, 1944, the Interstate Commerce Commission authorized the abandonment of the Webb City Branch. The line was described as being approximately 3.798 miles long.

Coming into Joplin, the KCS line begins to pass over and under a number of roads and streets. At Milepost 152, the remains of an old concrete headwall show where one road used to pass over the tracks.

152.9 TURKEY CREEK BRIDGE – This bridge consists of a single through truss span, located not far west of North Main Street. The bridge still has its builders plate that indicates it was manufactured by the American Bridge Company of New York in 1911. The stream forms to the east and flows westward into Spring River. Various stories claim that it was named for several flocks of wild turkeys found along its course.

Just south of the bridge is **Control Point North Joplin**, the north end of the Joplin Siding complex at Milepost 153.0.

This through truss span crosses Turkey Creek just a few feet north of the siding switch at Control Point North Joplin.

Heavener Sub Route Guide

Kansas City Southern makes sure that train crews can read their signs, such as this large one at Control Point North Joplin.

153.8 JOPLIN UNION DEPOT COMPANY NORTH CONNECTION – Today, North Main Street bridges over the KCS mainline at this location. There is a series of nearby parks, but the landscaping includes a large number of trees that hide the railroad from view.

For many years, this was the north end of the Joplin Union Depot property. KCS employee timetables stated that at Joplin, "all first-class and extra passenger trains will use the Joplin Union Depot Company's tracks between Main Street and Third Street."

154.3 JOPLIN UNION DEPOT (JO) – In 1893, the Kansas City, Pittsburg & Gulf Railroad completed its 24.98-mile rail line between Pittsburg, Kansas, and Joplin, Missouri. When it arrived at Joplin, there was already a booming mining town served by other railroads.

The City of Joplin is today split between southern Jasper County and northern Newton County, and is still the largest city in Jasper County, Missouri. Located at the junction of Interstates 44 and 49, Joplin is the home of several trucking and trucking service companies. It is located on the mainline of the Kansas City Southern railroad, and is also served by branches of BNSF and the Missouri & Northern Arkansas Railroad. The population is approximately 50,000.

One of the first settlers in the area was Reverend Harris G. Joplin, who built near a spring and small stream about 1840, both of which soon took his name. The creation of the City of Joplin can be traced back to the discovery of lead in the Joplin Creek Valley before the Civil War. However, the lack of good transportation prevented the development of the area. In 1871, after the Civil War, John C. Cox filed a plan for a city to serve the mines that were starting to develop. The town was soon named Joplin City.

With Cox's town being on the east side of the valley, Patrick Murphy created the town of Murphysburg on the western side. Almost immediately, the two towns merged to form Union City, but a court ruling declared the merger illegal. A new set of documents led to a legal merger on March 23, 1873, creating the City of Joplin. Joplin attracted railroads, businesses and other services needed to support the lead and zinc mining industries. Declaring itself the lead and zinc mining capital of the world, Joplin soon featured some of the finest saloons in the region. Probably the most famous was the House of Lords, a three-story complex with a bar and restaurant on the first floor, gambling rooms on the second floor, and a brothel on the third. Mining methods included open pit and deep mining, resulting in huge spoil piles to the north and west of town, and almost 75% of Joplin sitting over underground mines. This didn't stop the town from growing or modernizing, quickly obtaining lights and electricity. However, there was still enough of the rough edge that the notorious Bonnie and Clyde spent several weeks in Joplin in 1933, even robbing a number of local businesses for spending money. When their apartment (3347½ Oak Ridge Drive) was raided by police, they were forced to leave behind many of their possessions. Included in these items was a camera. The film was quickly developed by the *Joplin Globe*, resulting in some of the most famous pictures of the outlaw couple. These included the picture of Bonnie with her foot on a car fender, posed with a pistol in her hand and cigar in her mouth, and Bonnie holding Clyde at mock gunpoint. The apartment is now on the National Register of Historic Places.

Route 66 was becoming a boom for Joplin by the mid-20th century. However, most of the mines closed after World War II, and like most cities, residents moved to the suburbs. Much of downtown was destroyed by attempts at urban renewal, but some buildings from the era still stand. Many of these are listed on the National Register of Historic Places. Mother Nature has even been a challenge to Joplin, with a major tornado damaging much of the town on May 5, 1971, and another EF5 tornado on May 22, 2011, damaging almost every building in the area. A reported 8400 homes, 450 businesses, and 18,000 cars were damaged or destroyed by this storm. The 2011 storm kicked off the second phase to return Joplin to its boom times. Its location at the junction of two Interstate Highways had already led to new industry, and nearly $800 million in reconstruction spending continued the progress.

While many of the older buildings are gone, much of Joplin's history remains. Pauline Starke, an early silent-film actress, was born in Joplin on January 10, 1901. On June 4, 1924, *Gunsmoke* and *McCloud* star Dennis Weaver was also born in Joplin. Sports stars Hale Irwin, 3-time U.S. Open golf champion, and NASCAR driver Jamie McMurray have also called Joplin home. Finally, Blondie and Dagwood Bumstead are from Joplin, according to their creator Chic Young in an interview with the *Joplin Globe* newspaper.

Joplin Union Depot Company

Located at KCS Milepost 154.3 is a major 300-foot-long and 80-foot-wide concrete union station that once served Joplin, Missouri, as well as a 7930-foot-long siding. The original KCS Joplin station was located on the west side of the tracks south of 4th Street. Other railroads had their own stations, and as the twentieth century began, the Santa Fe and KCS were discussing a new joint station and terminal. Other railroads also entered the discussion, and in 1907 the Missouri & North Arkansas proposed that they be included in the plans.

The Joplin Union Depot Company was incorporated on June 23, 1908, to build a joint station to serve the Atchison, Topeka & Santa Fe Railway; Kansas City Southern Railway; Missouri, Kansas & Texas Railway; and the Missouri & North Arkansas

Railroad. According to the *Missouri, Kansas & Texas Railway Company Report to the Stockholders for the Year Ended June 30th, 1910*, the company was created "to acquire suitable freight and passenger terminals in Joplin for the joint use of the four railroads named, each of which subscribed for $10,000 capital stock of the Depot Company. The construction of the terminals is financed by an issue of bonds which has been made and sold by the Depot Company, such bonds being guaranteed, both principal and interest, by the four proprietary railway companies above mentioned." Much of the land chosen had been the site of the William Brugger Custom Ore Crusher.

A later report stated that the Joplin Union Depot Company owned 0.740 miles of main track and 5.657 miles of sidings and yard tracks, 26 acres of land, plus the station buildings. These buildings included the Union Passenger Depot, Union Freight Depot, and assorted support structures. While few of the tracks remain, the shell of the station building still stands near downtown Joplin. Plans for the station started in the 1900s, and Canadian-born architect Louis Curtiss was chosen to head the design work. Curtiss had a long history designing railroad stations, including many for the AT&SF, the Fred Harvey Company, and the Union Terminal in Wichita, Kansas. Curtiss was also known for his many buildings in the Kansas City area. There, his Boley Clothing Company Building is considered to be "one of the first glass curtain wall structures in the world." He was sometimes known as "the Frank Lloyd Wright of Kansas City."

The design of Joplin Union Depot called for reinforced concrete, mixed with local mine waste. The buildings were considered to be absolutely fireproof, and all had walls designed to allow the construction of additional stories. The design was featured in the January 1912 edition of *Popular Mechanics*, as well as several other magazines of the time. On June 5, 1910, it was announced that the Manhattan Construction Company of New York, through their branch office in Fort Smith, Arkansas, had been awarded the contract to build the Union Depot. According to the *Joplin Daily Globe*, construction started on June 24th.

Almost immediately, construction on the complex was slowed as excavation work uncovered a major seam of zinc. Some of the workers organized a mining company and soon mined and sold off the ore. Once the zinc was gone, construction progressed rapidly, except for several weeks when winter cold halted work. The tracks were completed enough that a work train entered the property on May 19, 1911. During the evening of July 1, 1911, Missouri, Kansas & Texas passenger train No. 83 became the first train to use the station. Reportedly more than 2500 local residents met the train at 10:30pm, and fireworks and numerous railroad torpedoes made sure that the rest of Joplin's citizens knew that the first passenger train had arrived.

Multiple sources provided descriptions of the building. Some described it as being an "old Roman type, antedating the classic style." The building was made of concrete, with oak finish. The passenger depot consisted of three parts, the central section measuring 180 feet long, with 60-foot-long north and south wings. The two-story central section housed the ticket office; general, women's and men's waiting rooms; and related offices and rooms. The second floor featured office space for the various railroads. The south one-story wing housed the dining room, later converted into the Railway Express Agency office, while the north one-story wing featured the express and baggage rooms. The local newspaper stated that the "general arrangement of the depot is very much similar to that of the union depot in St. Louis, although the interior is more beautifully decorated than its larger counterpart." Outside, the complex included train sheds, a roundhouse, and a number of tracks.

According to the 1936 KCS employee timetable, rules of the Joplin Union Depot Company applied between the yard limit boards at Joplin. A train register, bulletin books, and a standard clock were all located in the Joplin Union Depot Telegraph Office.

In early 1964, the southbound *Southern Belle* (No. 1) was scheduled to depart Joplin at 12:25pm, a schedule that had been in place for several years. The last passenger train, KCS' *Southern Belle*, served the station on November 4, 1969. The complex was soon abandoned, but with numerous proposals for museums, restaurants, and other businesses to fill the space. However, none of the proposals actually resulted in the building's use, and the station slowly deteriorated. The passenger depot was placed on the National Register of Historic Places on March 14, 1973. It is currently owned by the Missouri Department of Natural Resources and plans continue to pop up for its use. For those wanting more information about the Joplin Union Depot, the *Historic Joplin* website has a large article on its planning, construction, and possible future.

While many might have thought that the Joplin Union Depot Company was long gone, it was the subject of an Interstate Commerce Commission hearing in 1989. On January 30, 1989, the ICC granted authority to the Kansas City Southern to acquire sole control of the Joplin Union Depot Company, effective March 9, 1989.

In 1989, Joplin Union Depot was clearly abandoned, but there appeared to be some preservation work underway.

This photo from 1997 shows deterioration to the Joplin Union Station.

This view is what many passengers would have seen as they arrived at the Joplin Union Station. This is the covered walkway from where the tracks once were into the main lobby of the station.

By 2018, the Joplin Union Depot was simply a concrete shell, but fencing had been installed to try to save what was left of the structure.

Missouri & North Arkansas Trackage Rights

The Missouri & North Arkansas Railroad, and later the Missouri & Arkansas Railway, used trackage rights over the Kansas City Southern to travel between Joplin and Neosho, both in Missouri. Heading south from the Joplin Union Depot property, M&NA trains used the KCS mainline for both passenger and freight trains. The May 31, 1936, KCS *Northern Division Employee Timetable* included information on these rights. By this time, only M&A freights No. 211 and No. 212 used the trackage rights, listed as Third Class trains. A timetable note stated that Missouri & Arkansas trains leaving Neosho were required to obtain train orders with the information required in the KCS Book of Rules before departing.

Trackage rights over the KCS from Neosho to Joplin were acquired by the Missouri & North Arkansas as part of their 1908 expansion plans. The rights included the use of KCS facilities at Neosho and Joplin, rights that were used until the Missouri & Arkansas Railway shut down in 1946 and abandoned the line to Neosho the following year.

Other Joplin Railroads

While the Kansas City Southern, the route used by the Missouri & North Arkansas and the Atchison, Topeka & Santa Fe to reach Joplin, is the main north-south railroad that passes through Joplin, the large number of lead and zinc mines attracted other railroads. Today, many of these routes still exist, along with some of their history. However, a majority of the rail lines that once reached Joplin are gone.

Heavener Sub Route Guide

Reviewing these lines clockwise from the KCS line north to Kansas City, there were once more than a dozen lines out of town. The KCS line through Joplin is the Heavener Subdivision, part of the main route from Kansas City south to Shreveport, Louisiana, the original core of the company. Clockwise, the next line was the former Frisco line that ran northeast to the mainline at Oronogo, Missouri. This line was built by the Missouri & Western Railway Company and acquired by the Frisco in 1879. A few miles of this line remains in the Joplin area and crosses the KCS south of Joplin Union Station. It is today operated by the Missouri & Northern Arkansas, a regional railroad owned by the Genesee & Wyoming.

Immediately to the east of the former Frisco line was the Southwest Missouri Electric Railway, an interurban that operated from Carthage to Webb City, then southwest to Joplin, and then west to Galena, Kansas. Created in 1892, this interurban railroad absorbed local routes in several cities, but was bankrupt and in receivership by 1927 and was selling off property and moving to buses. It crossed the KCS just south of today's MNA Crossing, wandered through Joplin, and then headed west, following today's BNSF route to Galena.

The next two lines bridge over the KCS route. Using joint track in this immediate area, they include a short Frisco branchline to Webb City, and the former Missouri Pacific line from Carthage. The MP line is today operated by the Missouri & Northern Arkansas. Further south is another former line of the Southwest Missouri Electric Railway which curved around the southeast side of Joplin using 15th Street.

Continuing in a clockwise direction from the KCS line south, there was once a short Missouri Pacific branch to Grand Falls. Grand Falls is a large waterfall on Shoal Creek where a hydroelectric plant and a park were built. The park included a theater, boat houses, a German Village and a dance pavilion, and Missouri Pacific used to run special excursion trains to and from the falls over this line. Next were the Southwest Missouri Electric Railway and Frisco lines heading west to Galena, Kansas. The interurban line, acquired from the Joplin & Galena Electric Railway in 1896, is long gone. The Frisco line, once known as the Joplin & Galena Branch, is still in place and is operated by BNSF. Two other lines also headed west toward Galena. One was another Frisco line that reached Galena via Horn (all now abandoned), and the other was the Missouri-Kansas-Texas (MKT) line, now partly operated by BNSF. The MKT (Katy) Joplin Line was built from the Kansas City-Texas mainline at Oswego, Kansas, by the Walsh-List-Gifford Construction Company to serve the various mines in the area. Katy abandoned much of their own route to Joplin in the early 1980s, using trackage rights over BN's line from Galena.

Heading west from downtown, and then north from Schiffendecker Park, was the Joplin & Pittsburg Railway, another interurban company. This line was a combination of several electric lines and was built to Joplin from Pittsburg to the north. Finally, between the Joplin & Pittsburg Railway and the KCS line was another Frisco line, this one also heading north to Pittsburg. This was originally the Joplin Railroad, built between Joplin and Girard (just west of Pittsburg, Kansas), and acquired by the Frisco in 1879. The Joplin Railroad, built by local mine owners, has the claim of being the first railroad to reach Joplin. To serve this and other lines in the area was a turntable and small roundhouse, located south of 11th Street and east of Byers Avenue. It sat in the middle of a large wye just north of the Galena Branch. All of the Frisco lines in this area are now gone.

Existing Joplin Railroad Facilities

Probably the most documented railroad structure in town besides Joplin Union Depot is the St. Louis-San Francisco Railroad Building, also known as the Frisco Building. Located at 601 South Main Street, this was the second Frisco station in Joplin. The first was a small wooden structure a block to the east, but this building is a nine-story, "L"-shaped, brick and stone trimmed station, built under contract for the local Odd Fellows Lodge Hall. Spending approximately $1 million on what was described as Joplin's first modern, high-rise, fireproof office building, the Odd Fellows agreed upon a fifty-year lease with the Frisco for the first two floors, and then leased office space on the upper levels, mostly to doctors. The railroad used the first floor as the station, and the second floor featured company offices and a public café. The station opened to rail service on November 30, 1913, and construction on the platforms, tracks, and train shed were completed by the end of the year. At its peak, the station served as many as 52 passenger trains a day, using tracks that came in from the east. However, the last train departed in 1955, and a new medical building caused most of the doctors to depart the same year. The building then went through multiple owners and uses.

The building was added to the National Register of Historic Places on October 22, 2002. Among some of its historic features is its design in what was known as the "Chicago Style" by the St. Louis architectural firm of Mauran, Russell and Crowell. The firm was noted for its many St. Louis buildings, including the Railway Exchange Building, the Federal Reserve Bank Building, the St. Louis Globe-Democrat Building, and the Missouri Pacific Building. The firm also designed a number of the Carnegie libraries across the Midwest. Today, the building is known as the Frisco Station Apartments and provides affordable housing for senior citizens.

The former Odd Fellows Lodge Hall is still in downtown Joplin. It once housed the Frisco station, giving it the name of the St. Louis-San Francisco Railroad Building.

Heavener Sub Route Guide

There are also several former Missouri Pacific (MP or MoPac) structures still standing in Joplin. The most recognizable one is the former 8-stall roundhouse at 1070 Missouri Street. The railroad long ago sold off the building, It no longer includes tracks or a turntable, and it is used by a local business for storage and manufacturing. The original MoPac brick depot once stood nearby on the southwest corner of Main and Tenth Streets. In 1916, a new cut stone station opened on the east side of Main Street. This station has since been torn down and then rebuilt at 29th and Rangeline as a restaurant. While not restored fully to its original design, the beautiful stone building now stands next to the KCS mainline.

The Missouri Pacific roundhouse still stands at Joplin, but is no longer used by a railroad.

The Missouri Pacific train station was torn down and moved as part of plans to build a new restaurant. During early 2022, the building sat empty but the entryway clearly shows part of the building's history.

Several of the interurban railroad facilities are also still in Joplin. The Joplin & Pittsburg Railway's brick carbarn stands on the northwest corner of 4th Street and Maiden Lane, just west of downtown. Further west on 4th Street is Schifferdecker Park. This large park today includes golf, swimming, trails, and about anything else a park should have. During the early 1900s, the park, known as Electric Park, was built by the Joplin & Pittsburg Railway as a destination for the trolley and interurban system.

The interurban carbarn for the Southwest Missouri Electric Railway also still stands, today a part of the Tamko Building Products manufacturing complex on North High Avenue. Tamko is one of the largest roofing manufacturers in the nation, and the carbarn is almost surrounded by additions and new buildings.

154.5 JOPLIN FREIGHT STATION – This was the location used by Kansas City Southern for their freight station at Joplin during the 1940s.

154.6 CONTROL POINT SOUTH JOPLIN – This is the south end of the Joplin siding that was once part of the Joplin Union Depot complex, and was once known as Joplin Union Depot Company South Connection. It is located just north of East Fourth Street. The KCS Joplin station was once on the west side of the tracks near here, just south of Fourth Street.

Located just north of Fourth Street is Control Point South Joplin.

The August 1945 issue of *Railway Signaling* covered this part of the line when it reported on the installation of Absolute Block Signals (ABS) between Gulfton and McElhany. Just south of the Joplin station track, the KCS main track was crossed by two separate single-track lines of the St. Louis-San Francisco. These crossings were not protected, and therefore, all trains on both railroads had to stop and whistle at these crossings.

The Heavener Sub: History Through the Miles

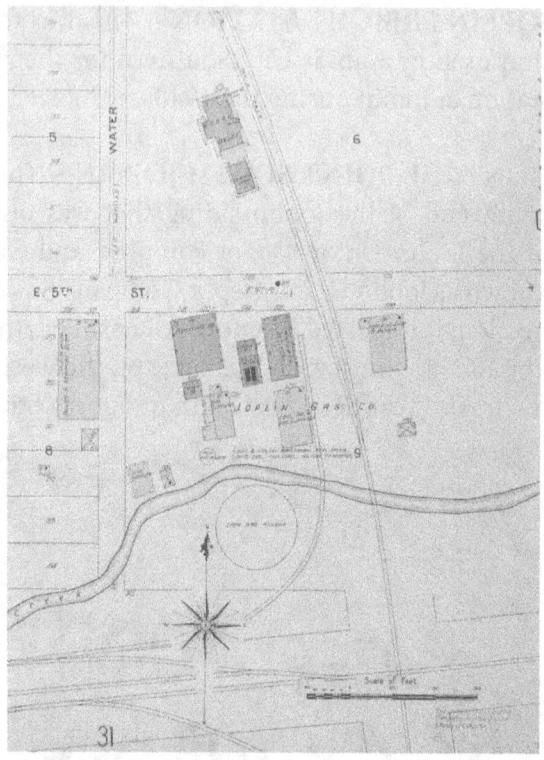

Before the construction of Joplin Union Depot, KCS had their passenger station located just south of East 4th Street. *Sanborn Fire Insurance Map from Joplin, Jasper County, Missouri.* Sanborn Map Company, 1906. Map. Retrieved from the Library of Congress, https://www.loc.gov/item/sanborn04718_006/.

154.8 STL&SF CROSSING – At one time, the Frisco had an industrial lead that went west to serve several industries like The Redell Manufacturing & Supply Company, Thomas Fruit Company, and the C. M. Spring Wholesale Drug Company. It was located just south of Sixth Street. More importantly, it served the Frisco passenger depot and the freight depot. It later served the St. Louis-San Francisco Railroad Building when it opened in 1913.

Heavener Sub Route Guide

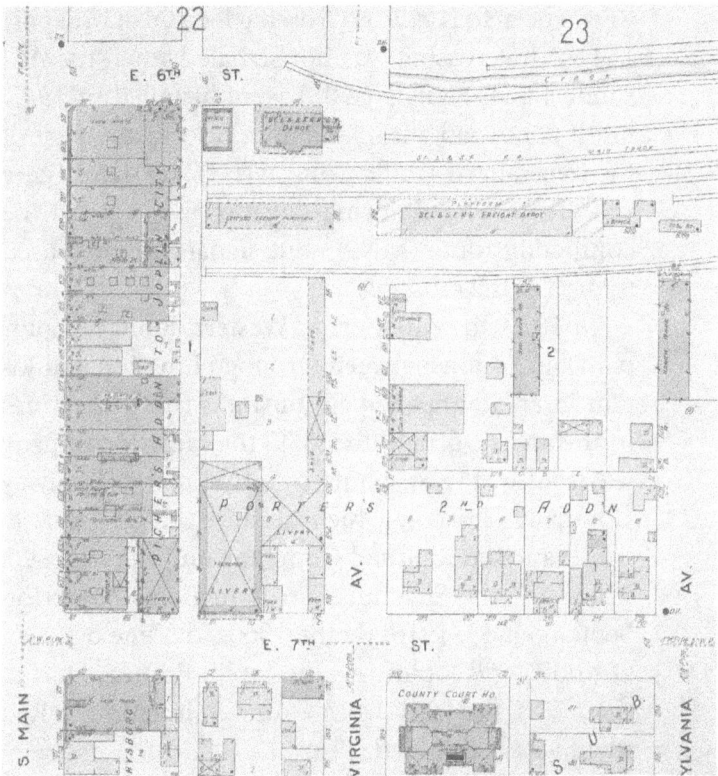

Just west of the KCS mainline was once this complex of Frisco tracks and buildings, many replaced in 1913 with the opening of the St. Louis-San Francisco Railroad Building on Main Street. *Sanborn Fire Insurance Map from Joplin, Jasper County, Missouri.* Sanborn Map Company, 1906. Map. Retrieved from the Library of Congress, https://www.loc.gov/item/sanborn04718_006/.

154.8 MNA RAILROAD CROSSING – This diamond, located just north of the Seventh Street/Route 66 overpass, is for the former Missouri & Western Railway Company line from Oronogo, now used by the Missouri & Northern Arkansas to reach the Tamko Building Products manufacturing complex just northeast of town. Timetables from the 1960s show this to be a St. L. & S. F. Crossing located at Milepost 154.9. The crossing was not signaled when the Absolute Block Signals (ABS) were installed in 1945, but it is now an automatic interlocking as a part of the Centralized Traffic Control (CTC) system. There was a gate whose normal position was against the conflicting route (MNA), but signals are now used to protect the crossing.

In 1879, the Missouri & Western Railway Company built a line between Oronogo Junction and Joplin in an attempt to gain business from the mines in the area. During July 1879, the railway company was sold to the St. Louis & San Francisco Railway Company (Frisco), which became the St. Louis & San Francisco Railroad Company on June 29, 1896. It became the St. Louis-San Francisco Railway on September 15, 1916. By the 1960s, the line between Oronogo and Joplin was the Joplin Branch. During the 1970s, the track from Oronogo Junction to Red Plant was abandoned.

In 1980, the Frisco became part of the Burlington Northern Railroad, which abandoned the track from Red Plant to Webb City in 1984. On December 31, 1996, Burlington Northern and the Atchison, Topeka & Santa Fe Railway merged to create the Burlington Northern & Santa Fe Railway (BNSF). During September 1998, BNSF sold a few miles of isolated track in Joplin to the Missouri & Northern Arkansas Railroad. The line curves to the northeast to serve the Tamko Building Products facility. North of there, the grade is now the Frisco Greenway Trail. It is described as being a 3.5-mile trail that "consists of firmly packed gravel on top of an old railroad bed and is suitable for walking, running, or biking. It ex-

Heavener Sub Route Guide

tends from North Street in Joplin, MO to Highway 171 in Webb City, MO."

Just south of the diamond, a modern bridge crosses the tracks. This is Seventh Street, which also serves as the business route of Interstate 44, and as the designated Route 66 through Joplin. On the north side is a nice walkway, providing a safe place to photograph the rail activity. If you look closely at the diamond, you will see that it is a modern flange-bearing crossing frog. Also known as a lift frog or a jump frog, this diamond frog has a solid rail for the KCS mainline, and a route for the Missouri & Northern Arkansas that requires the locomotives and cars to ride on their wheel flanges. This type of frog reduces the pounding on the frog as the higher volume KCS route has no open flangeways to bounce across.

This view of the MNA Railroad Crossing at Milepost 154.8 was taken from the Seventh Street overpass, located just south of the crossing.

The Wreck at the St. L. & S. F. Crossing

This railroad crossing was part of an accident investigation in 1942. As stated by the Interstate Commerce Commission: "On January 19, 1942, there was a rear-end collision between a Kansas City Southern Railway freight train and a Missouri & Arkansas Railway freight train on the line of the Kansas City Southern Railway at Joplin, Mo., which resulted in the death of one employee and the injury of three employees." The northbound trains involved were KCS Extra Freight No. 762 and Missouri & Arkansas (M&A) freight No. 212. Extra No. 762 included 97 cars (33 loaded and 64 empty) and a caboose, and was pulled by KCS #762, a 2-8-8-0 oil-burning steam locomotive built in 1924 by Alco-Brooks. The following train, M&A No. 212, included 15 cars and a caboose, pulled by M&A #50. This steam locomotive (2-8-2) was built in 1913 by Baldwin for the Atlanta, Birmingham & Coast Railroad, and was sold to the M&A in 1939.

The accident took place 1.6 miles south of the station at Joplin on the Second District (Watts-North Yard at Pittsburg). "As the point of accident is approached from the south there are, in succession, a tangent 5,004 feet in length, a 4 degree 12' curve to the right 1,359.1 feet, a tangent 1,605.7. feet, a 1 degree curve to the right 814.2 feet to the point of accident and 965.6 feet beyond. The grade for northbound trains varies between 0.414 percent and 1.162 percent descending a distance of 2,250 feet to the point of accident, and is 1.162 percent at the point of accident."

The accident was "caused by failure to provide flag protection for preceding train." In this case, Extra No. 762 "stopped at the St. L.-S. F. crossing, located 0.6 mile south of the station at Joplin, at 9:12 p.m. The caboose stood 287.5 feet south of the south yard-limit sign." Three minutes later, M&A No. 212 ran into the caboose of Extra No. 762 at about 20 miles per hour, killing the KCS conductor. Because of switching service to be performed at Joplin, the flagman was at the head end to assist in this work and the conductor should have provided the flag protection.

The Missouri & North Arkansas, later the Missouri & Arkansas, used the Joplin Union terminal until the end of September 1946 for freight operations, with an agency in the Union Depot that used the telegraph call of "JO". In 1939, M&A Freight No. 212 was scheduled to arrive at 5:05pm, a time that was used for nearly a decade. The locomotive and caboose were serviced at the shops of the Union Depot. While M&A freight service lasted until the end of the railroad, passenger service ended in 1934, instead using Neosho, Missouri, as a connection with the Kansas City Southern trains.

The Frisco-KCS Crossings

Throughout southwest Missouri, the St. Louis-San Francisco and the Kansas City Southern served the same basic territory and their railroads crossed in a number of places. Each of these crossings required an agreement, with normally the second railroad arriving bearing the costs of any facilities. On December 14, 1888, the St. Louis & San Francisco Railroad Company (Frisco) and the Kansas City, Fort Smith

& Southern Railway Company (KCFS&S, later KCS), entered into an agreement on what was called the "South Frisco Crossing" at Joplin. The agreement allowed the KCFS&S to construct and maintain, at its expense, a good and sufficient crossing at the point of intersection.

Over the years, the agreement was updated and expanded to include that KCS would install and maintain four crossing gates, three at crossings in Pittsburg, Kansas, and one at a crossing in Joplin, Missouri. All four of these gates were to have their normal position across the tracks of the Frisco, allowing KCS trains to move over the crossing without stopping. The agreements spelled out that Frisco crews were required to ensure that their trains could safely move across the crossing before opening the gates, and that they were required to restore them to their normal position across the Frisco tracks after the train has passed.

A 1960 supplement to the agreement also added that an interlocking plant could be installed at the "South Frisco Crossing" at Joplin. The agreement stated that Frisco may, at the sole cost and expense of KCS, furnish and install an interlocking plant. While a four-year requirement was stated for installing the interlocking plant, the agreement actually stated that the Frisco could install it at any time, even after the four-year period had passed. The improved gates were almost immediately installed, but the automatic interlocking plant was not installed until Centralized Traffic Control (CTC) signaling was placed into service on the Kansas City Southern.

Heavener Sub Route Guide

155.1 MNA CONNECTION – Located just north of Ninth Street, this connecting track serves as an interchange track between KCS and the Missouri & Northern Arkansas Railroad Company (not to be confused with the earlier Missouri & North Arkansas Railroad Company). The line connects to the former Missouri Pacific line from Carthage, as well as indirectly with the remains of the abandoned Frisco Webb City branch. Just south of the switch, the former Missouri Pacific line bridges over the KCS.

The Missouri Pacific line was built by the Carthage, Joplin & Short Creek Railway Company. The railroad was incorporated on September 6, 1881, and soon built an 18-mile line from Carthage through Webb City to Joplin. On September 12, 1883, the railroad was sold to The Missouri Pacific Railway Company. The railroad established a yard, a small frame passenger station, and a freight station between 10th and 11th streets. On August 9, 1909, a number of railroads were consolidated into The Missouri Pacific Railway Company, which became the Missouri Pacific Railroad Company on May 12, 1917.

After Missouri Pacific became a part of Union Pacific, duplicate and lightly-used lines were sold or abandoned. A number of the lines in the Arkansas-Missouri area were sold to the Missouri & Northern Arkansas Railroad in 1992. Today, the Missouri & Northern Arkansas is a part of Genesee & Wyoming, and operates more than 500 miles of track. The main route is Diaz Junction, Arkansas, to Pleasant Hill, Missouri. There are several significant branch lines, including the Carthage-Joplin line that crosses above the KCS.

South of here at KCS Milepost 156 (just south of the 20th Street overpass) was the Joplin Buff Brick Company, located to the east of the tracks. The firm sold brick across the region, and a number of buildings in Kansas City were built using the company's brick.

During April 2022, a number of Canadian Pacific locomotives could be found leading trains across the Heavener Subdivision. This one is heading north under the former Missouri Pacific bridge and past the MNA Connection at Joplin, Missouri.

155.4 STL&SF CONNECTION – Once located south of Twelfth Street, this junction between the Kansas City Southern and the Frisco railroads was shown in timetables and company documents for several decades.

157.5 LONG BELL AMERICAN – Look for where Rangeline Road bridges over the railroad. A track heads off to the east to serve an industrial park. One of the major companies served by this track is Gilster-Mary Lee, a firm that "produces over 8,000 items in over

500 different private label brands, as well as its own Hospitality label." In March of 1999, the company purchased Jasper Foods of Jasper/Joplin, Missouri, giving it a larger presence in the private label microwave popcorn and cereal industry.

157.6 REX – This station was listed in the *Thirty-Fourth Annual Report of the Railroad and Warehouse Commissioners of the State of Missouri, Year Ending June 30, 1909*. Documents from the time show that the area was known as Rex City, and the area is still known as the Rex Voting District of Jasper County. Several area histories state that this planned mining suburb of Joplin was thought to be so well located that it would boom and be the "king" of the mining camps. Therefore, it was named Rex (Latin for king) by its founders. The Rex Mine, a lead and zinc mine, was once located here and operated by the Rex Mining & Smelting Company.

158.0 COUNTY LINE – Leaving Joplin, the KCS line heads to the southeast and goes from **Jasper County** and into **Newton County** at the 32nd Street grade crossing. **Jasper County** was created on January 29, 1841, with the first government organized on February 25, 1841. A new town, Carthage, was created as the county seat on March 28, 1842. At the time, Jasper County also included what eventually became Barton County. Like many area counties, it was mostly abandoned during the guerrilla wars of the Civil War. Later, the county boomed due to lead and zinc mining.

The county honors Sergeant William Jasper, a Revolutionary War hero. During the battle of Sullivan's Island in June 1776, the British pounded the

American fort, eventually shooting down the flagpole bearing the Fort Moultrie Flag – a blue flag with a white crescent used by South Carolina forces. William Jasper, a member of the Second South Carolina Regiment, jumped out of the fort, walked the entire length in full view of the British, and then cut the flag from its pole. Climbing the wall, he fastened the flag to a cannon sponge-staff and planted it in the wall, all while in the face of deadly fire. For this feat, South Carolina President John Rutledge presented Jasper with his dress sword at a review held soon after the battle and offered him a commission. Jasper turned this down, instead preferring to serve as a scout for the American forces. Jasper was also recognized later for his scouting efforts against the British until he was killed at Savannah in 1779 while planting the colors of the Second South Carolina Regiment on the British lines. He was buried somewhere near the scene of the battle in a mass grave with many of his comrades.

Newton County dates to December 31, 1838, and is today the eighteenth most populous county in Missouri, with about 60,000 residents. Neosho is the county seat. The county's name has an interesting history, as it is often used along with Jasper as a county name. The name Newton comes from John Newton, a somewhat fictional hero who fought in the Revolutionary War. Newton served in the forces of Brigadier General Francis Marion, the famous and legendary "Swamp Fox." While officers who served with Newton called him a "thief and villain," he was made famous in the early 19th century schoolbooks written by Parson Weems. Weems claimed many great achievements for Newton, a number of which seem almost identical to those of William Jasper.

With the fame created from the schoolbooks, many western states have a county or town named for John Newton.

158.3 GULF STATES PAPER – Located just north of Interstate 44 is a spur track to the east that serves the WestRock facility. For many years, this was Gulf States, a privately held company founded in 1884 by the Warner and Westervelt families. Gulf States Paper Corporation manufactured cartons and boxes for industrial users. In 2005, Gulf States sold its manufacturing assets to the Rock-Tenn Company, a firm founded in 1936 that has assets in the same industry. In 2015, Rock-Tenn merged with MeadWestvaco to form WestRock. WestRock is now the second largest packaging company in the United States, and one of the largest in the world.

Not far to the southeast, the railroad passes under Interstate 44 at Milepost 158.6. The railroad continues to the southeast until reaching Thurman Creek, where it turns to the southwest and follows the creek to Shoal Creek. The area from here south also has a number of cuts, and much of the dirt (more than 125,000 yards) was moved to Joplin as fill for the Joplin Union Depot project.

160.0 SAGINAW – The KCS has a short 2450-foot siding to the east (north switch at Milepost 159.7, south switch at Milepost 160.2). The community of Saginaw started with a country store operated by a Mr. Thurman, giving the community the name of Thurman. A post office with that name opened here in 1873. The post office was renamed Saginaw in 1889, apparently named after Saginaw, Michigan. The Mine and Quarry News Bureau stated in 1897 that The Saginaw Mine of the Saginaw Lead & Zinc Company was located here. The company was based in Saginaw, Michigan, and had ten employees.

During the 1930s, a railroad mail crane was located at Milepost 160.7 to serve the post office. This allowed mail to be picked up by trains without stopping. Today, the population of Saginaw is approximately 300.

The grade of an old quarry spur track can be made out in the woods to the east. This track once headed more than a mile east to where several bar pit ponds can now be found. These ponds were created when dirt was dug up and moved for other projects, including the Joplin Union Depot project, filling in a number of old mines, and fill for several highway overpasses. So where did the term "bar pit" come from? A bar pit is actually a borrow pit. It received the shorter name typically in the southern and southwestern parts of the United States, where it is often pronounced that way. It also became a way to shorten the time taken to make notes and document the movement of materials, so it is even written "bar pit" in many cases, and has grown to be used across the country.

Just south of Saginaw, the railroad turns to the southeast and follows Shoal Creek uphill to Neosho, Missouri. The railroad crosses a number of bridges and culverts over several roads and small streams flowing in off the hillside to the east.

Heavener Sub Route Guide

Several roads pass under the Heavener Subdivision using large concrete culverts, including Amy Road at Milepost 160.3.

At Milepost 162.0, Saginaw Road, the old Highway 71, passes under this small deck plate girder span of KCS.

164.8 INTERSTATE 49 – Just north of Tipton Ford, the railroad passes under the new Interstate 49. This highway replaced U.S. Highway 71 in the area, which had already been rebuilt to Interstate standards.

Kansas City Southern has worked to continue to upgrade the Heavener Subdivision. This series of concrete culverts is located immediately north of the grade crossing at Tipton Ford, Missouri.

165.0 TIPTON FORD – Look for the grade crossing with Old Highway 71 and the Undercliff Grill and Bar to the east. There was once a short siding here and a platform to the west. The name Tipton Ford (also Tipton's Ford, Tiptonford, or simply Tipton) comes from a ford across Shoal Creek to the west that was once near the home of the Tipton family, especially James William Tipton. The Tipton Ford post office opened here in 1890, but the town never grew very large and the post office closed in 1923. Today, the community is unincorporated and the railroad has no side tracks here. Heading south, the railroad closely follows Shoal Creek.

The Wreck of August 5, 1914

On August 5, 1914, just before 6:00pm, Tipton Ford became the center of attention of the Kansas City Southern and the Missouri & North Arkansas. KCS Pacific-type locomotive 805 pulling a northbound passenger train (Train First No. 56, actually a much delayed No. 2) had just hit southbound M&NA 70-foot-long "gas-electric motor car of light steel construction" #103 (Train No. 209), apparently after the M&NA crew misinterpreted their orders to meet the KCS train at Tipton Ford. The M&NA motorcar telescoped more than twenty feet and was thrown back 650 feet by the impact. The collision and resultant fire from the fuel tank killed 43 (38 passengers and 5 employees) of the 77 persons onboard. Many of those killed were buried in the Neosho cemetery, all victims of the worst accident ever on the KCS and the M&NA.

The collision actually took place about 3500 feet south of the south switch at Tipton Ford, which the M&NA train crew passed despite their train orders. The Interstate Commerce Commission (ICC) conducted a detailed study of the accident, spending much of their time examining the handling of train orders for the two trains. The report produced a description of M&NA operations on the line, stating that "(T)he 20 miles of track between Joplin and Neosho is used jointly by trains of the Kansas City Southern and Missouri & North Arkansas Railroads. Four first-class and two third-class trains of the latter road are scheduled to pass over this section of track daily, subject to the operating rules of the Kansas City Southern Railway."

The accident was also a historic one for the ICC, as indicated by part of their report. "This is the first accident investigated by the commission wherein a gasoline motor car was involved. On account of the fire caused by ignition of this highly inflammable substance, the casualty list in this accident was much larger than it otherwise would have been. The rapidly increasing use of these motor cars, carrying large quantities of gasoline, introduces such an additional element of danger as to demand extraordinary precautions against the possibility of collisions wherever such cars are used."

While the report covered a grisly subject, it did provide a great deal of information about the trains of the Kansas City Southern. It stated that "Kansas City Southern passenger train, first No. 56, operating between Heavener, Okla., and Pittsburg, Kans., consisted of mail and baggage car No. 38, baggage and express car No. 21, baggage and express car No. 3, express car No. 1709, day coach No. 159, chair car No. 277, and one Pullman sleeping car, hauled by locomotive No. 805." This showed that the train had three passenger cars and four cars for baggage, mail and express. These cars were typical for the era and mainly were built of wood, some with steel underframes. The ICC reported that car "Nos. 38, 21, 1709, and 277 had steel underframes, while the remainder of the cars were of wooden construction."

This small memorial is a reminder that Tipton Ford was the site of one of the worst wrecks ever on the KCS.

169.0 BOYDEN – This station, spelled Boydan in 1890 and Boyden in 1903, no longer exists on the railroad. It was located where the north switch of Dalby siding is now. The name Boyden likely came from the Boyden family who lived in the area.

170.1 DALBY – Timetables from the 1930s show Dalby to be at Milepost 170.5. In 1964, it was listed as being a siding that was 134 cars long. In that year, Dalby wasn't shown as a passenger station, but KCS No. 1 (southbound *Southern Belle*) was scheduled to be here at 12:46pm.

The siding was extended in 2007 and Dalby was shown to be located at 170.1, with **Control Point North Dalby** at Milepost 168.9 and **Control Point South Dalby** at Milepost 170.8, for a total of 8900 feet. D. B. Dalby was the Freight Claims Agent for Kansas City Southern in 1915, but there is no clear record of the history of the siding's name.

Control Point South Dalby can be seen from Lime Kiln Drive north of Neosho, Missouri. The siding is often used to meet trains that work the industries at nearby Neosho and McElhany.

Heavener Sub Route Guide

KCS 2961 leads a southbound Dodger out of the siding at Dalby after meeting a northbound coal train on this April 2022 day.

172.2 OZARK TERMINAL SPUR – While gone today, there was once a steep spur track to the east. This facility began as a series of limestone caverns, mined since at least the 1930s for the production of calcium oxide. In 1936, the Southwest Lime Company had a 40-car spur track here.

The road that serves the facility is still named Lime Kiln Drive. According to the July 15, 1956, issue of the *Neosho News*, the limestone company was turning their underground facilities into a series of warehouses, operated by a new company known as Ozark Terminal, Inc. The article also stated that the "Kansas City Southern Railroad will lay a 4030-foot spur track from its main line, which passes just west of the lime plant, into the warehouse to permit under ground loading and unloading of entire trainloads of materials to be stored."

The 1966 KCS employee timetable provided instructions on using the spur track. It stated: "All movements on the Ozark Terminal Spur Mile 172.1, are restricted to 6 mph and because of the heavy grades in this track no movement will be made until the automatic brakes are cut in and operative."

The tracks of the Ozark Terminal Spur are long gone, and just a few abandoned rails in the brush still mark the location.

Lime Kiln Drive can be used to follow the Heavener Subdivision from Neosho northward past the Ozark Terminal and to the south end of Dalby siding.

172.4 SHOAL CREEK BRIDGE – This bridge includes a through truss span on the north end, and eleven relatively new precast concrete ballast deck spans. Shoal Creek is more than 80 miles long and is one of the largest tributaries of the Spring River. Shoal Creek begins near Cassville, Missouri, and flows to the southwest to here, where it turns to the northwest to near Joplin, and then west to the Spring River. Shoal Creek reportedly gets its name from its fast, rocky ledges and falls. The Missouri Department of Conservation reports that the stream is great for fishing, including "all three species of black bass, black and white crappie, a variety of sunfish, rock bass, and both flathead and channel catfish."

172.7 BNSF RAILROAD CROSSING – Once known as STL&SF Crossing, this is the BNSF mainline between St. Louis, Missouri, and Tulsa, Oklahoma, and on to Avard, Oklahoma, and a connection with the BNSF Transcontinental Line between Chicago and Los Angeles. There is an interchange track between the two railroads in the southeast quadrant of the diamond.

To protect the trains using the crossing, an operator was once assigned to a tower to direct trains through the diamond. The two-story tower was located on the north side of today's BNSF tracks, and the crossing tracks were protected by a semaphore and a split-rail derail controlled by the tower operator. With the 1945 ABS signal installation, the semaphore signals at the crossing were replaced by color-light signals, and the operator was replaced by an electro-mechanical interlocking.

The Heavener Sub: History Through the Miles

In 1990 when the locomotives of KCS were mostly white, KCS 654 is shown crossing the BNSF Railroad Crossing heading northbound with coal train No. 92.

The BNSF route has a somewhat complicated history, going through the hands of a number of companies in the period of late 1860s – late 1870s. Planning and construction on the line dates back to July 27, 1866, when the Atlantic & Pacific Railroad Company (A&P) was chartered to build a railroad from Springfield, Missouri, to the Pacific Ocean. As the years passed and track was built, the line was divided into several divisions. The Missouri Division extended from Franklin (now Pacific, near St. Louis), Missouri, to Seneca (west of Neosho), Missouri, about 292 miles. On October 26, 1870, the route was described as being in service as a "standard-gage, single-track railroad" from Franklin to Pierce City, Missouri. West of Pierce City, there were 39 miles of graded roadbed to Seneca, Missouri.

On October 23, 1875, a suit was filed against the A&P due to unpaid interest on certain Missouri Division bonds, and receivers were soon assigned. The Missouri Division was sold by auction on September 8, 1876, to a representative of the St. Louis & San Francisco Railway Company. On June 30, 1896, the railroad was sold to the St. Louis & San Francisco Railroad Company, which was sold to the St. Louis-San Francisco Railway Company (Frisco) on September 15, 1916. The Frisco became a part of the Burlington Northern Railroad on November 21, 1980, and then the Burlington Northern & Santa Fe Railway (BNSF) with the merger with the Atchison, Topeka & Santa Fe Railway on December 31, 1996.

Heading south from the crossing, there is a track to the east that serves as the interchange track between KCS and BNSF. The switch for this track, known as BNSF Interchange, is at Milepost 173.2. This is the north end of Neosho and the railroad passes by several blocks of housing.

173.6 OLD NEOSHO RAMP – Starting during the 1950s, many railroads installed intermodal ramps to handle local truck traffic. Much of this was caused by the movement of many types of freight from boxcars to truck trailers. Additionally, the Interstate Commerce Commission started to create rate and service standards for the movement of highway trailers by rail.

Kansas City Southern installed a ramp at Neosho just south of the College Street grade crossing. As the service was examined, intermodal terminals were centralized and the Neosho ramp was closed. Not far south of where the ramp once stood is the north switch for the Neosho siding.

North of the tracks along College Street at Neosho is what is advertised as the "World's Largest Flowerbox." It is made from a retired railroad gondola freight car.

173.7 MISSOURI & ARKANSAS NORTH CONNECTION – Neosho was a junction between the Kansas City Southern and the Missouri & Arkansas Railway (M&A – operated under different names over the years) from 1908 until the railroad closed in 1949. The M&A at first shared the KCS facilities and then built their own to the east. This switch was important as the M&A had trackage rights over the KCS northward to Joplin Union Depot. There were several connections at Neosho, and they were clearly identified in various documents.

174.1 NEOSHO (ON) – In the April 1922 issue of KCS' *Agricultural and Industrial Bulletin,* an article about Neosho stated that it was "the best known town of 5000 in the United States." It stated that the town featured "iron foundry and plow works, planing mill, florist, fruit and ornamental nursery, two flour mills, feed mill, cigar factory, garment factory, concrete block and tile factory, broom factory, tripoli factory, advertising slide company, vegetable canning factory, bottling works, ice plant and cold storage, ice cream factory, laundry, marble works, wholesale candy company, two wholesale grocery companies, two poultry and produce companies, fire-proof storage and warehouse, and two motion picture theatres."

Today, Neosho has a population of approximately 12,000, making it the largest city in Newton County, Missouri. It is also the county seat. White settlers began to move into the area during the 1820s and 1830s, generally of English, Scottish, Welsh, Scots-Irish and German ancestry. The area was open prairie on the top of the Ozark Plateau, making it perfect for hay and livestock production. The first communities were to the east, but John W. McCord and Levie Lee located near Walbridge Spring in an area known as "Six Bulls" for the six roaring streams in the area ("Six Boils").

Walbridge Spring, also known as Bell's Iron Spring, indirectly provided the name of Neosho, an Osage word that means "clear, cold water," generally from a spring. Besides Walbridge Spring, the largest spring in the area – Clark or Big Spring – became the center of the community and is now located in Big Spring Park. Both were used for many purposes, including industrial and residential, giving Neosho the nickname "City of Springs." The town was platted in 1833, incorporated on August 20, 1847, and incorporated as a city in 1878. Part of the initial growth of Neosho was due to the discovery of lead and zinc. Much of the ore was shallow, and miners could mine it and move it to the Arkansas River in Indian Territory (Oklahoma) for water shipment to New Orleans. This attracted stores, taverns, and other industries to Neosho to support the needs of the miners and their mines.

The town's importance can be seen by the creation of a monthly Pony Express mail route from Neosho to Albuquerque, New Mexico, on August 3, 1854. However, the Civil War ended the region's importance with four years of guerrilla warfare and multiple military campaigns. The courthouse was burned, as was much of the town as it changed hands on a regular basis. The decade after the Civil War saw Neosho regrow, with many buildings constructed using brick. A new courthouse opened in 1878, and the population surpassed 2000 by 1890. Much of the boom during the late 1800s was due to the improved transportation available when the Atlantic & Pacific Railroad (Frisco) reached Neosho in 1870. A second railroad arrived in 1887 – the Kansas City, Fort Smith & Southern Railroad, later the Kansas City Southern Railroad. A third railroad, the Missouri & North Arkansas, arrived in 1908.

A unique and historic event links Neosho to the great vineyards of Europe. In 1882, vineyards across France, Spain and Portugal died from the deadly phylloxera louse, a small pale yellow sap-sucking insect. After searching for answers, it was discovered that Neosho winemaker Hermann Jaeger was growing a new grape that was resistant to the phylloxera louse. Cuttings from Jaeger's vineyards near Monark Springs were shipped to Europe, ending the destruction of the wine industry. Because of his assistance, Jaeger was awarded the French Legion of Honour, the highest award that France can bestow on a civilian.

On August 7, 1914, a funeral was held at the Newton County courthouse for the victims of the M&NA-KCS accident at Tipton Ford. Many of the victims were not identified, and more than 30 were buried in a mass grave in the Neosho Independent Order of Odd Fellows Cemetery, located southeast of downtown.

This monument in the Neosho Independent Order of Odd Fellows Cemetery marks the burial site of many of those killed in the train wreck at nearby Tipton Ford, Missouri.

The 1950s and 1960s saw a growth in local industry, and national recognition. For example, Neosho won the 1957 All-America City Award from *Look* magazine and the National Municipal League for its beautification efforts, making it "The Flower Box City." Much of downtown Neosho is known as the Neosho Commercial Historic District and is listed in the National Register of Historic Places.

In 1872, Missouri law required a school for African Americans. The small wooden school at Neosho was known as the Lincoln School. One of the students was an orphan with the name of George Washington Carver. Carver had been born nearby as a slave in 1864, and after the war moved as a child to attend school. He was known as Carver's George at the time for his one-time owner, Moses Carver, but had his name changed to George Carver by a teacher at the school. He attended school at Neosho for about five years before moving for more advanced education. In time, he became a prominent agricultural scientist and head of the Agriculture Department at the Tuskegee Institute.

Another student educated in Neosho was humorist Will Rogers. Rogers was born in 1879 in the Cherokee Nation of Indian Territory. His parents were both of mixed-race and Cherokee ancestry, and identified as Cherokee. His father was a Confederate veteran, an attorney and Cherokee judge, and a successful rancher. To help with his education Will Rogers attended the Willow Hassel School at Neosho, where he claimed that he "studied the Fourth Reader for ten years."

Railroads at Neosho

The railroad era at Neosho began in 1870 when the Atlantic & Pacific Railroad arrived. This line later became part of the Frisco Railroad's St. Louis to Tulsa route, and is today operated by BNSF. The line loops around the north and west side of Neosho. The stucco Frisco passenger and freight depot was at Benham Avenue and Commercial on the north side of town. Today, a modern metal office building and a communications tower stand where the old station once was located.

The second railroad to reach Neosho was the Kansas City, Fort Smith & Southern Railroad, later the Kansas City Southern Railroad. It arrived in 1887 and runs north-south on the east side of downtown. The large brick station, built in 1922-23 and located at KCS Milepost 174.1, was once where the large communications tower now stands between East Coler and East Brook on the west side of the mainline along North Washington. Built of brick in 1923, the depot housed bulletin books, a train register, and a standard clock. Like many of the KCS stations, there was a covered porch on the passenger end. In 1938, the movie *Jesse James*, starring Tyrone Power and Henry Fonda, was filmed in the area and several scenes were filmed at the KCS depot.

For several decades, Neosho was the site of an emergency icing station, which was very active during the berry movement season. This station loaded refrigerator cars with ice to help keep the contents cool while moving to market.

Neosho was also once the home of the Neosho Dodger, a Monday through Saturday local that served customers between Tipton Ford and Lanagan, and handled any station switching. This assignment changed greatly as the railroad moved from steam to diesel locomotives. During the late 1900s, Neosho was also the base for several sets of pusher locomotives that were used on the steep grades to the south.

In 1990, the railroad was changing from white locomotives to grey ones. At the time, Neosho was the base of several sets of pusher locomotives to assist trains over the hilly Heavener Subdivision. This photo of KCS 706 and 796 shows the changes underway at the time.

In 1908, the Missouri & North Arkansas reached Neosho and shared the KCS facilities for many years before building their own basic facilities in 1933, and then abandoning the line in 1947. In 1936, M. & A. southbound Freight No. 211 was scheduled to arrive here at 10:20am to meet KCS northbound Second Class Manifest Freight No. 42. The M&NA's north-

Heavener Sub Route Guide

bound was scheduled to depart daily at 4:20pm as Freight No. 212.

Neosho was a scheduled stop for the *Southern Belle*, the premier train on the Kansas City Southern. This train operated between Kansas City and New Orleans and was the first diesel-powered lightweight passenger train on the railroad. The schedule that was published on January 5, 1964, showed that the southbound train No. 1 was scheduled to depart at 1:00pm.

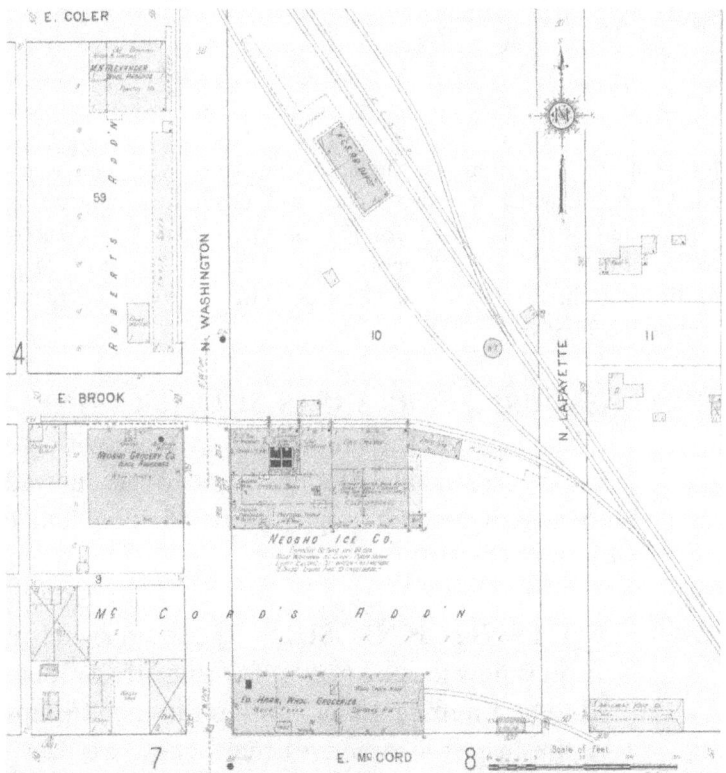

This Sanborn map from 1916 shows the general area around the KCS station at Neosho, Missouri. A number of shippers were in the area, including the Neosho Ice Company and the Ed Haas Wholesale Groceries warehouse. *Sanborn Fire Insurance Map from Neosho, Newton County, Missouri*. Sanborn Map Company, April 1916. Map. Retrieved from the Library of Congress, https://www.loc.gov/item/sanborn04794_006/.

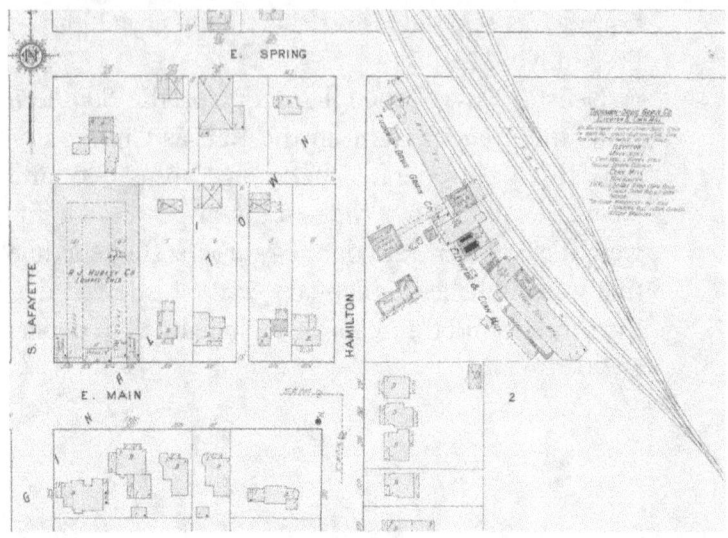

Just south of the station was the large Thurman-Davis Grain Company complex, which included a corn mill, elevator, manufacturing facility, and warehouse. *Sanborn Fire Insurance Map from Neosho, Newton County, Missouri*. Sanborn Map Company, Apr, 1916. Map. Retrieved from the Library of Congress, https://www.loc.gov/item/sanborn04794_006/.

174.2 MISSOURI & ARKANSAS SOUTH CONNECTION – This was the southern connection with the Missouri & Arkansas Railway, and once allowed both passenger and freight trains to interchange with the KCS.

174.3 SOUTH SWITCH NEOSHO – The south switch at Neosho is now located north of Spring Street. There used to be a number of facilities in this area to support the helper locomotives that once were based here. This is the north end of a 1.31% grade that ends at Milepost 177.7 near the former location of Fort Crowder, also known as Camp Crowder. It can be impressive to watch southbound trains fight this short uphill grade as they leave Neosho.

From Neosho to McElhany, the railroad once had a number of industries and the Fort Crowder facility to serve. The justification for installing the ABS signals south to McElhany included a reported six to eight daily switching moves between Neosho and Camp Crowder.

174.6 MCKINNEY STREET – This street is also Missouri Highway 86. To the east is the Neosho National Fish Hatchery, the oldest Federal Fish Hatchery still operating. This facility opened in 1888 on East McKinney Street, and eventually was located next to the tracks. The hatchery at first used water from Hearrell Spring, and expanded to using McMahon Spring in 1907, giving the facility 1000 gallons of water a minute. Since then, the hatchery has raised more than 130 different species of fish, with rainbow trout, pallid sturgeon, and Topeka shiners the primary species currently being raised.

On the south side of McKinney Street is Hearrell Spring, and the 1.3-acre Hearrell Spring Unit National Wildlife Refuge, a part of the Ozark Cavefish National Wildlife Refuge. The railroad passes on the west side of a low, wooded hillside. For the next several miles, the southbound railroad is heading uphill as it passes through a series of residential areas.

The Heavener Sub: History Through the Miles

One of the most unique buildings that KCS passes at Neosho, Missouri, is certainly that of the Neosho National Fish Hatchery.

177.1 LINDE SPUR – To the west is a long industrial lead (5599 feet) that serves a number of customers, including Praxair and several agricultural companies. Not far south of here, a long track once looped to the east to serve several industries along Doniphan Drive and then further east on the Fort Crowder property. This track is gone, but a few vestiges remain where the Doniphan Drive grade crossing once was.

177.5 AERO JET SPUR – This 12-car track is no longer here. The old grade can be seen to the west.

177.6 GLAZER SPUR – This was a 32-car-long track that was listed in the March 22, 1970, employee timetable. Maps from the time show a track heading to the west.

Heavener Sub Route Guide

Just south of here at Milepost 177.7 is the top of the 1.31% grade that started at Milepost 174.3 at the South Switch Neosho.

178.2 MCELHANY PASSENGER STATION – Located where the railroad bridges over today's Lyons Drive, the railroad had a passenger station to the east during the 1940s. This station was located here so that it would not sit in the middle of the new Fort Crowder.

The Lyons Driver underpass was once the location of the McElhany passenger station.

178.5 MISSOURI SUGARS TRACK – To the east is a siding that serves the facility of Missouri Sugars. The firm located here in 2006, and prior to that the track was known as the Coach Track. Missouri Sugars is part of a company that includes Indiana Sugar, New England Sugars, New York Sugars, and Sweet Specialty Solutions. These companies provide high-quality ingredients to the food manufacturing industry. The facility at Neosho includes a sugar processing plant (bulk and powdered sugars) and a liquid sugar processing plant (bulk liquids and low color liquids).

Through the 1960s, there were still a number of tracks that served Fort Crowder. By 1970, the only track shown was the Fort Crowder Coach Track. It was shown to have a length of 34 car lengths and had switches on each end, making it a short siding.

179.1 CONTROL POINT NORTH MCELHANY – Located not far south of Austin Avenue is the north end of the 3.5-mile-long McElhany siding. This part of the railroad was redesigned and rebuilt about 2012 to add capacity to the line, essentially creating a short stretch of two main tracks.

179.5 FORT CROWDER PASSENGER PAGODA – This location was shown in KCS employee timetables during the 1940s and 1950s.

179.6 FT. CROWDER NORTH CONNECTION – A 45-car-long track once went to the west and served a number of warehouse buildings that were part of Fort Crowder, also known as Camp Crowder until the 1950s.

Camp Crowder was built south of Neosho in 1941 as an armored training center. It was converted by 1943 to be a U.S. Army Signal Corps training center. It was also used as an infantry replacement center and as a German prisoner-of-war detention facility. The name Crowder came from General Enoch Crowder, who developed the draft during World War I. One of the famous alumni of Camp Crowder was Carl Reiner. In *The Dick Van Dyke Show*, Camp Crowder was where Rob (Dick Van Dyke) and Laura (Mary Tyler Moore) met. The plot had Rob as a sergeant in

Heavener Sub Route Guide

Special Services and Laura was a USO dancer. Camp Crowder was also the model for Camp Swampy, the base of the comic strip *Beetle Bailey*. This was due to the well-known nature of the facility, and cartoonist Mort Walker's assignment there during WWII. The camp was deactivated in 1951, with much of the base sold off. The location is now an industrial park, the home of Crowder College, and the Fort Crowder Conservation Area. During the past decade, there has been a great deal of development on the former base, but Kansas City Southern serves only a limited part of it.

180.7 OZARK WOOD – To the east is the former site of Ozark Wood Fiber, a firm created in 1997 to operate a chip mill. Initially, the company purchased slabs from local sawmills and processed them through a chipper to produce hardwood chips. These chips were then loaded into railcars and sold to various paper mills. The company expanded to manufacturing lumber, railroad crossties, oak mulch, sawdust, pallet cants, and various framestock. The company annually manufactured more than fifteen million board feet of hardwood products and 50,000 tons of byproducts like mulch, chips, and sawdust. It closed several years ago.

By 2022, most of the processing facilities were gone and the location was producing large utility poles, many shipped out by rail. Several new Stella-Jones signs were at the gates. As described by the company, "Stella-Jones is North America's leading producer of industrial pressure-treated wood products. Responding to the vital infrastructure needs of our economy, we manufacture and distribute rail-

The Heavener Sub: History Through the Miles

way ties, utility poles, residential lumber and industrial wood products across the continent."

Milepost 180.7 is actually the north switch to the siding that served Ozark Wood Fiber. The track is shown to be 2366 feet long. Cars loaded with hardwood poles and logs are often spotted here.

180.7 FT. CROWDER SOUTH CONNECTION – This was another connection into Camp Crowder, measuring 10 cars long and also located to the west. Today, a 5400-foot-long Government Lead is shown to exist here. The track passes through a series of old warehouses and several newer industry complexes.

The Government Lead at McElhany winds through a number of old warehouse buildings to serve several customers.

Heavener Sub Route Guide

180.8 MCELHANY – McElhany was an original station on the line, and was named for the McElhany family who lived in the area. In 1890, the railroad station was briefly named McElheny, likely a spelling mistake. The McElhany post office opened in 1896, but the town didn't grow enough to keep it from closing in 1911. A platform and station was located to the west at this location. Today, McElhany is a rural unincorporated community south of Neosho.

In 1964, McElhany was shown to be a 111-car-long siding. There was also a 17-car spur track. Today, there is a crossover between the siding and mainline at Milepost 180.8, shown as being Control Point 181 McElhany. No passenger service was provided in 1964, but at the time train Nos. 15 and 16 (*The Flying Crow*) were scheduled to meet here at 2:37am. Riding the southbound *Southern Belle*, the train was scheduled to pass here at 1:09pm without stopping.

Control Point 181 McElhany marks the location of the crossovers near the center of the long section of two tracks south of Neosho, Missouri.

Pools Prairie

This area has been known as Pools Prairie for more than 100 years. It has been a popular area for grazing livestock, and during the Civil War was a frequently used encampment by both armies. Part of the prairie is now an EPA Superfund site due to several projects at Fort Crowder. During the 1950s, part of the fort was used by the Air Force as a rocket engine manufacturing plant (Air Force Plant No. 65). The plant operated 1957-1968, and was then used to manufacture, test, and refurbish jet airplane engines. The plant was sold in 1980 to a private company who used it to test and refurbish jet and helicopter engines. The facility has been cleaned and is currently used for other manufacturing.

Because of the grades in the area and the frequent congestion at Neosho, the siding at McElhany has been a popular place to meet trains. In 1990, southbound grain train No. 701, with KCS 650 leading, waits for a northbound train at McElhany. The area is a growing industrial park and photos like this are getting harder to take as new buildings are erected.

Heavener Sub Route Guide

182.6 CONTROL POINT SOUTH MCELHANY – This is the south switch of the long siding at McElhany.

182.9 COUNTY LINE – Not far south of South McElhany is the county line between **Newton County** (to the north) and **McDonald County** (to the south). **Newton County** dates to December 31, 1838, and is today the eighteenth most populous county in Missouri, with about 60,000 residents. Neosho is the county seat. The name Newton comes from John Newton, a somewhat fictional hero who fought in the Revolutionary War. Newton served in the forces of Brigadier General Francis Marion, the famous and legendary "Swamp Fox." While officers who served with Newton called him a "thief and villain," he was made famous in early 19th century schoolbooks written by Parson Weems. Weems claimed many great achievements for Newton, a number of which seem almost identical to those of Sergeant William Jasper. Jasper is a well-documented hero of the Revolutionary War. He showed bravery at battles like Sullivan's Island and Savannah, and was awarded several honors before he was killed in 1779. With the fame created from the schoolbooks, many western states have a county or town named for John Newton.

McDonald County is located in the very southwestern corner of Missouri. It has a population of about 23,000 and Pineville is its county seat. The county was originally created as Seneca County by the Missouri State Legislature on January 1, 1847, but attached to Newton County for government purposes. The county was independently organized on March 3, 1849, as McDonald County, but the government stayed connected to Newton County until 1856. The name McDonald apparently comes from Sergeant Alexander McDonald, a soldier in the American Revolutionary War. However, why it was named after him is unclear. Like many courthouses across the region during the Civil War, the Pineville courthouse was burned in 1863 and most records were lost. While farming and ranching have always played a large role in the local economy, tourism is now also significant.

183.5 DONOHUE – Names came and went throughout this area as the land was being settled and the railroad was built. This station was one of those places that seemed to move and change its name on a regular basis during the late 1800s. The mileposts also moved a mile or more as the railroad was completed, making it even more difficult to clearly identify each station. This location involves at least four stations – Erie, Wade, Donohue, and Goodman.

Various railroad timetables state that Erie was at Milepost 183 in 1890, which would put it about Milepost 184 today. The name was apparently changed to Wade by 1893, which was listed as being at Milepost 184.5 that year. A George A. Ogle & Company map from 1909 showed Wade as being located at the north end of Goodman, and that its alternative name was Erie Station.

In 1896, the station of Donahue was shown to be at Milepost 181, but the post office was in McDonald County, several miles further south. Various reports state that Donahue was originally called Wade, but the Kansas City, Fort Smith & Southern had a station named Wade about three miles to the south of the listed milepost. Reports also state that Donahue eventually became part of Goodman.

A post office opened at Donahue on May 13, 1895, with Alonzo W. Burton as its postmaster. The railroad showed a station named Donahue here by 1896. The post office closed in 1897 and was replaced by the one at Goodman on October 23, 1897. The source of the name Donahue is not clear, but it is believed to have come from an early settler.

183.8 ERIE – Erie, or Erie Station, was listed as a railroad station by 1890. The first post office opened in the area at the home of John M. Harmon on August 10, 1858. John M. Harmon was a leader in the development of the area; he had the community of Erie surveyed and built the first home here. However, the Civil War kept the community from growing, and actually ran off many of its residents. The post office remained until Harmon's death in 1862. A new post office opened on June 8, 1871, thanks to Dr. John L. Sellers.

When the railroad was built, it was several miles west of Erie, and a station was planned for where it could be reached by a road. The stop soon took on the name of Erie Station. As Goodman grew, it replaced the stop for Erie.

This traditional concrete post marks Milepost 184. Located north of today's Goodman, it once was located between Erie and Wade, both in Missouri.

184.5 WADE – Wade was a station listed by 1893 and was part of the complex history of the Goodman area. A Wade post office was established on November 29, 1889, and closed on October 28, 1893 (although some sources state 1895). The name came from William Henry Wade, a successful area farmer who served in the Missouri House of Representatives (1881-1884) and then the U.S. House of Representatives (1885-1891).

Maps from the early 1900s show Wade as being at the north end of Goodman. They showed that the location was also known as Erie Station, and was located at the Garner Street grade crossing at what is today Milepost 184.0.

Starting here, southbound trains almost fall off the ridge on a 1.32% grade, which ends near Elliff at Milepost 188.3.

184.6 GOODMAN (MS) – Goodman is the remaining name of the stations that were once here. The history of Goodman states that when the railroad was built, a depot was located within the Village of Donahue. As the railroad began operating, the depot, several section houses, and the post office were moved a short distance to be closer to the planned center of the growing town. Soon, the Ozark Orchard Company began buying land and planting trees in the area. Eventually the firm owned land north, west and south of the community, as well as half of the town site. On October 23, 1897, Henry Stites opened a post office that he named for Lowell A. Goodman, who came to Donahue about 1890 to develop the orchard business.

Goodman had been in the fruit business for years, and worked with several partners to eventually have more than 2500 acres of orchards in Goodman and the surrounding areas. Acres of strawberries were also planted. Goodman's work led to the creation of the Ozark Orchard Company in 1895, and then the naming of the new post office after himself a few years later. Goodman eventually became the vice-president and general manager of the Ozark Orchard Company, living in Kansas City, Missouri. On June 25, 1917, he passed away in the village of Goodman while on a business trip to inspect the company's fruit and berry acreage.

The influence of Goodman could be felt for decades. During the 1920s, organizations like the Goodman Fruit Growers Association, Goodman Berry Growers Association, and Independent Berry Growers Association sold and shipped apples, grapes, strawberries, blackberries, and Bermuda onions from Goodman. Additionally, Hawkins Canning Company handled tomatoes.

The Great Depression ended much of this business, and many trains simply passed through town. The depot, located at the west end of Main Street, was closed. The section house located on the southeast corner of Stites and Second streets was eventually sold, but still stands today. Goodman became Goodman Spur and a mail crane was installed so that trains could pick up the mail without stopping. The Village of Goodman incorporated as the City of Goodman (Fourth Class City) on November 6, 1956. However, the town didn't get much bigger, and in 1964 Goodman was only a flag stop for train Nos. 15 (2:42am) and 16 (2:31am). *Southern Belle* No. 1 simply passed by at 1:13pm without stopping. Goodman now has a population of about 1200 and is a rural community, with a number of residents commuting to larger cities nearby. The new Interstate 49, built west of town, has supported this recent growth, and the Goodman Elementary School stands just north of the tracks.

In 1964, there was a 62-car-long siding at Goodman, plus other tracks with a capacity of 75 cars. Today, at the southwest end of Goodman, located north of Splitlog Avenue, is a 1200-foot spur track to the southwest. This spur is what is left of the line that once headed west to the community of Splitlog, one of the projects of Mathias Splitlog.

Heavener Sub Route Guide

Heading south, the railroad follows Beaver Branch all the way to Anderson, Missouri.

A small park in downtown Goodman is perfect for watching northbound trains as they reach the top of the steep grade from Anderson. This is KCS 4698 with a Norfolk Southern and another KCS locomotive finally getting a breather as they pass the small pavilion at Goodman after a long and slow climb up the 1.32% grade.

For decades, Goodman, Missouri, has been locally famous for this neon sign that points the way to the small community.

The signal at Milepost 184.8 stands at the south end of Goodman, Missouri.

The short spur track at the south end of Goodman is actually the original mainline to Splitlog, Missouri.

Heavener Sub Route Guide

186.4 INTERSTATE 49 – The railroad passes under the roadway at this location. Interstate 49, a north-south highway, was not part of the original 1957 Interstate Highway plan. During the 1960s, Missouri, Arkansas and Louisiana pushed for the roadway as an improved U.S. Highway 71. Initially, it was to be an extension of Interstate 29, but it became Interstate 49 when construction began in Louisiana in 1984. The use of the name Interstate 49 in Missouri became official on December 12, 2012, replacing U.S. Highway 71 which had already been rebuilt to Interstate standards. When completed, Interstate 49 will connect New Orleans, Louisiana, with Kansas City, Missouri.

186.7 MISSOURI HIGHWAY 59 BRIDGE – The railroad passes over Missouri Highway 59 on a three-span concrete bridge. The bridge has for years had a KCS shield on the center span.

Highway 59 has slowly replaced the earlier U.S. Highway 71 over much of its route through the area. Highway 59 heads south from the I-49/I-44 junction east of Joplin, near Fidelity, Missouri. At the Arkansas state line south of Noel, it becomes Arkansas Highway 59. Missouri Highway 59 started between Arkansas and Lanagan in 1960 when U.S. Highway 71 was moved east to the former Route 88. As U.S. 71 was moved and upgraded to Interstate Highway standards, Highway 59 took over the old road. From Neosho to Noel, Missouri Highway 59 closely follows the tracks of the KCS.

The Heavener Sub: History Through the Miles

In 1990, train No. 5 was a daytime freight over the Heavener Subdivision, and one that photographers could depend on. Here, it is crossing Missouri Highway 59 near Elliff at a popular photography location.

In 1990, one of the big news items on the Heavener Subdivision was the testing of several Denver & Rio Grande Western SD40T-2 locomotives in pusher service. Here, black D&RGW 5401 is bracketed by white KCS locomotives as they push train No. 701 southbound over Missouri Highway 59 near Elliff, Missouri.

188.1 ELLIFF – Elliff was an 82-car siding and a short 13-car spur track for many years. The siding was extended to 100 cars long by the late 1950s, but was removed 1962-1964. The railroad passed through the property of Jesse L. Elliff north of Anderson. Elliff moved to McDonald County in 1866 with his parents at the age of 11. As an adult, he was a local leader, having been principal of a nearby school system, a clerk of the Baptist Church at Anderson, and a noted member of the Independent Order of Odd Fellows (IOOF). For more than a year he was the appointed clerk at Quapaw Agency, chosen by President Cleveland. He was also a representative to several state conventions, and served as a Probate Judge 1884-1886.

In 1906, the railroad reported that they built a second track here for J. L. Elliff, so he obviously also operated a business that required rail service.

189.2 BEAVER BRANCH BRIDGE – Located behind the Missouri Department of Transportation office, the railroad crosses Beaver Branch. Like a number of streams in the area, it was named for the beavers found along the waterway. Beaver Branch starts as a small wet-weather stream near Goodman. While generally not much more than a dry, stony waterway, Beaver Branch is known for its flooding during heavy rains. The stream flows southward and the railroad uses its valley which reaches Indian Creek at Anderson.

189.8 BEAVER BRANCH BRIDGE – Normally a fairly dry creek bed, Beaver Branch is crossed using a 4-span 4-steel-beam bridge not far south of Hagee Road (Milepost 189.7). This bridge is new, having been installed in 2017 to replace a series of older timber spans. During the past decade, KCS has replaced a number of its older bridges.

191.7 ANDERSON (RS) – What you see at Anderson today is nothing like what it was during the early 1900s. It seemed that every few years, the town's layout changed. About 1900, the train station was located north of Beaver Street, on the west side of the mainline. The Portland Hotel was a block to the north, and the railroad stock yards were to the south at First Street. The main road through town that is now Missouri Highway 59 did not exist.

In 1910, Kansas City Southern built a new brick station south of the Beaver Street grade crossing. The north end of the building housed the passenger waiting room, while the south end was the freight room. In 1920, the brick station was on the west side of three tracks. The Anderson Roller Mills was just south of the depot and to the east. The Chamberlain Canning Company was located further south and also to the east. There was also a long beer loading platform on the east side of the tracks, located north of Beaver and south of Main.

By 1928, the Portland Hotel was the Tandy Hotel, and the beer loading platform was being used for fruit shipping. A second fruit shipping facility had also been built opposite the depot. A mail crane was installed about this time, and lasted until the end of passenger service.

Heavener Sub Route Guide

Anderson remained a staffed office into the 1970s, with it having telegraph services 8am-5pm weekdays. Anderson's population of less than 1000 had it a nighttime flag stop for the *Flying Crow* (Nos. 15 and 16) in 1964, but southbound No. 1 (*Southern Belle*) was scheduled to simply pass through at 1:22pm.

For years, timetables listed North Switch Anderson at Milepost 191.8 and South Switch Anderson at Milepost 192.1. Today, the siding is gone, but there is still an 1150-foot spur track to the east that serves the Fairview Mills elevator. The Anderson station still stands between the tracks and the downtown Anderson Park, used as the Anderson City Hall.

The northbound Dodger (Local) is shown passing the Anderson depot on February 17, 1990. Note the use of the former F7B slug #4077 in the consist.

This photo shows the north end of the brick depot at Anderson. The building now serves as Anderson's city hall.

The south end of the Anderson depot was used for freight, as shown by the large end door on the building.

The City of Anderson

Anderson traces its history back to 1886 when Robert Anderson opened a general store, and then a post office on September 21, 1886. The site was near a series of springs above the Indian River, shown as Indian Creek in most documents today. When the railroad was built through a nearby gap, Marshall E. Meador platted the town of Anderson along the route. Within a few years, the Anderson Fruit Growers Association began shipping strawberries, attracting new businesses and residents. With the growth of the community, the City of Anderson was incorporated on December 7, 1909.

The strawberry industry had its beginning in the fall of 1903 when berries were shipped from the Anderson Fruit Growers Association. This industry would grow until Anderson became known as the "Strawberry Capital of the World." By the early 1950s, this local industry waned due to severe competition from the Western/Southern states. The Chamberlain Canning Company canned millions of fresh vegetables from around the area. The Seven Valley Cheese Company also processed milk from area farmers. Due to excellent rail connections, Anderson boasted a Hatchery and Feed Mill.

The Anderson Fruit Growers Association started in 1903 with only 15 members and 35 acres of Aroma strawberries. That first year, a total of seven cars of strawberries were shipped from Anderson. By 1923, Anderson Fruit Growers was the largest fruit growing association in the Ozark country, and it shipped 300 carloads of strawberries in 1926. The association handled strawberries, blackberries, apples, peaches, and grapes. Other firms shipped green beans, canned tomatoes, and evaporated apples from Anderson.

The largest of the canning companies was Chamberlain Canning. During the fall of 1924, the cannery turned out 16,000 cans of tomatoes a day. The firm reported that at its peak that year on September 11th, they canned 41,326 No. 2 cans (such a can holds 1 pound 4 ounces, or 2 ½ cups of product). Almost 400,000 cans of tomatoes were produced that year, requiring almost 400 railcars to ship. Tomatoes and the canning business were a frequent subject of the Kansas City Southern Railway's *Agricultural and Industrial Bulletin*. In one issue, it reported the following about the tomato industry.

> In 1925, the acreage in McDonald County alone had reached three thousand acres, and great acreages were also planted in Newton County, Missouri, and Benton County, Arkansas, and the production of the canneries at Anderson, Goodman, Lanagan, Neosho and Noel, Mo., Decatur, Gentry, Gravette, Siloam Springs, Ark., and Stilwell, Westville and Watts, Okla., reached 459 carloads, valued at approximately $1,249,770.

Due to the volume of strawberry shipments, Anderson called itself the "Strawberry Capitol of the World." This business is mostly gone, but the community still celebrates its strawberry history with the Anderson Berries, Bluegrass & BBQ Festival. With a population of 2000 it also has other industries, such as the Fairview Mills elevator at the south end of town just south of Canning Factory Road. The Hiland Dairy Foods facility is not far to the north.

This grain elevator stands towards the south end of Anderson, Missouri, and receives regular railroad service.

The town wraps around the north side of a sharp bend in Indian Creek, with a number of old buildings located near the depot. Several newer businesses are located on U.S. Business 71 north of town. Interstate 49 has recently been built east of town, helping with its slow but steady growth in population.

195.2 LANAGAN (AG) – Lanagan is located on a low ridge west of Missouri Highway 59, the tracks of the Kansas City Southern, and Indian Creek. The area is now mostly wooded, but like much of the area, fruit and berries once were grown everywhere. A few early publications used the spelling "Lanegan," but legal documents always used Lanagan.

Lanagan dates its history back to 1886 and a failed oil well. In that year, the New York Petroleum Company drilled an 834-foot well searching for oil, but instead struck a powerful sulphur-water spring. The search for oil ended, but 40 acres of the lease were acquired by a group of speculators, including T. C. Lanagan, M. R. DeGroff, and I. D. Galbraith, in 1887. The town of Sulphur Well City was immediately platted, with plans to be on the railroad being built through the area.

The railroad built along Indian Creek in 1889, but the town was not an immediate success. A few years later, the Ozark Orchard Company bought land all around the small community, and T. C. Lanagan added the Lanagan's Addition to the south end of the Sulphur Well City plat. It was here that a train depot was built between the community and the tracks, located at the bottom of Pebble Street. A series of parks were built nearby, all featuring fountains fed by local artesian wells and springs.

On March 6, 1891, the Lanagan post office opened, and the community took the name Lanagan. There were soon several resorts in the area using the various springs. By 1897, Lanagan was described as being a "prosperous little village with three stores, two hotels, a new church and school house, and is doing a large timber business."

The town grew to about 300 residents by the 1920s. In the April-May 1926 issue of *Agricultural and Industrial Bulletin*, a short article described Lanagan.

> The village of Lanagan has 400 inhabitants, is south of Kansas City 195 miles and has an altitude of 900 feet. The general business of the village depends upon the agricultural and forest resources in the vicinity. Near the railway, fruit and berry growing, poultry raising and dairying are the predominating pursuits; further out general farming and stock raising receive much attention. There are in the village several stores, two hotels, a garage, a cannery, an up-to-date school building and a power dam across Indian River, with an electric plant from which Lanagan and a number of summer resorts are supplied with light and power.

In 1925, the railroad hauled a number of agricultural products from Lanagan, including strawberries, tomatoes, grapes, apples, canned goods, cream and other dairy products, and eggs, Much of this was shipped by the Lanagan-Pineville Berry Association and the J. W. Gooding Tomato Cannery. The railroad also promoted "miles of fine fishing waters" in the Lanagan area.

While the railroad promoted Lanagan, it never grew to much more than just a small rural village. Its population in the 1930 census was 347, and it stayed near that until 1980 when it jumped to 440 residents. In 1990, the census showed 501 people living in Lanagan, but that has dropped to about 400 recently. Little of the original Sulphur Well City remains, with most of the town being south of Flint Street in Lanagan's Addition.

In 1936, Lanagan had a staffed station from midnight until 4pm, seven days a week. It was a regular station stop for passenger trains, but it also featured a mail crane. There was a 102-car passing track, plus 63 car-lengths of other tracks. Oil, water, and coal were also available at the time.

The siding was removed 1962-1964, and only a 20-car spur track remained. The station agency was also closed, and passenger trains had reduced their service at Lanagan; the *Southern Belle* (No. 1) simply passed by at 1:27pm. The wooden KCS depot was sold to the town and moved several blocks away to the southeast corner of Pebble and Second streets. It is now used as the city hall, and the freight end has been modified. The spur track still sits along Missouri Highway 59.

Although no longer located next to the tracks, the Lanagan depot still stands on the southeast corner of Pebble and Second streets.

Heavener Sub Route Guide

Located to the southeast of the Heavener Subdivision, the Lanagan City Park is a good spot to sit and watch trains moving over the line.

195.5 COUNTY ROAD EE - The railroad passes under this concrete beam bridge, built in 1928. The bridge is a popular photo location with the green ridge in the background. Heading south, the railroad squeezes between Indian Creek and a low ridge. On top of the ridge alongside Missouri Highway 59 is Indian Creek Roadside Park. Before the trees grew, there were views down onto the railroad.

The Heavener Sub: History Through the Miles

KCS 650 pulls a grain train southward through Lanagan, Missouri, and then under the County Road EE bridge back in early 1990.

196.7 TEN DEGREE CURVE – Reportedly, this is the sharpest mainline curve on the railroad. There have been numerous studies to reduce the curvature, but all require removing the end of the ridge, which sources state is made of granite. The curve is part of a 25-mile-per-hour speed restriction between Mileposts 195.9 and 196.7.

197.0 ELK RIVER BRIDGE – The bridge that you see today includes a dozen deck plate girder spans. Note that those across the river are smaller than those on the south end of the bridge. Also note that there are more modern piers between the older stone piers. At one time, several through truss spans were used to cross the Elk River, but those came down due to a freight train derailment in the early 1980s. Besides crossing the very active Elk River, this bridge also crosses Elk Springs Road using the south bridge span.

The Elk River is formed from two major sources – Big Sugar Creek (forms near Seligman, Missouri) and Little Sugar Creek (forms near Bentonville, Arkansas). The two streams merge near Pineville, Missouri, and the Elk River then flows generally westward 35 miles before entering the Neosho River, now part of the Grand Lake O' the Cherokees. The river has become a popular float stream and there are numerous cabins, campgrounds, and outfitters along the route. Next to this bridge are several campground and float operators, and this area can be very busy.

The name of the river has a romantic version and a practical version. Most sources state that the river was originally known as the Cowskin River. This name dates from the early 1800s when a settler lost a number of his cows. He reportedly skinned them and left the skins out on the bank of the river to dry. Another version of the Cowskin name states that the river was christened by a Catholic priest when a buffalo cow was killed there, and the skin made into a robe. No matter the source of the Cowskin River name, the river's current name is the Elk River.

By 1845, the names of Cowskin River and Elk River were being used jointly. The romantic version of the Elk name comes from several stories that elk roamed the riverbanks when the first settlers arrived. This is certainly true as elk were common in this area until the mid-1800s. The less romantic version for the naming states that Steve Elkins, a local politician, had the Missouri Legislature name it after himself.

One of the most popular photo spots along the Heavener Subdivision is the long bridge across the Elk River. Here, KCS 706 leads southbound No. 5 across the bridge over the popular floating stream.

During the early 1980s, part of the Elk River Bridge was destroyed by a train derailment, and replaced with several deck plate girder spans. This view shows the new concrete piers that were installed as part of this work.

197.3 ELK SPRINGS – Just south of the Elk River bridge is another one of those places that has gone through a number of names, yet never grew beyond being a simple rural community. The community started as Rutledge, and Larkin McGhee opened a post office using that name on September 18, 1849. By this time, Rutledge had won an election to become the county seat of McDonald County. Some describe the selection process as a civil war, a feud, and more. It was basically a fight between Rutledge and Maryville (later Pineville) that became a struggle between the two ends of the county. During the campaigning, there were a number of fights and several murders. Rutledge won the election narrowly, and a small log courthouse was erected.

Despite being the county seat, Rutledge never grew and was considered to be too rural and rowdy. In 1857, the Missouri General Assembly passed several acts requiring that the county seat be near the geographical center of the county. This eliminated Rutledge, and Maryville, almost immediately renamed Pineville, became the new county seat. Despite losing the business related to being the county seat, Rutledge was still located in a favorable location alongside the Elk River, with large pastures nearby. Because of this, Rutledge was used as an encampment by military forces during the Civil War. During August 1864, several Civil War skirmishes were fought here between forces using the area for livestock feed and rest. After the war, Rutledge failed to recover, and its post office was closed on June 27, 1867.

Madge, Missouri

Little remained here until the railroad built through McDonald County. With this, a new town was formed known as Madge. John K. Parish was an important leader in the community, and he established the Madge post office on August 22, 1891, but the railroad was using the name of Rutledge. A sawmill was in operation, and several quarries opened to handle the high-quality limestone under the nearby ridge that forced the Elk River to make a sharp curve. By 1899, the Kansas City, Pittsburg & Gulf was using the name Madge for this location. The post office was discontinued on March 31, 1903, but the quarrying activities continued.

In 1904, the Missouri Bureau of Geology and Mines published *The Quarrying Industry of Missouri*, which reported on the quarries at Madge. It stated that the "Madge Stone Co. and the Joplin-Elk River Stone Co. operate quarries located on the same hill east of the Kansas City Southern railroad at this place." The Joplin-Elk River Stone Company quarry opened about 1902 and was located on the north side of the hill. Its stone was used as heavy bridge stone or capped into range and curbing. KCS had a spur track to the quarry and there were two derricks and a hoist for loading the stone.

The older and larger quarry was operated by the Madge Stone Company, having started about 1898. In 1904, it had a "west face of about 500 feet along the hill." The firm made stone for bridges and street curbing, and the waste was crushed for road macadam and railroad ballast. The quarry had "a No. 3 Gates crusher, 35 horse power engine, 40 horse power boiler, two steam drills, and two derricks." It was also served by the Kansas City Southern.

In 1905, the legal case *Foster v. Kansas City Southern Railway Co.* had a detailed description of Madge and how the railroad operated there. The case involved a horse that was killed by a train, and the laws as they related to fencing at railroad stations. Therefore, it was important in the case to determine if Madge was a railroad station, or simply a switching point for a shipper. The reader will be able to tell that there is a bit of sarcasm in the report about the importance of Madge.

> *The evidence shows that in the long ago Madge, a city of mythical name, had a depot and post office and some inhabitants, but that many years since the railroad removed the depot, the post master moved away and took the post office with him or turned it back to the government, the inhabitants arose, took up their belongings, moved away and have not returned; and that the dark arms of the wilderness have encircled her and the hoot of the owl is heard at night in her precincts; that even the site from which she reared her mythical head would have been lost to future generations had not the railroad company marked it by an enduring monument of creek gravel, one hundred and forty-four inches long, forty-eight inches wide and twelve inches in thickness, planted near its track. This monument of stone serves the double purpose of marking Madge Station and*

of furnishing a standing block on which the would-be passenger may mount and with a red flag in his hand cause a train to stop long enough for him to get aboard; here also freight trains will drop off such packages as are consigned to that point. But the evidence also shows there are two rock quarries, one on either side of the railroad, not a great distance from the Madge monument; that the appellant has built switches to these quarries, over which it pushes cars into the quarries to be loaded with stone whenever required.

Elk Springs, Missouri

In 1909, another attempt was made to develop a town here, and the Elk Springs post office opened. The name came from a nearby spring that was reportedly used by elk when the region was first settled. Legal documents from as late as 1913 still called the location "Madge or Elk Springs." The railroad showed Elk Springs to be a flag stop, but the traffic could be quite heavy during hot summer days due to the development of several nearby resort hotels.

About 1905, W. H. Fleming opened the Riverside Inn at Madge/Elk Springs. Reports from the time stated that the hotel featured a tastefully appointed inn and rustic cottages not far from the trains of the Kansas City Southern Railway. The resort provided relief from the heat of summer and provided fishing, boating, and bathing in the Elk River. According to several area histories, the "more adventurous would find 'surrounding mountains covered with heavy timber' which afforded 'plenty of opportunity for exploring parties, and a number of caves' that were within a half hour's walk from the inn."

Other places such as Witt's Resort and the Ginger Blue Lodge provided similar services. However, the Depression was hard on Elk Springs and the post office closed in 1935. Nevertheless, for years, KCS timetables still showed Elk Springs as a flag stop for train Nos. 15 and 16 (*The Flying Crow*) from May 1st through September 30th. The location wasn't even listed by 1964.

200.7 NOEL (NE) – Noel is a summer vacation community that also gets busy as truckloads of Christmas cards get brought here for that special postmark ("Noel, Mo. – The Christmas City in the Ozark Vacation Land"). Like many towns in the area, Noel grew because of timber and farming. While it didn't have the large fruit and berry business, it did have a number of limestone quarries.

The Noel name gives this small community a bit of Christmas fame each year.

The name Noel (pronounced "no-ul") came from the Noel family, who were among the earliest settlers that came west from Kentucky in 1846. C. W. and W. J. Noel raised livestock and owned a sawmill on the Elk River. Thomas Marshall was actually the person who first platted the community, and he went through the names of Cedar Grove and Marshall, both of which were rejected as those names were already being used in Missouri. In early 1886, he submitted the name Noel in honor of "Uncle Bridge" Noel, and a post office opened on February 1, 1886.

The early 1900s saw Noel expand into the summer resort and entertainment business. This started during the 1890s when employees of the Kansas City, Pittsburg & Gulf built the O Jo Fishing Club on the Elk River. In 1925, Marx Cheney bought the club house and formed Shadow Lake with a beach, swimming area, and stage. Fame really reached Shadow Lake when Henry Fonda, Tyrone Power, Nancy Kelly and Randolph Scott stayed there while filming the movie *Jesse James* in 1938. Reports state that as many as 30,000 people showed up one weekend to see the stars. The visitors allowed several new cafes and other businesses to open at Noel. World War II saw crowds of troops from Camp Crowder and other nearby military bases. Bands played nightly throughout the 1950s. However, Oklahoma began allowing alcohol sales in 1957, and U.S. Highway 71 was moved east through Pineville. The park slowly saw attendance drop, and it reverted to a local swimming and fishing area. Tourism has increased over the past few decades, and Shadow Lake is again popular, along with several other lodges, resorts, and activity centers.

Heavener Sub Route Guide

In 1920, the census showed a population of 324. In 1922, Kansas City Southern described the town in their company magazine. "Noel has a bank, three general merchandise establishments, three grocery stores, one hardware, one drug store, two meat markets, one garage and filling station, one bakery, fine cafe, two good hotels, theatre, two produce houses, a 250 barrel flour mill, an ice plant, oil station, lumber yard, a fine water power plant providing power and light, a dancing pavilion, a consolidated high school and several churches." Crops like strawberries, grapes, apples and tomatoes were shipped from Noel, but not in the volumes of other nearby towns.

Like most Ozark communities, the Great Depression was a painful wound. In an attempt to attract business, Noel promoted its name and became "The Christmas Card Center." This became easier when radio and television singer Kate Smith began to tell the "Noel Story" during her broadcasts each year.

The population of Noel was 685 in 1950, and then 736 in 1960. In 1961, Missouri left Noel off of its official state map of vacation areas. In reaction, McDonald County proclaimed its secession from Missouri, creating the McDonald Territory. Despite this, Noel regained its tourism status and the population reached more than 2100 in the 2020 census. Helping this is a large Tyson Foods facility, located across the Elk River in the growing area north of downtown. The Tyson Foods plant has also brought a great deal of diversity to Noel as a number of Somali and Sudanese refugees moved here to work for the company.

The Railroad at Noel

For the Kansas City, Pittsburg & Gulf, and later Kansas City Southern, Noel was a regular station agency and siding that was used by many trains, It was also the source of significant volumes of freight and passengers. In 1909, maps showed that the Montour Charcoal Company, Ellis & Putman mill, and a large stockyard all were served by the railroad. At the time, the railroad had a depot between the mainline and siding about where Main Street now crosses the tracks.

During the early 1920s, the railroad built a number of new stations and stronger bridges. Noel received a new brick station in 1923, located a block south of Main Street (Milepost 200.6). In 1936, the station had an agent 8am-5pm Monday through Saturday. A mail crane stood nearby so trains could pick up mail without stopping. Timetables showed that there was an 82-car-long siding, plus other tracks with a capacity of 22 freight cars.

As freight trains got longer, and passenger train service was reduced, things changed at Noel. The siding was shown to be 135 cars long in 1964, and the other tracks had been expanded until they could hold 41 freight cars. The agency had also been expanded, and now had two shifts: 8am-5pm and 10pm-6am daily. Noel was a stop for all passenger trains. *The Flying Crow* stopped northbound (No. 16) at 2:06am and southbound (No. 15) at 3:08am. For the *Southern Belle*, Noel was a flag stop. Southbound No. 1 was here at 1:36pm, while northbound No. 2 was here at 3:24pm.

Heavener Sub Route Guide

On August 3, 1969, a 115-car Kansas City Southern freight train exploded while passing through Noel. The train crew reported that at 3:45am they saw a fire on one of the cars moments before it exploded. A second and larger explosion took place shortly afterwards. The explosion, which damaged the KCS station, was apparently caused by a hot box on a boxcar of ammonium nitrate fertilizer. A six-block area of Noel was damaged, forty people were hurt, and one person was killed. Newspaper reports stated that parts of the train flew throughout town and landed as far away as half a mile, including an 800-pound railroad car wheel that soared three blocks and landed in a house. The site of the explosion was marked by a hole 15 feet deep and 50 feet across.

KCS 724 pulls a train southbound past the Noel depot the day after Christmas in 1992.

Downtown Noel has never fully recovered, although most of the old stone and brick buildings are still filled with local businesses. For the railroad, Noel features a siding of 8513 feet (Milepost 200.4 to 202.1). There is also a 675-foot spur track to the east known as the Noel Team Track, or Noel Gas Track. The Noel train station still stands and is used as the Noel City Hall.

The brick depot at Noel now serves as the city hall. This photo from 1989 was taken before the fencing around the station was installed.

Heading south, the railroad follows Butler Creek from Noel all the way to Sulphur Springs, Arkansas. The stream was named for Charles Butler, an early settler in the area. The route was considered to be some of the most scenic on the line due to the railroad running between the creek and a line of high ridges to the east. One of these was promoted as Butler's Bluff, and the location was used for a number of promotional photographs.

202.4 ARMSTRONG QUARRY – The grade crossing with South Kings Highway has long been known as Armstrong Quarry. While the area was once full of active quarries, only JHE Granite remains to remind people of the area's history. JHE Granite is actually a seller of granite, marble and quartzite slabs that are used for counter tops and showers. The firm is relatively new, dating from 2003. However, the mining history is a century older.

The Quarrying Industry of Missouri (Missouri Bureau of Geology and Mines – 1904) reported that there were three large quarries along the railroad south of Noel. The report stated that they were quarrying the strongest limestone in Missouri. At the time, the John P. Hughes quarry "was located just west of the Kansas City Southern, three-fourths of a mile south of town." The firm chiefly produced stone blocks for bridge abutments. By 1909, much of this area was shown to be owned by the McDonald Land & Mining Company. A second quarry was operated by Armstrong and Cravens. This quarry was located one mile south of Noel, on the east side of the KCS.

Starting about 1900, the Kansas City Southern railroad had their own quarry here, "located just east of the railroad, joining the Armstrong and Cravens quarry on the south." The quarry worked a 330-foot face, and had been cut 240 feet to the east. The limestone was easy to get to as it was buried under only two to six feet of gravel and clay. The principal output was stone for bridge abutments, needed as the railroad upgraded its line. The Missouri Bureau of Geology and Mines stated that the quarry featured two derricks, two drills, a steam hoist and a boiler, plus a rail spur off of the mainline.

Limestone has played several roles in the area. To the west is the Bluff Dwellers Cave, an area attraction since 1927. This limestone cave had been used by ancient Archaic-aged Native Americans (Bluff Dwellers), but the two entrances had been covered by landslides for at least two thousand years. In 1925, Arthur Browning felt a cool breeze while he was checking traps on his property. He brought in help to move rock and vegetation so he could explore the cave. The first entrance was the size of a basketball, but as debris was removed, larger entrances were discovered. The cave is still available for tours and is owned by the grandchildren of Arthur Browning. The family home is now used as The Cavern Inn.

Located just south of the Armstrong Quarry is Butler's Bluff, a scenic location used by the railroad for a number of promotional photographs.

Heavener Sub Route Guide

203.7 DEER CREEK SPUR – During the quarrying days, a spur track headed east and curved up Deer Creek. Today, the grade is a private access road.

203.9 MISSOURI-ARKANSAS STATE LINE – This is the border between McDonald County, Missouri, and Benton County, Arkansas. **Missouri** borders eight different states – no state borders on more. Missouri became the 24th state on August 10, 1821. Today, Missouri is the 21st largest and the 18th most populated of the states. Known as the "Gateway to the West," Missouri was the starting point and the return destination of the Lewis and Clark Expedition, as well as the starting points of the Pony Express Trail and Oregon Trail. Its capital is Jefferson City, one of the smaller cities in the state and named for Thomas Jefferson, the third President of the United States. There is actually no official state nickname, but the "Show Me State" has appeared on its license plates. The phrase "The Lead State" has been used, and is explained by the lead mining history around the Joplin and Neosho part of Missouri.

McDonald County is located in the very southwestern corner of Missouri. It has a population of about 23,000 and Pineville is its county seat. The county was originally created as Seneca County by the Missouri State Legislature on January 1, 1847, but attached to Newton County for government purposes. The county was independently organized on March 3, 1849, as McDonald County, but the government stayed connected to Newton County until 1856. The name McDonald apparently comes from Sergeant Alexander McDonald, a soldier in the American Revolutionary War. However, why it was named after him is unclear. Like many courthouses across the region during the Civil War, it was burned in 1863 and most records were lost. While farming and ranching have always played a large role in the local economy, tourism is now significant.

The Territory of **Arkansas** was admitted to the Union as the 25th state on June 15, 1836. It is the 29th largest state, and the 34th most populated. This part of the state is the Ozark Plateau/Mountains. This is part of the interior highlands region, the only major mountainous region between the Rocky Mountains and the Appalachian Mountains. Arkansas is also the only state where diamonds are mined, and you can go mine them yourself at the Crater of Diamonds State Park. The former nickname of the state was the Land of Opportunity, but it now uses The Natural State. Little Rock, located near the center of Arkansas, is the capital and largest city in the state.

Located in the extreme northwest corner of Arkansas is **Benton County**. The county was created in 1836 from lands in Washington County and was named after Thomas Hart Benton, a prominent U.S. Senator from Missouri. The county seat is at Bentonville. Benton County was the home of Walmart founder Sam Walton, as well as the home of the trucking firm J. B. Hunt. Reportedly, in 1901, Benton County led the nation in apple production, producing 2.5 million bushels of apples and becoming known as the "Land of the Big Red Apple." By 1938, Benton County was the largest chicken broiler producing county in the nation, fueled by Tyson Foods and Peterson Hatchery. Today, with a population of a quarter-million, Benton County is the second-most populous county in Arkansas.

204.4 ARKANSAS HIGHWAY 59 – The railroad passes under Arkansas Highway 59, which follows the railroad to Siloam Springs, Arkansas. When Arkansas created its highway system in 1926, Highway 59 was to be located between the Louisiana state line and Eudora in southeast Arkansas. That route became Highway 159, and Highway 59 was moved to northwest Arkansas. By 1936, it connected Van Buren and Siloam Springs. It was expanded northward when U.S. Highway 71 was relocated eastward. Arkansas Highway 59 now connects Missouri Highway 59 with Barling, located southeast of Fort Smith. The highway is 93 miles long and parallels U.S. Highway 59 between Siloam Springs and Fort Smith. The highway causes some confusion as it is the only Arkansas state highway that shares its number with a federal highway that goes through Arkansas, and the two are very close at a number of locations.

During the 1940s, a spur track served the Independent Gravel Company. The company mined dolomite and crushed and ground it for local farmers. Farmers used it to mix into soils as a pH buffer and as a magnesium source. Because of this, shipments were made to a number of fertilizer plants in Houston, Texas, and to cotton gins in Texas, Louisiana and Arkansas. Independent Gravel also shipped stone to several glass manufacturers in Fort Smith, Arkansas, and Henrietta, Oklahoma. The report *Wartime Developments and Postwar Prospects of Arkansas Mineral Industry* (War Minerals Report No. 385, published in April 1945 by the United States Department of the Interior – Bureau of Mines) stated that the dolomite was in a "16-foot bed underlying 200 acres" and were "estimated to be sufficient for 20 years."

205.2 BUTLER CREEK BRIDGE – This 13-span concrete ballast deck bridge was once known as Bridge A-206. Butler Creek forms in the hills to the southeast of Siloam Springs, and flows here. It then heads north and flows into the Elk River on the west side of Noel, Missouri. The railroad follows Butler Creek between Noel and Siloam Springs. An early settler, Charles Butler, gave his name to the stream.

During the late 1800s and early 1900s, there was a wye to the east, located just north of the Butler Creek bridge. The grade can barely be made out today. A benchmark was also placed on the bridge, stating an elevation of 899 feet. To the west was the Johnson & Givens sawmill.

KCS 724 leads a mix of power and paint southbound across the Butler Creek Bridge in late 1992.

205.3 SULPHUR SPRINGS (SU) – The railroad passes through the west side of Sulphur Springs, where there was once a staffed train station, The original station was located on the east side of the tracks, north of Spring Street. In 1910, a large stone station was built with a covered pavilion south of Spring Street (the grade crossing no longer exists). The building was the only native stone depot on the line, and it looked somewhat like the Missouri & North Arkansas station at Eureka Springs, Arkansas. The station has been gone for decades, but its foundation can still be found.

Spring Street was a busy place. During the early days of the railroad, there was an eating house on the west side of the tracks south of Spring Street, with a park to the west. At the time, trains generally didn't carry dining cars, so stops were designated where meals could be obtained. The railroad also had stock yards further south. They were located on the west side of the tracks at the west end of Patterson Street.

In 1936, the station was staffed 9am-6pm on weekdays, and a mail crane stood nearby. By this time there were two sidings, both about 54 cars long. The agent was gone by the 1950s, but a short 30-car siding had been installed, as well as a house track that could hold 18 freight cars. In 1964, only *The Flying Crow* could be flagged, and the *Southern Belle* No. 1 passed southbound at 1:42pm.

Sulphur Springs, Benton County, Ark., well and favorably known as a delightful health and pleasure resort, and visited annually by hundreds of people who spend the summer months there, has some features, worthy of mention, which are not generally known.

Among its sources of income are general farming, stock raising, dairying and the production of poultry and eggs, strawberries, tree fruits, grapes and commercial truck. While none of these agricultural pursuits have reached very large proportions, they have been generally profitable and worth while. Climate and other conditions are ideal for poultry raising and dairying. Sulphur Springs ships considerable quantities of poultry and eggs, besides which it has an excellent home market. The Van Noy Interstate Company which operates all the eating houses on the K.C.S. Railway buys its poultry and eggs for the entire system here, using a truck to gather its supplies at the farms in the surrounding country. This company alone purchases $50,000 worth of poultry and eggs per year. The dairy business can be developed indefinitely. Some revenue is derived from the cultivation of strawberries and commercial truck.

Heavener Sub Route Guide

This is how the Kansas City Southern described Sulphur Springs in its January 1, 1922, issue of the *Agricultural and Industrial Bulletin*. The flat land around a series of springs began to attract settlers by the Civil War. The Whinnery family acquired the land where the springs bubbled up. A few cabins were built to house health seekers visiting the springs and a post office opened on April 26, 1878, as Sulphur Springs. In 1884, Charles H. Hibler visited the springs and began buying land to establish a health resort. Using family money and money from investors, Hibler laid out the townsite and opened the Park Hotel and Bathhouse. In 1885, a city was officially laid out and the post office moved a short distance to the new townsite. Today's Sulphur Springs got its start that year as a mineral spa resort using a series of natural mineral springs. One of these was a rare lithium spring. A number of healing properties were advertised and the stories about those who were cured were shared with newspapers nationwide. The *Sulphur Springs Speaker* newspaper, later the *Sulphur Springs Record*, started publishing during Fall 1888. As the community grew and the railroad neared the site, Sulphur Springs was incorporated on August 26, 1890.

In 1891, the railroad arrived, but construction halted for several years. Being the end of the railroad helped Sulphur Springs become an important station, and a number of businesses opened here. By the turn of the century, Sulphur Springs was the third most popular resort in Arkansas, after Eureka Springs and Hot Springs. It was also a popular meeting place for the Chautauqua Society, a group that had as its goal to provide educational enrichment and inspiration in a picturesque natural setting. Their meetings included lectures, speeches, debates, music, and theater in a rural and healthy environment.

The 1900 census reported 315 residents living at Sulphur Springs. At the time, there were also eleven hotels, three sanitariums, and numerous doctors. More attractions were being built, and Butler Creek was dammed forming Lake LaBalladine. The lake featured a boathouse and a piece of high ground that became known as Amusement Island. This area included a roller skating and dancing pavilion that drew crowds throughout the summer. The town continued to grow and the Bank of Sulphur Springs opened in September 1906. The Burger Bathhouse, now used as the Sulphur Springs Community Museum, was just one of several that were built. Finally, the Sulphur Springs Sanitarium Hotel and Bath Company built a five-story native limestone building called the Kihlberg Hotel, but it was too fancy and too expensive for many of the working-class visitors to the community.

The population temporarily peaked at 500 citizens in 1910, but fires in 1911 and 1912 burned much of the town, and it wasn't until 1915 that electrical power returned and downtown was rebuilt. By this time, other resorts had attracted the health seekers and Sulphur Springs didn't recover, with the population steadily dropping to 404 in 1930.

Heavener Sub Route Guide

The Sulphur Springs Community Museum uses the former Burger Bathhouse building, and displays this Burger Baths sign.

A few businesses remained at Sulphur Springs and were reported in the *Arkansas Marketing and Industrial Guide of 1921*. These included the G. W. Clifton canning factory, the Western States Lumber Company, and the J. G. Gatton lumber company. In 1924, John Brown University opened in the Kihlberg Hotel. The university was created by evangelist John Brown, who also bought much of downtown Sulphur Springs. The plans were to educate both local students and the children of wealthy supporters. However, the plans changed as the revenues didn't cover the costs. Brown used the facility as a high school academy and a junior college for women. Neither plan worked, and the university was consolidated with John Brown College in Siloam Springs. The university complex at Sulphur Springs then became the Julia A. Brown School for Children, which in 1937 became the Brown Academy, a military academy. Other efforts such as a linguistics school (Camp Wycliffe of the Wycliffe Bible Translators) were also started in town.

The Great Depression hurt the community greatly, and businessman W. R. Eaton founded the Ozark Craftsmen's Guild in Sulphur Springs to employ out-of-work factory laborers. The project also helped area farmers as local fruit was used to make jams and jellies. The Works Progress Administration (WPA) was also active in the area, helping to build a new schoolhouse.

The 1960s saw another religious group move to Sulphur Springs. The Shiloh Community from Sherman, New York, bought and restored the former Kihlberg Hotel, the thirty-room Livingston Hotel, and another property which had been built by John Brown, which became the Shiloh House Parsonage. By 2020, the population was back above 500, and a few businesses are again open. The Harbor House still operates as a religious bed and breakfast, and the Sulphur Springs Old School Complex Historic District was listed on the National Register of Historic Places in 2001. The Sulphur Springs Park Reserve is also on the National Register, and includes some of the original springs.

Heading south, the KCS climbs a ridge by following Horse Creek, through an area seldom documented due to the lack of road access. Starting at Milepost 206.2, southbound trains climb a 1.42% grade to Milepost 209.8. The railroad peaks out at about 1200 feet at Gravette, before dropping again on a 1.29% grade to Milepost 212.6 near the bridge over Spavinaw Creek. This is part of a series of grades that have for more than a century been a challenge to the railroad.

209.7 SECOND AVENUE TUNNEL – Approaching Gravette from the north, the railroad climbs through a narrow cut to the west of Hillcrest Cemetery. It then passes under Second Avenue, Arkansas Highway 72, using a tunnel created from a large steel culvert. This improvement replaced the curvy Main Street grade crossing, which is now closed.

The top of the 1.42% grade is a short distance to the south near the former Main Street grade crossing, so southbound trains are working hard as they pass through the culvert.

209.8 STL&SF CROSSING – This crossing was with a lightly used branchline of the Frisco, and it once sat in the middle of Main Street. The Frisco came in from the east along Main Street and looped south of Broadway (today's Atlanta Street) before turning back north to make the crossing. Heading west, it curved and passed its station about a half block north of Main Street. The station was just west of Powell Street (today's Third Avenue SW) in what was known as the Pearson & Karr's Addition. A berry shed and stockyards were once further to the west.

The crossing involved the Bentonville Branch of the St. Louis-San Francisco, and was shown in timetables to be an interlocking with a connection. The connecting track was in the southwest quadrant of the crossing. While this junction was an early goal of the railroad, the Frisco abandoned their line through Gravette in 1940.

What became the Bentonville Branch dates to February 11, 1882, when a few citizens incorporated to build a railroad to the western boundary of Benton County, Arkansas. Instead, they built a crude private railroad between Rogers and Bentonville. On May 23, 1891, the railroad was sold under decree of the Circuit Court and reorganized as the Bentonville Railroad Company. During March 1898, the railroad was sold to J. M. Bayless of Cassville, Missouri. Bayless had plans to extend the line westward and create a junction with the Kansas City, Pittsburg & Gulf. As a part of the financial arrangements, the City of Bentonville had offered a $25,000 bonus to aid the construction.

On April 1, 1898, the Arkansas & Oklahoma Railroad Company was incorporated in Arkansas, and quickly absorbed the seven miles of the Bentonville Railroad Company. The line was extended to Gravette that year, creating a shorter route to Kansas City for the fruit grown in the Bentonville and Rogers area. Gravette didn't remain the end of the line for long as the Arkansas & Oklahoma Railroad again incorporated in Arkansas on March 8, 1899. The purpose of the change was a planned extension westward. On April 3, 1899, the Arkansas & Oklahoma Railroad began work on extending the line to Southwest City, Missouri, work that was completed in October 1899. The railroad was now 35 miles long.

On November 17, 1900, the Bentonville Railroad Company was officially sold to the Arkansas & Oklahoma Railroad. Bigger changes took place on November 20, 1900, when the Arkansas & Oklahoma was acquired by the St. Louis & San Francisco. It was officially merged into the larger railroad on June 21, 1901. An extension of the line was soon completed to Grove, in Indian Territory, and plans were announced that it would be built on to Afton, also in Indian Territory. The extension didn't take place, and service on the Bentonville Branch remained pretty basic.

The ownership of the line changed again on September 15, 1916, when the St. Louis & San Francisco Railroad was sold to the newly organized St. Louis-San Francisco Railway Company. However, the change had little effect on the line. At the time, the line was served by the daily roundtrip known as the *Western Express* and the *Eastern Express*. Regular passenger-only service over the Bentonville Branch ended in 1927, replaced by a daily mixed train. In 1933, this service was reduced to three times weekly: Tuesday, Thursday and Saturday.

The line was in trouble by the 1920s as the fruit business died off. Fewer than 1500 carloads of freight were normal each year during the 1920s, and reports state that it was about 500 carloads a year during the 1930s. Things did pick up in 1938 when Twentieth-Century Fox rented the Bentonville Branch for a few scenes of the movie *Jesse James*. Old freight and passenger cars were brought in by the Frisco, and an old locomotive from the Dardanelle & Russellville Railroad was used, Most of the filming took place at Hiwasse, Arkansas, and Southwest City, Missouri.

The Heavener Sub: History Through the Miles

The line's fame didn't help any, and on December 22, 1939, the Frisco applied to abandon the 41 miles of track from Bentonville to Grove. On July 31, 1940, the Interstate Commerce Commission approved the abandonment, and the diamond at Gravette was soon gone.

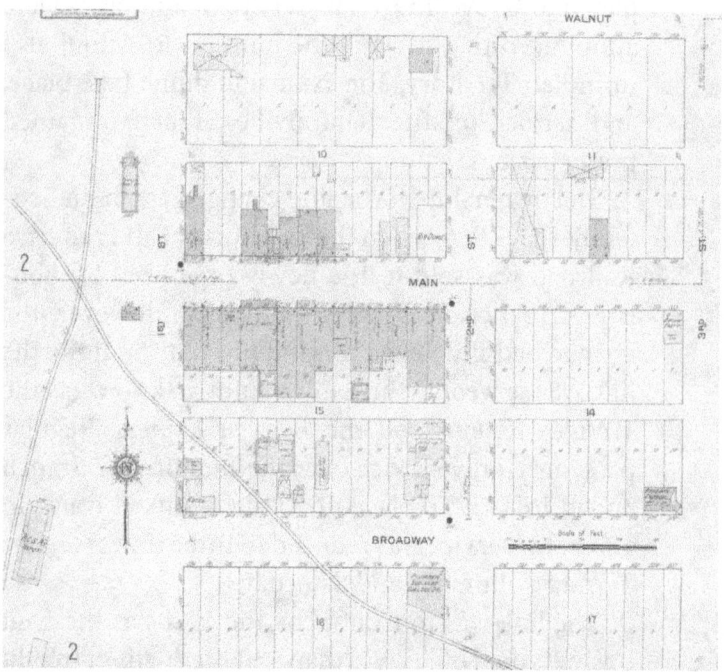

As shown in this Sanborn map from 1913, the KCS station was to the south of the diamond at Gravette, Arkansas. *Sanborn Fire Insurance Map from Gravette, Benton County, Arkansas.* Sanborn Map Company, Sep, 1913. Map. Retrieved from the Library of Congress, https://www.loc.gov/item/sanborn00252_001/.

209.9 GRAVETTE (BO) – Until 1940, Gravette was a junction town served by the Frisco and the KCS. Because of this, there were a number of rail facilities. During the early 1900s, the Kansas City Southern had a wooden station at Gravette on the east side of the mainline. It was at the end of Broadway (today's Atlanta Street), with a house track looping around the east side of the structure. South of the KCS depot were a KCS fruit shipping shed, a grist mill, an ice house, and a crate warehouse. Further south were the railroad's stockyards. The station housed an agent and telegraph services 8am-5pm weekdays in 1936. The same year, there was a 70-car siding, plus several other tracks with a total capacity of 58 freight cars. A mail crane also stood near the depot.

By 1964, the siding had been extended to 133 cars, and the industry tracks could hold 39 railcars. The agent was gone and Gravette was not a scheduled or flag stop for the Southern Belle, so Train No. 1 would pass through Gravette at 1:50pm without stopping. Today, the station building and siding are gone, and only a short team track remains. However, Kansas City Southern caboose #383 is on display at Centennial Park, near where the old depot once stood. The bay window caboose was built by the Louisiana & Arkansas, a part of the Kansas City Southern, in 1952. It was retired on August 2, 1990, and donated to Gravette in May 1991. The caboose was restored over a two-year period and dedicated along with Centennial Park in 1993. KCS #383 was added to the National Register of Historic Places in 2010. Since then, the caboose has sat at Gravette, squeezed between a fence, landscape vegetation, and the food trucks that often are found at the park.

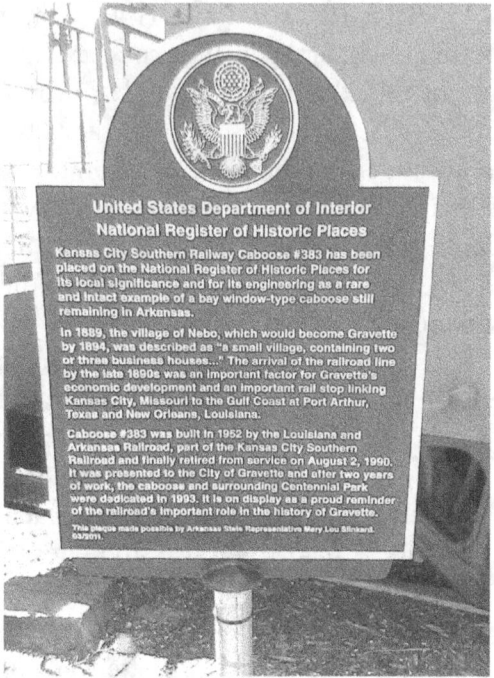

This marker explains the history of KCS Caboose 383, as well as the relationship between the railroad and the town.

Heading south, the railroad drops down several hundred feet in elevation, passing through Railroad Hollow. This narrow valley exposed several large limestone deposits, at least one of which was developed commercially.

City of Gravette

As stated by the city's website, "Gravette is a City of the First Class with an estimated population of over 4,000 and a land mass of nearly 14-square miles." However, it has not always been that way. The town started nearby in Chalk Valley using the name Nebo. Located about a mile east of Gravette, the town was platted during the 1870s by Joseph P.

Covey, who later moved to Southwest City, Missouri. The Nebo post office opened in 1874 and lasted until 1894.

In 1891, much of Nebo moved west to be on the route of the Kansas City, Pittsburg & Gulf (KCP&G). This move was led by Ellis Tillman Gravett, who operated a general merchandise store and the Chalk Valley Distillery at Nebo, and soon in the new community of Gravett. On July 17, 1893, Ellis Tillman (E. T.) Gravett and Laura Gravett sold land to the Missouri Coal and Construction Company, that was building the railroad for the KCP&G. With the right-of-way established, E. T. Gravett platted the new town, with papers filed on July 26, 1893. A charter was received on August 9, 1893. In 1894, the post office at Nebo officially moved to the new town and took the name Gravett. On January 27, 1899, Gravette was incorporated and the population was shown to be 447 in the 1900 census, the year the post office changed the spelling of its name, a change that has never been fully explained.

Since its founding, Gravette has had a steady growth in its population. By the 1920 census, the population was up to 754 residents. In that year, Gravette had a number of local industries that benefitted the town and the railroad. The stockyards featured two pens. The Marr Canning Company and the Morton Canning Company handled much of the local vegetable and fruit business. In particular, Morton Canning produced hundreds of thousands of cans of tomatoes each year. With apples being grown in the area, the Speas Vinegar Company (earlier Gregory Vinegar Factory) produced cider vinegar and shipped it off to several processing plants. W. T. Nickell operated a flour and feed mill, and the

Gravette Custom Mills operated a feed mill, flour mill, and grist mill. Finally, the Gravette Lumber Company cut local timber.

The population passed 1000 in the 1970 census, and then 2000 in the 2010 census. Today, the population is close to 4000 as Benton County and northwest Arkansas have boomed over the past few decades. For years, Gravette was the home of Lloyd "Arkansas Slim" Andrews. Arkansas Slim was an American actor, singer, composer, and host of a series of children's television shows. He was born in Gravette on December 8, 1906. By age 17, Andrews stood 6'8" and started doing a comedy routine, learning from other artists like Watso the Musical Wizard. At one of his shows he ran into Tex Ritter, who invited him to come to Hollywood and star in movies with him. Eventually, Andrews performed in 15 movies with Tex Ritter. One of the unique parts of his various roles was riding a mule, a situation caused by his fear and hatred of horses. As western movies became less common, he moved to television, often playing cowboy roles on children's shows. He also toured, singing and writing new songs with various artists. When he retired, Andrews and his wife Lucille returned to Gravette, where they lived until his death on April 3, 1992.

212.4 OZARK WHITE LIME COMPANY – During the early 1900s, the Ozark White Lime Company had a quarry and a series of lime kilns in this area, located to the east of the KCS mainline. On June 14, 1905, the lime company was part of an investigation by the Railroad Commission of the State of Arkansas. The study and hearing looked at the rates being charged by the Kansas City Southern Railway Com-

Heavener Sub Route Guide

pany "between the depot at Gravette, Arkansas, and Lime Kiln Spur, two and one half miles south." The commission determined that the movements were actually a "switching haul, and subject to the Commission's rules and rates."

Not far south of where Ozark White Lime once operated is the grade crossing with Limekiln Road (Milepost 212.6). It is pretty clear where the road's name came from. This area also has the name of Railroad Hollow, obviously a reference to the Kansas City Southern.

Following Limekiln Road will get you to the Heavener Subdivision near both the former site of the Ozark White Lime plant, and the Spavinaw Creek bridge.

212.8 SPAVINAW CREEK BRIDGE – Spavinaw Creek forms in northwest Arkansas and flows westward into the Neosho River at Lake Hudson in Oklahoma. The stream is primarily spring-fed, but heavy rains can fill normally dry channels several miles further up the hillsides. Spavinaw Creek has historically been known for its trout fishing, and the waters east of Arkansas Highway 59 have been stocked and can be fished with special permits. Research shows that trout have been here for more than a century, and at one time there were several commercial hatcheries along the stream.

The name Spavinaw Creek dates back to early French explorers and traders. While exploring northeast Oklahoma, they noted patches of tall trees which they called cepee vineux, or a young stand of trees. These trees were commonly used to build cabins, and thus were an important resource. The name eventually meant the general hills in the area, and then the waterway that flowed through them.

On the west side of the bridge, Wolf Creek flows into Spavinaw Creek from the south. The railroad follows this stream to near Decatur, Arkansas.

KCS 724 south was caught again in December crossing the Spavinaw Creek Bridge.

The Spavinaw Creek "A" Bridge

The elevation here is 1027 feet, about 175 feet lower than nearby Gravette. At one time, Spavinaw Creek was crossed by the railroad using a Waddell "A" through truss bridge. This style of bridge was built during the late 1800s and early 1900s because the bridge had great rigidity in all directions, it was easier and cheaper to erect, and there was less metal required when compared to other designs that provided the same strength and rigidity.

The bridge design was created and patented by John Alexander Low Waddell (sometimes spelled Waddel), author of one of the definitive books on bridge building. During the early 1880s, Waddell served as a visiting professor of civil engineering at Tokyo University. While there, he worked with railroad engineers on building new bridges. At the time, bridges of about 100-150 feet were very expensive and time-consuming to build, and he looked for a cheaper design that could be built faster. His research led to the "A" truss, commonly used for building roofs. His work led to him receiving the rank of Knight Commander in the Order of the Rising Sun.

Returning to the United States, J. A. L. Waddell looked for railroads to work with. During April 1893, Waddell "was retained by the General Manager of the Kansas City, Pittsburg and Gulf Railroad Company to design some bridges. After a little persuasion, the General Manager was induced to agree to build a 100-ft. 'A' truss span as an experiment; but when he saw the completed plans he ordered at once four bridges to be built therefrom, and this style of structure was soon afterwards adopted as the standard 100-ft. span for the road."

With this success, a number of railroads in the United States and Japan used the design. However, as train weights increased and other designs improved, the design went out of favor by 1920. Today, bridges of this design are extremely rare, with only a few preserved. This bridge is an example, as it has been replaced by a Pratt through truss span. There is some humor in this as Waddell considered Pratt trusses as "being too light and vibratory." However, he later stated that his design was old and that improvements in other trusses had made them preferable. In addition to the "A" truss being replaced, the long timber trestle approach on the north end has been replaced with steel spans.

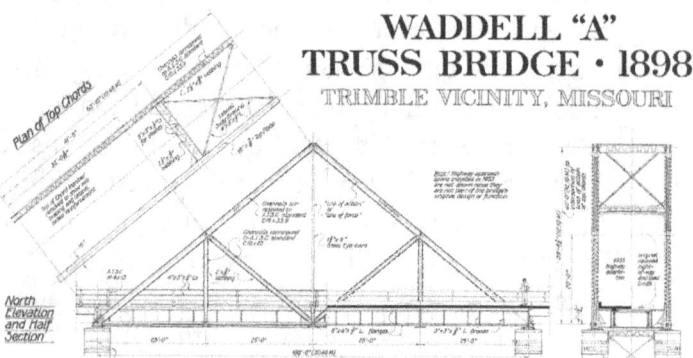

This Historic American Engineering Record drawing of a Waddell "A" Truss Bridge shows its unique design. This particular span was built for the Quincy, Omaha, & Kansas City Railway near Trimble, in Clinton County, Missouri. Historic American Engineering Record, Creator, John Alexander Waddell, Quincy Omaha, A & P Roberts Company, Pencoyd Bridge Company, Donald C Jackson, Richard K Anderson, and Thomas M Hocker. *Waddell "A" Truss Bridge, English Landing Park, Parkville, Platte County, MO. Missouri Platte County Parkville, 1968. Documentation compiled after. Photograph. Retrieved from the Library of Congress, https://www.loc.gov/item/mo0162/.

The October 1919 issue of *Railway Maintenance Engineer* had an article about strengthening several of these KCS bridges. The work was carried out by the Kansas City Bridge Company, using parts from several A-truss spans that were located in various KCS storage yards.

> *During the latter part of 1918 two 100-ft. single track railway spans on the Kansas City Southern were reinforced for modern standard loading by adding extra trusses and stringers from like spans which had previously been taken out of service. The spans recently reinforced are in two different bridges and had been continued in service for some years under traffic much in excess of the loads for which they designed by maintaining slow orders. Formerly there were a number of spans of this type on the road, but all had been removed except these remaining two. They are pin-connected spans of the so-called A-truss type, with four 25-ft. panels.*

214.2 DORSEY – Dorsey is a relatively new 8580-foot siding that stretches between **Control Point North Dorsey** (Milepost 213.2) and **Control Point South Dorsey** (Milepost 215.1). Here, the railroad is closely following Wolf Creek, once known as Dry Fork, which created the steady grade up to Decatur, Arkansas.

Maps from 1903 show that a sorghum mill was once located just west of the tracks. However, the community wasn't listed as a KCS station, and shipments were directed to nearby Decatur. Just to the east was once the community of Clementine, which had a post office 1891-1906. By 1945, Dorsey was shown to be at Milepost 213.7. At Milepost 213.8, Mt. Olive Road crosses the railroad.

Between Mileposts 215.3 and 219.1, southbound trains again fight a steep grade, this one being 1.43%. Combined with the attractions at the old Decatur train station, this makes the area a popular train watching location.

216.1 PETTERSON SPUR – While this 4665-foot spur track is often known as Petterson Spur, it once served the facilities of Peterson Farms. Lloyd Peterson founded Peterson Farms in 1939, and expanded into poultry breeding in 1950. Lloyd Peterson was ahead of his time as he hired experts from around the world to work on the genetics of his birds, creating a breeding rooster known as the Peterson Male. By the mid-1990s, the Peterson Male commanded 70 percent of the domestic market for breeders and 50 percent of the international market. The demand was so great that the company built a 3863-foot runway on the shore of Crystal Lake (just south of the feed mill and to the east) so that days-old chicks could be flown to market. After suffering some financial setbacks, the firm sold its broiler operations, propane company, and other assets to Simmons Foods Inc. of Siloam Springs, Arkansas. The Peterson Male line was sold to Aviagen in 2010. What remains of Peterson Farms is owned by L&L Farms, and the company still has a cattle breeding operation and produces broilers for several companies.

Today, Petterson Spur serves the Simmons Foods feed mill and dry pet feed facilities north of Decatur,

Arkansas. According to the company, "Simmons Pet Food is a leading North American private-label and contract manufacturer of wet and dry pet food and treats." The company also supplies poultry, pet, and ingredient products.

This sign for the Simmons Feed Mill is located at the entrance to the facility.

In 1991, Peterson Farms was restoring KCS 4060, an F7A locomotive built in August 1950, and KCS caboose #385 at their feed mill north of Decatur.

217.0 DECATUR (DE) – Decatur is almost a required stop for visiting rail enthusiasts for three reasons – a KCS train station, a KCS caboose, and a KCS F7A locomotive. All three are listed on the National Register of Historic Places. Located between the tracks and Arkansas Highway 59 is the Kansas City Southern depot, built about 1920 as the town began to grow. The station is unique in that it is a single-story structure built out of concrete blocks. Most major stations along the line were built of brick. The Decatur station was also less decorative than most such structures, with a hip roof with Craftsman-style brackets and decorative fishscale wood shingles over the three-sided telegrapher's bay. The depot was added to the National Register of Historic Places in 1992.

The KCS depot still stands at Decatur, Arkansas, but it is very unique having been built of concrete blocks instead of brick, as shown in this 1989 photo.

Heavener Sub Route Guide

Everything is all-white in this photo as KCS 658 pulls train No. 97 southward past the white Decatur depot on May 29, 1990. This was a few years before a KCS locomotive and caboose were placed on display at this end of the depot.

Next in age is KCS locomotive #73D, a classic F7A built by the Electro-Motive Division of General Motors in August 1950. Assigned construction number 12322, the locomotive was part of an order for six F7As and 10 F7Bs. During March 1956, it was rebuilt to be an F9 and renumbered as #90. After serving a career across the railroad, it was turned into a slug in April 1978 and became #4060. Slug-type locomotives had their prime mover (engine) removed and received electrical power from an adjacent locomotive to turn its wheels. Slugs were especially popular when railroads ran heavy trains at low speeds, much like the Kansas City Southern did over the many ridges in northwest Arkansas. The locomotive was retired about 1991.

The newest railroad attraction at Decatur is KCS caboose #385. Like the display caboose at nearby Gravette, it was built in 1952 by the Louisiana & Arkansas, a part of the Kansas City Southern. The bay-window caboose was retired about 1991.

KCS 4060, an F7A locomotive, and KCS caboose #385, are now on display at the Decatur, Arkansas, depot.

Both the caboose and locomotive were acquired by Peterson Farms. They were moved to the Peterson Farms grain elevator north of Decatur during September 1991, where employees of the company spent about two years restoring the railroad equipment. On May 25, 1993, the locomotive was placed on a short section of track next to the Decatur depot, which at the time was used by Peterson Farms. Today, the train station is the Decatur Museum, and the locomotive and caboose were listed on the National Register of Historic Places in February 2006.

The KCS at Decatur

In 1893, the Kansas City, Pittsburg & Gulf Railroad built through northwestern Arkansas, including a route through Decatur. By 1903, the railroad had a depot on the east side of the tracks at the corner of Main Street (Hill Avenue) and Second Street (South Main Street). A house track ran around the east side of the depot, while a siding was on the west side of the mainline. The siding's north switch was near the stockyards at North Street (Roller Avenue).

During the 1910s-1920s, Kansas City Southern upgraded the railroad and added new buildings at many of its stations. In 1920, the company built the concrete-block station that still stands today. That year, Decatur was a regular stop for the two daily passenger trains. In 1936, the station was staffed and had telegraph service 8am-5pm on weekdays. The siding was shown to have a capacity of 70 cars, and the various house and industry tracks had a capacity of 40 freight cars. A mail crane had been installed near the depot so that mail could be picked up by moving trains. Decatur was a scheduled stop for *The Flying Crow*, and northbound No. 16 was scheduled to be here at 1:28am, while southbound No. 15 departed at 4:58am.

By the 1950s, Decatur was simply a flag stop for *The Flying Crow* and the *Southern Belle* passed right through. Timetables from 1964 show that the siding had been shortened to only 36 car lengths, and the house track was down to being able to hold only 25 cars. However, the depot was still staffed with telegraph service available 8am-5pm on weekdays. *The Flying Crow* could be flagged early in the morning, but the southbound *Southern Belle* (No. 1) passed without stopping at 1:58pm. Today, the railroad agency is gone and a short 1860-foot track is located on the west side of the mainline, just south of the depot.

City of Decatur

Little from the earliest years of Decatur was documented, but it is known that William F. Burrow began farming around a fresh-water spring that later was known as St. Elmo Spring. While Burrow was here by the 1830s, he did not actually receive a formal deed to his forty acres from the U.S. government until 1854.

The Civil War slowed development in northwest Arkansas, and it wasn't until the 1880s that the community grew big enough to have a post office. In 1883, John Cotton became the first postmaster at what was then known as Corner Springs. However, the existing name was rejected, so Mitchell was tried, named in recognition of the work that Everard Mitchell did to obtain the post office. However, Mitchell was also already taken, so there was a community discussion to try to come up with a new name. Mitchell proposed that the post office, and the town, be named after Commodore Stephen Decatur, Jr., a hero of the War of 1812. Mitchell stated that relatives of Decatur lived in the area, so the name was justified. The post office name was accepted in 1883. When the town was created, the part of town north of North Street (today's Roller Avenue) was Decatur, with the part to the south being the original Corner Spring. Even today, many of the platted lots have never been developed.

Despite having a post office, Decatur remained small with just a few stores and houses. In 1893, the Kansas City, Pittsburg & Gulf Railroad built through Decatur, and farmers could ship their products out to market. The Ozark Orchard Company soon bought large tracts of land in the area, and shipments of strawberries, apples, peaches, and other crops went out by rail. Hotels, a sawmill, several churches, and a number of businesses soon opened. Decatur was incorporated on May 25, 1908, and the population was 246 in the 1910 census.

Decatur peaked about 1920 with a population of 424. That year, the peach and apple crops failed due to a disease, leaving the many packing houses and three apple evaporators with nothing to process. A few different vegetable crops like green beans were tried, but Decatur started a slow decline. Businesses like B. M. Bobb (brooms), Holland-American Canning Company, Decatur Canning Company, Good Canning Company, and H. L. Cotton (fruit evaporators) held on for a few years. The Ozark Fruit Growers' Association worked to sell local farm products. There was also a movement towards raising livestock, and the railroad had a three-pen stockyard to handle the business.

The Great Depression finished off most of the rest of the businesses at Decatur, but Lloyd Peterson turned things around by developing the poultry industry. He helped to create a national market for his chickens, and worked with others like the Bredehoelt family to create trucking companies to move his product. Peterson's company grew and eventually hired hundreds of people, helping Decatur to again grow. The 1960s saw a doubling of the population (415 to 847), and it has grown to about 2000 residents as all of northwest Arkansas has boomed. The city now features feed mills, processing plants, hatcheries, and offices that are related to the poultry industry.

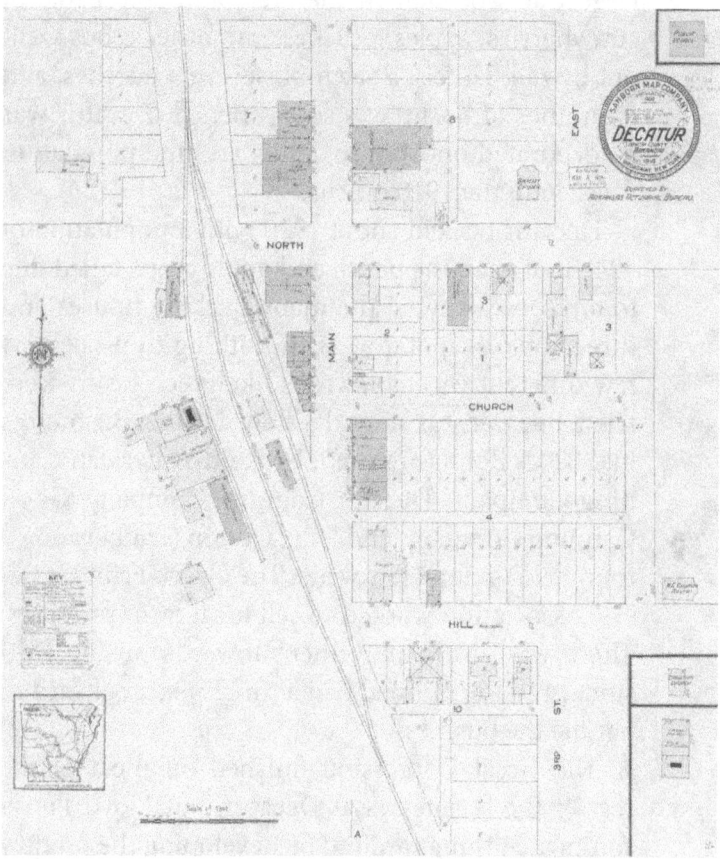

This Sanborn map of Decatur from 1914 shows the depot on the east side of the mainline, and a large canning and fruit packing facility to the west. *Sanborn Fire Insurance Map from Decatur, Benton County, Arkansas.* Sanborn Map Company, Jan, 1914. Map. Retrieved from the Library of Congress, https://www.loc.gov/item/sanborn00232_001/.

Heavener Sub Route Guide

Heading south from Decatur, the railroad closely follows Arkansas Highway 59 all the way to Gentry. Along the way it passes through miles of pasture, most of which once belonged to the Ozark Orchard Company. Cattle is very common today, and there are a number of large poultry house complexes. Several processing plants owned by Simmons are also close to the tracks.

221.3 CONTROL POINT NORTH GENTRY – Just south of a small farm crossing is the north end of the 7831-foot-long Gentry Siding. The south switch is at South Collins Avenue at Milepost 222.9.

222.1 GENTRY - MCKEE FOODS – To the west is a large manufacturing plant for the McKee Foods Corporation, producers of Little Debbie® snacks. This is one of three plants owned by the company across the country. McKee Foods was founded in 1934 by O. D. and Ruth McKee, who bought a small bakery at Chattanooga, Tennessee. The company moved several times as it expanded its market and created new products. One of the things that set the firm apart was selling "family packs" of boxes of individually wrapped baked goods.

Along the line, Bob Mosher, a packaging salesman, told the owners that the McKee name and packaging was boring, and that something more catchy would help product sales. O. D. McKee decided the idea was a good one, and using a picture of his granddaughter, Debbie, had an artist create a "Little Debbie" image of her in a straw hat as a logo. Thus was born the Little Debbie® snacks line of products in 1960.

In 1982, the Gentry plant opened and serves the western United States and Mexico. One of the points of pride is that "Little Debbie" herself once managed the plant. Later, Debbie McKee-Fowler became Executive Vice President of McKee Foods, still a privately owned company.

KCS serves the McKee Foods plant, also called the McKee Baking Company, with a 1380-foot industrial lead. Products like sugar, flour, and oils are delivered by the railroad. Six axle locomotives are prohibited from operating on the McKee Foods spur track.

This photo from February 17, 1990, shows the Siloam Springs Dodger working the McKee Baking Company at Gentry, Arkansas.

222.5 GENTRY (RY) – It is difficult to research Gentry since most of the east-west streets have been renamed. While Main Street has remained, the streets to the north and south have new names. For example, today's First Street (one block to the south) was once Fourth Street, and Second Street was once Fifth Street. Heading north from Main Street, what was once Third Street is now Arkansas Street, and Second Street is now Benton Street.

Heavener Sub Route Guide

Gentry is a true railroad town, created when the railroad built through the area and decided to locate a division point here. A town was platted and sold by the Arkansas Townsite Company, a Stilwell firm. The town's original name was Gentry when settlement began in 1894, but by 1897, Orchard and Orchard City were being used. By early 1900, the name Gentry was again in fashion, and the town became the residential and financial center for a vast fruit-growing industry. The name Gentry came from Richard Gentry, an initial incorporator of the Kansas City, Nevada & Fort Smith Railroad. Richard Gentry fought in the Civil War, and then graduated from Missouri State University in 1868.

Gentry worked as a civil engineer for several railroads, and also became involved with banking, real estate, cattle ranching and mining. In 1889, he became associated with the Kansas City, Nevada & Fort Smith Railroad. Gentry held a number of titles with the railroad, including general manager, chief engineer and vice-president. He was directly involved with building the first 300 miles of the railroad. In 1895, Richard Gentry sold his stock and retired from the railroad.

On May 21, 1894, the Gentry Post Office opened, but was known as Orchard 1897-1900. In the 1900 census, the population was shown to be 419. Many reports stated that Gentry had 1000 residents in 1903 when the fruit business picked up and the J. P. Roush Lumber Company was established to supply lumber for fruit boxes. However, the official population in 1910 was only 668.

The railroad was the heart of Gentry in 1903. As the railroad entered the north side of town, a canning factory was to the east at First Street, today's

Crawford Street. Switches for a siding to the east, and a house track to the west, were located at the original Second Street. From there to Main Street were a series of warehouses, grain elevators, and stockyards. Just south of Main Street, the depot was located between the house track and mainline to the west. The south switch of the house track was at Fourth Street while the siding's south switch was at Sixth Street.

A report from 1914 stated that Gentry had a population of 1200 and was at an elevation of 1252 feet. The principal sources of income were "the raising of live stock, fruit and berry growing. The fruit shipments in an ordinary season are valued at $200,000 to $250,000, consisting in the main of apples, peaches and berries. The egg shipments run from 4,000 to 6,000 cases and the poultry shipments from 70,000 to 90,000 pounds; the berry shipments vary from 5,000 to 15,000 crates. Large shipments of hogs, cattle, horses, mules, wheat, oats are also made. The butter shipments range between 10,000 and 15,000 pounds. Gentry has a bank, waterworks, electric light plant, roller flour mill, box and barrel factory, cannery and about twenty five mercantile establishments." In that year, 152 carloads of apples were shipped from Gentry on the railroad. Several newspaper articles reported that the Kansas City Southern was considering building a rail line east from Gentry into Boone County, Arkansas.

Just outside of town were miles of orchards and berry farms. Ozark Orchard Company owned many of the orchards and shipped the fruit out by rail from Gentry and several other nearby towns. Because of the nearby fruit and berries, Gentry featured a number of businesses related to shipping, evaporating and canning. Reports from about 1920 stated that Gentry had a booming agricultural economy, and the community "also boasted a canning factory, a bank, three hotels, two furniture stores, two drug stores, one millinery store, one confectionery store, one restaurant, three real estate firms, two meat markets, one produce house, one newspaper, two lumber yards, four evaporating plants and three coopering establishments."

By 1921, W. W. Griner; Hawks & Son; and Miller & January all operated evaporators. The Gentry Fruit Growers Association, earlier the Gentry Apple Growers Association, handled an assortment of fruits and vegetables like apples, grapes, tomatoes, strawberries, blackberries, raspberries, Bermuda onions, peaches, sweet potatoes, and cantaloupes. The J. P. Roush Lumber Company still made lumber for wooden boxes and other products. Finally, the Gentry Milling Company produced flour, and the railroad had a stockyard consisting of two pens.

With the growth of Gentry, a new train station was required. Bids were closed on August 7, 1926, for the construction of a brick passenger station at Gentry. The station opened in 1927, and a special train of railroad officials arrived to participate in the grand opening and banquet. The population peaked at 779 in the 1930 census before dropping back to less than 730 until the 1960s. By this time, the fruit and vegetable business had died out, and poultry and cattle began to dominate the local economy. The station came down a few years later as rail business went away. In 1982, the McKee Baking Company brought jobs to the area with the opening of their manufacturing plant. The general boom across northwest Arkansas has also brought new residents and businesses. The population now is about 4000 residents.

The original plat for Gentry had the entire town on the west side of the tracks, which run northeast-southwest through town. A number of additions were made to Gentry over the years, but most of the town is still west of the railroad. However, many of the local businesses are now located along Arkansas Highway 59, which is a block east of the Kansas City Southern.

The Railroad at Gentry

Initially, Gentry was a division point on the railroad, and it featured a number of railroad offices. However, this title soon moved and Gentry was simply a shipping and receiving point for the local farm business. Therefore, a number of industry tracks were initially built, plus a siding for trains to pass and switch. By 1936, most of these tracks were gone and there was an 82-car siding, plus other tracks with a total capacity of 52 cars. A mail crane had earlier been installed, which was the subject of special instructions in KCS timetables. These stated that "Trains 1 and 2 reduce speed not to exceed 30 mph passing mail crane in order to exchange heavy U.S. Mail."

During the 1950s, the siding was expanded to 93 car lengths, and then 154 cars by 1964. During the early 1960s, William Deramus III changed the railroad's operating plan to run very long trains, and many of the sidings were lengthened to allow the trains to pass. Traffic was still good at Gentry, and the industry tracks had a capacity of 47 freight cars. However, an Arkansas Commerce Commis-

Heavener Sub Route Guide

sion hearing was held on April 11, 1962, to review the petition of the Kansas City Southern to close and abandon the railroad's agency and station at Gentry.

In 1964, Gentry was no longer a stop for the *Southern Belle* passenger trains, and southbound No. 1 passed at 2:05pm. By the 2010s, most of the tracks were gone. The track into the McKee Foods complex is north of town. A short 575-foot house track remains in town, and the siding is shown to be 7831 feet long.

The Third Street overpass is a popular photography location, although the lack of a sidewalk and growing vegetation does make photography a challenge. This photo shows grain train No. 701 waiting for a meet at Gentry in 1990.

Heading south, the railroad today passes by new housing subdivisions, pastures and chicken houses. The route was once described as passing "through some ten to fifteen thousand acres of land devoted to orchards, truck gardens and berry patches."

The Heavener Sub: History Through the Miles

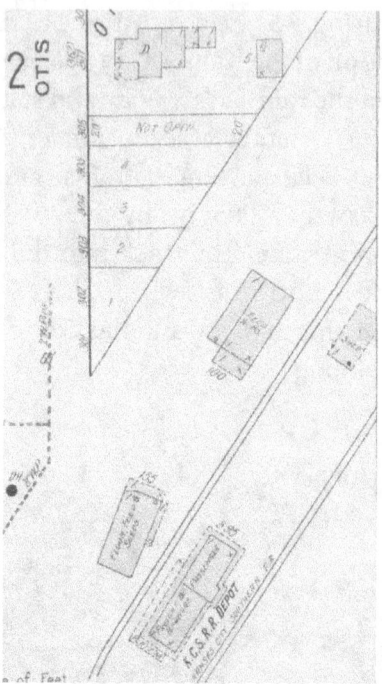

In 1918, Gentry was a small town of about 700 that featured a few fruit, feed and flour warehouses. The railroad also had a nice depot with a freight and baggage section to the south, and passenger facilities to the north. *Sanborn Fire Insurance Map from Gentry, Benton County, Arkansas.* Sanborn Map Company, Nov, 1918. Map. Retrieved from the Library of Congress, https://www.loc.gov/item/sanborn00249_003/.

223.7 CONTROL POINT FLINT CREEK – Look for the switch just south of the grade crossing with Pioneer Lane at the Gentry Cemetery. Here, a track heads to the west to serve the Flint Creek Power Plant, visible because of its 540-foot-tall smokestack. The tracks form a full loop around the plant through the coal unloading shed, and there is a small rail yard and several tracks used for loading and unloading shipments. An enclosed facility handles the loading of ash into railcars, and the plant has long had its own locomotive or car mover.

Heavener Sub Route Guide

This photo of the Flint Creek Power Plant shows the general layout of the plant, as well as train No. 95 unloading its Powder River coal.

This plant is a coal-fired, electrical power station that opened on July 1, 1978, and was jointly owned by SWEPCO/AEP and the Arkansas Electric Cooperative Corporation, although it is operated by SWEPCO (Southwestern Electric Power Company, owned by American Electric Power). This plant created an immediate traffic boom as 143 loaded coal trains were delivered during 1979.

The plant burns Powder River Basin (Wyoming) coal and produces 528 megawatts of electricity. The coal is delivered by Kansas City Southern trains, interchanged at Kansas City. Loaded coal trains come south as the C-KCFL (Coal – Kansas City to Flint Creek), while empties head north as the C-FLKC (Coal – Flint Creek to Kansas City). These trains were once Nos. 95 and 96.

Unlike many coal-fired power plants, this one has been upgraded with new emissions controls and there are plans to keep the plant open, although the ash pond will be closed. At the north edge of the 1600-acre property is the Eagle Watch Nature Trail, part of 700 acres that are wildlife habitat. Several years ago, the plant was awarded the Conservation Certification by the Wildlife Habitat Council due to its environmental stewardship.

225.0 FLINT CREEK BRIDGE – Flint Creek forms at Springtown, several miles to the east, when North Flint Creek and East Flint Creek merge. It then flows to the west, just south of Gentry. Flint Creek flows into the Illinois River not far south of Flint, Oklahoma. A small community developed to the east along the stream known as Flint. There was a Flint post office there 1890-1895.

In 1915, this bridge burned and was reported upon by several newspaper articles. At the time, Kansas City Southern published *Current Events – An Industrial and Agricultural Magazine*. The magazine was a collection of railroad news from newspapers, and articles by the railroad company. The article about the bridge burning and the work required to rebuild it described the bridge as "nearly 400 feet of trestling twenty feet high." Today, the bridge consists of a deck plate girder span across the stream, and seven concrete ballast deck spans to the north.

227.1 WEBB WHEEL – As the Kansas City Southern approaches Siloam Springs from the north, it starts to pass a number of past or current rail shippers. One of them is Webb Wheel Products, which has a Webb's Aftermarket Business Unit at Siloam Springs. This manufacturing plant produces brake drums, wheel hubs, rotors and spoke wheels for trucks, tractors, trailers, and buses as part of the commercial vehicle aftermarket. KCS no longer serves the facility as the turnout has been removed.

Just to the south is another large facility that has no rail service. This is a large warehouse for La-Z-Boy Furniture Galleries.

227.7 COBB SPUR – To the west is a small feedmill facility known as the Cobb-Vantress Siloam Springs Feed Mill. Cobb was established in 1916 and is now the world's oldest pedigree broiler chicken breeding company. The firm began on November 20, 1916, when Robert C. Cobb bought the Old Pickard Farm at Littleton, Massachusetts. From this, he created Cobb's Pedigree Chicks. By 1925, the company became the largest breeder of Barred Plymouth Rocks in New England. In 1947, the company began a breeding line of white birds called White Rocks, and then opened a hatchery at Siloam Springs in 1961. While the company stayed involved with poultry breeding, the ownership and management went through a number of changes.

In 1974, Cobb was purchased by the Upjohn Company while Tyson acquired the Vantress breeding lines. Less than a decade later in 1983, Tyson and Cobb created Arkansas Breeders as a joint venture. In 1986, Tyson and Upjohn jointly created Cobb-Vantress and moved the company to Siloam Springs. Tyson acquired all of the company's stock in 1994. Throughout this time, the company also opened a large number of international operations. In 2002, Cobb opened the Siloam Springs Feed Mill, a tall concrete structure visible for miles. It is served by an 1100-foot spur track off of the KCS mainline.

The elevator at Cobb, north of Siloam Springs, serves as a local landmark due to its height.

227.5 ARKANSAS, OKLAHOMA & WESTERN RAILROAD DIAMOND – From 1908 until 1918, Siloam Springs was actually served by a second railroad, which crossed the KCS at this location. This line started as the Rogers Southwestern Railroad, became the Arkansas, Oklahoma & Western Railroad, and then failed as the Kansas City & Memphis Railway Company. The Rogers Southwestern Railway was incorporated on January 16, 1904, to build from Rogers, Arkansas, to Siloam Springs. Money was hard to raise, and it wasn't until June 1906 that survey crews finally arrived at Siloam Springs. The town was slow to raise the money for a right-of-way and a

$15,000 subsidy. Numerous meetings were held, and more than $13,000 was raised by early 1907. Meanwhile, the Panic of 1907 prevented enough bonds from being sold to pay for all of the construction plans. This created numerous problems for Rogers banker William R. Felker, who was the principal financial backer of the railroad.

On February 13, 1907, the Arkansas, Oklahoma & Western Railroad was chartered to take over the work. The new company announced plans to build into Indian Territory, and also east to Eureka Springs, and even as far as Memphis, Tennessee. By April, construction began again on the line to Siloam Springs. Things were further delayed in September as the line needed to cross the Kansas City Southern mainline north of Siloam Springs. It took three weeks for an agreement to be reached, but the crossing was completed on October 15, 1907.

The story of the fight between the KCS and the Arkansas, Oklahoma & Western (AO&W) was covered in the October 17, 1907, issue of the *Arkansas Gazette*. Apparently the AO&W didn't have an agreement for the crossing when it reached the KCS on September 23, 1907. To prevent the crossing from being built, three boxcars blocked the route and fifty men guarded the site. The actions forced a contract in which the AO&W agreed to maintain the crossing and a gate that protected the KCS mainline. Another agreement between the two railroads was that the KCS would make available 20% of the gross earnings with the AO&W to meet any deficiency in interest charges. Essentially, some of the revenue that the KCS obtained from interchanging traffic with the AO&W would be made available to pay interest on the line's construction.

By January 1908, the Arkansas, Oklahoma & Western entered Siloam Springs from the northeast, following the south side of Sager Creek, shown as Spring Creek at the time. For those trying to follow the line, the route is now used as Washington Street. The railroad bragged that with its arrival, shippers had the choice of using either the Kansas City Southern or the Frisco railroad to get their crops to market. By March, the AO&W – known as the "Fruit Belt Line" – was providing Railway Postal Service between Rogers and Siloam Springs.

During early 1910, there were a number of reports about the AO&W being acquired by larger railroads. One of these rumors was about Missouri Pacific, with plans to extend the AO&W eastward to Bald Knob, Arkansas. Over the next few years, the AO&W built a few short branches and absorbed other smaller lines. However, grand plans continued to be announced. During May 1911, the AO&W acquired the Monte Ne Railway, and then was acquired by the Kansas City & Memphis Railway (KC&M – incorporated December 17, 1910) on May 1, 1911. It didn't take long for the KC&M to also fail and enter receivership on July 14, 1914. The Bondholders' Protective Committee of the Arkansas, Oklahoma & Western Railroad purchased the railroad on September 24, 1918. With the nationalization of most of the country's railroads, there was hope that the federal government would acquire the railroad and save it. This didn't happen, and the entire 57.77 miles of the Kansas City & Memphis were abandoned by the end of the year.

If you want to find where the Arkansas, Oklahoma & Western ended at Siloam Springs, look at the north side of the intersection between East Main

Street and North Washington Street. At the time, this was the location of the A.B.C. Flouring Mill. The mill was owned by Andrew Brown Current, who also handled retail coal sales. For those looking for the diamond, it was north of town, not far south of the Cobb feed mill.

229.3 SILOAM SPRINGS (SX) – The first European settlers at what became Siloam Springs arrived in late 1839. Simon Sager and family began farming along Sager Creek. A small community named Hico was here by the 1850s, created by Caldeen and Nancy Ward Gunter. The Gunters traded with the nearby Cherokee Nation and named their community after the Cherokee word for "clear water" or "sparkling water." The area took this name because of several springs that flowed into Sager Creek. In 1855, the Hico post office was established.

As with many towns in the region, much of the business and population moved away during the Civil War. The post office closed and then reopened during this time. In 1880, John Valentine Hargrove, a merchant at Hico, started up the town of Siloam City on land he owned along Sager Creek. The census that year showed a population of 95. The new town began to grow due to the reported health benefits of the local springs, trade with the Cherokee Nation, an increase in farming, and the many reports that a railroad would be built through the area. On December 22, 1881, Siloam Springs was incorporated and a post office opened in 1882, the same year the Hico post office closed. In 1885, the Hico post office reopened, but it closed again in 1894 as Siloam Springs expanded. The town's population hit 1748 in 1900, a few years after the railroad arrived.

So where was Hico and the original Siloam Springs? Hico was in the northeast part of today's Siloam Springs, near where the Simmons processing plant now stands. The original Siloam Springs was on the north side of Sager Creek, centered around today's city hall. The next question many have is where did the term siloam come from? It refers to the healing waters of the Pool of Siloam, found in the New Testament (John 9:6). With many early visitors coming for the healing waters, it was logical to borrow the name of a famous curative water.

The fading hopes for a railroad lit back up in 1893 when the Kansas City, Pittsburg & Gulf Railroad restarted construction after being stopped at Sulphur Springs. To make sure the railroad passed through Siloam Springs, a number of local businessmen pledged $20,000 to the railroad, and secured land for the depot and ten miles of right-of-way for the track. Late that year on December 20, 1893, the railroad reached Siloam Springs. This kicked off a big boom in population, with more than 1700 residents in 1900 and 2400 in 1910. The railroad also brought many visitors to the health resorts, and hauled out large volumes of apples, peaches, strawberries, and other fruits.

Education, summer camps, and industry developed throughout the early years of Siloam Springs. The Arkansas Conference College opened in Siloam Springs in 1898. The college was sponsored by the Arkansas Conference of the Methodist Episcopal Church, but it closed in 1919 and the main building became the Siloam Springs High School. As the Arkansas Conference College closed, evangelist John Elward Brown Sr. opened his Southwestern Collegiate Institute, which became John Brown University. The university is known for its mix of academic, spiritual, and vocational training in its curriculum. In 1921, Gypsy Camp was opened as a private summer camp for girls on the nearby Illinois River, several miles south of town. The camp closed in 1978, the buildings were listed on the National Register of Historic Places in 1988, and starting in 2018, the Gypsy Camp Historic District became the home of Gypsy Camp & Canoe.

The early and mid-1920s saw a continued growth in Siloam Springs, often simply called Siloam. The decade started with local businesses like the Siloam Springs Bottling Works, the Siloam Springs Ice Company, and J. A. Bloomfield (foundry and machine shop). There were three flour and feed mills (A. B. C. Milling, East Side Milling, and West Side Milling) and two lumber mills (Fountain City Lumber and Siloam Lumber). Kansas City Southern had four pens in their stockyard, and the Arkansas-Oklahoma Berry & Grape Growers Association had several docks and warehouses to handle the local produce. In 1922, the Ozark Creamery & Produce Company opened a facility, and in 1926 Earl Allen established Allen Canning Company to produce canned tomatoes.

The late 1920s saw hints of a growing economic crisis as much of the fruit business was hit by several diseases, floods, and then droughts. The Flood of 1927 impacted much of the country, and almost every community alongside a waterway in Arkansas has their story. Sager Creek had a reputation for flooding, and Siloam Springs fought the stream several times that year. The situation did not improve much after the Flood of 1927. Over the next several years, a series of tornadoes hit Arkansas, and then the stock market crashed in 1929. By the 1930 census, the population of Siloam Springs had dropped from 2569 in 1920, to 2378. This is the only census record of a population loss in the community.

Starting early in 1930, a drought hit twenty-three states across the Mississippi and Ohio river valleys and further east. According to the weather data from the time, Arkansas was the state hit the hardest. The rainfall dropped by thirty-five percent (parts of Arkansas saw no rain for seventy-one days) while temperatures set records. Food was scarce, with the Arkansas Agricultural Extension Service reporting that only Benton County (out of seventy-five counties) had "sufficient food for its farm population and livestock feed to tide it over the winter." Government programs were established to help, and a new post office, high school, community building, and roads were built. Additionally, the series of parks through town were expanded and improved.

The recovery after the Depression and World War II was helped greatly by the poultry industry, which grew throughout northwest Arkansas. For Siloam Springs, Simmons Foods built a processing plant and their headquarters in 1952. Almost every decade since has seen growth of more than twenty percent, with some decades seeing the town size double. Today, Siloam Springs has a population closing in on 20,000, and it features many restaurants, hotels, and retail chains. Trains can be hard to chase through town due to the highway traffic.

The KCS at Siloam

For decades, the station at Siloam Springs was shown simply as Siloam in KCS employee timetables. With the division point just a few miles away at Watts, Siloam wasn't the busiest station in the area, but there was plenty to do. It was generally a stop for all passenger and most freight trains. Jefferson Street at Milepost 229.3 was once the center of rail activity at Siloam Springs. North of the crossing and to the east in 1903 was the Siloam Springs Milling Company and their flour mill. To the west was a long spur track that went north up Hico Street to serve a fiber plaster plant, the H. P. Stanley & Company evaporators, and an ice plant and cold storage facility. The railroad station was on the south side of Jefferson and to the west of the mainline. Lumber yards were to the east and west. A planing mill, several grain elevators and fruit loading docks, and a number of small warehouses and sheds also lined the railroad.

Siloam Springs was an important fruit and berry station for the Kansas City Southern. It also produced ice for other area stations, and rates for carload movements were created in 1903 from Siloam Springs to Gentry, Decatur, Gravette, and Sulphur Springs. The fruit business was so important that special trains operated from here to handle the valuable foods. An example was in 1906, when the railroad announced that a special strawberry train would begin to operate on May 1, 1906. The train would operate daily from Siloam Springs, Arkansas, to Kansas City during the strawberry season. The train would run at passenger train speeds, leaving each evening from Siloam Springs to pick up fruit picked that day at Siloam Springs, Gentry, Decatur, Gravette and Neosho, Missouri. This special train would get the strawberries to Kansas City the next morning where they would be quickly sold, or shipped on to other large markets.

During early 1908, there was talk about moving the division point from Stilwell, Oklahoma, to Siloam Springs. The rumors started due to a water shortage at Stilwell, plus several surveys to realign the main line from Siloam Springs to Fort Smith. Land on the east side of Siloam Springs was apparently considered for a new yard and roundhouse, and the Siloam Springs Town Lot Company stopped surveying and selling property there until a plan was announced. However, the new mainline wasn't built and the division point moved to the new community of Watts, Oklahoma.

The original wooden KCS station was located just south of Jefferson Street, and it served as both a passenger and freight depot. In 1915-1916, the old station was moved farther south and converted into a freight station. A new single-story brick 24'x 148' brick station was built on the site of the old station, dedicated to passenger operations and train orders for the crews. In 1936, the station was staffed 8am-5pm workdays (Monday-Saturday). Because the station was staffed when most passenger trains stopped, there was no mail crane. Instead, mail was handled while the passenger trains were stopped at the station. Siloam Springs was also a water stop for many trains, filling the tender of the steam locomotive. Two sidings were in operation, the west siding (62 cars long) and the east siding (58 cars long). A small yard and a number of industry tracks also were in use.

Heavener Sub Route Guide

By the late 1950s, the depot was staffed 8am-9pm weekdays, and 1pm-9pm on weekends. A yard was still required to handle the local business, and one 93-car siding was listed. By 1964, when *Southern Belle* No. 1 was scheduled to stop at 2:20pm, the station agency was open 8am-5pm daily. The yard was still shown in timetables, and the siding had been extended to 163 cars long. Today, the siding stretches from North Siloam (Milepost 228.6) to South Siloam (Milepost 230.2) for a total of 8063 feet of clearance. This is the old east siding, while the west siding is now used as an industry lead and storage track. General orders/circulars and a base radio are available to serve train L-SS101, the Siloam Springs Local, historically called a Dodger.

Pardon all of the photos around the Siloam Springs depot, but this was a great place to start the day during the late 1980s and early 1990s. At the time the Siloam Springs Dodger was based here, and the depot was a good place to get a line-up for the day. This photo is of the depot on October 15, 1988.

The Siloam Springs Dodger parked behind the depot, requiring a move towards the small feedmill to start the day. This photo is from a productive day of photography on October 25, 1989.

Within a year, the Siloam Springs Dodger received new power – a set of grey of GP40-2 locomotives, plus a former F7B slug #4077.

The Siloam Springs Dodger parked behind the depot in an area that was often busy. This photo is from October 1989.

The last run of the *Southern Belle* was on November 3, 1969. With the end of passenger service, the agent's office simply handled local freight billing, train orders for crews, and the needs of the Siloam Springs Dodger. On June 20, 1971, the passenger waiting room began to be used by the Siloam Springs Museum, which moved a year later to larger quarters. While there were a number of plans for the depot after it closed, it was destroyed by fire in 1991. The Arkansas Welcome Center on U.S. Highway 412 was built to resemble the station and includes a few parts of the KCS depot. These include paving bricks and roofing tiles, the ticket window and counter, the agent's telegraph counter, and the semaphore levers.

Signs of the large number of rail shippers can still be found throughout Siloam Springs. North of Main Street and to the east is the Siloam Springs Ramp Track, the site of the former trailer-on-flatcar facility. Just north of Jefferson Street is the Powell Feed & Milling complex, and the large buildings of the Robinson Canning Company to the east. Other tracks once were Allen Canning (Milepost 229.4), the Siloam Springs Lumber Track (Milepost 229.5), and Allen Can (Milepost 229.9). A few foundations can still be found of shippers like Pet Milk, Phillips Petroleum, and Sinclair Refining.

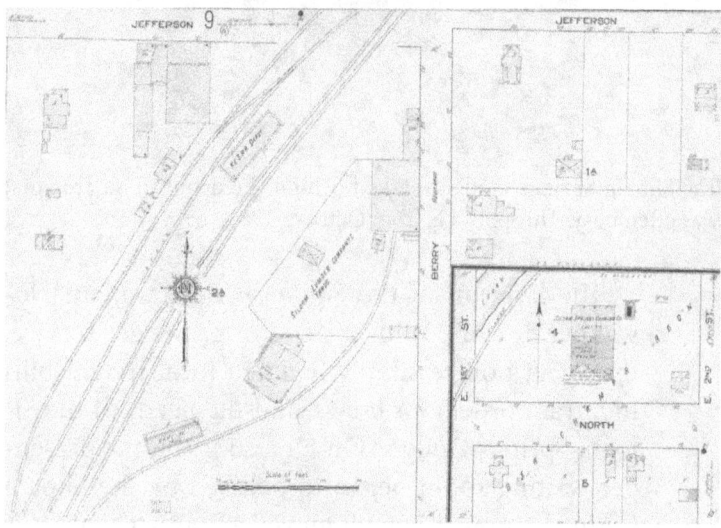

This Sanborn Map covers the busy area around Jefferson Street, including the KCS depot and the Siloam Lumber Company. *Sanborn Fire Insurance Map from Siloam Springs, Benton County, Arkansas.* Sanborn Map Company, Jan, 1914. Map. Retrieved from the Library of Congress, https://www.loc.gov/item/sanborn00343_004/.

Heavener Sub Route Guide

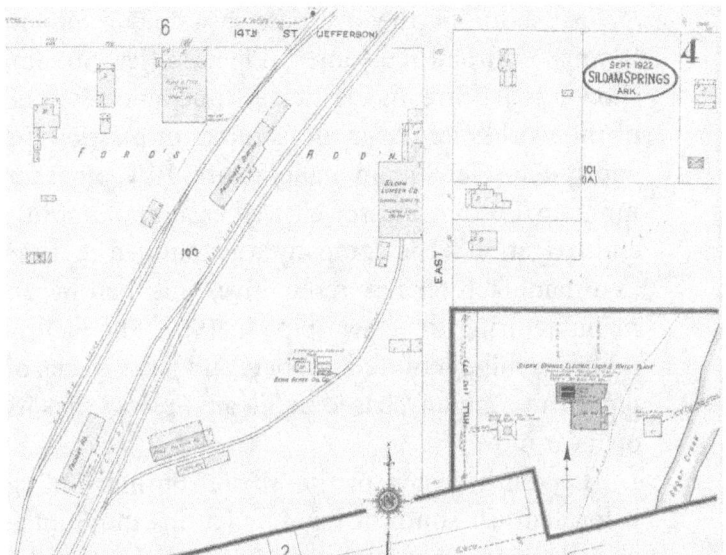

This Sanborn map from 1922 shows the KCS station and freight house, located on the east edge of Siloam Springs, Arkansas. *Sanborn Fire Insurance Map from Siloam Springs, Benton County, Arkansas.* Sanborn Map Company, Sep, 1922. Map. Retrieved from the Library of Congress, https://www.loc.gov/item/sanborn00343_005/.

230.0 U.S. HIGHWAY 412 – The railroad passes under U.S. Highway 412, which serves as a bypass around the south side of Siloam Springs. However, with the growth of the area, the highway can be very busy and it is lined with traffic lights.

U.S. Highway 412 is a relatively new route, commissioned in 1982. It now connects Interstate 25 at Springer, New Mexico, and Interstate 65 at Columbia, Tennessee, for a total of 1130 miles. The route through Siloam Springs and east to Alpena, Arkansas, was once Arkansas Highway 68. Most of the highway in the area is now a four-lane route, very different from what it was like before 1980.

Just south of the overpass is a major Siloam Springs railroad customer. PipeLife Jet Stream, shown as Jet Stream Plastics in timetables, is "one of the world's largest manufacturers of plastic pipe and systems. Jet Stream manufactures PVC pipes for municipal water and sewer, well casing, plumbing, and irrigation." The company was founded in 1948 as a manufacturer's representative, and then began manufacturing their own pipe in 1957. The facility is always full of covered hoppers and large stacks of pipe. The company, based in Siloam Springs, has its own car mover.

The south switch of the Siloam Springs siding is located just south of PipeLife Jet Stream. Southbound trains drop down a 1.36% grade from Milepost 230.6 to near the Illinois River at Milepost 233.6.

The Siloam Springs Dodger works the small yard just north of U.S. Highway 412 at Siloam Springs, Arkansas, in 1990.

232.6 ARKANSAS-OKLAHOMA STATE LINE – Heading south, KCS trains exit Arkansas and enter Oklahoma at an elevation of 971 feet. The Territory of **Arkansas** was admitted to the Union as the 25th state on June 15, 1836. It is the 29th largest state, and the 34th most populated. This part of the state is the Ozark Plateau/Mountains. This is part of the interior highlands region, the only major mountainous region between the Rocky Mountains and the Appalachian Mountains. Arkansas is also the only state where diamonds are mined, and you can go mine them yourself at the Crater of Diamonds State Park. The former nickname of the state was the "Land of Opportunity," but it now uses "The Natural State." Little Rock, located near the center of Arkansas, is the capital and largest city in the state.

Located in the extreme northwest corner of Arkansas is **Benton County**. The county was created in 1836 from lands in Washington County and was named after Thomas Hart Benton, a prominent U.S. Senator from Missouri. The county seat is at Bentonville. Benton County was the home of Walmart founder Sam Walton, as well as the trucking firm J. B. Hunt. Reportedly, in 1901, Benton County led the nation in apple production, producing 2.5 million bushels of apples and becoming known as the "Land of the Big Red Apple." By 1938, Benton County was the largest chicken broiler-producing county in the nation, fueled by Tyson Foods and Peterson Hatchery. With a population of a quarter-million, Benton County is the second-most populous county in Arkansas.

To the west (railroad-south) is **Oklahoma**, once known as Indian Territory (1834-1907), and later partly as Oklahoma Territory (1890-1907). The KCS annual report for the year ending June 30, 1906, provided information about the tracks in Indian Territory. The report stated that there were 127.59 miles of mainline track, 15.04 miles of branches, and 24.68 miles of yard track and sidings.

Oklahoma means "red people" in the Choctaw language, and the name was decided during an 1866 meeting between federal officials and leaders of the five Indian nations who had been moved there. During the late 1800s, the western part of what became Oklahoma was the Oklahoma Territory, while the eastern part was Indian Territory. The two merged and became the 46th state on November 16, 1907. It is the 20th largest state and the 28th most populated, with about four million residents. About two-thirds of Oklahomans live in the Oklahoma City (the state capital) and Tulsa metropolitan areas. The state is known as "The Sooner State" due to the number of white settlers who staked their land claims out before the official opening date in the western Oklahoma Territory.

The Railroad Act of 1886 opened the way for railroad construction across Indian Territory. The builders of the various railroads took advantage of this Act to build across the state, in what was actually a relatively late burst of railroad activity.

This is **Adair County**, located in northeastern Oklahoma. Like most of Oklahoma, the land that creates the county was settled, sold, traded, and re-settled. Numerous tribes lived and hunted in the area, and Creole trapper-traders visited during the late 1700s and early 1800s. In 1825 the Osage sold the land that is now Adair County to the United States, and various Cherokee groups began to arrive by 1825. At the Oklahoma Constitutional Convention in 1906, Adair County was created from the Going Snake and Flint districts of the Cherokee Nation. The name Adair came from a prominent Cherokee citizen, William Penn Adair, described as being influential in both white and Native American society. After three different elections, Stilwell became the county seat in 1910. The economy has historically been based upon farming (corn, wheat, oats, cotton, and cattle).

234.0 ILLINOIS RIVER BRIDGE – The Illinois River is the bottom of grades from each direction. The grade is as much as 1.50% heading north toward Siloam Springs, and 0.90% heading south to Westville. Once known as Bridge A-234, the current bridge features four deck plate girder spans on the north end, and a through truss span on the south end. Some records state that the through truss span dates from 1900. Builder plates from the American Bridge Company (Lassig Branch of Chicago, Illinois) with 1900 dates can still be found on several of the deck plate girder spans.

The Heavener Sub: History Through the Miles

The Illinois River Bridge, like a number of bridges on the Heavener Subdivision, consists of a mix of deck plate girder and through truss spans.

The former Chicago facility of Lassig Bridge & Iron, a part of the American Bridge Company, supplied this bridge structure in 1900. The Lassig Bridge & Iron Company of Chicago was founded by Moritz Lassig in 1881. Being located in Chicago, and with Lassig providing great service to his customers, most Midwestern railroads bought his bridges. The business boomed during the 1890s, making it a target for acquisition by the recently created American Bridge Company. In May 1900, Lassig sold his company to American Bridge. As the firm's history states: "American Bridge Company was formed as a JP Morgan & Company engineered merger of 28 steel companies in 1900." The Chicago Lassig plant was used by the American Bridge Company until early 1902 as their Lassig Branch plant.

Heavener Sub Route Guide

On the north end of the Illinois River Bridge are a series of deck plate girder spans set on tall concrete piers. Builder plates with dates of 1900 can still be found on several of the spans.

The Illinois River is about 150 miles long. It forms southwest of Fayetteville, Arkansas, and flows generally westward before entering the Arkansas River about twenty miles below Muskogee, Oklahoma. Like many streams in the area, the river has several different names. The Osage Indians called it Ne-eng-wah-kon-dah, or "Medicine Stone River." Early French explorers called it "rivière des Illinois," apparently for the Illinois Indians. However, the Illinois tribe didn't live here, so the name may have been a reference to a river elsewhere with a similar look. The Miami word Ilaniawaki, which means "real or original ones," was where the French word Illinois came from. The Miami were part of an alliance of different tribes which included the Illinois.

The seventy miles of the Illinois River between the Arkansas border and Lake Tenkiller are supervised by the Oklahoma Scenic Rivers Commission, and the river has been declared to be a Scenic River under the Oklahoma Scenic Rivers Act of 1977. There are a number of resorts and float suppliers along the route. Below Lake Tenkiller, the Illinois River is a designated year-round trout stream, stocked with rainbow and brown trout. The Oklahoma record rainbow trout was caught there. Readers of the novel *Where the Red Fern Grows* will recognize the Illinois River as the family farm was located on the stream, and much of the book's activities took place along its banks.

Lake Frances

Just upstream from the bridge was once Lake Frances, a resort that mainly attracted the wealthy from Tulsa and other regional cities. The resort started in 1926 when Julius K. Livingston and a few partners bought about 1200 acres along the Illinois River, not far south of Siloam Springs. They built a dam on the Illinois River and developed a resort they called Forest Park. When completed, the resort featured a 70-acre lake, a large hotel with indoor and outdoor dining, a swimming pool, a ballroom that could hold several hundred couples, a golf course and tennis courts, walking trails, and more. There were also a number of cabins, some in a small grouping and others scattered through the woods. Forest Park sold some of the cabins and rented others. Many of the initial guests were wealthy Tulsa oil executives, but visitors came from nearby towns to enjoy the dancing and outdoor recreation.

In 1927, James Wallace Sloan took control of the organization and renamed the resort Lake Frances after his daughter. A few years later, Sloan had the dam enlarged and strengthened, but the Great Depression slowed the work and reduced the interest in the resort. Several floods again damaged the dam, and parts of the resort fell into disrepair. In 1954, the City of Siloam Springs bought Lake Frances, making it a source for city water. The lake was also used for public recreation, including boating, swimming, fishing and camping.

Flooding remained a problem, and in 1989, the lake was drained to prevent the collapse of the dam. Much of the surrounding land was sold for private use. Only a few foundations and chimneys can be found at the site today. This may change as the Grand River Dam Authority (GRDA) has been considering the construction of a new whitewater park on the Illinois River. In 2017, an agreement was reached between the GRDA, the City of Siloam Springs, the Siloam Springs Water Resources Corporation, and the Walton Family Foundation to research the plan and to fund it if approved. Approval has still not been received from the U.S. Army Corps of Engineers and the Oklahoma Scenic River Commission.

235.0 ROGERS WHITE LIME COMPANY SPUR – About 1893, Fleming Freeman began operating limestone mines and kilns in several places in Arkansas. In 1902, he organized the Rogers White Lime Company at Rogers, Arkansas. The lime produced was advertised as being 99.4% pure and it was sold for stone and brick works, plastering and whitewashing, disinfecting and water purifying. In 1913, the company added pulverized agricultural lime to its line of products.

In mid-1917, the company acquired the Grove White Lime Company, and moved the plant to near Watts, Oklahoma. A report by the Oklahoma Geological Survey explained the move: "Grove is located at the end of a branch of the St. Louis & San Francisco Railroad which enters Oklahoma from Arkansas. Watts is much more favorably located on the main line of the Kansas City Southern Railway, and from this point shipments can be made to points in Oklahoma more quickly and with less expense."

This move may not have worked as planned as the Rogers White Lime Company entered bankruptcy in 1918. A reorganization was possible due to the demand for the product, and an 11-car spur track was still shown in KCS timetables into the late 1930s.

236.0 WATTS (WS) – Watts is a typical railroad town, created just a mile away from a town that already existed when the railroad was built. The area was once the location of Fort Wayne, established in 1838 by Captain John Stuart and the Seventh Infantry. Originally named Camp Illinois, the fort was designed to protect travelers and military movements, and to ease the fear of Cherokee raids on Arkansas farms. The fort was renamed after General "Mad" Anthony Wayne, was moved in 1840, then finally closed in 1842. A few years later, Captain Nathan Boone, youngest son of Daniel Boone, helped survey the area for a military road. When Fort Wayne was abandoned, it became the property of the Cherokee Nation and was used by Stand Watie and his followers. It became a Confederate post where Watie organized his regiment of Cherokee volunteers. The Battle of Fort Wayne in October 1862 was a defeat for

Confederate forces. Today, nothing remains from the fort.

The nearby community of Ballard developed from a small number of area farms. The railroad built through the town in 1895-1896, but little was ever located there. In 1912, Kansas City Southern was reorganizing the railroad and planned to close its division point at Stilwell, replacing it with a new location to the north. The town of Watts was created for this purpose, named after John Watts, a Chickamauga Cherokee chief. John Watts had died before the Cherokees were moved to Oklahoma, but members of his family settled in the area. When word leaked out about the new division point, settlers, land speculators, businessmen, and even KCS employees began buying up land. The town was quickly organized, and the post office opened in L. J. Anderson's store on March 30, 1912.

Known by many as Watts Switch, the town grew quickly, especially when most of the businesses at Ballard moved a mile to the north to be here. Several hotels and rooming houses, two drug stores, several general stores, a lumberyard, two livery stables, a hardware store, a bakery, several doctors, a bank, and a newspaper were soon at Watts. A three-story schoolhouse opened in 1913. Despite the early excitement, the town only grew large enough to support the railroad and its shops. The 1920 census showed a population of 396, the largest population ever recorded at Watts. Local farming led to the construction of a tomato processing plant by the Chamberlain Canning Company in the mid-1920s.

Initially, the railroad had a number of facilities at Watts, including a depot, roundhouse, coal chute, icehouse, water pump station and water tower. Many of these were torn down by the mid-1900s as steam locomotives were replaced with diesel locomotives by 1953. The population was down to 267 residents in 1950, when it began to slowly increase. The depot finally came down in the late 1980s. Today, Watts has a population of about 300, but its school (partly built with brick from the original 1913 schoolhouse) has almost 400 students in prekindergarten through twelfth grade. While the town has to compete with nearby Siloam Springs, it still features a post office, several churches, a few businesses, and a number of homes. The largest structure in town is the large feedmill alongside the mainline of the Kansas City Southern.

The Division Point at Watts

Being a division point meant that train crews got on and off trains at Watts. Steam locomotives would also be changed here, and local trains that served the area were based here. When created, Watts was the division point between the Second District (Pittsburg to Watts) and the Third District (Watts to Heavener). A depot was built in 1912, followed by a roundhouse, coal chute, water tower, three-story restaurant and hotel, and a small rail yard as part of the new division terminal. There was also an emergency icing station that was very active during the annual fruit and berry season.

In 1936, the railroad showed a yard, water tower, coal chute, turntable, oil facility, telephone, standard clock, and bulletin books at Watts. There was a 97-car siding, and the depot was staffed continuously to provide telegraph service and to provide orders to train crews. The number of tracks required some special instructions in KCS employee timetables.

> When first-class trains meet at Watts on special orders, that part of the passing track that lies between the north switch and the cross-over south of the depot will be used. If the trains are to meet at the south lead of the yard, the order must so designate. Passenger trains will not run through yard tracks at Watts without special instructions.

Little changed by the late 1950s, except the roundhouse was gone and diesel locomotives passed through on the trains. The depot was still staffed continuously and served as a register station with a standard clock. The yard was still active, but it only provided water and could turn locomotives on a turntable. A mail crane had been installed to handle local mail. Another change was that the siding had been extended to 153 car lengths as trains were running longer and longer.

By the 1960s, the siding was even longer at 251 car lengths. Other things were pretty much the same as there was continuous telegraph service at the station, and a mail crane stood nearby. Water was available at the yard. Watts was also still a scheduled stop for the passengers trains, with *Southern Belle* No. 1 departing at 2:30pm. Even though the passenger service ended on November 3, 1969, the station remained staffed for a number of years. The depot finally came down in late 1989, and the other services also ended, especially as the Second and Third subdivisions were combined to form the Heavener Subdivision.

Today, there is a small office on the west side of the tracks at Watts, opposite of the large grain mill and processing complex. General orders and circulars, plus radio communications, are available here. An 11,500-foot siding (Control Point North Watts at Milepost 234.3 to Control Point South Watts at Milepost 236.7) and a four-track yard are located alongside the mainline. The yard is known as Watts Storage, and the north switch is at Milepost 236.1, while the south switch is at Milepost 236.8.

A grain feed mill and processing complex at Watts stands on the east side of the tracks. The facility is a regular customer for the railroad.

Heavener Sub Route Guide

The Watts depot didn't have long to stand after it was photographed on October 25, 1989.

The former depot was replaced by this portable office, located just across the tracks from the largest shipper at Watts, Oklahoma.

237.1 BALLARD – Ballard, often locally called Ballard Hill, was the first town in this area. It is located where the railroad has a long curve, changing from heading southwest to heading southeast. A post office opened on May 13, 1896, as the town included a lumber yard and several businesses. During the early 1900s, a series of charcoal ovens operated here. On September 16, 1908, the Oklahoma Corporation Commission conducted a hearing on the necessity for a depot at the town of Ballard. The hearing produced a description of the railroad at Ballard.

> It is shown by the evidence that Ballard is situated on the defendant's line of road, nine miles south of Siloam Springs and seven miles north of Westville; that the town of Ballard contains less than one hundred population, and that there is a side track and platform for passengers, to get on and off trains, and that cars are set out for the loading of freight in carload lots. There is no telegraph communication.

The Oklahoma Corporation Commission determined that due to the distance from other railroad stations, "the establishment of a depot at this place, business will be sufficient to pay for the maintenance of the same." Therefore, KCS was ordered to build and maintain a depot at the town of Ballard, with its location agreed upon by the defendant and the citizens of the town of Ballard. The depot was to be constructed and ready for operation by December 15, 1908.

Heavener Sub Route Guide

However, in 1912, KCS opened its terminal less than two miles to the north at Watts, and most of the business and population moved there. The post office closed on June 15, 1916. There is no clear source of the name Ballard, but it is a fairly common name among the Eastern Cherokee. For example, William Ballard, a member of the Eastern Cherokee, moved into the area as part of the Trail of Tears movement of the tribe. At least one source stated that it was named for a slave by the name of Ballard.

This is now the Township of Ballard in Adair County, Oklahoma. The township is actually administered by the Watts city government. A few blocks of scattered houses cover the hillside to the west of U.S. Highway 59. To the east are the Kansas City Southern tracks and then Ballard Creek. Alongside the west bank of Ballard Creek can be found traces of the Ballard Creek Roadbed, now listed on the National Register of Historic Places. This road was active from the late 1830s until the Civil War as a trading route between Indian Territory and businesses in northwest Arkansas. The route was also used by a few of the Eastern Cherokee during their forced movement westward. As new roads were built after the Civil War, and trade patterns changed, the need for the Ballard Creek wagon road diminished.

Some sources state that the Ballard Creek Road could have dated hundreds of years earlier as it may have been built on an old Osage trail. The tribe created a number of trails across the region, using the left bank with the current at their back, exactly where the road was later located. The Osage ceded claims to their lands in the Indian Territory in 1828, and members of the Western Cherokees moved into the area.

237.3 BALLARD CREEK BRIDGE – Immediately east of the recently improved U.S. Highway 59, the railroad crosses the stream using a three-span deck plate girder bridge, known in some sources as Ballard Creek Bridge II. Ballard Creek was once known as Williams Creek. While there is no clear record of the stream's naming, the family of William Ballard, an Eastern Cherokee, did live in the general area.

Ballard Creek forms from several small streams several miles west of Lincoln, Arkansas. The stream flows westward and then turns northward, eventually flowing into the Illinois River north of Watts, Oklahoma. Ballard Creek has been described as a generally shallow, gravel-bottomed stream about forty to sixty feet wide, flowing past rolling hills, woods, pastures, and scattered farmhouses.

A benchmark on this bridge shows it to be at an elevation of 970 feet.

237.7 BALLARD CREEK BRIDGE – As the railroad climbs towards Westville, it follows the valley created by Ballard Creek. This bridge, known by some as Ballard Creek Bridge I, consists of two deck plate girder spans. It is also immediately east of the new U.S. Highway 59 route, located at an elevation of 974 feet. Heading south, the KCS mainline stays next to U.S. Highway 59 until Milepost 240.

241.2 FEEDER – To the east is the large Tyson Foods Westville Feed Mill which supports thirty poultry houses further east. North Feeder is at Milepost 240.7 and South Feeder is at Milepost 241.6, and the track is shown to have 4300 feet of capacity. This was once a Hudson feed mill, built during the 1980s. In 1997,

Tyson acquired Hudson and assumed ownership of this complex.

Tyson Foods is big, producing 20% of the chicken, beef, and pork in the United States. Tyson Foods started in 1931 when John W. Tyson moved to Springdale, Arkansas, and to feed his family, began buying chickens locally and selling them across the Midwest. The business grew rapidly during World War II as poultry was one of the few foods not rationed, and Tyson moved into chicken production. The company was incorporated in 1947 as Tyson Feed and Hatchery, Inc. During the late 1950s, the company built its first processing plant, meaning that it raised, processed and sold poultry, one of the first firms to control the entire process.

In 1963, Tyson's Foods went public, allowing it to continue to expand. The name became Tyson Foods in 1972, and other product lines were added throughout the 1980s. By 1990, Tyson Foods was the world's largest fully-integrated producer, processor, and marketer of poultry-based food products, and was quickly expanding its international market. Thanks to further expansion and several acquisitions, Tyson became the world's largest processor and marketer of chicken, beef, and pork by 2001. Since then, the company has continued to expand and the product names on the side of their trailers will surprise almost anyone.

The Heavener Sub: History Through the Miles

The Tyson feed mill at Feeder is easy to find as it towers over area farms.

241.5 BAPTISTE – This station was listed in schedules from 1899, but not for many more years. Baptiste, also known as Baptist Mission and Baptist, was once an important supply point and mission for the Cherokees. Today the site is marked by several historical markers, a white frame church building, and the Baptist Mission Cemetery. All of these are to the west of the tracks and U.S. Highway 59, not far south of the large Tyson feed mill. The location is easy to find as it is just north of Bushyhead Mountain.

This area has a history that is closely tied to the Cherokees. It started in 1839 when several Cherokee parties arrived here from the Trail of Tears and were issued supplies that were intended to sustain them during their first year in the Indian Territory. The supplies gave the location the name Breadtown. Soon, a Baptist Mission opened with missionary Evan Jones and Cherokee minister Jesse Bushyhead. There, they promoted Cherokee Christian evangelism and education, and published a number of books and documents for the tribal members. Reverend Jesse Bushyhead was also elected as one of the first members of the Supreme Court of the Cherokee Nation in 1839. He served until his death on July 17, 1844.

Jesse Bushyhead and Evan Jones had each served as a conductor of a Cherokee detachment as they made their way west. Bushyhead and Jones selected the spot where food and supplies had been issued as a centralized mission as their two groups settled in different locations. Reports indicate that originally the location was part of the Woodall farm. The two began training Cherokee Baptists to lead their own congregations, they opened a school to educate Cherokee school teachers, and established three schools at other locations. One of their major projects was translating the Bible into Cherokee. In 1843, they began printing eighteen books of the New Testament, a series of textbooks, a Cherokee hymnal, training materials, and more. They also published the *Cherokee Messenger*, the first periodical issued in the Indian Territory.

A small community grew up around the mission that was described in 1842 as "a flourishing and growing settlement" that featured "a respectable store, a saddler, a blacksmith shop" and plans for a school. A post office reportedly opened in 1844, but the Baptist Mission Post Office opened on July 5, 1850. As the Civil War started, a battle between different elements of the tribe began, and pro-Confederate Cherokees burned the mission buildings and their contents. The Baptist Mission Post Office was officially closed on June 22, 1866.

The town of Baptist remained after the Civil War, and grew enough to have a post office on March 9, 1881. The town was basically a rural community that had to compete against other nearby and larger towns. When the Kansas City, Pittsburg & Gulf built to the east and used Westville as the local station, Baptist lost most of its population. The post office closed on November 15, 1912. About all that remains are the old church building, the cemetery, and a few farms.

The Old Baptist Mission Church marks the hillside where many important Cherokee Christian events took place during the 1800s.

Heavener Sub Route Guide

There are several historical markers and signs at Baptiste that explain much of the community's history.

The Railroad Station Battle at Baptist

As the town of Baptist shrank, the railroad ended service to the community. In response, in 1915 a number of local citizens ("130 residents of this vicinity, who resided all the way from 1 to 10 miles from this point") protested to the Oklahoma Corporation Commission, demanding that the railroad be required to stop its trains at Baptist. The Corporation Commission, after a hearing and report, ordered the Kansas City Southern to stop two trains a day at this point, one going in each direction, upon being flagged. During the first six months, the average number of passengers per month (inbound and outbound) was 37, and the average total revenue per month was 23 cents per passenger.

Based upon the operating data, the railroad petitioned the Supreme Court of Oklahoma to overrule the requirement. Information about Baptist and the nearby towns of Watts and Westville was evaluated, as well as the use of the passenger train service that was being provided. Several statements from the case are included here.

> The facts of the case, as shown by the record, are that Baptist, so far as being a town or village is concerned, is a myth, but is a thickly settled farming community. At this place there is no store, post office, school, blacksmith shop, or business of any kind, no side tracks, switches, or section house, but is merely a point which has been designated as Baptist.
>
> If this were a station or a village that would justify some one in establishing a business of some character, there might be some justification for the people demanding or requesting the trains to stop at this particular point, but the record discloses that this is nothing more than a farming community between two stations which are between 8 and 9 miles apart.

Not surprisingly, the Supreme Court of Oklahoma overruled the Oklahoma Corporation Commission and ended the requirement for the Kansas City Southern's passenger trains to serve Baptist.

Heavener Sub Route Guide

244.0 STL&SF CROSSING – To the north of Buffington Road on the north side of Westville was once a crossing between the mainline of the Kansas City Southern and the Muskogee Subdivision of the St. Louis-San Francisco Railway Company. The Frisco grade once curved across the KCS to the northwest, passing through the north end of the Westville Community Park. A gate lined against the Frisco protected the mainline of KCS. Both freight and passenger connections were located here. During the early 1900s, timetables promoted connections with KCS passenger trains by stating "Eastbound train makes good connection with Kansas City Southern railway at Westville for Neosho, Joplin, Pittsburg, Kansas City and all points north and west; also Texarkana, Shreveport and all points south."

On November 29, 1899, the North Arkansas & Western Railroad was chartered in Arkansas. The goal of the company was to connect Fayetteville with the timber and fruit businesses in the Illinois River Valley in Indian Territory. As construction progressed, funding ran short and the railroad was renamed the Ozark & Cherokee Central Railway Company (O&CC) on April 19, 1901. The railroad reached Prairie Grove, Arkansas, on August 31, 1901, and apples and strawberries began to be shipped. The line was extended to Lincoln, Arkansas, on January 22, 1902, and then to Westville, Oklahoma, during late March. On July 12, 1902, the railroad reached Welling, Oklahoma, and then Tahlequah on August 2, 1902.

Further westward construction got the railroad to Fort Gibson on December 10, 1902, and then Muskogee on February 1, 1903. Some of the last construction took place using two other companies.

The Muskogee City Bridge Company built the steel bridge over the Arkansas River, while the Shawnee, Oklahoma & Missouri Coal and Railway Company completed the line on to Okmulgee on March 13, 1903.

The railroad had success hauling local farm products and shipments from the Stark Brothers nursery at Farmington, Arkansas, and planned on further expansion. A *New York Times* article on April 15, 1903, stated that the O&CC had acquired the Shawnee, Oklahoma & Missouri Coal and Railway Company to get into Okmulgee. The railroad had also received permission from the Arkansas Railroad Commission to build 400 miles of track from Fayetteville eastward to Jasper, from Muskogee to Fort Smith, and westward to Oklahoma City.

With the railroad's immediate success, the St. Louis & San Francisco Railroad Company gained control through a lease on July 1, 1903, and then bought the Ozark & Cherokee Central Railway Company fully on July 15, 1907. The ownership of the line changed again on September 15, 1916, when the St. Louis & San Francisco Railroad was sold to the newly organized St. Louis-San Francisco Railway Company (Frisco). In 1926, the railroad was operating two sets of passenger trains between Fayetteville and Muskogee – a morning and an afternoon train in each direction. To cut costs, a large motorcar took over the business, including the Railway Post Office services. Passenger service ended in May 1940.

While often busy, the line didn't produce a profit and much of the line, known as the Muskogee Subdivision, was abandoned in 1942 under the orders of the War Production Authority and the Interstate Commerce Commission. The abandonment came about due to losses on the line and the need to move almost ten miles of the line because of the construction of Fort Gibson Lake. The track from Fayetteville to Fort Gibson saw the last train operate on July 10, 1942, ending the need for the crossing at Milepost 244.0.

244.4 WESTVILLE (VI) – Westville is another townsite created by the Kansas City, Pittsburg & Gulf as the railroad built southward towards the Gulf of Mexico. Reportedly, the town was named by Jim West, Jr., a railroad attorney, for his father Jim West, who lived just across the border in Cincinnati, Arkansas. Several small towns were already in the area. The town grew as the Kansas City Southern began full operations, and then the Ozark & Cherokee Central Railway Company built through the north side of town.

In 1930-1931, Kansas City Southern "spent a large sum of money in building a new station and re-arranging its tracks" after an August 25, 1930, agreement with the City of Westville. The agreement required the railroad to make the improvements if the city closed several grade crossings, including Cherry Street. After the railroad built its new station, Westville reopened Cherry Street (now Buffington Street) and several other streets. KCS then sued the city to have the streets closed since the grade crossings "would require it to cut its freight trains on the passing track, slow down its operation, interfere with and reduce the usefulness of its steam track and increase hazards to the traveling public." Although it was agreed that Westville didn't keep their side of the bargain, the Oklahoma Corporation Commission also determined that Westville had never received official permission to close the crossings and they were to be reopened. The case later went through the Oklahoma Supreme Court to the U.S. Supreme Court.

In 1936, the station was staffed 8am-5pm, providing telegraph service. A mail crane stood nearby to handle the mail when the station wasn't staffed. There was an 89-car siding plus a number of other tracks with a capacity of 81 freight cars. The station stayed open on weekdays through the end of passenger service. As the railroad ran longer trains, the siding was extended to hold 138 cars, but the industry tracks were down to 58 cars in 1958. By the 1960s, the siding was capable of holding 168 cars. In 1964, the *Southern Belle* (southbound No. 1) served Westville as a flag stop, scheduled to be here at 2:41pm. In 2014, the siding was gone. A long track (Milepost 243.9 at North Westville to Milepost 244.5 at South Westville) on the west side of the mainline is used to serve the H. J. Baker & Brother elevator.

During March 1990, KCS 685 was photographed heading north past the Westville station sign.

Heavener Sub Route Guide

The foundations still remain from the old KCS depot at Westville, Oklahoma. In the background is the H. J. Baker & Brother Elevator.

The City of Westville

The City of Westville was founded as one of a number of railroad townsites laid out in the 1890s by the Kansas City, Pittsburg & Gulf. The area was a natural meeting point that had been used for centuries by roaming hunters. One of the earliest documented events at today's Westville was the Trail of Tears, the forced Cherokee immigration to Indian Territory (eastern Oklahoma) during the 1830s. At least one immigration party disbanded near here and headed to a resupply point that later became Baptist, Oklahoma. One study states that twelve Trail of Tears detachments disbanded in early 1839 near here, while a recent study has concluded that only three detachments disbanded in the area. Few actually settled at Westville, and no community grew up here until the railroad built through eastern Oklahoma.

The railroad began building through the Cherokee Nation and Indian Territory in 1895, and railroad construction gangs were at Westville by that summer. Located in the Going Snake District of the Cherokee Nation, the KCP&G platted a 175-acre townsite that became Westville. The town name honored Jim West, who lived one mile south of nearby Cincinnati, Arkansas, and whose son, Jim West, Jr., was an attorney for the Kansas City Southern Railway. With town lots selling quickly, the Westville post office was established on November 18, 1895. The William D. Williams Addition and the Pat Dore Addition soon added to the community's size. Some reports state that lots were sold to Cherokee citizens at half of the appraised value and to others at the full appraised value.

In 1900, Westville's population was 296, and in March 1902, the Ozark & Cherokee Central Railway built through the north side of town. Already, Westville was growing and the first bank (First National Bank) opened in 1901. The Peoples Bank was founded on January 3, 1903, Westville's first school term began in fall 1903, with the first high school student graduated in 1908. As Westville developed, businesses from surrounding communities moved to here, making it the only area town along the Kansas City Southern to gain in population in the years after 1897.

When Oklahoma became a state on November 16, 1907, Westville was made the county seat of the newly formed Adair County. This status didn't remain long as votes in 1908 and 1910 supported the move of the county seat to Stilwell. The census recorded 802 residents in 1910, the year the brick, two-story Buffington Hotel (added to the National

Register of Historic Places in 1984) was built at Main and Williams, two blocks east of the KCS tracks. About this time, the Kansas City Southern Railway Company Immigration Department published the booklet *Eastern Oklahoma along the Kansas City Southern Railway*. The booklet included a number of interesting statements about Westville.

> Westville, Adair County, is a crossing point on the Kansas City Southern Railway and a branch of the St. Louis & San Francisco Railway. It is 244 miles south of Kansas City, Mo., and has an altitude of 1,137 feet. The location is a very good one, owing to the very large scope of fertile country surrounding it. The present population is about 1,200. The town is now rapidly growing, because the adjacent lands are now in market and can be had at a moderate price. During the year 1910, twenty new dwellings, costing $18,000, two hotels, $4,000, an electric light plant, $4,000, were completed, and bonds for a water works plant to cost $28,000 were voted. Concrete sidewalks have been ordered for all parts of town.
>
> The shipments of surplus products from Westville amounted during the past year to thirty carloads of wheat, 5,000 bales of cotton, worth about $75 per bale, 20,000 pounds of poultry, 2,000 cases of eggs, 44 carloads of cattle, 15 carloads of hogs, 5 carloads of oats, 8 of apples, and 30,000 pounds of hides, pelts and furs.

> *In addition to some fifteen or twenty mercantile establishments, the town has a large modern flour mill, an electric light plant, two banks, a large modern school building and several churches.*

The population peaked in the 1920 census at 956, a number that it wouldn't exceed until the 1980 census (1049 residents). The 1920s started positively as Westville was incorporated in 1920, and the fruit and vegetable business remained strong. During this time, the Westville Fruit Growers Association handled products like peaches, apples, strawberries, grapes, blackberries, green beans, tomatoes and sweet potatoes. KCS reported in 1925 that annual shipments from Westville included 60 carloads of wheat, 125 carloads of cattle and hogs, and 65 carloads of corn, plus cotton, flour, oats, forest products, poultry, eggs and cream. The Westville Cannery Company packed tomatoes and other vegetables from the area. In 1926, several oil storage plants were built at Westville.

The late 1920s saw things take a turn for the worse as crops began to fail, the 1927 flood impacted the region, and the Great Depression started. By 1930, the population of Westville had dropped by almost a third to 691. As the economy slowly recovered, businesses began to return. The Baron Canning Company (1940) and The Griffin Canning Company (1941) opened to handle local vegetables and fruits. Several other small manufacturing businesses opened during the latter part of the twentieth century, and Westville's population started to grow.

Heavener Sub Route Guide

Not all of the history is along the tracks. At Westville, the historic Buffington Hotel stands several blocks to the east.

With the construction of the new U.S. Highway 59 about a mile west of town, many of the businesses have moved along the highway. The population is about 1600 and the H. J. Baker & Brother elevator is still served by the railroad, located in downtown Westville.

The H. J. Baker & Brother Elevator stands next to the Heavener Subdivision in downtown Westville, providing a bit of business for the railroad.

Heading south, the railroad follows Shell Branch until the waterway flows into Baron Fork near the community of Baron, Oklahoma. Not far south of Westville, the railroad passes the west side of Alberty Mountain, which stands about 300 feet above the tracks.

249.9 BARON – You can almost start a fight when researching this former railroad station. Over the years, this station has had several versions of the name, including Baron, Barron, and Barron Fork (Oklahoma Corporation Commission in 1910). Many sources state that the name was actually Barren Fork (Oklahoma Corporation Commission in 1908), named for the Barren Fork tributary of the Illinois River. However, even here there is conflict as it is documented as being the Baron Fork of the Illinois River, but current highway signs state that it is the Barren Fork Creek.

Whatever the earlier name, when the Kansas City, Pittsburg & Gulf built through the area, the company created the townsite of Baron. The Baron post office opened on November 12, 1895, as one of four KCP&G townsites that gained a post office that year. A small depot was installed for $1126.97 in 1925. While the town was only a flag stop for passenger trains, there was an 88-car siding, other tracks with a capacity of 27 freight cars, plus a mail crane in 1936. This was about the peak of the community as the post office closed on December 31, 1942. The siding remained until about 1960, and only a spur track with a capacity of 21 cars was shown in 1964. Today, a 1050-foot spur track is located on the west side of the mainline and Baron is an unincorporated community along U.S. Highway 59.

Baron versus Barren

The fight about whether the name is Baron or Barren (or even Barron) is not new, and both names were being mixed by the early 1900s. The United States Geological Survey of the Department of the Interior published *A Gazetteer of Indian Territory* by Henry Gannett in 1905 that only adds to the confusion. It stated that Baron was a post village in the Cherokee Nation, while Barren was a railroad station on the Kansas City Southern Railway in the Cherokee Nation. It was also reported that there was a Kansas City Southern Railway station named Barren Fork. Finally, the book stated that Barren Fork was a left-hand branch of the Illinois River, rising in Arkansas and flowing into the Illinois a few miles south of Tahlequah, Cherokee Nation.

250.5 BARON FORK BRIDGE – This bridge features two Pratt through truss spans on the south end and five deck plate girder spans on the north end. Baron Fork, known also as Baron Fork Creek, Baron Fork River, and even Barren Fork Creek, is only about 35 miles long. It begins about Lincoln, Arkansas, and flows west to the Illinois River near Welling, Oklahoma.

Despite most current and railroad documents showing that it is Baron Fork, very early documents state that it is Barren Fork of the Illinois River, named such because early explorers often found the stream to be almost dry. The stream is heavily influenced by area rainfall, and the large gravel beaches that are found along most of Baron Fork can often disappear during periods of rain.

The bridge over the Baron Fork, often known as Barren Fork, features a series of deck plate girder spans, plus two Pratt through truss spans.

The spelling of the name of this stream has varied over the years. Historically, the railroad has used Baron Fork, while modern highway signs have it Barren Fork.

Heading south, trains begin to climb a steady grade. According to a 1917 Interstate Commerce Commission report, "with the exception of one or two sags, the grade is ascending for southbound trains practically all of the way between Barron Fork and Stilwell, a distance of 8.4 miles, most of it being between .75% and 1%."

251.1 PEAVINE CREEK BRIDGE – The railroad crosses Peavine Creek on a single-span bridge at an elevation of 885 feet. The railroad climbs the valley of Peavine Creek to near Maryetta, Oklahoma. At Milepost 252.8, the railroad passes the Peavine School. Peavine is a census-designated place with a population of less than 500, and a small community of about 400. It is basically a collection of rural homes and farms.

Peavine Creek is one of the major tributaries of Baron Fork. The stream is about ten miles long and forms in the hills northeast of Stilwell. Peavine Creek has been used to irrigate crops in the area, including the appropriate green beans.

253.6 PEAVINE LUMBER COMPANY SPUR – The Oklahoma Corporation Commission showed that this station was 3.7 miles south of Barren Fork in 1908. The spur was listed in the rates published by the Central Freight Association until the late 1910s.

254.3 CHERT BALLAST PIT – This ballast pit was listed by the Oklahoma Corporation Commission about 1910. During this time, the railroad was spending a great deal of money improving the track structure, and a number of ballast pits were opened along the line.

The 1906 KCS annual report mentioned this location as part of its coverage of efforts to better ballast the railroad's track. It described chert as "a disintegrated rock found near Stilwell (MP 255) handled by the company steam shovel; capacity, about 60 cars per day, if sufficient cars are furnished."

255.8 CONNER INDUSTRIES – A spur tracks heads to the west to serve the mill of Conner Industries. The firm is about forty years old and provides industrial wood and packaging solutions such as custom pallets, crates, boxes, and other wood packaging products. The company claims that using both softwoods and hardwoods, they can produce thousands of different wood products at their fourteen facilities from Nebraska to Florida.

This area has also used the name Tyler Spring, and the Tyler Spring Cemetery is not far to the east.

256.6 MARYETTA – This was never a station on the railroad, but the Maryetta School is just to the west. Also in the area is the Indian Capital Technology Center, a technical school system headquartered in Muskogee, Oklahoma, that is affiliated with the Oklahoma Department of Career and Technology Education.

258.2 STILWELL (Z) – Stilwell is the most successful of the four KCS railroad townsites that received post offices in 1895-1897. The town was created by the railroad on land once owned by Martha Johnson and Elizabeth Freeman and replaced Gentry, Arkansas, as a division point in 1895. According to the National Register of Historic Places, the Kansas City, Pittsburg & Gulf "erected a small, wood-frame depot building and other, more elaborate facilities befitting a centralized location of railroad maintenance activities. These included an eight-stall roundhouse with a turntable, a coal chute and loading ramp, and various small shops." The railroad brought in train crews, machinists, managers, and a number of other employees, allowing the Flint post office to be moved northward three miles and changed to Stilwell on May 12, 1896. Stilwell was incorporated on January 2, 1897, and its population was 770 in the 1900 census. After several elections, Oklahoma Governor Charles N. Haskell declared Stilwell to be the seat of Adair County on May 6, 1910. That year the population was recorded as being 1039.

The railroad and town also benefitted from the local agricultural economy. Being the largest town in the region, the local businesses attracted customers from smaller towns and farms from miles away. Most of what was bought and sold was moved by the railroad. Farm products included wheat, corn, cotton, apples, peaches, poultry and eggs. By 1909, the Stilwell Ginning Company (cotton) and the Whittaker Brothers (flour and feed mill) were served by the railroad and located just south and north of Ash Street. Within a few years, Stilwell "had thirteen general merchandise stores, four grocers, two hardware stores, a lumber mill, and numerous other enterprises flourished. An electric light system and waterworks had been installed."

While the population of Stilwell continued to grow, 1912 was the peak of railroad activity at the town named after the founder of the KCP&G: Arthur E. Stilwell. In 1912, Kansas City Southern again moved the division point, this time to the new town of Watts, Oklahoma. This meant that the roundhouse and other mechanical shops were closed and moved away, as well as some of the offices. This left just the original wood-frame depot representing the railroad company. The station was on the west side of five KCS tracks just south of Maple Street. It was a combination structure, with the baggage room to the north and the passenger waiting room to the south. By this time, there were reports that the station had deteriorated. The depot also didn't comply with the 1907 Oklahoma "Jim Crow" law that required segregation of blacks and whites. Hearings about this station and others were held by the Oklahoma Corporation Commission and the Oklahoma Supreme Court, which required railroads to maintain stations that were "in keeping with the size and general characteristics of the communities in which they operated."

At Stilwell, the KCS felt that the station was sufficient, but many citizens and the Oklahoma Corporation Commission felt differently, ordering the railroad to build a new brick or concrete station. Plans were required by February 1915, and construction began in October of that year. The station was similar to a series of stations built by the railroad over the next decade. The 129-foot-long and 26-foot-wide building was brick, built in a "late nineteenth-early twentieth century revival style called mission." The station had its passenger waiting areas and ticket office in the north end, and rooms for baggage/express and freight to the south. The building still stands along U.S. Highway 59, two blocks north of the original station location. It was placed on the National Register of Historic Places on September 8, 2015, and serves as a museum and visitor center. For those who want to know more about the KCS station, the National Register application provides a great deal of history and design information.

In 1997, the Stilwell depot was an abandoned building sitting between the Heavener Subdivision and the construction of an improved U.S. Highway 59 through town.

During the past decade, the Stilwell depot has been restored and now houses the KCS Depot Museum.

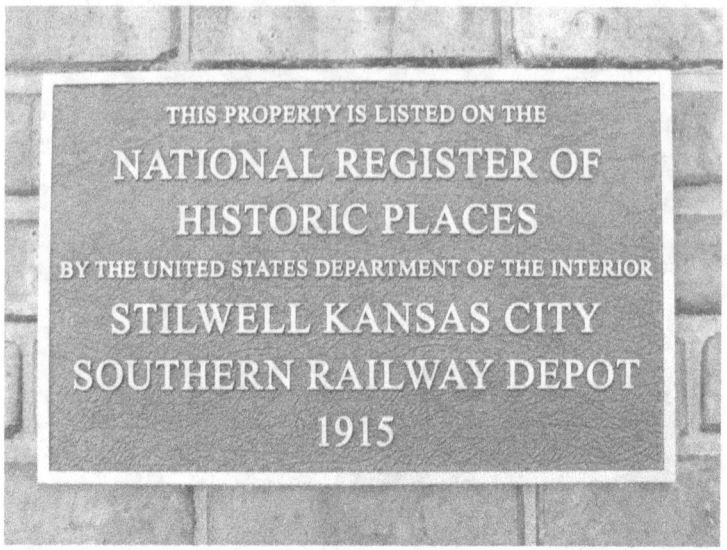

The KCS depot at Stilwell was placed on the National Register of Historic Places in 2015.

Despite the loss of railroad jobs, Stilwell continued to grow, having a population of 1155 in 1920. Then, as now, the railroad was basically the east end of town, with the downtown business district to the west of the railroad station. Businesses and warehouses lined Front Street where U.S. Highway 59 now passes through town. Several blocks to the west was the three-story, native-stone courthouse on Division Street. It was completed in 1920, but burned on December 30, 1929. A new granite, steel, and concrete courthouse opened in January 1931, and was placed on the National Register of Historic Places on August 23, 1984.

During the 1920s, a number of companies shipped agricultural products by rail from Stilwell. These included the Stilwell Fruit Growers Association, Ozark Fruit Growers Association, Stilwell Berry Growers Association, P. F. Hughes (16,000 bushels of sweet potatoes in 1926), and the McCoy Produce Company. On April 26, 1925, the railroad completed a spur track to serve the Stilwell Canning Company, adding canned tomatoes to the list of products moved. In 1926, the Kansas City Southern Railway's *Agricultural and Industrial Bulletin* had an article about Stilwell that described the town's development and businesses.

> *The industrial undertakings in Stilwell are the Whittaker Bros. Flour Mill, the Stilwell Cannery, a handle factory, stave mill, saw mill, two cotton gins, two corn and grist mills and a sweet potato curing plant of 16,000 bushels capacity recently contracted for. The mercantile enterprises consist of two banks, twenty general merchandise firms, three hardware, three drug firms, two newspapers, one hotel. There are here also five churches, one grade and one high school.*

The railroad allowed farmers to reach new markets, and strawberries became a major cash crop. As the Great Depression hit the economy, more acres of strawberries were planted, with more than two thousand acres being picked each spring. In 1948, the Stilwell Strawberry Festival was started by the local Kiwanis Club, and by 1949, the Oklahoma state legislature and governor had declared Stilwell and Adair County to be "the Strawberry Capital of the World." The festival is still held, but the acreage is much less.

This sign on the edge of Stilwell proclaims the town to be the Strawberry Capital of the World.

Also during the 1940s, a company started up that still has a strong presence at Stilwell. Stilwell Foods was formed in 1942 to can tomato products for the federal government. In 1976, the firm was acquired by Flowers Industries, and the canning ended in 1980, replaced by a growing frozen foods line. In 1999, Mrs. Smith's Pies, part of Flowers, acquired Stilwell Foods and renamed the company Mrs. Smith's Bakery of Stilwell, producing about 600,000 pies and cobblers daily. In 2003, Mrs. Smith's frozen dessert business was sold to The Schwan Food Company. The large plant just east of the KCS station still makes fruit pies and other desserts for several of the Schwan's product lines.

A major change in the agricultural activities in the area was notable by the 1960s. Less farmland was available as ranching and poultry began to take over.

The population of Stilwell first passed two thousand in the 1970 census, with a recorded number of 2134 residents. Better roads allowed trucks to handle much of the business, and residents could travel to larger cities for employment. Stilwell still serves as a market and supply point for much of Adair County. The population recently passed 4000, and the city still features a full school system, a technical college, and a number of retail stores and chains.

The KCS at Stilwell

As stated, Stilwell became a railroad division point in 1895, featuring a small yard, roundhouse, mechanical facilities, and offices. This ended in 1912 when Kansas City Southern moved the division point to the new town of Watts, Oklahoma. After that, Stilwell was simply a shipping point along the line. In 1936, the train station was staffed and had telegraph service from 11pm until 3pm the next afternoon. There was still a rail yard and turntable, plus a water tower. A mail crane allowed mail to be picked up anytime, and an 83-car siding allowed trains to meet and pass each other.

After World War II, little changed except the turntable was removed. The yard remained so that a Dodger (local train) could handle local switching. In 1958, the station was staffed 8am-5pm daily except Sundays. The siding had been expanded to 134 car lengths to allow the operation of longer trains. By 1964, the staff hours were 7am-4pm, but little else changed except the siding was shown to be 158 cars long. Even though Stilwell had one of the largest populations of any KCS station in Oklahoma, it was only shown to be a flag stop for Train No. 1, the

Southern Belle. Timetables showed that it was to be at Stilwell at 2:58pm. The last run of the *Southern Belle* was on November 3, 1969, but the station agent remained for a few more years. With no passenger train to serve, the station hours changed to 5am-2pm on weekdays by 1970. In 1971, the railroad gave the station building to the City of Stilwell.

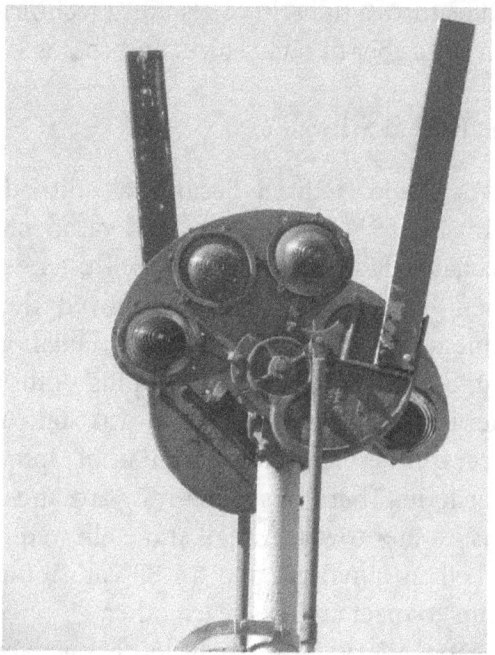

The Stilwell depot still features a set of train order signals, although inactive, as shown here.

By the 2010s, the railroad at Stilwell was down to a 7794-foot siding located between Control Point North Stilwell (Milepost 257.0) and Control Point South Stilwell (Milepost 258.6). South of South Stilwell is an industry track to the east that serves Henningsen Cold Storage (Milepost 258.8). The firm handles the storage and distribution of refrigerated and frozen foods.

Heavener Sub Route Guide

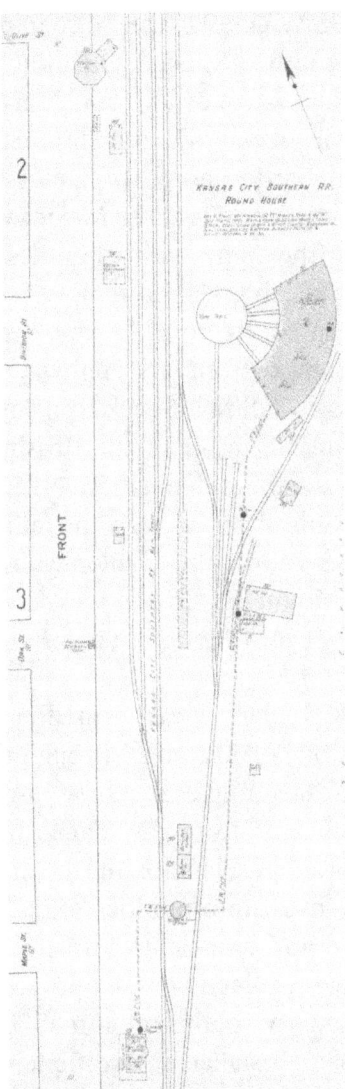

This Sanborn map from 1909 shows the former KCS roundhouse that was once located at the east end of Division Street on the east side of the mainline. An icing platform was located to the south with a coaling platform just to its west. The KCS railroad station was south of the roundhouse near the water tower, pump house, and sanding facility. *Sanborn Fire Insurance Map from Stillwell, Adair County, Oklahoma.* Sanborn Map Company, Jun, 1909. Map. Retrieved from the Library of Congress, https://www.loc.gov/item/sanborn07259_004/.

259.1 U.S. HIGHWAY 59 – The railroad passes under the highway south of Stilwell, Oklahoma. U.S. Highway 59 is a border-to-border route, part of the NAFTA Corridor Highway System. Its north end is at the Canadian border north of Lancaster, Minnesota, while its south end is at the Mexican border at Laredo, Texas. The highway is 1911 miles long and passes through eastern Oklahoma.

Heading south from Stilwell, the railroad turns southwest away from U.S. Highway 59. The railroad then follows Sallisaw Creek to near Sallisaw, Oklahoma, avoiding most of the Brushy Mountains in southern Adair and northern Sequoyah counties. Between Stilwell and Bunch, the railroad passes west of Fletcher Mountain, Dahlonegah Mountain, and Hudson Mountain. To the west are Gitting Down Mountain, Lyons Mountain and Bunch Mountain.

262.1 BLANCK – Blanck was located around the grade crossing with E850 Road. Through the 1930s, there was a 60-car siding and a short 9-car house track. The name came from the Blanck family of nearby Stilwell. Frank A. Blanck came to Stilwell in 1894 and began to invest in a number of businesses, including a land and real estate firm that became Burch & Blanck, a regular advertiser promoting land along the Kansas City Southern Railroad. In 1906, KCS reported that it installed an additional track here for P. A. Blanck, likely a typo that should have read F. A. Blanck. There is little here today to let anyone know that Blanck and a railroad siding ever existed.

The name Blanck did confuse many people, and even the Oklahoma Corporation Commission sometimes referred to the location as Blanch Spur.

Heavener Sub Route Guide

Maps by the U.S. Geological Survey have shown the location as Blanch for decades.

263.8 FLINT – Flint was a district of the Cherokee Nation, created by the Cherokee National Council on November 6, 1840. A post office was established at the community of Flint on August 1, 1846. The post office lasted here for almost fifty years before moving three miles north and being renamed Stilwell on May 12, 1896.

Flint was located where Hanging Dog Creek flows into Sallisaw Creek. Look for the grade crossing with S4660 Road, shown as RD 4760 by the Federal Railroad Administration. Most of the town followed the post office to Stilwell during the 1890s, and the location stopped being a train stop soon after. This area is now simply a mix of pasture and woods with no homes or other structures.

Not far north of here is 40-acre Sallisaw Creek Site 19 Reservoir, shown as Stilwell City Lake on many maps. It is one of 34 dams and lakes constructed in the Sallisaw Creek Watershed Project that are designed to reduce flooding and erosion. Reports state that the lake can be fished for bluegill, largemouth bass, and black bullhead.

Heading south, the railroad loops west to go around the west side of Fletcher and Dahlonegah mountains. Through this area, the railroad follows Sallisaw Creek, which it does heading southward for a number of miles.

265.7 LYONS – Lyons is an unincorporated community alongside Sallisaw Creek, located between Fletcher and Gitting Down Mountains. Its elevation is 838 feet, much lower than the almost 1100 feet at Stilwell. The community has never been large, nothing really more than a few businesses and houses. However, it was big enough for a post office to open on January 29, 1909.

Lyons, know as Lyons Switch for many years on the railroad, was the subject of a 1916 investigation by the Oklahoma Corporation Commission. The subject was whether the railroad should provide better services at Lyons. The report included some interesting details about the community.

> The Commission finds that Lyons Switch is located on the line of the Kansas City Southern Railway Company between Stilwell and Bunch and that it is about seven miles from either place; that at Stilwell and Bunch stations are maintained whereat freight is handled and tickets are sold; that Lyons is not incorporated; that there are two stores near the switch; that excepting said stores there is little to differentiate the place from the remainder of the surrounding country; that trains of the defendant are stopped at Lyons Switch for the accommodation of the community thereabout and that freight has been accepted and delivered at said place.
>
> It appears that the company has heretofore used a box car for a depot but has not kept the same in clean and comfortable condition, and that in forwarding freight shippers have been required to call either at Stilwell or Bunch for bill of lading.

The record shows that before matters, finally presented to the Commission, were first agitated E. S. Hill, for and on behalf of the defendant company, went to Lyons Switch and had a conference with George W. McLemore, et al., and that they came to a tentative understanding, whereby the company would establish a level about half way between the two stores at said Switch and cover the same with cinders, chatts or other suitable material and make the same smooth, and thereupon locate one box car to be used as a freight station and another box car to be used as a passenger depot. The company would light the passenger station at night and place a stove therein for use during cold weather and keep the same properly fired. The company would also stop its night passenger trains on flag.

The Commission after hearing and considering the case is of the opinion that it would not be justified in requiring the company to make an outlay of expenditures on the service at Lyons Switch much in excess of what, as above indicated, has been agreed upon.

Another investigation about the Lyons area took place in 1919. This one was conducted by the Interstate Commerce Commission in response to a train derailment. The report included a detailed description of the track structure. "The track in the vicinity of the point of accident is laid with 85-pound rails, 33 feet in length, on about 20 ties to the rail, the ties being 97 per cent. white oak and 3 per cent. walnut and pine. The rails are single spiked and tie plates are used on curves. Four-hole, 24-inch angle bars are used and are fully bolted, the bolts being in good condition and tight. The ballast consists of 2 to 5 inches of gravel on top of 8 inches of chat on a sub-grade of rock formation with 8 to 12 inches of ballast to shoulder outside ends of ties."

The Lyons post office closed on November 30, 1923. A listing in the 1925 *General Rating Book of The Shoe & Leather Mercantile Agency, Inc.* stated that Lyon's population was 25. It also stated that W. L. Halloway operated a small general store at Lyons. In 1936, Lyons had a dispatcher telephone and was a flag stop for *The Flying Crow* passenger train, with a platform on the west side of the tracks. There was a 120-car siding and an 8-car house track. The only change by the late 1950s was that Lyons was no longer a flag stop for passenger trains, and the siding was shown to have the capacity of 143 freight cars. The siding length was up to 153 cars in 1964, and the *Southern Belle* (No. 1) kept moving southbound as it passed at 3:06pm. Within a few decades, all tracks but the mainline were gone. Today, Lyons Switch is a census-designated place in Adair County that has a population of about 300.

268.9 CAVE SPRINGS – The 8620-foot siding at Cave Springs was built in the 1990s to split up more than 22 miles between the sidings at Stilwell and Marble City. The siding extends from Control Point North Cave Springs (Milepost 267.3) to Control Point South Cave Springs (Milepost 269.0).

This large sign clearly identifies the location of Control Point South Cave Springs.

At the South Cave Springs switch is the Cave Springs Public Schools complex. The school system was founded in 1926 by consolidating three kindergarten through eighth grade schools, and was originally called Union Grade School. One of the first structures used was built by the Works Progress Administration (WPA) from area stone using local labor. After World War II, it became the Cave Springs School District and added a high school to the system. With the change, the school mascot became the Hornets, using the colors green and white. The school system has about two hundred students, with about 90% being American Indian.

This view of the signals at Control Point South Cave Springs shows the Cave Springs Public Schools complex in the background.

Cave Springs is a part of the Cherokee Nation and the population was shown to be 74 in the 2020 census. There is a small cemetery in the community, known by some as the Scott Cemetery for the family with the earliest grave markers (Alex Scott – died September 6, 1869). While there is no clear explanation for the name of the community, there are a number of small springs that flow out of area caves.

Heading southward towards Bunch, the railroad is normally tree-lined, even as it passes through valley pastureland. At Milepost 270.8, the valley to the east is named Lead Mine Hollow.

271.8 BUNCH (BN) – Bunch was an early settlement, but it was not an organized community until the Kansas City, Pittsburg & Gulf built through the area. As stated in several sources, the railroad "made Bunch an outpost of the modern world in the middle of one of the most isolated and traditional areas of the Cherokee Nation." However, it couldn't have been too undeveloped as a post office opened at Bunch on May 26, 1886.

The name Bunch came from Rabbit Bunch, a member of the Cherokee Senate and then Assistant Principal Chief of the Cherokee Nation (West) from 1880 to 1887. Rabbit Bunch lived in this area during the 1880s and was buried in the Bunch Cemetery after his death. In an article about Rabbit Bunch in the November 2, 1899, issue of *The Fort Gibson Post*, he was called the "wisest and most far seeing full blood Cherokee that ever lived."

Rabbit Bunch, the source of the name for the community of Bunch, was buried in the Bunch Cemetery, located on the hill north of town.

In 1912, the KCS Immigration Department stated that Bunch was at an elevation of 772 feet and it had a population of 125. "An immense bed of marble is situated a few hundred yards from this station. There are in Bunch, two hardwood saw mills, a grist mill, Methodist church, public school and three mercantile firms. Lumber and live stock, about 300 car loads of the former and ten of the latter, poultry, eggs, corn, farm produce are the principal shipments from this point." Companies like the Bunch Produce Company, R. B. Choate & Son, and H. Johnson shipped products like strawberries, green beans, peaches, Irish potatoes, cantaloupes, Bermuda onions, radishes, and string beans. Today, Bunch is an unincorporated community in southwestern Adair County and consists of a scattering of homes and churches.

Bunch was in the news during the 1910s. For example, *The Excavating Engineer* (November 1915) reported that the List & Gifford Construction Company of Kansas City, Missouri, was "making good progress on their contract for the Kansas City Southern Railroad, here. The work is grade reduction, the raising of tracks and the widening of banks, the excavation amounting to about 250,000 cubic yards. They are using one 70-ton Bucyrus shovel, four locomotives and forty 12-yard Western dump cars. The work will be finished about February 1st."

In 1936, Bunch was actually an important railroad station. There was a 75-car siding, plus other tracks with a capacity of 33 freight cars. It was a flag stop for both the northbound and southbound passenger trains (*The Flying Crow*), and there was a mail crane. The depot was staffed for telegraph service 6:30am-3:30pm Monday-Saturday, and 6:30am-8:30am on

Heavener Sub Route Guide

Sundays and Holidays. Early each morning, Bunch became a very busy place. First, northbound Manifest Freight No. 56 would arrive at 6:35am. A few minutes later at 6:42am, *The Flying Crow* (No. 15) would arrive southbound. At 6:55am, southbound Manifest Freight No. 55 would pass through Bunch. Finally, at 7:10am, southbound Merchandise Special No. 77 would arrive at Bunch, and No. 56 could finally head north again.

By 1958, the agent was gone, replaced by a dispatcher telephone, and passenger trains didn't stop at Bunch. There was a 62-car siding and a house track with a capacity of 20 cars. Bunch was still a meeting point as northbound Manifest Freight No. 88 would meet southbound Manifest Freight No. 81 at 12:53pm. The siding was gone by 1964, but a 28-car house track remained. The southbound *Southern Belle* (No. 1) passed through Bunch at 3:13pm without stopping in 1964. The 1400-foot house track has survived into the 2020s.

272.1 SALLISAW CREEK BRIDGE – The railroad crosses Sallisaw Creek using a five-span deck plate girder bridge. The bridge also crosses a farm road under each end. The railroad once had a water tower here that was used to water steam locomotives.

Sallisaw Creek is almost fifty miles long, starting near Stilwell between Taylor and Doublehead mountains. It flows to the southwest and into the Arkansas River at Robert S. Kerr Lake. Sallisaw Creek forms a natural route through the mountains in this area, and the Kansas City, Pittsburg & Gulf built its line along the valley to obtain easier grades.

This bridge is cited in a survey of Adair, Cherokee and Sequoyah counties. "Bunch, 1¼ miles south of bridge over Sallisaw Creek; on northwest corner of south abutment – 736.515 feet of elevation."

The railroad crosses Sallisaw Creek using this five-span deck plate girder bridge.

The two north spans of the Sallisaw Creek Bridge at Milepost 272.1 have unique beveled ends to fit on the headwall and pier. This design generally indicates a span replacement, in this case with a heavier span as train weights increased.

Heavener Sub Route Guide

273.8 GREASY CREEK BRIDGE – Greasy Creek is one of the four main tributaries to Sallisaw Creek. It forms to the east up Starkiller Hollow near Welch Mountain. The stream is about ten miles long but is generally well-watered. Two lakes are along its course, Greasy Lake and a large reservoir just east of here.

The community of Greasy is located about halfway up the stream. There was a post office there 1920-1921. In 1922, *Bullinger's Postal and Shippers Guide for the United States and Canada* stated that the rail service for Greasy was at Bunch, Oklahoma. During the 1800s, Greasy was a tribal subdivision for the Cherokee Nation.

Like many bridges along the route, a number of deck plate girder spans set on concrete piers are used to cross the waterway. In this case, there are three deck plate girder spans.

The Greasey Creek Bridge is located two miles south of Bunch, Oklahoma, and consists of three deck plate girder spans.

275.5 COUNTY LINE – In the middle of a small patch of woods, the Kansas City Southern exits Adair County and enters Sequoyah County as trains head south.

Adair County is located in northeastern Oklahoma. Like most of Oklahoma, the land that creates the county was settled, sold, traded, and resettled. Numerous tribes lived and hunted in the area, and Creole trapper-traders visited during the late 1700s and early 1800s. In 1825 the Osage sold the land that is now Adair County to the United States, and various Cherokee groups began to arrive by 1825. At the Oklahoma Constitutional Convention in 1906, Adair County was created from the Going Snake and Flint districts of the Cherokee Nation. The name Adair came from a prominent Cherokee citizen, William Penn Adair, described as being influential in both white and Native American society. After three different elections, Stilwell became the county seat in 1910. The economy has historically been based upon farming (corn, wheat, oats, cotton, and cattle).

To the south is **Sequoyah County**. This started as the Skin Bayou District, and became the Sequoyah District of the Cherokee Nation in 1851, named for George Guess (Sequoyah), who invented a Cherokee alphabet. The area was one of the most popular access points into what later became Oklahoma as the federal offices at Fort Smith are just to the east in Arkansas. The county includes the Arkansas River valley, as well as the Ozark Plateau to the north and the Ouachita Mountains to the south. Many of the local names date to French explorers and the Cherokee who started to acquire the land through Lovely's Purchase in 1816. In 1829, the area officially became part of the Western Cherokee Nation. Sallisaw is the county seat and the county's population is about 45,000. The county features mostly farming, ranching and poultry, but tourism and industry also play an important role.

Heading south to near Marble City, the railroad is away from all roads. However, it does closely follow Sallisaw Creek most of the way.

276.2 CHOATE'S SPUR – This spur track was listed by the Oklahoma Corporation Commission about 1910. The Choate family has been in the area since the early 1800s, and there is a Choate Cemetery located southwest of Marble City.

277.6 WINDSOR – During the first part of the twentieth century, there was a siding here. It was listed as a shipping station in 1925, and there was a dispatcher telephone and 89-car siding here in 1936. Everything was gone by the 1950s.

280.1 DRY CREEK BRIDGE – This is another one of the four major tributaries of Sallisaw Creek. The stream forms to the northeast in the Brushy Mountains. Just upstream from here is Sallisaw Creek Site 28 Reservoir, another one of the 34 dams and lakes constructed in the Sallisaw Creek Watershed Project that are designed to reduce flooding and erosion.

281.1 MARBLE CITY – This area has a somewhat complex history as it once reported to Arkansas, and this was once part of Lovely County, Arkansas. A post office using the name Nicksville opened near here in 1828, but it was closed in 1829 when white settlers were removed so the Western Cherokees living in Arkansas could move here. About the same time, the Arkansas Territorial Legislature terminated its claim to the land, and the Dwight Mission took over

Nicksville as part of its evangelistic venture. With education and a basic store available, a small community grew up in the area. A series of names and post offices resulted with the Kidron post office established on September 17, 1835. On September 8, 1858, the post office moved to a new location and was renamed Marble Salt Works, which closed October 23, 1871.

A Kidron post office again opened on October 27, 1859, but it closed on January 22, 1869. As the area developed, the Kedron post office opened on May 26, 1886. The name Kidron/Kedron obviously has some relationship with the Dwight Mission. The name Kidron is a stream found in the Bible, referred to in II Samuel 15:23 and John 18:1. Kedron remained the name until surveyors and then construction workers for the Kansas City, Pittsburg & Gulf Railroad passed through the area. The town and post office moved next to the railroad and the post office was renamed Marble on January 16, 1895. To serve the local business, the railroad installed a station and a few side tracks. Change continued when the town and post office became Marble City on April 2, 1906.

The first census of the community (1910) showed that there were 342 residents. According to the KCS, the principal asset of the community was an enormous marble deposit, situated about three-quarters of a mile from town. Seventy carloads of dressed and polished marble were shipped out in 1911. The railroad also stated that there was "a hardwood saw mill, the Kelley Cotton Gin, with a capacity of forty bales per day and an annual output of 700 bales, a grist mill, printing office and a newspaper. There are also in town twelve mercantile firms, a bakery, hotel, church and good public schools." Other sources added a bank, "telephone exchange, five general stores, numerous livestock dealers, and many other retail outlets."

Several signs like this, carved out of the local stone, welcome visitors to Marble City, Oklahoma.

The Ozark Marble Company mined the stone at Marble City from 1906 until 1914. Some of the stone was used in the construction of Oklahoma City's Pioneer Telephone Building and at the Rice Institute (later Rice University) in Houston, Texas. The marble beds were reportedly 142 feet thick, but the challenge was moving the stone to the nearby railroad.

Starting during the 1910s, Watie Davault began to be a major factor in the business world of Marble City. He handled the sale of products from area farms, shipping out strawberries, radishes, cucumbers, peaches, and green beans to various markets. Davault was elected mayor in 1914, and held the position until 1961. A KCS report from 1923 stated that the population was about 300 and that the town had been incorporated in 1910. Other information was also provided. "The village has a high school, three churches, the E. Yocum Lumber Co. sawmill, sawing oak and rough wagon timbers, cotton gin and a great deposit of marble which has been developed, but is not worked at present. The adjacent country is hilly, rolling and level in places, and produces cotton, corn, poultry and eggs and commercial truck."

Despite the efforts to make Marble City a farm market, it was the nearby stone that kept the town busy, and the closed quarries during the 1920s had the town's population down to 168 in 1930. At that time, business was returning and there were two limestone companies and two sawmills operating. The area limestone became the focus of manufacturing. Starting in 1939, the Sinclair Lime Company was mining limestone near Marble City. The firm built a plant to convert limestone into quicklime in 1964. Three nearby kilns manufactured charcoal briquettes.

At this time, the population of Marble City was between 200 and 300, where it has remained to this day. However, mining of the local rock has continued. The Oklahoma Mining Commission reported in 2002 that Global Stone Saint Clair and Marble City Gravel were mining limestone. Today, the two mining companies are U.S. Lime Company – St. Clair and Polycor's Oklahoma Quarry. Although the two operations are close by, only U.S. Lime Company – St. Clair is rail served.

U.S. Lime Company – St. Clair is a part of United States Lime & Minerals, based in Dallas, Texas. The firm was founded in 1948 and incorporated on Oc-

Heavener Sub Route Guide

tober 4, 1950. The company has plants and facilities in Arkansas, Colorado, Louisiana, Oklahoma and Texas. The U.S. Lime Company – St. Clair facility includes an underground mine and a plant to produce lime, pulverized limestone, and quicklime on two rotary kilns. The company states that "annual production capacity of pulverized limestone is 150 thousand tons and the plant is serviced by the KCS railroad."

Marble City is still a small agricultural and industrial center with a post office, a few scattered businesses, and a number of houses. The Dwight Mission Camp and Conference Center still uses the site and buildings of the earlier Dwight Mission (three miles to the southwest), which is listed on the National Register of Historic Places. The stone two-story Citizens State Bank building on the northwest corner of Main Street and Seminole Avenue is also on the National Register.

South of Dwight and out of sight of the tracks is the Dwight Mission, an early educational and religious center in Indian Territory.

Located several blocks to the east of the Heavener Subdivision is the former Citizens State Bank Building, listed on the National Register of Historic Places.

The Railroad at Marble City

There are actually two parts of the railroad at Marble City – the tracks near downtown and the tracks near the marble and limestone quarries. The tracks downtown include the mainline of KCS, as well as a number of storage tracks and a siding.

For the first decade after the railroad was built, a boxcar served as the depot at Marble City. After several years of complaints and petitions, the Oklahoma Corporation Commission held a hearing on July 27, 1908, about the need for an improved station. The hearing determined that Marble City was incorporated and that there were "four hundred inhabitants, fourteen business houses and saw mills, and a marble quarry and other industries." An agreement was reached where an additional boxcar would be installed as a waiting room until a new station building opened by early October 1909.

This view looking south from the Seminole Avenue grade crossing shows the tracks at Marble City, Oklahoma. From left to right is the KCS mainline, Marble City siding, and the Marble City Storage Track.

During the first few decades, the depot staffing depended upon the marble and limestone business. In 1936, there was no agent and the business was handled from Sallisaw. There was a mail crane to allow passenger trains to pick up mail from the Marble City post office. The railroad had an 88-car siding as well as other tracks with a total capacity of 18 cars. An interesting detail in the railroad's schedule was that *The Flying Crow* (southbound No. 15) had Marble City as a flag stop at 6:58am, but it was a scheduled stop for northbound No. 16 at 11:23am.

By 1958, the railroad had an agent handling telegraph services 8am-5pm Tuesday through Saturday. At that time, the station used the code "MR" and also had a dispatcher telephone. The timetable that year had interesting instructions for passenger service at Marble City.

> *Nos. 15 and 16 will stop on flag at Bunch, Marble City and Panama for revenue passengers to or from Siloam or beyond and for revenue passengers to or from Heavener or beyond.*

The siding had been extended to 139 car lengths by 1958, and the industry tracks were shown to be long enough to handle 49 freight cars. In 1964, the siding was shown to be 165 cars long. The mail crane was still in use, and train Nos. 15 and 16 had Marble City as a conditional flag stop. *Southern Belle* No. 1 passed the depot southbound at 3:24pm without stopping. The only thing that really changed by 1970 was the end of the passenger service. Today, the Marble City siding (Mileposts 280.5 - 282.2) is shown to be 8333 feet long. There is also the 2403-foot Marble City Storage Track (Mileposts 280.7 - 281.3).

The second set of tracks at Marble City had several different names over the years, but they left the KCS mainline south of town, crossed Sallisaw Creek, and then headed north to the various mines and quarries. The end of the line was near the appropriately named Quarry Mountain.

281.4 MARBLE CITY QUARRY SPUR – This track has had a number of different names over the years, including the Sinclair Lime Spur during the 1940s and 1950s, the Marble City Quarry Spur 1950s-1980s, and simply Quarry Spur (today). For years, the track was shown to have a capacity of 189 cars, and today 6600 feet.

The spur track heads northwest off of the Marble City siding just south of the south switch of the Marble City Storage Track. The track crosses Seminole Avenue and then Sallisaw Creek. The primary span of the bridge is a pin-connected, seven-panel Parker through truss which originally crossed the Poteau River at Fort Smith, Arkansas. The span was moved here when the Fort Smith route was abandoned.

U.S. Lime actually switches their plant at Marble City, and operates the Quarry Spur. These carloads of crushed lime have been moved to the KCS switch for pickup.

The Quarry Spur at Marble City crosses Sallisaw Creek using an old through truss span that once crossed the Poteau River at Fort Smith. The bridge still features a tell-tale, easily photographed from local roads.

This U.S. Lime plant is the reason that the Marble City Quarry Spur still exists.

Heavener Sub Route Guide

U.S. Lime operates the Marble City Quarry Spur using several old diesel locomotives. The locomotive with TXNW 107 markings is former Texas North Western Railway Company 107, and originally Pennsylvania Railroad 9369. It was built during June 1950 by EMD as an SW7 diesel locomotive.

The tracks then come alongside N4610 Road, which it crosses before reaching the U.S. Lime Company – St. Clair facility. A spur track curves west and under the loader, while the Quarry Spur continues north, providing a short storage track and switching lead.

For those following the railroad, N4610 Road and Bunch Road connect Bunch and Marble City.

282.9 SALLISAW CREEK BRIDGE – With the railroad closely following the winding and curving Sallisaw Creek, it is no surprise that the railroad crosses the stream several times. In the middle of thick woods just northeast of the old Dwight Mission, this Pratt through truss span with a through plate girder span off each end is used to cross the stream.

Immediately north of the bridge, the railroad is squeezed between Sallisaw Creek, to the west, and Andes Mountain, to the east. Andes Mountain is part of the higher ground to the east that forces the railroad to use the valley of Sallisaw Creek.

284.8 SALLISAW CREEK BRIDGE – This is a Pratt through truss span with a deck plate girder span off each end. Some reports state that it dates from 1906.

285.0 BRUSHY CREEK BRIDGE – The railroad passes over Brushy Creek, one of the four large tributaries of Sallisaw Creek. The stream starts in the Brushy Mountains north of Brushy, Oklahoma. Not far upstream from here is the Brushy Lake Reservoir (Sallisaw Creek Site 29 Reservoir). On its eastern shore is the Brush Lake State Park with RV campsites, picnic pavilions, boat dock, and other facilities.

To the west of the tracks is Hastings Mountain with an elevation of 742 feet. This low mountain forces Sallisaw Creek and the railroad to curve to the southeast.

286.5 BRUSHY – By 1910, there was a siding located near here simply known as Passing Track. Later, the siding took the name of Brushy. Located at the grade crossing with E1040 Road, the railroad station of Brushy was many miles from the community of Brushy over on today's U.S. Highway 59. The railroad Brushy was the location of an 88-car siding during the 1930s, shown as 62 cars in 1958. There was also a dispatcher telephone here that could be used by train crews and track workers. Brushy was a busy place at 4:30am in 1958 as passenger train No. 15 met manifest freight No. 42 here daily.

The siding at Brushy didn't last much longer as in 1961, KCS ordered and starting installing 69 miles of CTC signals between Gentry, Arkansas, and Sallisaw, Oklahoma. The equipment came from the General Railway Signal Company, and a control machine at Heavener, Oklahoma, was expanded to handle the additional miles. The CTC signals from Heavener to Sallisaw had been installed in 1960. The installation of CTC signaling allowed train dispatchers to better schedule train movements. At the same time, the railroad was operating longer trains, so the company lengthened some sidings and eliminated others, and Bushy was one of those that was removed.

Just west of the tracks at Brushy is the McCoy Cemetery. West of here at Sallisaw Creek is McCoy Ford. The E1040 Road also carries the name McCoy Ford Road. McCoy Ford was one of several places where survivors of the Trail of Tears gathered to start claiming property for their homes. McCoy was a somewhat common name among the Cherokee, Chickasaw, Choctaw, Creek, and Seminole.

Heading south, the railroad curves its way to Sallisaw. While much of this area is still woods and pasture, the growth of the area can be seen by the number of new houses that are being built near the railroad. To the west of the tracks at Milepost 288 is Badger Mountain, standing about 880 feet above sea level, almost 300 feet above the railroad.

The Brushy Derailment

On January 5, 1932, it was "dark, misty and raining at the time of the accident, which occurred about 5.30 a.m." The accident occurred along the bluffs "at a point approximately 2,400 feet north of the north switch of the passing track at Brushy." At this location, where the railroad is squeezed between Sallisaw Creek and the hillside, about sixty tons of rock fell from more than thirty feet up on the bluff. This created a pile of rock about forty feet wide and five feet thick on the tracks. When the train hit the rock slide, the steam locomotive and its tender, plus the first two cars and the forward truck of the third car, all derailed. They fell towards Sallisaw Creek, resulting "in the death of 1 employee and the injury of 10 passengers, 1 baggageman and express messenger, 2 mail clerks, and 1 employee." The accident led to a thorough investigation by the Bureau of Safety of the Interstate Commerce Commission (ICC), which determined that there was no previous record of rock slides at this location.

The train involved was northbound passenger train No. 16, which "consisted of 1 combination mail and baggage car, 2 coaches, and 2 Pullman sleeping cars, in the order named, hauled by engine 809." The combine and the first Pullman car were of all-steel construction, while the remainder were of steel-underframe construction. The locomotive was built by Alco-Schenectady in 1919 as a 4-6-2, and was one of a series that were assigned to *The Flying Crow* passenger trains. These steam locomotives featured a tuned air horn that emitted a crow's caw, gold trim, special lettering, and *The Flying Crow* emblem on the tender. KCS #809 was repaired after this accident, and finally scrapped in April 1952.

The report also provided some details about the track structure at the time. "The grade for northbound trains is 0.18 per cent ascending. The track is laid with 85-pound rails, 33 feet in length, with an average of about 20 treated hardwood ties to the rail-length, single-spiked, fully tie-plated, and ballasted with chatts and gravel to a depth of about 12 inches; six rail anchors per rail-length are used." Today, the railroad uses heavy welded rail and lots of stone ballast. The location of the derailment, described by the ICC as a bluff 1600 feet long with a maximum height of about 155 feet, is basically inaccessible with wooded hills to the east and Sallisaw Creek and ranches to the west.

287.8 PASSING SPUR – This location was listed in 1908 by the Oklahoma Corporation Commission and was shown to be 3.3 miles north of Sallisaw.

289.4 OKLAHOMA CREOSOTING COMPANY – While the track was shown as the Oklahoma Creosoting Company in KCS timetables, other documents showed it to be the Creosoting Company Spur. Located to the west of the Kansas City Southern and south of West Redwood Avenue, this facility opened in September 1946 to treat poles and piles with straight creosote, or a creosote and petroleum solution. The initial owner and operator was the Oklahoma Creosoting Company, which installed an 8-foot diameter by 75-foot-long cylinder to do the timber treatment. A growth in the business led to an 8-foot diameter by 110-foot-long cylinder being installed in 1956.

Soon after the plant was enlarged, it was acquired by the Southwest Wood Preserving Company, which expanded the older treatment cylinder to 110 feet long in 1958. Crown Zellerbach Corporation acquired the plant in 1976 and ended creosoting, replacing it with pentachlorophenol. In 1984, production ceased at the plant and clean-up began. In 1987, Crown Zellerbach became Cavenham Forest Industries, which completed the work of closing the plant.

Nothing remains of the former Oklahoma Creosoting Company plant at Sallisaw except for a few foundations and lots of treated dirt.

For the Kansas City Southern, tracks came in from the north and then into the various buildings of the treatment facility. No capacity was ever provided; timetables simply listed the switch as a connection to the tracks of the creosoting company.

290.4 UNION PACIFIC CROSSING – This is a crossing and junction with Union Pacific Railroad (UP RRX) that is currently known as Control Point North Sallisaw. It was previously known as Mo. Pac. Crossing. In 1936, the crossing was shown by KCS as being interlocked and as a connection. By 1958, the crossing was shown to be staffed continuously with the telegraph code of "AW". It was still shown as a connection. The CTC signals installed in 1961 ended the need for a staffed interlocking, and it was automated. The interchange track was once in the northeast quadrant, but is now in the southwest corner of the diamond.

The initial planning for the Union Pacific route took place using the Kansas & Arkansas Valley Railway (K&AV), incorporated in Arkansas on November 27, 1885. The owners of the K&AV were the owners of the existing Little Rock & Fort Smith and the Little Rock, Mississippi River & Texas. The initial plan of the new railroad was to connect lines in Kansas with those in Arkansas, creating a route to move products to and from the Southwest. In 1886, the United States Congress held hearings and then approved a railroad "from Fort Smith, in the State of Arkansas, across a small portion of the reservation belonging to the Choctaws, and a considerable distance through that belonging to the Cherokees, in a northwesterly direction to the southern line of Kansas, at or near Arkansas City, with a branch designed to make connection with existing railroads at or near Coffeyville, in the State of Kansas."

The area around Union Pacific Crossing is also Control Point North Sallisaw. In April 2022, a number of track gangs were working in the area, requiring manual operation of the crossing signals. The track closest to the photographer is the interchange track between the KCS and Union Pacific railroads.

A KCS tamper was heading north through the Control Point North Sallisaw area during April 2022. Below the tamper is an old concrete culvert, and several signal foundations can also be found nearby. All of these show the many changes that have happened along the Heavener Subdivision.

Heavener Sub Route Guide

Construction of the K&AV began in 1887, and the company's contractor began laying track west of Lee's Creek near Van Buren, Arkansas. They were expected to complete the line "to Fort Gibson, Indian Territory by October 1, 1887," according to the *Daily Arkansas Gazette*. Passenger trains began operating from Van Buren to Wagoner in Indian Territory on August 13, 1888. The railroad was completed to Coffeyville, Kansas, by November 21, 1889, and it was leased to the Little Rock & Fort Smith for fifty years on January 1, 1890. The consolidation of the railroads continued when the Kansas & Arkansas Valley was acquired and merged into the St. Louis, Iron Mountain & Southern on September 1, 1909. This merger involved a number of railroads, all of which were owned or leased by the Iron Mountain and its subsidiaries. On February 11, 1910, the Iron Mountain began fully operating the K&AV.

The Iron Mountain entered receivership on August 19, 1915, and was sold to its creditors at foreclosure on February 21, 1917. Then, combined with The Missouri Pacific Railway Company, which had been created in 1909, the two railroads merged to create the Missouri Pacific Railroad Company on May 12, 1917. For years, the trackage from Van Buren, through Sallisaw, and on to Coffeyville operated as the Wagoner Subdivision. On January 8, 1980, the Union Pacific Corporation announced an agreement to buy the Missouri Pacific Railroad. Approval was finally received on September 13, 1982, after a series of hearings and lawsuits. It finally took a Supreme Court ruling to allow the merger on December 22, 1982. A unique detail not known by many was that the Missouri Pacific had a number of outstanding bonds that prevented a full merger of the two companies. The bonds were finally closed during the mid-1990s, and the merger became final on January 1, 1997. Union Pacific still uses the name Wagoner for this subdivision. The brick Missouri Pacific station still stands in downtown Sallisaw and is used as a library.

The former Missouri Pacific depot still stands in downtown Sallisaw, Oklahoma, now used as a library.

Not far south of the diamond/Control Point North Sallisaw, the railroad bridges over U.S. Highway 64. During the Great Depression, the Works Progress Administration funded the construction of a steel span to eliminate the grade crossing. At the time, U.S. Highway 64 was a major highway, and it still connects northeast Arizona with Nags Head, North Carolina, a total of 2326 miles.

Heavener Sub Route Guide

The KCS bridge over U.S. Highway 64 at Sallisaw was originally built during the early 1930s as part of a series of projects funded by the Works Progress Administration to eliminate busy railroad-highway grade crossings.

291.1 SALLISAW (WA) – The area that became Sallisaw started out as a trail on the hills above the Arkansas floodplain, and later was a steamboat landing. Several small towns in the region have claimed to be the source, but the name apparently came from the French word salaison, which means "salt meat" or "salt provisions." The term was recorded as early as 1819 when English naturalist Thomas Nuttall wrote about his travels across the territory and used the name "Salaiseau."

By the 1840s, the name Sallisaw was being used for a steamboat landing on the Arkansas River, as well as a nearby stream. The name also appeared in different Civil War reports about battles and troop movements in the Indian Territory. After the war, a settlement grew up in the area, and a post office opened in 1878 using the name Childer's Station. During the late 1880s, Cherokee Will Watie Wheeler and early white settler Argyle Quesenbury laid out an organized one-half mile square town. On December 8, 1888, the Childer's Station post office changed its name to Sallisaw. At the same time, a Sallisaw post office (1873-1888) in Adair County to the north changed its name to Mays (1888-1896), and then closed before the turn of the century.

While Wheeler and Quesenbury sold lots, they never incorporated the town, which soon became known as a Cherokee town and trading center. In 1888, the Kansas & Arkansas Valley Railway built through the town on its way to Coffeyville. This was followed by the Kansas City, Pittsburg & Gulf Railroad in 1895-1896. At the time, the village was a significant community thanks to the help of Wheeler, who had started up a series of businesses including a cotton gin, sawmill, gristmill, lumberyard, and a coffin shop (today's Wheeler Funeral Home). Other businesses in Sallisaw at the time included a bank, drug store, grocery, and several mercantile and general stores.

Sallisaw was incorporated in 1898, and the population was recorded as being 965 in the 1900 census. It was the seat of Sequoyah District, and made the county seat of Sequoyah County when Oklahoma was organized as a state. The town grew quickly and the population reached 2479 by the time of the 1910 census. In 1912, Kansas City Southern promoted the town through its Immigration Department, which wrote the following about the community.

Heavener Sub Route Guide

> This is the county seat of Sequoyah County, Okla., and has a population of about 4,400 people. It was platted about thirteen years ago at the junction of the Kansas City Southern and Missouri Pacific Railways. Its location is 291 miles south of Kansas City, Mo. Sallisaw has made a steady growth from year to year, until the tribal lands were allotted to the individual members of the tribes, when a more rapid growth became possible. In the last three or four years the growth has been very rapid. There are in Sallisaw about seventy-five mercantile establishments, five hotels, four restaurants, five cotton gins, one cottonseed oil mill and three prosperous banks. It has stores in which stocks of $25,000 to $40,000 are carried and a business of $125,000 is annually transacted. A majority of the leading stores do a business of $40,000 to $80,000 a year. It is a modern little city, having a water works system, electric light plant, telephone service, well graded streets and paved sidewalks, etc., and is expanding in all directions. The two trunk lines of railroad passing through Sallisaw transport annually from 12,000 to 15,000 bales of cotton.

Cotton was important to Sallisaw during the early 1900s, and other crops soon joined it. Firms like McDonald & Matthews and the Truck Growers Association shipped peaches, spinach, green beans, strawberries, cabbage, Irish potatoes, sweet potatoes, and Bermuda onions. As the economy moved away from cotton, the population dropped through the early 1930s. Other industries like poultry, lumber, coal and petroleum products started to play a role in the community. The population bottomed out with 1785 residents in 1930. Soon after, the *Sequoyah County Times* started publishing under the ownership of the Wheeler and Mayo families. It is still published by the Mayo family. Seven auto-related businesses, a bakery, two blacksmiths, a bottler, four gins, several mills, and two printing companies supported the town during the Great Depression. However, John Steinbeck's *The Grapes of Wrath* hurt the reputation of Sallisaw when he used the town as the Dust Bowl community where the fictional Joad family suffered and then headed west for California. The problem was that Sallisaw was not in the Dust Bowl and many locals were insulted by the shiftlessness of Oklahoma residents that Steinbeck played up. Another Great Depression event at Sallisaw was the funeral of local resident and gangster Charles Arthur "Pretty Boy" Floyd. Floyd grew up in the area and an estimated twenty thousand to forty thousand people attended his funeral on October 28, 1934. Floyd had been shot and killed at East Liverpool, Ohio, on October 22, 1934. His body was shipped back home by rail, moving from Kansas City to Sallisaw on the Kansas City Southern.

Canning, furniture manufacturing, and a few other industries developed during World War II, and the population reached 2885 in 1950. Horse racing also supported Sallisaw, with Blue Ribbon Downs and a number of local horse training facilities. In 2003, the Choctaw Nation bought Blue Ribbon Downs and eventually added a casino, but

Heavener Sub Route Guide

closed the horse track in 2010. During the last few decades, Sallisaw has steadily grown, being on the edge of the booming Fort Smith and North Arkansas area. Its population was 8439 in the 2020 census, and the town is the home of many of the typical retail and restaurant chains, and a number of locally-based businesses.

The importance of the Kansas Southern Railroad to Sallisaw is demonstrated by this sign for Port Arthur Avenue.

Sallisaw and Kansas City Southern

The Kansas City, Pittsburg & Gulf arrived at Sallisaw by January 31, 1896. Located at an elevation of 526.051 feet (benchmark on the south end of the station platform), the railroad was finishing its descent from the Ozark Mountains down to the Arkansas River. The town was a significant cotton shipping point, and fruits and vegetables also moved from here. Later, lumber and various timber products joined the movement. The volumes were never significant enough to justify much more than a small rail yard, several industrial tracks, and a passenger and freight depot. A coal chute was located in the center of the tracks between Maple and Ash streets, north of the station, and a water tower was to the south. A benchmark on the station showed that the elevation was 533 feet. By the south switch, it was 517 feet.

On May 18, 1914, the Oklahoma Corporation Commission ordered Kansas City Southern to build a new railroad station because the "present one is too old, too small and unsanitary, and not up to the present requirements in many other ways." The order required that the station open on or before January 1, 1915, a date that was almost met. Just a few years earlier, the Commission had ordered the St. Louis, Iron Mountain & Southern to also build a new station at Sallisaw.

In 1936, Sallisaw had a few KCS train facilities like oil, coal and water. There were two sidings: the north siding had a 56-car capacity while the south siding could hold 67 cars. Other tracks had a total capacity of 82 cars. The stucco station was staffed and provided telegraph service 7am-4pm daily using the office call of "WA". A mail crane stood south of the depot at Milepost 291.3.

A National Railroad Adjustment Board report dated December 17, 1958, provided a description of Sallisaw in 1952. It stated that there "is no Yard Limit Board at Sallisaw, there is no switching limits, as there is no yard there, the tracks at Sallisaw consists of a passing track with two or three tracks breaking off the passing track. The Sallisaw Station is located at mile post 291.2, the north passing track switch is at mile post 290 plus 1906.3 feet, the Missouri Pacific connection is at mile post 290 plus 548.6 feet and the Sinclair Lime Spur is at mile post 290 plus 411.2 feet, both the Missouri Pacific connection and the Sinclair Lime Spur is some little distance north of the passing track switch." It also stated that there were two connections with the Missouri Pacific near the diamond at Sallisaw.

In 1958, Sallisaw was a scheduled stop for all passenger trains. At the time, the station used the office call "CK" and was staffed 8am-5pm daily. The siding was shown to be 118 cars long, and there were other tracks with a capacity of 169 cars. A dispatcher telephone, mail crane, and track scale were also located here. Little changed by 1964 when the southbound *Southern Belle* (No. 1) was scheduled to stop at Sallisaw at 3:40pm. The only noteworthy change by 1970 was the end of all passenger service. This allowed the removal of the mail crane, and the agent's hours were changed to 8:30am-5:30pm.

In 1987, the KCS timetable made things look more barren at Sallisaw. The siding was shown to be 5880 feet, or 107 cars, long. It also listed a yard and a house track at Milepost 291.2. The station was shown to be a train register for some crews. During this time, a TOFC (trailer-on-flat-car) facility was located here to handle trailer traffic to and from Fort Smith. The 2002 timetable showed that the siding had been turned into a storage track (Mileposts 290.4-291.6). By 2014, even the storage track was gone from the timetable, which showed a Union Pacific interchange track at Milepost 291.0 and General Orders/Circulars at a railroad office.

In 1990, a cut of piggyback cars await pickup at Sallisaw, Oklahoma. This facility was designed to serve the manufacturing business at nearby Fort Smith, Arkansas.

On September 30, 2003, KCS 4301 was photographed switching the Sallisaw piggyback yard. The piggyback yard, located on the west side of the mainline where track materials are now stored, has been removed and little indicates that it ever existed except photos like this.

Heavener Sub Route Guide

The former Sallisaw piggyback yard is now used to store company materials, like these signals in June 2021.

In April 2022, a KCS trailer was located at the former piggyback yard in Sallisaw, used to store supplies for area track and signal gangs.

A quick drive around the former yard area shows how little remains. To the north is the Chickasaw Avenue grade crossing. On the east side is Port Arthur Avenue (once North Railroad), while on the west side is Port Arthur Place (once South Railroad), which has a grade crossing at the south end of the yard area. The foundation of the KCS station can still be found on the east side of the tracks at Main Street. A few modular office buildings are located on the property for maintenance gangs and train crews. Lots of track materials are also located here.

Remains of the Sallisaw station still remain, but they are located behind fencing.

Heavener Sub Route Guide

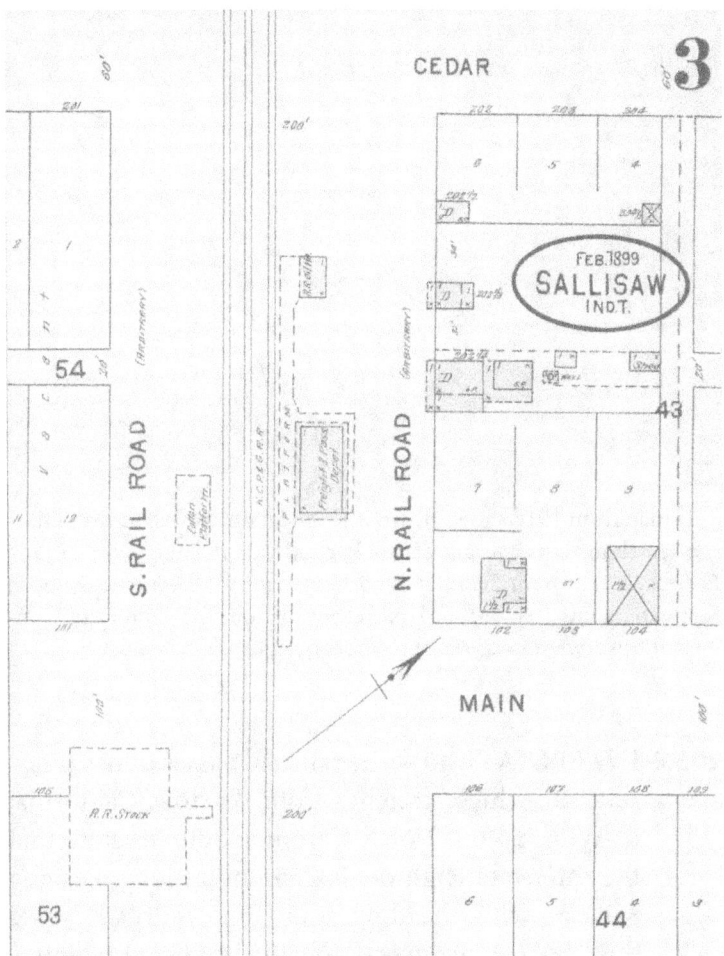

This Sanborn map from 1899 shows the area around the Kansas City, Pittsburg & Gulf depot at Sallisaw, Oklahoma. *Sanborn Fire Insurance Map from Sallisaw, Sequoyah County, Oklahoma.* Sanborn Map Company, Feb, 1899. Map. Retrieved from the Library of Congress, https://www.loc.gov/item/sanborn07240_002/.

The Heavener Sub: History Through the Miles

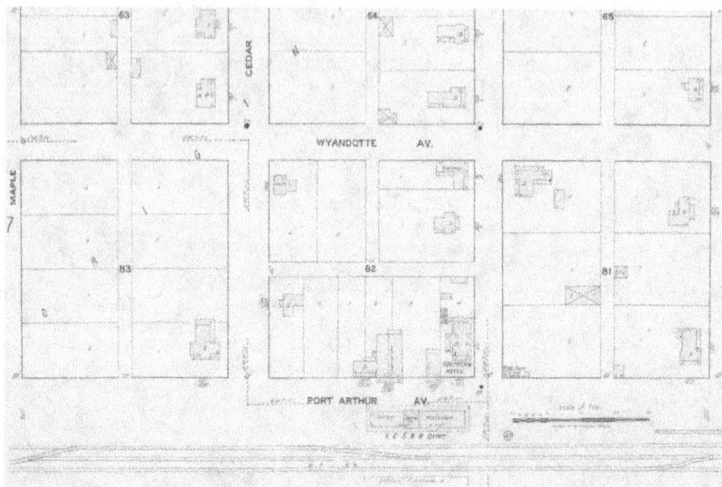

This map from 1918 shows the new KCS station, as well as the Southern Hotel and a restaurant across Port Arthur Avenue. *Sanborn Fire Insurance Map from Sallisaw, Sequoyah County, Oklahoma.* Sanborn Map Company, Dec 1918. Map. Retrieved from the Library of Congress, https://www.loc.gov/item/sanborn07240_007/.

292.0 INTERSTATE 40 – The railroad passes under Interstate 40, which stretches from Barstow, California, to Wilmington, North Carolina. Sources state that the Interstate Highway is 2555 miles long. Leaving Sallisaw while heading south, the railroad passes the closed golf course of the Shadow Creek Country Club, crosses Little Sallisaw Creek, and then passes the baseball fields of the Sallisaw Sports Complex.

292.7 LITTLE SALLISAW CREEK – Little Sallisaw Creek is the last of the four large tributaries of Sallisaw Creek. The creek starts just east of Brushy, Oklahoma, not far from the source of Brushy Creek. From there, Little Sallisaw Creek flows to the southwest and merges into Sallisaw Creek and the Arkansas River at Robert S. Kerr Lake.

Heavener Sub Route Guide

The Kansas City Southern bridge consists of a Pratt through truss span, with shorter deck girder spans off each end.

This bridge is used to cross Little Sallisaw Creek south of Sallisaw, Oklahoma.

297.0 HICKORYNUT RIDGE – This was not a railroad station, but the ridge had a major impact on the construction of the Kansas City, Pittsburg & Gulf. Hickorynut Ridge, as well as Wildhorse Mountain to the north, and Pine Mountain to the south, forced the railroad to turn to the southeast at Sallisaw. The same challenge forced Interstate 40, and earlier the Kansas & Arkansas Valley Railway (Union Pacific), to use this winding valley some distance north of the Arkansas River.

About Milepost 297, the KCS turns to the south and squeezes between Hickorynut Ridge to the west and Krumpe Mountain to the east. Not far south of this narrow valley, the railroad enters Gans.

299.2 GANS – Most histories of the area state that Gans began as a "dispersed settlement in the Sequoyah District of the Cherokee Nation in Indian Territory." One of the most common names for the community was Jack Town. During the late 1800s, Cherokee brothers Charlie, Swimmer, and Tom Gann settled in the area and took an active role in the community, which began to use their name. A post office using the name Gann was established on March 21, 1896, just as the Kansas City, Pittsburg & Gulf Railroad built through the community.

This railroad station sign marks the location of Gans.

The history of the community states that the railroad already had a Gann on the line, and requested that it be changed to Gans. The community approved the change and the post office followed suit on September 8, 1899. The first census, done the next year, reported a population of 136. In 1902, the town incorporated in the Cherokee Nation. The area was already used for farming, and the railroad allowed a wide range of products to be shipped to market.

Among the fruit and vegetables found in the KCS records, strawberries, blackberries, grapes, peaches, watermelons, cantaloupes, Irish potatoes, green peas, green beans, cucumbers, radishes, turnips, and spinach were all routinely shipped from Gans. Cattle, hogs and cotton were also grown locally and shipped to market.

In 1910, Gans hit its peak of population with 351 residents. At the time, the town had a bank, two cotton gins, a sawmill, six general stores, three doctors, two drug stores, two blacksmiths, a restaurant, three churches, and a short-lived newspaper named *The Gans Reporter*. The 1920s were both good and bad for Gans as gas and oil well drilling began in the area, but the bank moved to nearby Sallisaw and the population dropped to 204 in the 1930 census. With the Great Depression underway, Gans lost its incorporation in 1933.

In 1953, Gans reincorporated, and by 1960 it had a population of 234. The town has grown and shrunk ever since, with the population staying between 200 and 350. Gans still has a post office as well as its Gans School District, which serves more than 300 kindergarten through high school students. Probably the most famous student is Bryant "Big Country" Reeves, a seven-foot player for the National Basketball Association's Vancouver Grizzlies (1995-2001). When Reeves retired from basketball and returned home, he donated a new city hall to Gans.

NBA basketball player Bryant "Big Country" Reeves is from Gans, as shown by this highway sign.

Gans was never a major railroad station, but there has always been a siding here. In 1909, there was an Oklahoma Corporation Commission hearing about the need for commercial telegraph service through the railroad at Gans. It was determined that at the time the telegraph office was open during the cotton season and closed when business dropped off and that commercial telegraph service amounted to about 50 cents of revenue per month. Additionally, Gans was about seven miles north of Redland and eight miles south of Sallisaw, which were the nearest telegraph stations. The Commission determined that reasonable service could not "be rendered the people at Gans and vicinity without the maintenance of a telegraph operator in the conduct of its business."

Heavener Sub Route Guide

Gans is a railroad town created when what became the Heavener Subdivision was built. This street sign shows that even a local road is named after the railroad.

In 1936, the siding at Gans was 88 cars long, and there were other tracks with a capacity of 22 cars. The station was not staffed, there was a small platform on the east side of the mainline, and there was a mail crane and a dispatcher telephone. At the time, Gans was a flag stop for the daily passenger trains.

By the late 1950s, passenger trains no longer stopped. A dispatcher telephone was available for train crews as they used the 73-car siding. The house track was down to 8 car lengths. As CTC signaling was installed in 1960, many sidings were extended. The one at Gans was extended to 164 car lengths. In 1964, the *Southern Belle* passed southbound (No. 1) at 3:49pm. In 1987, the siding was shown to be 148 cars long, and then 8144 feet long in 2014 (Control Point North Gans at Milepost 298.4 and Control Point South Gans at Milepost 300.1). The siding and the short team track are both on the west side of the mainline.

Heading south towards Foremans, the railroad is straight and uses a series of fills and cuts to maintain a relatively steady downhill grade. In 1913, there were several reports in *The Contractor* that stated that KCS would build a new line from Gans to the Iron Mountain at Cherokee Junction, Oklahoma. The purpose of the new line would be to provide a new route into Fort Smith, Arkansas.

Gans Line Diversion

In 1911, KCS announced that forty-one per cent of the Kansas City Southern was on a grade of 0.5% to 1% and that there were plans "to put the entire remainder of the road on practically this same basis, except in the mountain district." There were plans to sell $21 million dollars in bonds to pay for the work. While there were great plans to build a better route through parts of Arkansas and Oklahoma, in reality only a few line diversions and work to reduce the grades on several hills actually took place. One of these line diversions took place at Gans, creating two miles of straighter and flatter track. While much of this was shown in accounting reports, little general publicity ever took place about the work.

During 1911, the Burke & Joseph Contracting Company had several contracts with KCS, including at Gans, Oklahoma. The construction of the new 2-mile-long grade through the east side of Gans started where the railroad curves to the southeast at the southwest corner of Krumpe Mountain. From here, the railroad once headed straight to the west side of Gans. This grade is now used as farm roads, and then as D4689 Road north of town. Through Gans, much of the grade is now used by KCS Road. Heading to the south, the grade is now D1124 Road, also known as Old Dump Road. Dump is an old term for a fill or grade created by dumping dirt to build it up. The south end of the railroad realignment can be found where the county road turns south and away from the current Kansas City Southern tracks. This work allows KCS enthusiasts to actually drive a part of the original Kansas City, Pittsburg & Gulf.

The very north end of the old grade near Gans, Oklahoma, passes through a series of pastures.

Heading into Gans, the old grade becomes KCS Road.

South of Gans near current Milepost 300.3 is an old stone culvert that passes under the original grade. This culvert allows water to flow into nearby Onion Creek from the hills to the northwest.

Heavener Sub Route Guide

303.7 FOREMANS – Foreman, Foremans, or Foreman's Spur, was an early railroad stop that didn't last much later than World War II. The community was named for Zachariah "Zack" Foreman, a local merchant, and a post office opened on October 31, 1898. Zach Foreman had started his life as a slave, and like all slaves of the various tribes in Indian Territory, was given tribal rights after the Civil War. When tribal lands were allocated, Foreman claimed almost three thousand acres in the area and began farming and raising cattle. A town grew here using his name. His family was large and he was considered to be a rather wealthy gentleman. His son, Zach Foreman, Jr., played for the famous Kansas City Monarchs of the Negro League. Zach, Jr., was killed at a poker game in Foreman in 1921, but his cousin Sylvester Foreman played catcher for the Monarchs for another decade.

A mail crane lasted at Foremans until August 31, 1936, when the post office closed. The railroad never had a station or siding here, but Foreman, considered to be a "Black Cherokee" town, was a passenger train flag stop during the first part of the century. What remains of Foreman is located at the grade crossing with E1155 Road and along S4710 Road. In total, there is a church and about a dozen scattered houses.

Little remains at Foremans except a few houses, a church, and a new building for the Redland Fire Department.

306.4 REDLAND – This area has had the name Redland Bottoms since the time of the first explorers, named for the area's red soil. Much of the area is floodplain and has developed into rich bottom lands which were farmed by Native Americans, early settlers, and even today. Fishing and hunting were also good, and the Arkansas River and area streams provided multiple transportation routes.

The high grounds on the north shore of the Arkansas River allowed a settlement to form that was above the annual floods, and on May 17, 1883, the Redland post office opened. Redland was considered to be a ginning center due to the growth of cotton in the area, plus a trading center due to the presence of several stores opened by Alfred Foyil. Things changed some as the KCP&G built through the area. Redland became a base for railroad construction crews building a bridge across the river, and it was a telegraph station from the start.

In 1912, the Kansas City Southern stated that Redland was "situated near the Arkansas river in Sequoyah County and has 100 inhabitants, most of whom are engaged in agricultural pursuits. The country surrounding it is very fertile and produces abundantly of corn, potatoes, cotton and livestock of which large shipments are made. In the village are five mercantile establishments and a cotton-wood saw mill." It was also stated that the altitude of Redland was 455 feet.

Several businesses shipped on the railroad at the time. Geren & McNabb, as well as W. O. Olintine, farmed, brokered, and shipped Irish potatoes, radishes, and sweet potatoes. In 1912, the Kansas City Southern built a track for the Hines-Kobel Sand Company. By 1936, there was an 80-car siding plus several industry and team tracks with a capacity of 26 cars. Redland was a flag stop for passenger trains, it had a mail crane to send out mail, and there was a dispatcher telephone for the crews to use. The mail service ended on June 30, 1937, when the post office closed.

By the late 1950s, the siding had been extended to handle 134 cars. Other tracks could hold 23 cars. A note in employee timetables stated that train "Nos. 15 and 16 will stop on flag at Redland for revenue passengers to or from Kansas City." This was the only passenger service listed for Redland. When CTC signaling was installed, the siding was removed, leaving only a short 15-car team track. In 1967, the Garland Coal Company publicly stated that it was going to build a large coal shipping facility at Redland to use both rail and water, but no construction ever took place. In 1970 during the work on the McClellan–Kerr Arkansas River Navigation System and the new KCS bridge, the team track was expanded to 23 car lengths. Soon, with the work completed, all of the tracks were gone except for the mainline, and Redland was left as an unincorporated community consisting of a scattering of houses overlooking the Arkansas River.

306.8 ARKANSAS RIVER BRIDGE – Also known as the Redland Bridge and Bridge A-307, this large continuous box-girder structure stands high above the Arkansas River, having opened in 1971. The bridge today looks nothing like the many previous bridges that once stood here. Reports state that the first bridge was a "wooden trestle type bridge" that was washed out in numerous floods. Other reports state that the bridge used several 127-foot deck truss spans, built in the time period 1895-1896. The bridge was such an issue that Arthur E. Stilwell mentioned that the Arkansas River was the most expensive bridge on the railroad.

In 1922, Kansas City Southern began taking bids on a new Arkansas River bridge. The July 27, 1922, issue of *The Iron Age* reported that the railroad had ordered 1900 tons of steel for the bridge from the McClintic-Marshall Company. McClintic-Marshall was founded and operated by Howard McClintic and Charles Marshall, graduates of Lehigh University as civil engineers in 1888. The company made structural steel which was used in the building and bridge trades, including the Waldorf-Astoria Hotel, the George Washington Bridge, the Golden Gate Bridge, and the Panama Canal. The firm was based at Chicago, Illinois, and Pittsburgh, Pennsylvania, and became a Bethlehem Steel Corporation subsidiary in 1931. Various newspapers and magazines reported that "another new steel bridge capable of carrying heavy power now under construction over the Arkansas river, will cost in the neighborhood of $270,000." *Railway Age* reported in January 1924 that the bridge work was "94 per cent completed." Several of the older deck trusses were shipped to Shreveport, Louisiana. They were used on the Cross Bayou bridge in 1926, where they remain today, listed on the National Register of Historic Places.

When completed, the new 1593-foot-long bridge was at Arkansas River mile 389.2 and included nine fixed spans and improved approaches. The primary channel had a clearance width of 240 feet, with a vertical clearance of 19 feet at high water, and 52 feet at mean low water. Although the bridge was new, an old problem also had to be solved. For years, the Arkansas River had changed channels and was washing out the area around the bridge, and along the branchline to Fort Smith at nearby Braden's Bend. During the late 1920s and early 1930s, Kansas City Southern undertook a number of projects to stabilize the river channel. An article in *Railway Age* (August 27, 1932) entitled "Taking the Threat Out of a River" covered the work in detail, which included 2046 linear feet of log cribbing and 11,327 linear feet of revetment (stone-lined shoreline).

From 1944 until 1947, the bridge was again worked on, leaving it with three through truss spans, plus many deck plate girder spans. Reports state that the bridge was reconstructed and lengthened at a cost of $851,264. The bridge survived another twenty years until the McClellan–Kerr Arkansas River Navigation System required the construction of a new bridge to provide the clearances desired for the improved waterway.

The railroad took a bold decision and built what became the first major steel-deck, box girder design railway bridge in the United States. The bridge was designed by the firms Forrest and Cotton, Inc., and Walchuk and Mayrbauri, with Bethlehem Steel Corporation serving as the steel fabricator and superstructure contractor. The substructure was handled by Peter Kewitt & Sons. The bridge won the American Institute of Steel Construction Award of Merit (1972) for medium span, high clearance structures.

The new continuous welded box girder bridge (20 feet by 15 feet) used a unique design where sections were built in lengths of 42 feet to 117 feet. Each section was then attached to an existing section and pushed (launched in what were called trains) across the piers from both north and south. Looking at the bridge today, the ribs on the outside are stiffeners needed to strengthen the bridge as it was pushed across between concrete piers. This design had the advantage that no falsework was needed below the bridge, which would have blocked the river, or the large number of cranes that are usually required to install a bridge span. Several studies reported on the $4.3 million bridge and its construction, which was a subject of the book *Bridge Engineering: Construction and Maintenance* (edited by Wai-Fah Ghen and Lian Duan).

The first major steel-deck railway bridge in America, the 2110-ft. single-track Kansas City Southern Railway bridge over the Arkansas River near Redland, Oklahoma, is a continuous box-girder structure having nine spans. Approximately 2400 tons of ASTM A588 (50-ksi yield) weathering steel, left unpainted, were used. The 24 individual box units, ranging in length from 42 ft. to 117 ft. and in weight from 44 tons, were shop-fabricated by welding. At the site, box units were bolted together in trains behind each abutment and rolled or launched across the spans, supported on sliding-type (skidway) units located at the abutments and piers. The two trains met and were spliced at the middle of the channel span. An extensive erection strength investigation was required, because each girder panel had to pass across one or more skidway units and therefore had to be adequate to withstand the various combinations of moment, shear, and reaction that occurred. Web and flange erection strengthening and stiffening were found necessary. Pier and abutment stresses and stability were reviewed.

Access to the Redland Bridge from the north is good when the river is at normal or low levels. Baldridge Road, N4720 Road, crosses the tracks and then heads down to the river, ending under the bridge. A number of places along the shoreline allow great photography, especially during the late afternoon. Access from the south requires using farm access roads like D4723. Low water conditions are also preferable for access to the shoreline.

This photo of the north end of the Arkansas River Bridge shows a new concrete pier and the unique welded box girder design of the bridge, built during the early 1970s.

KCS 4709 leads a southbound train across the Arkansas River Bridge in June 2021.

The Heavener Sub: History Through the Miles

The welded box girder spans of the Arkansas River Bridge are large, as shown by this southbound freight.

In a sign of things to come, Canadian Pacific locomotive 9837 pulls a train northbound over the Arkansas River Bridge in September 2021.

The Arkansas River

The Arkansas River is a 1469-mile tributary of the Mississippi River, flowing from Lake County, Colorado, near Leadville, southeast across Kansas, Oklahoma and Arkansas until entering the Mississippi River near what was once Napoleon, Arkansas. The river is the second-longest tributary of the Mississippi-Missouri River system, the sixth-longest river in the country, and the 45th longest river in the world. The Arkansas River was once part of the border between the United States and Mexico, as created by the Adams–Onís Treaty of 1821. The treaty established the western border of the United States as being the Sabine, Red, and Arkansas Rivers to the Rocky Mountains, then west along the 42nd parallel to the Pacific Ocean. This ended with the Annexation of Texas (1845) and the Treaty of Guadalupe Hidalgo (Treaty of Peace, Friendship, Limits and Settlement between the United States of America and the Mexican Republic – 1848), which ended the Mexican-American War.

The Arkansas River is now used by the McClellan-Kerr Arkansas River Navigation System. The commercial river system was named for Senators John L. McClellan of Arkansas, and Robert S. Kerr of Oklahoma. Work by the U.S. Corps of Engineers has made the river navigable from the Mississippi River as far west as the Tulsa Port of Catoosa.

McClellan–Kerr Arkansas River Navigation System

The construction of this bridge came about because of navigation improvements on the Arkansas River. This project was designed to provide regular barge service between the Mississippi River and the Tulsa Port of Catoosa in Oklahoma. Small boats had operated on the Arkansas River since the first settlements were made in Arkansas and Oklahoma, but many only during high water conditions. For almost one hundred years, sternwheelers provided freight and passenger service up and down the river, and along many of its tributaries. By the 1920s, there were proposals to improve the river system to allow larger boats to operate all year long.

The first major step forward took place with the passage of the Rivers and Harbors Act on July 24, 1946. This Act authorized the Arkansas-Verdigris Waterway, but provided little funding for the Catoosa to Mississippi River route. However, it did specify that the project would provide navigation, hydropower, flood control, and recreation along the route. After several more small fundings, major construction began in 1958 with the Lake Dardanelle Lock and Dam, the route's largest. On October 4, 1968, navigation with a nine-foot deep channel opened to Little Rock, and the rest of the system opened on December 30, 1970. Additional projects continued for years, but when finished, the renamed McClellan-Kerr Arkansas River Navigation System was 445 miles long and included eighteen locks and dams. It climbs 420 feet along its length.

During the construction, the project was renamed for its two largest supporters - Senator Robert S. Kerr of Oklahoma, and Senator John L. McClellan of Arkansas. An official dedication ceremony took place on June 5, 1971, with President Richard M. Nixon attending. The waterway is operated by the U.S. Army Corps of Engineers, and was the largest civil works project undertaken by the Corps of Engineers to that time.

While the McClellan-Kerr Arkansas River Navigation System covers the Arkansas River, it includes a few miles on the Verdigris River in Oklahoma, and the White River in Arkansas. The White River is straighter than the Arkansas River near the Mississippi River, thus was the preferred waterway route. The Arkansas Post Canal was built to connect the White and Arkansas rivers, and still allow access to the White River for navigation. The Montgomery Point Lock and Dam (Lock 99) was the last structure built (in 2004) and is located at Navigation Mile 0.5 on the White River.

The County Line

To the north is **Sequoyah County**. This started as the Skin Bayou District, and became the Sequoyah District of the Cherokee Nation in 1851, named for George Guess (Sequoyah), who invented a Cherokee alphabet. The area was one of the most popular access points into what later became Oklahoma as the federal offices at Fort Smith are just to the east in Arkansas. The county includes the Arkansas River valley, as well as the Ozark Plateau to the north and the Ouachita Mountains to the south. Many of the local names date to French explorers, and the Cherokee who started to acquire the land through Lovely's Purchase in 1816. In 1829, it officially became part of the Western Cherokee Nation. Sallisaw is the county seat and the population is about 45,000. The county features mostly farming, ranching and poultry, but tourism and industry also play an important role.

To the south is **Le Flore County**, Oklahoma. The land became owned by the Choctaw Nation after they ceded much of their homelands with the Treaty of Doak's Stand in 1820, and then the rest with the Treaty of Dancing Rabbit Creek in 1830. While this was Indian Territory, it was part of the Moshulatubbee and Apukshunnubbee districts of the Choctaw Nation. Coal and timber attracted settlers, industry and railroads to the region. The county has about 50,000 residents, and Poteau is the county seat.

The county is named for the LeFlore family, which dates back to Frenchman Louis LeFleur, who married the daughter of the renowned Choctaw warrior Pushmataha. LeFleur became a wealthy trader and fought with Andrew Jackson in the War of 1812. His son, Greenwood LeFlore, was a leader in education and Christianity for the Choctaws. He married Elizabeth Coodey, sister of Cherokee leader William Shorey Coodey and a niece of Chief John Ross. LeFlore later signed the Treaty of Dancing Rabbit Creek, thinking that moving west would enable the Choctaws to retain their sovereignty. The family continued to play a leading role in tribal matters, both in Indian Territory and in Mississippi.

Heavener Sub Route Guide

307.5 SAND SIDING – In 1908, the Oklahoma Corporation Commission listed this as a station on the mainline of the Kansas City Southern. At the time, Sand Siding was shown to be 1.1 miles south of Redland, and appears to be one of many locations used to obtain fill materials for the railroad. A large bar (borrow) pit is located on the east side of the tracks.

Throughout this area are a number of old Arkansas River channels, and the lands have taken the name Redland Bottom. Farming is very popular here.

311.5 OAK LODGE – When the Kansas City, Pittsburg & Gulf was built, a station known as Oak Lodge was established in 1896. The station didn't last long and was replaced by Spiro, Oklahoma.

Oak Lodge went through several names during its first forty years of existence. Choctaw Agency, the first in the west, was established here in 1832 by Major Francis W. Armstrong. The agency was to supply Choctaws during their removal from the southeast to the new Indian Territory. The Choctaws named the agency "Iskuli," which means a piece of money. Soon, the small community was being called Skullyville or Money Town. For a time, the town also served as the capital of the Choctaw Nation. A post office opened on June 26, 1833, using the name Choctaw Agency.

As other tribes were moved west, they also stopped at Choctaw Agency. These included Seminole and Chickasaw families, who were also resupplied here. Another activity at Skullyville was the Butterfield Overland Mail route, which created a stop here by 1856. Butterfield Overland Stage created their own name for the station – Walker's Station. The name came from Tandy Walker, a Choctaw Chief who later was the Governor of the Choctaw Nation. Tandy Walker lived in part of the old Choctaw Agency at the time, the site of a large gathering of Choctaw leaders in 1857. The result of the conference was the creation of the Skullyville Constitution of 1857, which established a government for the Choctaw Nation.

During the late 1850s, the Indian agency moved to Fort Washita, and on August 16, 1860, the post office changed its name to Scullyville. The misspelled name (Scullyville instead of Skullyville) didn't last long before the post office changed back to Choctaw Agency on December 4, 1860. Not long afterwards, the Civil War began, the Butterfield Overland Stage ended service, and Confederate and Union forces fought over the area. After the war, the community never regained its importance and became a small farming community. The Choctaw Agency post office closed on October 10, 1871, and a new name – Oak Lodge – was assigned to a post office on December 22, 1871. When the railroad was built to the west during the mid-1890s, Spiro gained an advantage and Oak Lodge slowly faded away. The post office closed on October 10, 1917, and today nothing remains of the town except for the cemetery. Instead, the area includes a few farms and a number of poultry houses. In 1972, Walker's Station/Choctaw Agency was added to the National Register of Historic Places.

The Kansas City, Pittsburg & Gulf used the name Oak Lodge for the station stop in this area until late 1898 when the Spiro post office opened. After that, the railroad station stop was Spiro.

311.7 SPIRO (DG) – Spiro is the first community the railroad passes through south of the Arkansas River and in the Choctaw Nation. Kansas City Southern stated the following about Spiro in 1912.

> It is the junction point of the main line of the Kansas City Southern Railway and its Fort Smith branch. The population for 1912 is given at 2,600, showing an increase of 140 over the preceding year. During 1911-12 fifteen new dwellings and two substantial business buildings were erected at a cost of $34,500, preceding year. During the year fifteen new dwellings and one substantial business building were erected at a cost of $18,000. The municipality also installed a water works plant costing $40,000, and improved its electric light plant and city park at a cost of $8,000. In the adjacent country one hundred and ten families have settled on farms and have brought under cultivation 2,800 acres of new land, involving an outlay of $30,000 for improvements.
>
> The annual production of cotton in the immediate vicinity of Spiro is from 10,000 to 12,000 bales, and large quantities from other places are also handled here. Potatoes are grown on a large scale, the annual shipments varying from 100 to 600 carloads. The bottom lands near Spiro are most excellently adapted to the cultivation of these crops. The hill lands or uplands are good for general farming

operations and also splendidly adapted to the cultivation of fine fruits and commercial truck. A few miles west of Spiro are large areas of prairie lands, well adapted to general farming and stock raising. Along the Arkansas River and north, east and south of Spiro there is much good oak, hickory and cottonwood timber, which could be manufactured. A good quality of coal is convenient to town, but is being mined only in a small way. In the township there are 6,000 acres of coal land and one vein between four and one-half and five feet thick is known to extend to within one-half mile of the city. Coal is being hauled direct from the mines, three to five miles away. Within a half mile of town is an inexhaustible deposit of fine brick shale, and building stone of excellent quality is found on the edge of town.

There are in Spiro two large cotton gins and a compress, two prosperous banks, two churches, an opera house, local and long distance telephone service, a brick plant, some thirty mercantile establishments, the largest of which do a business of $60,000 to $75,000 annually.

So how did Spiro get started? As Choctaw families moved into the region during the 1830s, some settled in this area on a low ridge that separates the Arkansas and Poteau rivers. Nearby was Choctaw Agency, known as Skullyville by many of the tribal members. When the railroad was built through the area, it was several miles west of Skullyville

Heavener Sub Route Guide

but through the farming community that became Spiro, then located in Skullyville County, a part of the Moshulatubbee District of the Choctaw Nation. Some settlers moved to the new railroad station, and a post office opened on September 21, 1898.

This railroad town was not the first settlement here. North of Skullyville near the Arkansas River are the Spiro Mounds, the remains of a Mississippian culture that was active here between the ninth and fifteenth centuries (AD 800 to AD 1450). A 150-acre site is now part of the Spiro Mounds Archaeological Center.

The question now comes up as to how the name Spiro came about. Truthfully, no one really knows. The word has several meanings, including respiration or breathing, or "relating to a compound or system that contains two rings having a single atom in common." Neither of these probably played a role in the naming of the city. However, there are a number of explanations and all relate to the name of someone. One version says that Spiro was the maiden name of the first postmistress. A second explanation states that Spiro was the name of the father-in-law of a successful Fort Smith merchant. The third story states that Spiro was the maiden name of a Fort Smith banker's mother.

From the start, cotton was a driver of the local economy. The Choctaw tribe had long been involved in owning and operating cotton plantations, and they brought the crops and slaves with them when the moved to Indian Territory. In 1901, there were three cotton yards and a cotton gin (Indian Territory Cotton Producers Company) at Spiro, plus a bank, five hotels, and a number of other businesses. The population had grown to 1173 residents in 1910, when there were three cotton gins (Oklahoma Gin Company, Planters Gin Company, and Redwine & Kobel Gin), but only two banks.

Petroleum products began to play a role at Spiro by 1927, when both the Beard Oil Company and Mid-Continent Petroleum Corporation leased KCS property to install bulk oil stations. Tracks were also built to serve these facilities. The 1920s and 1930s saw a large loss of population as tractors and other machines began to be used on area farms, reducing the need for farm laborers. The population was down to 969 in 1930, and didn't get back to more than the 1920 population until the 1950 census (1365 residents). By then, four gristmills handled grain, and timber and livestock were also becoming important to the Spiro economy.

The current population of Spiro is about 2200, with the town serving as a local business and retail center. There are a number of gas stations, restaurants and small businesses, but nearby Fort Smith is a major source of jobs and trade. Spiro also still has its own school district and several government offices.

The Railroad at Spiro

When the Kansas City, Pittsburg & Gulf arrived at Spiro, it created a small complex due to the plans for a branch line to Fort Smith. A depot was built on the east side of the mainline just south of the north wye switch. A meals and lodging facility was located south of the depot, used until the KCS started adding dining car service on its trains. The meals facility was closed by 1913. Further south was a freight house, moved in 1913 to the west side of the yard where a cotton platform once stood. Near the freight house and the south wye switch was the Indian Territory Cotton Producers Company, renamed the Oklahoma Gin Company after statehood. Also to the west of the four-track yard was the Port Arthur Hotel, which featured a dining room and a lunch room. It was located west of the station on the southwest corner of Hickory (today's SE 5th Street) and Washington (today's South Ash).

The movement of the freight house to the west side of the mainline (town side of the tracks) was done to comply with an order of the Oklahoma Corporation Commission. Also in 1913, the Commission ordered the railroad to "build a new passenger depot at Spiro, the same to be located on the side of its railroad next to the town of Spiro, Oklahoma." Because of the connecting service to Fort Smith, the new brick depot was built in the wye on the mainline to the east. The new station was a very typical KCS brick structure with a covered patio to the south, and a baggage and express room to the north.

Building the new depot on the east side of the tracks required hearings all the way to the Oklahoma Supreme Court. This 1914 hearing provided a great deal of information about the KCS operations at Spiro. The following is just some of the court's findings.

> On this main line the Kansas City Southern daily operates four through passenger trains. The Kansas City Southern has a branch line from Spiro to Ft. Smith, and each of the through trains on the main line is met at Spiro by one of its trains from Ft. Smith; the branch line

train that arrives to meet each through train counts as one train, and the train that leaves Spiro going back to Ft. Smith as each through train departs is another train, thereby making twelve passenger trains daily to handle this passenger traffic. In addition thereto there are two Kansas City Southern passenger trains running between Ft. Smith and Mena, Ark. which pass through Spiro. In addition to this the Ft. Smith & Western Railway Company operates two passenger trains westward and two eastward through Spiro, to and from Ft. Smith over the Kansas City Southern Railway Company tracks, thereby making eighteen passenger trains daily for the town of Spiro.

Under the present conditions it is necessary for the citizens of Spiro to cross four tracks to get to the passenger depot. The company has moved its freight depot as required by the order to the west side of the track, and they propose to locate the new passenger depot inside the "Y" on the east side of the main line, and to construct a building adequate for the accommodation necessary at a point of that importance, and propose to eliminate two of the four tracks now between the town and the depot, and construct a concrete sidewalk leading from the town over to the railway company's property and tracks to the depot for the accommo-

> dation of the town of Spiro. It is shown by the testimony that more than 500 people are transferred daily from the main line to the branch line and vice versa; that a great many more passengers are transferred at Spiro than take passage to or from Spiro.
>
> Three or four passenger trains may frequently be at Spiro at the same time; the main line train must stop at the station, and under the present and proposed arrangement of the company, passengers getting off of the main line or either leg of the "Y" on the branch line may transfer without crossing any tracks.

The Oklahoma Supreme Court hearing included a large discussion about the tracks that would have to be added or moved to allow a station to be built on the west side of the main tracks, siding and yard. There was also a reference to surveys which had been made that could lead the railroad to moving its mainline to Fort Smith, thus bypassing Spiro completely. However, the Oklahoma Supreme Court agreed that an improved depot was required, but that its location within the wye track on the east side of the mainline was justified. Therefore, both the Oklahoma Corporation Commission and the Kansas City Southern got half of what they wanted.

During the 1930s, Spiro was a scheduled passenger stop where mainline trains met the mixed trains to and from Fort Smith. To handle the passenger and freight business, there was a continuous agency. The siding was 87 cars long, the team track could handle

15 cars, and there was a small yard where water was available. The Fort Smith Wye was east of all of the other tracks in town.

Things changed a great deal during the 1940s and 1950s, and in 1958 Spiro was a regular flag stop for *The Flying Crow* (Nos. 15 and 16) and a conditional flag stop for the *Southern Belle* ("Nos. 1 and 2 will stop on flag at Westville, Stilwell, Spiro, Poteau and Howe for revenue passengers to or from Neosho or beyond and for revenue passengers to or from Spiro or beyond"). Because Spiro was just a flag stop, a mail crane had been installed to put mail on trains that did not stop. The agency was also only open 8am-5pm daily, so a dispatcher telephone was available. The Spiro siding had been extended to hold 160 cars, and there was diesel fuel available in the yard. While the line to Fort Smith had been abandoned, the wye still remained to turn locomotives and equipment.

In 1964, the only changes were that there was no telegraph agency service, no diesel fuel available, and that the terms of the conditional flag stop had changed for the *Southern Belle*. Scheduled for 4:03pm, the timetable now stated that "Nos. 1 and 2 stop on flag at Westville, Stilwell, Spiro and Howe for revenue passengers to or from regular stops." The end of passenger service meant that all there was at Spiro was the 160-car siding, yard, and wye. The wye was gone by the mid-1980s.

Today, the railroad remains the southeast boundary of Spiro, with little to the east except for the businesses along U.S. Highway 271. The siding starts south of the railroad bridge over U.S. Highway 271, with Control Point North Spiro at Milepost 311.4. The south switch, Control Point South Spiro, is at Milepost 312.8. On the west side of the tracks at

South Main Avenue are a series of large concrete slabs that have been used by Emerson Transload, A track through the area is known as Spiro/Emerson and extends between Mileposts 311.5 and 312.0.

The siding at Spiro is often used to meet trains, as happened on June 22, 2021, when southbound KCS 4671 met a northbound freight being pulled by KCS 4006, the railroad's SD70ACE "Veterans Day Salute" locomotive.

Fort Smith District

When the railroad south out of Kansas City was first being planned, Fort Smith was to be a mainline station. The city was so important that its name was used in several of the incorporations that built parts of what became Kansas City Southern. Names such as Kansas City, Nevada & Fort Smith Railroad Company and Pittsburg, Fort Smith & Southern Railroad Company showed that Fort Smith was important to the railroad. However, surveyors discovered the rugged hills to the north of the city, and found that an easier route was available through the eastern edge of Indian Territory.

The City of Fort Smith was not happy and it pulled back much of its financial and political support. As early as May 1893, Fort Smith was asked to raise $80,000 for right-of-way and depot grounds. The plan was for the railroad to build shops, a roundhouse and make the city a division point on the railroad. The railroad was to have trains running into Fort Smith by December 31, 1894. In March 1895, it was clear that at best Fort Smith would be at the end of a branch, and the plan was rejected by city leaders. Bonus money of $100,000 was then offered by Fort Smith to be on the mainline, but plans changed to getting a branch line by early 1896 when the railroad received federal permission to build across Indian Territory and to bridge the Poteau River. During October 1897, Fort Smith offered the Kansas City, Pittsburg & Gulf a $25,000 bonus if the 16.4-mile branch was built. Construction began on December 28, 1897, and there was a celebration of its completion on June 1, 1898. This didn't end the hopes of Fort Smith to be on the mainline as several surveys between 1906 and 1910 investigated moving the railroad.

Initially, a few mainline passenger trains operated in and out Fort Smith, but soon just connecting trains provided the service. In 1936, two mixed trains in each direction provided service each morning and late evening to connect with *The Flying Crow* at Spiro. Even this passenger service ended on August 31, 1941, and bus service to Sallisaw handled the business. Several local freight trains continued to operate over the line until May 1943 when heavy flooding washed out the Spiro to Fort Smith line. Temporary trackage rights over the St. Louis-San Francisco's Poteau to Fort Smith line were obtained.

On December 12, 1944, the Interstate Commerce Commission granted authority to abandon the KCS line to Fort Smith and approved permanent trackage rights over the Frisco out of Poteau, Oklahoma. The grade of the Fort Smith District is often used today by U.S. Highway 271.

Some of the rails for the wye to the Fort Smith District can still be found in the brush east of the Heavener Subdivision at the Ash Street grade crossing at Spiro, Oklahoma.

Fort Smith & Western Railroad Company

The Kansas City Southern had another railroad that used its Spiro to Fort Smith line from 1901 until 1939. This railroad was the Fort Smith & Western Railroad Company (FS&W), chartered in Arkansas on January 25, 1899. The company planned to build a railroad westward from Fort Smith (and points east) to Guthrie and other points in Indian and Oklahoma territories. As an effort to speed up construction and lower costs, the FS&W decided to use the twenty miles of track owned by KCS to what became Coal Creek, Oklahoma. The railroad started operating on December 1, 1901, and eventually owned 197 miles of track from Coal Creek to Guthrie, plus the KCS trackage at Fort Smith and 42 miles of track owned by subsidiary St. Louis, El Reno & Western Railway between Guthrie and El Reno, Oklahoma.

The railroad was soon in financial trouble and entered receivership on October 9, 1915. A foreclosure sale was ordered in 1916, but it didn't take place. A second order led to the railroad being sold for $900,000 on January 16, 1923. The railroad was reorganized as the Fort Smith & Western Railway on February 1, 1923. This didn't help much as the new company entered receivership on June 1, 1931. In an effort to save money, the receiver ended most passenger service on the railroad during December 1931. In 1932, several Reconstruction Finance Corporation loans were made, but the railroad hadn't paid them off by their due dates in 1935. The last of the passenger, mail and express service ended on October 12, 1938. All operations ended on January 19, 1939, by court order. An application was made to abandon the entire railroad in March, and permission was received on August 7, 1939. Most of the line was sold for scrap, with only some Fort Smith trackage, and the tracks west of Coal Creek, saved for operations by other carriers.

Fort Smith and Western Railway Company rail pass, front and back, circa 1930. From the author's collection.

The Heavener Sub: History Through the Miles

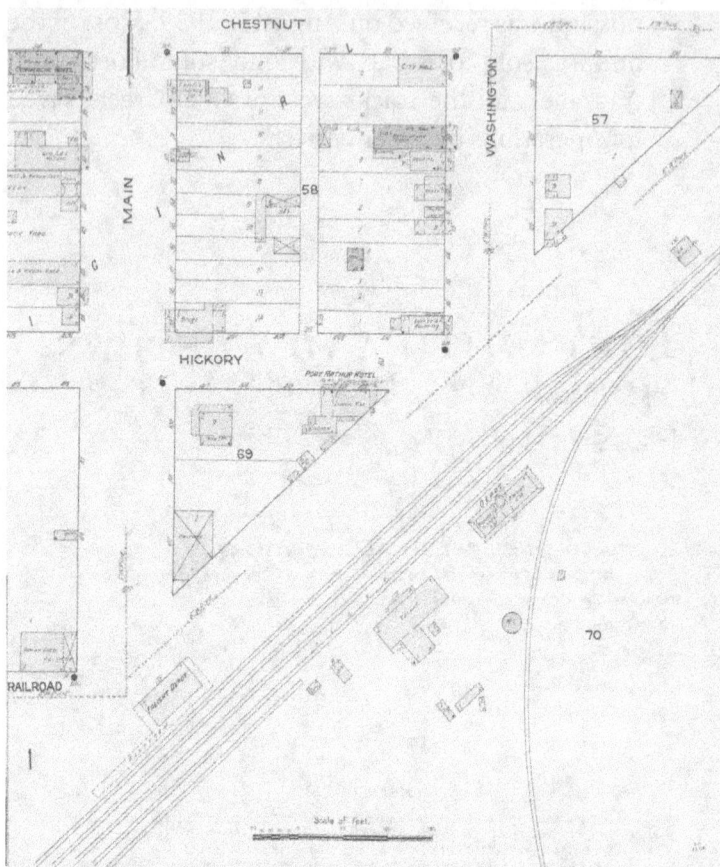

In 1913, the KCS station at Spiro was located just south of the north wye switch, convenient for both mainline and branch line trains. The freight house was further south on the west side of the small yard. *Sanborn Fire Insurance Map from Spiro, Le Flore County, Oklahoma.* Sanborn Map Company, Dec 1913. Map. Retrieved from the Library of Congress, https://www.loc.gov/item/sanborn07255_003/.

Heavener Sub Route Guide

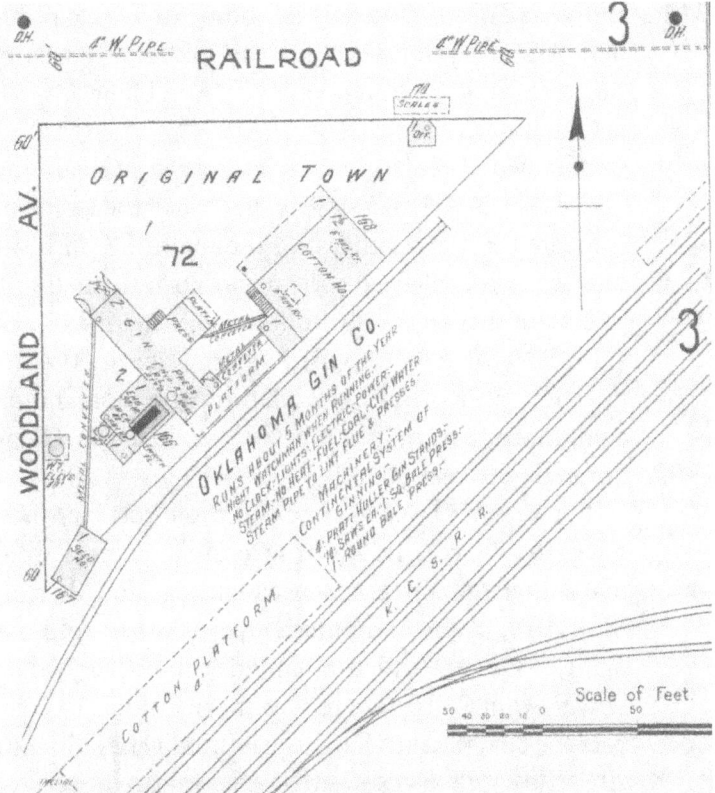

By 1913, Spiro was a busy agricultural town with at least three large cotton gins. This Sanborn map shows the Oklahoma Gin Company just west of the south wye switch at Spiro. *Sanborn Fire Insurance Map from Spiro, Le Flore County, Oklahoma.* Sanborn Map Company, Dec 1913. Map. Retrieved from the Library of Congress, https://www.loc.gov/item/sanborn07255_003/.

314.7 BONANZA – Bonanza is the home of a large number of poultry houses, plus the Oklahoma Gas & Electric (OG&E) River Valley Power Plant. OG&E is Oklahoma's oldest (founded 1902) and largest investor-owned electric utility and serves Oklahoma and western Arkansas. This electrical power plant is located to the southeast of the mainline, and was built as two coal-fired 175-megawatt units in 1990. The plant was originally built by AES Shady Point, a subsidiary of AES (Applied Energy Services) Corporation. When built, the plant burned Oklahoma coal, more than half of the coal produced in Oklahoma by the year 2000.

For years, AES sold much of the electricity produced to OG&E. In 2018, several statements were made that the agreement was ending, and then in May 2019, it was announced that AES had sold the plant to OG&E, which renamed it the River Valley Power Plant. While there have been studies to convert the coal plant to natural gas-fired generation, in 2020 the company requested proposals to move Wyoming and Montana Powder River Basic coal to the power plant in 115-car unit trains. An interesting requirement was that there could be no minimum volumes required. Currently, coal is interchanged to the KCS which delivers the trains from the north, the direction that the Bonanza switch was built.

The railroad line into the plant passes around the west and south side before reaching a large loop around the coal storage pile. A coal unloading shed is located on this loop next to the power plant.

Heavener Sub Route Guide

The Bonanza station sign was photographed on a foggy morning in June 2021.

Passing Bonanza, Oklahoma Gas & Electric's River Valley Power Plant can be seen to the east.

315.7 COAL CREEK – Coal Creek is located just south of a cut through the southeast end of Nubbin Ridge. This location has also been known as Fort Smith & Western Junction. A wooded grade for a wye can still be found to the west for the former Fort Smith & Western line to Guthrie, Oklahoma. The Fort Smith & Western Railroad Company operated this line from December 1, 1901, until February 1, 1923, when the Fort Smith & Western Railway took over. The railway company ended operations on January 19, 1939. Most of the railroad route was sold for scrap, but on September 8, 1939, the Interstate Commerce Commission approved the sale of the 20.9-mile line from Coal Creek, Oklahoma, west to McCurtain, Oklahoma, to the Fort Smith & Van Buren Railway. This part of the railroad served a number of coal mines, and the purchase allowed them to continue to operate. For years, the line was shown to be the Fort Smith & Van Buren Branch in KCS employee timetables.

The Fort Smith & Van Buren Railway (FS&VB) owned 3.3 miles of industrial tracks at Fort Smith that were operated by Kansas City Southern. In reality, the FS&VB was owned and controlled by KCS, but still kept its own incorporation. On July 8, 1992, the Interstate Commerce Commission approved the merger of the FS&VB into the Kansas City Southern Railway. The Coal Creek line didn't last much longer, as it was abandoned from Milepost 20.12 at Coal Creek, Oklahoma, to Milepost 40.27 at McCurtain, Oklahoma, on October 27, 1994.

Heavener Sub Route Guide

FT. SMITH & VAN BUREN BRANCH

	SOUTHWARD	NORTHWARD

Tracks not shown on face of time table	Distance from Coal Creek	TIME TABLE No. 2 Effective SUNDAY, JAN. 5, 1964	Mile Post
		STATIONS	
M.P.	0.0	.....COAL CREEK.....	20.0
Panama Vein Spur 29.6		7.0	
Milton 31.7	....	...M. V. Ry. Crossing...	....
Evans Coal Co. 38.4	7.0	.......BOKOSHE.......	27.0
Lone Star Spur 40.1		11.0	
	18.0	..... McCURTAIN	38.0
		2.7	
	20.7	.......End of Line.......	40.7
		20.7	

Ft. Smith & Van Buren Branch timetable from *Kansas City Southern Lines Time Table No. 2*, effective January 5, 1964. Employee timetable from the author's collection.

The rails in the Coal Creek Road grade crossing are about the last sign of the former Fort Smith & Western Railroad tracks at Coal Creek, Oklahoma.

When the Fort Smith & Western built the line in 1901, it allowed a number of coal mines to develop. Several of these were around the community of Panther (post office June 11, 1890-April 5, 1902), which was renamed McCurtain to honor Green McCurtain, the last principal chief of the Choctaw. With the arrival of the railroad, the San Bois Coal Company built four hundred company houses and a number of businesses opened in the community. The town's mining took a heavy blow when an underground explosion in Mine Number Two killed seventy-three miners. The March 20, 1912, explosion sent the San Bois Coal Company into bankruptcy. Some mining continued, with most using open-pit or strip mining techniques. Eventually, the lack of regular mining and coal shipments meant the end of the rail line, and most of McCurtain, Oklahoma.

This hot journal/dragging equipment/oversize load detector can be found at Coal Creek, located just south of where the switch for the Fort Smith & Western's westward line once was.

Where the wye once was, KCS now has a hot journal/dragging equipment/oversize load detector. At the location where the south wye switch was located, the railroad crosses Coal Creek on a small deck plate girder span.

317.3 PANAMA (JA) – Heading south, the railroad is entering coal country, and that is the reason Panama was created. The original town in the area was to the southwest on Buck Creek and was created by a mining company. The company built a number of mining shacks that were painted red, leading to the name of Red Town. When the Kansas City, Pittsburg & Gulf built through the area, a small community began to grow alongside the tracks, shown as Hobart in some early schedules. Somehow the new town took the name Panama by 1898. Most histories about the area state that it took the name from the Panama Canal, but the Panama Canal was built by the United States from 1904 until 1914. However, the French worked on building the canal 1881-1889, so it is possible that the name came from the French effort.

The Ozark Coal and Mining Company located here in 1898, helping the community to grow. A post office using the name Panama opened on January 14, 1898, but there was some sort of trouble with the operation as the post office closed it on February 23, 1898. A year later, the Panama post office reopened on February 21, 1899. While the post office was established, it wasn't until 1902 that the first store and cotton gin opened alongside the tracks. The gin attracted other businesses and a subscription school was established in 1903.

By 1904, Panama had a second railroad as the Midland Valley Railroad built westward from Excelsior, Arkansas. A number of homes and businesses moved to the area just north of the crossing, creating a downtown. The two railroads shared a wooden depot that was located in the northwest corner of the diamond. The 1910 census recorded a population of 310, and the town of Panama was a telegraph station served by a number of passenger trains on each railroad. Coal production was picking up, and farms in the area were producing cotton, livestock, and grain. Panama then featured a cotton compress, cotton gin, grist mill, two hotels, five mercantile stores, churches, a school, several local newspapers, and a bank. The 1920s were good to Panama as new coal mines opened in the area, supporting four general stores and two grocers. Not all of the business was on the Kansas City Southern as shown by the Hanraty Smokeless Coal Company on the Midland Valley Railroad Company just a mile west of the diamond.

Coal mining began to end by 1930 when Panama's population was 754. Despite the reduction in coal mining, Panama's population continued to grow except during the 1950s. Other businesses started to replace coal, with a creosote plant opening in 1937. Farming and ranching increased, with poultry production coming into favor by the 1960s. Some coal strip mining returned, but they employed few workers due to the machinery used. Even these, like the Panama Coal Company, closed during the 1970s and 1980s. Panama now serves as a local shopping center with stores, restaurants and gas stations along U.S. Highway 59. There is still a full public school system, and the town's population is about 1500.

The Kansas City Southern at Panama

According to a statement by a senior manager of the Midland Valley Railroad, "Panama was a terminal and they had a large interchange of business between their line and the Kansas City Southern Railway." During the first several decades of the twentieth century, a wooden depot stood in the northwest corner of the diamond between KCS and the Midland Valley Railroad. The depot was shared by both railroads. While the Midland Valley had a single track, KCS had two tracks with a crossover just north and south of the depot and diamond.

In 1936, KCS had a station agent-operator to handle ticket sales, freight paperwork, train orders, and telegraph service. The hours assigned were 7:45am-4:45pm workdays, and 7:45am-9:45am Sundays and holidays. For when the agent-operator wasn't there, a dispatcher telephone was available for train crews and track maintenance employees. Panama was a scheduled stop for all passenger trains, and there were two sidings listed in the employee timetable. The north siding was shown to be 54 cars long, while the south siding was 82 car long. The Midland Valley Crossing was gated for the KCS. An interchange track was in the southwest quadrant of the diamond, and connected to a yard that was south of the crossing. For some years, there was also an interchange track in the northwest quadrant passing behind the depot.

If you look in the brush just south of the Tecumseh Street grade crossing you will find the base of the former crossing gate for the Midland Valley Crossing.

Several changes had taken place by 1958. The agent-operator worked 8:30am-5:30pm weekdays, and Panama was only a conditional flag stop for *The Flying Crow* – "Nos. 15 and 16 stop on flag at Bunch, Marble City and Panama for revenue passengers to or from Siloam or beyond and for revenue passengers to or from Heavener or beyond." The two sidings had also been combined into a single 128-car siding. The siding was shortened as part of the installation of CTC in 1960, and it was shown as being 62 car lengths in 1964. The conditional flag stop had changed slightly to read "Nos. 15 and 16 will stop on flag at Bunch, Marble City and Panama for revenue passengers to or from regular stops." The premier passenger train, the *Southern Belle*, passed right by heading south at 4:09pm.

On April 1, 1967, the Midland Valley Railroad was merged into the Texas & Pacific Railroad (T&P), a Missouri Pacific subsidiary, which abandoned the line east of Panama in 1968. This ended the need for the diamond, but Panama remained a connection to the T&P line to the west. The end of KCS passenger service with the last run of the *Southern Belle* on November 3, 1969, changed more details at Panama. In 1970, the KCS agent-operator still provided telegraph service and handled train orders 11:00am-8:00pm weekdays. By the mid-1980s the siding was shown to be 3252 feet long and capable of holding 59 cars. The Midland Valley/Texas & Pacific line to the west remained in service, although it became owned by Missouri Pacific in 1983 as part of a merger with Union Pacific. Union Pacific received permission to abandon thirty miles of the line from Panama west to the Kerr-McGee mine near Stigler, Oklahoma, on April 27, 1988. On July 1, 1988, Kansas City Southern acquired the first ten miles between Panama and the Fort Smith & Van Buren crossing near Bokoshe. On September 21, 1994, KCS received permission to abandon what they called the Midland Valley Branch between milepost 20.80 at Panama, Oklahoma, and Milepost 30.30 at Bokoshe. Soon, all of the tracks were removed, leaving only the KCS mainline at Panama.

The Midland Valley Railroad

The Midland Valley Railroad touched the Kansas City Southern several times at Panama. Connections were shown at Mileposts 317.2 and 317.3, plus there was a crossing at Milepost 317.5. The Midland Valley Railroad was one of those regional railroads that seemed to have had nine lives, and used them all. The Midland Valley Railroad (MV) was incorporated on June 4, 1903, with the grand goal of building a railroad from Hope, Arkansas, through Muskogee and Tulsa, Oklahoma, to Wichita, Kansas. The real purpose was to serve a series of coal fields owned by C. Jared Ingersoll, a Philadelphia industrialist. The railroad was built quickly from western Arkansas (Fidelity, it never reached Hope, Arkansas) to Silverdale, Kansas, a total of 292.7 miles. Additional branches were built to serve coal mines and new oil fields. The Midland Valley acquired trackage rights over the Frisco between Maney Junction and Fort Smith to reach larger markets. However, coal from western Arkansas and eastern Oklahoma was the primary product handled by the railroad. It was so important that the railroad reportedly took the name Midland from the important coal mining town of Midland, Arkansas.

To reach new markets, the railroad leased the Wichita & Midland Valley Railroad on July 29, 1910, allowing the railroad to operate between Arkansas City and Wichita. In 1925, the Midland Valley acquired the Kansas, Oklahoma & Gulf Railway. The owner of the Midland Valley, the Muskogee Company, acquired the Oklahoma City-Ada-Atoka Railway in 1929, and operated all three railroads as the Muskogee Roads. The combined rail system was sold to Missouri Pacific in 1964, and then merged into the Texas & Pacific (owned by Missouri Pacific) on April 1, 1967. In 1968, the tracks eastward from Panama to Excelsior, Arkansas, were abandoned. Much of the old grade is now the Midland Valley Road.

East Midland Valley Road, located at Panama, uses the former railroad grade to the east of the Heavener Subdivision.

The track to the west of Panama remained as the Midland Valley Branch, which became part of Missouri Pacific when it absorbed the Texas & Pacific in 1983 as part of the merger with Union Pacific. On January 8, 1980, the Union Pacific Corporation announced an agreement to buy the Missouri Pacific Railroad. Approval was finally received on September 13, 1982, after a series of hearings and lawsuits. It finally took a Supreme Court ruling to allow the merger on December 22, 1982. A unique detail not known by many was that the Missouri Pacific had a number of outstanding bonds that prevented a full merger of the two companies. The bonds were finally closed during the mid-1990s, and the merger became final on January 1, 1997.

On April 27, 1988, Union Pacific received permission to abandon the Panama to Kerr-McGee near Stigler line. The first 9.5 miles of track to the Fort Smith & Van Buren crossing at Bokoshe were sold to Kansas City Southern on July 1, 1988. The line was saved to serve a few coal mines, but the business went away within a few years. On September 21, 1994, KCS was given approval to abandon the line effective October 27, 1994. A few pieces of the Midland Valley Railroad still remain in a few of the larger cities, but almost all of the railroad is now abandoned.

317.7 OZARK – This station was shown to be 0.4 miles south of Panama in 1908 by the Oklahoma Corporation Commission. The *Annual Report of the Mine Inspector for Indian Territory to the Secretary of the Interior for the Year Ended June 30, 1901*, called this the home of the Ozark Coal and Railway Company. The report stated that Ozark Coal "operates a slope mine which has been sunk 1,000 feet and was opened in 1898." The firm employed about 65 people at the time. The report also stated that the coal company "has constructed a railroad from Panama station, on the Kansas City Southern Railway, about 1 mile in length, which gives it excellent shipping facilities with that railroad." For the year ending June 30, 1900, the mine produced 37,276 tons of coal, and then 36,367 tons of coal for the year ending June 30, 1901. It produced 18,044 tons the next year before becoming the Henderson Smokeless Coal Company.

This mine became the Henderson Smokeless Coal Company on May 1, 1902. The coal was described as being a seam 3 feet 10 inches thick. For the year ending June 30, 1902, the mine produced 3770 tons of coal.

318.9 BRAZIL CREEK BRIDGE – This bridge consists of a series of deck plate girder spans. Brazil Creek forms in the Sans Bois Mountains north of Red Oak, Oklahoma. It flows generally eastward to the Poteau River, a short distance to the east of this bridge.

320.0 SHADY POINT – The first settlement in the area was a Choctaw Nation school developed by the tribal government and the Presbyterian Church. The community that grew up around the school was at first known as Double Springs. When a post office was assigned to the location and opened on September 17, 1891, it used the name Harrison, named for Choctaw attorney and leader William H. Harrison. Much of the town moved to the east to be on the route of the railroad being surveyed and built through the eastern side of Indian Territory. With the move, the town took the name of Shady Point (sometimes spelled Shadypoint), and the post office officially moved and changed its name on December 11, 1894.

Initially, timber and agriculture funded the community, but coal soon dominated. One of the first major projects of the coal industry was the construction of the Poteau Valley Railroad from Shady Point to Sutter (renamed Calhoun in 1914). Built in 1900-1901, the railroad was slightly more than six miles long, but served several large coal mines. The population of Shady Point had grown to be about 200, and there were four general stores, a blacksmith, a cotton gin, a gristmill, a grocery store, a drugstore, and two doctors. The Kansas City Southern described Shady Point in 1912 as follows.

> This is a coal mining town at the junction of the K. C. S. Railway and the Poteau Valley Railroad. The town has a population of 300 and is 320 miles south of Kansas City, Mo. The surrounding country is fertile and produces annually from 600 to 800 bales of cotton and from 25 to 50 carloads of livestock, mostly cattle and hogs. The Sequoyah Coal Mining Co., operating at Sutter, Okla., ships daily from six to ten car loads of coal. In the town are three substantial mercantile firms, a cotton gin, grist mill, Baptist church and public school.

The coal industry began to decline by the mid-1920s, and the Poteau Valley Railroad was abandoned in 1926. Several other mines in the area began to truck their coal to tipples alongside the Kansas City Southern mainline at Shady Point, including Poteau Machine Coal Company, the mine of Walter Pate, the mine of Charles Goodwin, and the strip mine of Webb, Covington and Beard.

Agriculture again became the dominate industry, with farmers growing Irish potatoes, blackberries, and cotton. A cotton gin and three grain mills operated at Shady Point through the Depression of the 1930s. However, even these businesses consolidated in larger nearby cities and Shady Point was down to just three grocery stores, a general store, and a service station by the end of World War II. To help make city improvements, Shady Point finally incorporated in 1970. A brief resurgence in the coal business took place in 1978 when the Evans Coal Company opened a deep shaft mine, but the mine closed in 1980 when the population of Shady Point was 235.

Two positive characteristics of Shady Point are that it still has its own school system through eighth grade, and it is located on U.S. Highway 59. Both have helped make Shady Point a growing suburb of nearby Poteau. The population grew to 597 in the 1990 census, and is now slightly over one thousand. The Shady Point School was constructed of cut and roughly coursed native sandstone in 1936 by the Works Progress Administration, and was placed on the National Register of Historic Places in 1988.

The Poteau Valley Railroad Company

The Poteau Valley Railroad Company was incorporated in Oklahoma on October 19, 1900, to "build a standard-gauge railroad from Fort Smith, Ark., via Shady Point, Sutter, and McAlester, Okla., to Guthrie, Okla." Instead, it simply built 6.61 miles of mainline track from a connection with the Kansas City Southern westward to a series of coal mines around Sutter (renamed Calhoun in 1914). There were also 1.273 miles of other tracks, according to the Interstate Commerce Commission.

The Interstate Commerce Commission (ICC) stated that the railroad was actually built by the Choctaw Coal & Mining Company, which became the Sequoyah Coal Mining Company in 1905. The ICC stated that "Evidently the coal companies used the property as a plant facility in their operations for no separate records of its operation as a common carrier were kept until June, 1907."

During late 1910, the Poteau Valley Railway Company petitioned the Oklahoma Corporation Commission to allow it to lease its line to the Kansas City Southern Railway Company. The reason cited was that "the business of said railroad is not sufficient to justify the operation of the same under the present conditions." The Corporation Commission approved the lease since it found that its charter didn't give it the authority to deny the lease. On January 14, 1913, Kansas City Southern took control of the Poteau Valley Railroad by buying its stock, but left it as an independent operation. KCS changed the Poteau Valley's charter on that same date to reduce the amount of capital stock authorized and to move the company office from Calhoun to the KCS office in Kansas City.

A hearing by the Oklahoma Corporation Committee in 1921 provided more information about the relationship between the Poteau Valley Railroad and the KCS. It reported that the "branch line operated as a feeder to the Kansas City Southern and is shown by the record in this case to be a subsidiary of the latter," and "the Kansas City Southern Railroad Company uses substantially the whole output of coal from the mines of Calhoun." However, unlike many railroads in eastern Oklahoma, the Kansas City Southern did not own the mine that supplied their locomotive coal.

The reason for the hearing was that morning passenger service had been stopped on the line on July 18, 1921, due to losses caused by the schedules and the required overtime pay to the train crew involved. The schedules had been established to meet the mainline trains, but that required a morning and an evening departure from Calhoun. The daily except Sunday trains departed Calhoun at 9:00am and 4:00pm, arriving at Shady Point at 9:45am and 5:00pm. Heading back west, they left Shady Point at 10:45am and 5:30pm, getting back to Calhoun at 11:00am and 6:00pm. The cancellation of the morning train left just the evening passenger train, plus one or more daily freight trains that mainly handled coal, with the scheduled coal train departing Calhoun at noon. The fight over the passenger service didn't last long as the railroad was abandoned on April 23, 1926, after a full purchase and merger with the Kansas City Southern Railway.

Shady Point and the Kansas City Southern

The railroad passes along the very east side of town. Although small, Shady Point was important to the Kansas City Southern Railway. First, until the mid-1920s, much of the locomotive coal used by the railroad came from the Shady Point area. Next, there has been a siding here since the railroad was built. In 1936, the siding was shown to be 88 cars long, and there were 41 car lengths of other tracks used to load coal and handle local rail business. Passenger trains no longer stopped here, so a mail crane was used to put mail onto the passing trains. Little changed by the late 1950s except that a dispatcher telephone had been installed, and the larger freight cars had the siding now listed as being only 73 cars long.

CTC signaling was installed north of Heavener starting in 1960, and those sidings that were kept were lengthened to handle longer trains. The Shady Point siding was extended to hold 150 cars. For those following the southbound *Southern Belle* (No. 1), it was scheduled to pass here at 4:12pm in 1964. By the mid-1980s, Shady Point siding was listed as being 7674 feet long, or 140 car lengths. The length hasn't changed much today, and Control Point North Shady Point is shown as being at Milepost 319.2, while Control Point South Shady Point is at Milepost 320.7.

You never know what you will find moving on the Heavener Subdivision. During early 2022, a KCS track inspector heads south through Control Point South Shady Point and then crosses the large through plate girder span immediately to its south. This is a nice photo location, but be warned that the local road fords Rock Creek, which is generally impassible after a heavy rain.

Heavener Sub Route Guide

The south switch of the Shady Point Siding can be found on the north bank of Rock Creek, located at Milepost 320.7.

Heading south, the railroad is forced to turn to the southeast to loop around Cavanal Mountain. Several coal companies mined the coal along the side of this mountain.

320.8 ROCK CREEK BRIDGE – Located just south of Control Point South Shady Point, Rock Creek forms on the northwest side of Cavanal Hill and flows to the north and then eastward. It enters the Poteau River a short distance to the east from here. The bridge that crosses Rock Creek is new, having been installed in 2018. It now includes a short concrete ballast deck span on the north end, and a large through plate girder span over the waterway.

321.3 A. D. CLARK COAL MINE SPUR – The A. D. Clark Coal Company had several operations in Oklahoma. In 1937, the coal company was shown to have mines at Panama (Upper Hartshorne coal seam) and Tahoma (Lower Hartshorne coal seam). By 1945, the company had an operation here. It was not listed by the railroad during the late 1950s.

322.5 POTEAU MINING COMPANY – This 30-car industry track was listed in employee timetables from the mid-1930s, but it was gone by the 1950s. Old maps show several mines on the west side of the tracks north of today's U.S. Highway 59 Bypass around the west side of Poteau. This area is now full of homes, hotels, and a casino.

325.0 LEFLORE COAL COMPANY – Railroad timetables from as late as the 1930s show a seven-car track at this location. While the railroad timetable called the company the Leflore Coal Company, the *Federal Register* of 1937 stated that it was the Leflore Poteau Coal Company. Other coal companies in the Poteau area mining what was called Panama Coal included the Black Diamond Coal Company; Dane Coal Company; J. F. Turnipseed Coal Company's Mine Nos 1, 2 and 3; Pioneer Coal Company; Quality Coal Company; and Royal Smokeless Coal Company.

Reports were that this was a small tipple that was supplied by trucks from area mines. Nothing remains of the tipple today.

325.5 FORT SMITH BRANCH JUNCTION – Located just south of Witte Street, Old State Highway 112, is a switch for the Fort Smith Branch of Kansas City Southern, a location now known as Control Point

Poteau. This is the former STL&SF Crossing that was once at the north side of Poteau. Timetables stated that this was an interlocked crossing in 1936, and an automatic interlocking by 1958. This was part of the original St. Louis-Texas route of what became the Frisco, the St. Louis-San Francisco Railway Company.

This large sign marks the location of Control Point Poteau, located next to Old State Highway 112 at Poteau, Oklahoma.

The Frisco built their line between St. Louis and Texas by buying several railroads and creating a number of new ones. The start of the company was the Atlantic & Pacific Railroad (A&P), created by the U.S. Congress in 1866 as a transcontinental railroad. On October 23, 1875, a suit was filed against the A&P due to unpaid interest on certain Missouri Division bonds, and receivers were soon assigned. The Missouri Division was sold by auction on September 8, 1876, to a representative of the St. Louis

& San Francisco Railway Company (Frisco, StL&SF, or SL-SF).

The Frisco's first route toward Texas came south from Monett, Missouri. As was typical at the time, the construction involved a number of paper companies coming together to build and initially operate the railroad. The first of these companies was the St. Louis, Arkansas & Texas Railway Company of Missouri, incorporated June 4, 1880. By summer 1881, the company owned and operated 32 miles of track from Monett to the Missouri-Arkansas state line. The second company involved was incorporated on July 17, 1880. This company, the St. Louis, Arkansas & Texas Railway Company of Arkansas, built approximately 37 miles of track from the Missouri-Arkansas state line to near Fayetteville, Arkansas. In September 1880, the Frisco created a third railroad subsidiary, the Missouri, Arkansas & Southern Railway of Arkansas. The new subsidiary was authorized "to build in a southerly direction" – likely from Fayetteville (Washington County) – "to some point on the Little Rock and Fort Smith Railway, not east of Clarksville, with total mileage of about 55 miles." Within a year, the railroad had 63 miles of track under construction between Fayetteville and Fort Smith.

On June 28, 1881, these three railroads were merged to create the St. Louis, Arkansas & Texas Railway Company. Seven months later, the St. Louis, Arkansas & Texas Railway Company was sold to the St. Louis & San Francisco Railway Company on January 21, 1882. The line from Fort Smith south to the Arkansas-Oklahoma state line was built by the Ft. Smith & Southern Railway Company, incorporated in 1886 and absorbed by the Frisco in 1887.

An important part of this plan was the incorporation of the Fort Smith & Van Buren Bridge Company in March, 1885, capitalized by the Frisco to build a bridge over the Arkansas River at Van Buren. From the state line through Poteau to Paris, the line was built by the St. Louis & San Francisco Railway Company and the Paris & Great Northern Railroad Company. The Monett to Paris line was completed on July 1, 1887, connecting with the Texas & Pacific Railway to Dallas and Fort Worth. On June 30, 1896, the railroad was sold to the St. Louis & San Francisco Railroad Company, which was sold to the St. Louis-San Francisco Railway Company (Frisco) on September 15, 1916.

After the Frisco's improved mainline was built to the west across Oklahoma during the late 1890s and early 1900s, the line between Monett, Missouri, and Paris, Texas, took on the role of a secondary line mostly serving local businesses. By 1926, six passenger trains headed west out of Springfield (MO) on a daily basis, but only two turned south at Monett to cover this route, although the Fort Smith route was still part of Table 1 in the *Official Guide*. By 1934, Table 1 was the route through Tulsa, with the route to Paris now on Table 1a. In 1949, the Fort Smith route had fallen to Table 5.

Heavy flooding washed out the Spiro to Fort Smith KCS line in May 1943, and the railroad obtained temporary trackage rights over the St. Louis-San Francisco's Poteau to Fort Smith line. On December 12, 1944, the Interstate Commerce Commission granted authority to abandon the KCS line to Fort Smith and approved permanent trackage rights over the Frisco out of Poteau, Oklahoma.

During the early 1960s, the National Railroad Adjustment Board had a number of hearings where the Poteau-Fort Smith line was cited. The hearing noted that train orders were "issued by Frisco train dispatchers to Kansas City Southern Railroad telegraphers governing movement of Kansas City Southern trains over the lines of this Carrier between Fort Smith and Poteau." Specifically, the operations were described, stating that "Kansas City Southern trains have been given train orders at Heavener, to a Kansas City Southern telegrapher, which allowed such trains to move from the connecting track at Poteau to the Frisco station, where they receive other train orders to enable them to move from Poteau to Fort Smith."

In 1961, the line from Fort Smith through Poteau to Paris was the Arthur Subdivision, Central Division, of the St. Louis-San Francisco Railway Company. The Frisco became a part of the Burlington Northern Railroad (BN) on November 21, 1980, and the abandonment of the line soon began. During 1983, BN abandoned the line south of Wister all the way to Antlers, Oklahoma, making the line north through Poteau the 6th Subdivision – a branch line of the Springfield Division. On March 15, 1984, BN abandoned the line northward from Wister to Poteau. The line south of Antlers is now the Kiamichi Railroad, while the track from Poteau to Fort Smith is owned by the Kansas City Southern. Fort Smith to Monett is the Arkansas & Missouri Railroad.

With BN getting rid of the Monett to Paris line, KCS officially leased the Poteau-Fort Smith trackage from BN on February 9, 1985. During 1986, the Arkansas & Missouri Railroad completed a lease-purchase agreement on the line as far south as South

Heavener Sub Route Guide

Fort Smith at Milepost 422.50. On June 19, 1987, the Interstate Commerce Commission approved the sale of Burlington Northern track to Kansas City Southern between Milepost 453.14 at Wister, Oklahoma, to Milepost 422.50 near Fort Smith, Arkansas. From South Fort Smith to their terminal in Fort Smith, KCS uses trackage rights over the Arkansas & Missouri Railroad. Details on the Fort Smith Branch are found on Page 473.

326.4 POTEAU (AU) – The Poteau area was along a trade and hunting route used by the Osage, and probably earlier tribes for thousands of years. The nearby Poteau River provided access to the Arkansas River, and the lands upstream and downstream. In 1719, the expedition of French explorer Bernard De Harpe visited the area. A series of trading posts were built along the Poteau River in the early eighteenth century, trafficking in furs and hides. This area was well-mapped and documented by these explorers and traders. Several explanations of the Poteau name exist as the word translates into English as "post." Some histories state that the post was a large post or marking along the Arkansas River that told travelers where to turn to reach the Poteau River. Other versions state that it was named after the military posts or outposts along the river.

When the Choctaws were removed to Indian Territory in the 1830s, many passed through Skullyville and up the Poteau River. A few settled in the valley between the Cavanal and Sugar Loaf mountains. During the late 1870s, white families began to move into the region, including Bud Tate who opened a general store. The community began to grow as the St. Louis & San Francisco Railway built southward to Fort Smith, with plans to build on to Texas. Poteau was located on high ground above the Poteau River, and farms quickly sprang up on the nearby prairie. Timber and stone were available locally for construction. The flat ground also allowed the railroad to build facilities that the mountainous country north of Fort Smith prevented. When the contractor arrived at today's Poteau, a number of buildings were erected. These included a depot, section houses, and a number of tool houses. By 1887, a town began to grow around the Frisco depot, and a post office using the name Poteau opened on October 27, 1887.

By May 3, 1896, a second railroad arrived at Poteau – the Kansas City, Pittsburg & Gulf Railroad, later the Kansas City Southern. On May 31st at 10:00pm, the *Arkansaw Traveler*, described as a KCP&G "flyer" passenger train, departed Kansas City for the end of the line at Poteau. The train consisted of a baggage car, smoking car, reclining chair car and Pullman sleepers and was expected to arrive at noon on June 1st and provide a connection to Houston and Galveston via the Frisco's line. By August 6th, the KCP&G had been extended another 54 miles to Mena, Arkansas. Despite this expansion, Poteau boomed and the KCP&G built a station at the east end of Parker Street, some distance from the Frisco station located at Beard Avenue, about one-half block south of Dewey Avenue. The business area moved from the northwest and began to locate along Dewey Avenue, the area that is still today the heart of the city.

Poteau was incorporated on October 8, 1898, and a native-stone school was built. The town continued to grow, and the 1900 census reported 1182 residents. The federal court moved to Poteau from

Cameron in 1900, and Poteau became the seat of the new Le Flore County when Oklahoma became a state on November 16, 1907. A telephone company (1904), electric company (1906) and water works (1906) added to the modernization of the town. In 1908, Poteau reached the population required to be a first-class city, and its official population in 1910 was 1830.

The growth of business between the two railroads led to the construction of a wye to the west off of the KCS north of Whitney Avenue. A track headed west off of the wye to a westbound connection with the Frisco. This track provided an interchange between the two railroads, and a number of industries located on spur tracks off of a small 5-track KCS yard that developed. The first industry to locate there was G. H. Harper, which operated a cotton gin, saw mill, and feed mill just west of Witte Street on the north side of the yard by 1904. By 1909, the area north of the yard and south of Reynolds Avenue was busy, with the Poteau Lumber & Manufacturing Company, Ingram Lumber Company, and Poteau Grain Produce Company from east to west. By the mid-1910s, the area was heavily developed. To the north were W. Bush & Son (ice factory), Poteau Lumber & Manufacturing Company, and the Osage Cotton Oil Company. To the west of Harper Street and south of the tracks was the Lapel Bottle Manufacturing Company. While these tracks are gone today, this area still features manufacturing with Kenco Plastics.

Coal and brick also became important during the first few decades of the twentieth century. The Poteau Pressed Brick & Tile Company located on the Fort Smith, Poteau & Western Railway north of Town Creek. Much of the coal business focused on the mines on Cavanal Mountain, but other mines were located all around the region. Agriculture was also important, especially cotton, various types of potatoes, and livestock.

With all of the business, both major railroads built new stations. In 1914, Kansas City Southern built a modern brick station at Dewey Avenue. At the time, the Frisco right-of-way was located between Peters and Broadway, and their station was on the west side of the mainline at Beard Avenue, a half-block south of Dewey Avenue. Their station had the passenger section to the south and a freight and baggage section to the north. A water tower and then stockyards were to the north of the building. The tracks of the Fort Smith, Poteau & Western Railway were west of the Frisco, using the same right-of-way through Poteau. In 1915, the Frisco built a new reinforced concrete ("fire proof construction") station on the east side of the mainline at Clayton, north of Dewey. Its waiting rooms were to the south and the baggage area to the north. This building still stands, restored as the Poteau City Hall and located at 111 N Peters Street.

The old Frisco station, located at 111 N Peters Street, is now used as the city hall of Poteau, Oklahoma.

Poteau is somewhat unique in Oklahoma as its population has grown every decade except during the 1950s. Being a county seat and the largest city in the area, Poteau has attracted numerous banks, hotels, retail stores, restaurants, gas stations, and other businesses. Poteau is also the home of Carl Albert State College, several offices of the Choctaw Nation, and Poteau Public Schools. Several industries still remain, but none currently served by the KCS. The population today is about 9000, and a four-lane highway bypass has been built around the west side of town.

The Kansas City Southern at Poteau

The Kansas City Southern was the second railroad at Poteau, and it remained the junior railroad until about 1980 when Burlington Northern began to abandon and sell the Monett to Paris route. Because of this, KCS normally had fewer facilities than the Frisco here. Initially, the railroad focused on its depot at Parker Avenue. In this area was a cotton platform, track scales, a water tower, and several maintenance-of-way sheds. In 1914, a more modern station was built at Dewey Avenue.

The early 1930s represented the peak of KCS infrastructure and service at Poteau. There was an agent-operator at the depot 8am-5pm except Sundays and holidays. For other times, there was a dispatcher telephone that could be used by train crews, plus a mail crane for the post office. Passenger train Nos. 15 and 16 had Poteau as a scheduled stop. There were two sidings – East Siding could hold 70 cars and West Siding held 57 cars. The yard and wye were shown in the timetable, as well as locomotive water.

During the early 1950s, KCS eliminated its steam locomotives, and many of the facilities required to support them. At Poteau, this just affected the water tower. By 1958, only a 56-car siding, the yard, and the wye remained. Two agents were assigned to Poteau Monday through Saturday, with the hours of 8:30am-1:30pm and 3:30pm-11:30pm. Poteau was still nicely served by the railroad's passenger trains, with *The Flying Crow* (Nos. 15 and 16) making regular stops, and the *Southern Belle* (Nos. 1 and 2) making conditional flag stops – "Nos. 1 and 2 will stop on flag at Westville, Stilwell, Spiro, Poteau and Howe for revenue passengers to or from Neosho or beyond and for revenue passengers to or from Spiro or beyond."

Little changed by 1964, except the agent-operator was assigned 8am-5pm Monday through Saturday. Poteau was again a stop for all passenger trains, with No. 1 here at 4:23pm. With the end of passenger service, the agent's hours were cut back to Monday through Friday. Another change took place with the Frisco abandoning its tracks, and KCS cutting back its facilities to a yard and a 1771-foot siding by the late 1980s. Soon after, Poteau was simply a few short industry tracks and the junction with the Fort Smith Branch.

If you are looking for signs of the KCS, besides its mainline, little remains. Probably the most unusual is KCS caboose #365, used as a bank building near the Walmart at the north end of town. The caboose is one of thirty such cars (#350-#379) that the railroad rebuilt from box cars. It has a steel frame and a wooden, outside braced body. It also features steel bay windows and rode on conventional freight car trucks.

Heavener Sub Route Guide

While there were once a number of tracks at Poteau, today there are few more than simply the mainline.

KCS caboose #365 is located north of downtown Poteau, and is used by a local bank.

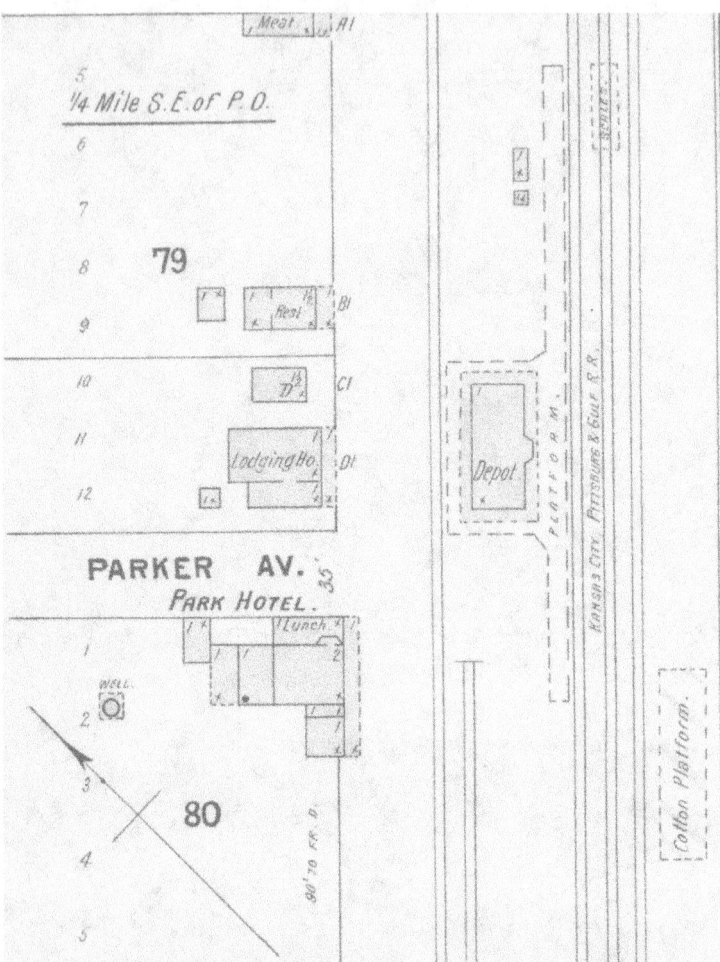

While both the Frisco and KCS served Poteau, each had their own station about ten blocks apart. The Frisco depot was on the west side of their mainline at Beard Avenue, about a half-block south of Dewey Avenue. The KCS depot was on the west side of their mainline at Parker Avenue in 1901. *Sanborn Fire Insurance Map from Poteau, Le Flore County, Oklahoma.* Sanborn Map Company, Jan, 1901. Map. Retrieved from the Library of Congress, https://www.loc.gov/item/sanborn07219_002/.

Heavener Sub Route Guide

This map shows the Poteau connecting track between Kansas City Southern and the Frisco. *Sanborn Fire Insurance Map from Poteau, Le Flore County, Oklahoma.* Sanborn Map Company, Oct, 1904. Map. Retrieved from the Library of Congress, https://www.loc.gov/item/sanborn07219_003/.

Poteau & Cavanal Mountain Railroad

Besides the Kansas City Southern and the St. Louis-San Francisco Railway, for a number of years during the early part of the twentieth century, there was a third railroad at Poteau. This line extended "from a connection with the St. Louis-San Francisco Railway at Poteau in a westerly direction to a point at or near Witteville, a distance of 3.5 miles all in Le Flore County, Okla." The railroad came in to Poteau from the north and came beside the Frisco line about College Avenue and then followed it south to about Cherry Avenue.

The railroad was built about 1893 by the Cavanal Coal and Mining Company to serve the coal mines near Witteville, Oklahoma. Located just three miles from Poteau, Witteville was once a prosperous mining town. The mines were actually further up the mountain and inclines were used to lower the coal to the tipples that were used to load the coal into rail cars. The primary operator of the mines changed several times over the years, and included the Cavanal Coal and Mining Company, Indianola Coal, and the Poteau Coal and Mercantile Company. On January 24, 1906, Poteau Coal's No. 6 Mine suffered a methane gas explosion. The number of deaths is unknown, but fourteen miners in Slope Mine No. 4 were killed nearby. The mines continued to operate for another decade or more, but they never reached the volumes from before the explosion.

These mines were located on the northeast side of Cavanal Mountain, often known as Cavanal Hill. The mountain is known locally as the "World's Highest Hill" based upon the concept that a hill stands less than 2000 feet above its surroundings. In this case, Cavanal Hill has an elevation of 2385 feet while the nearby Poteau River is 1960 feet lower. The name Cavanal comes from French explorers who used the mountain as a landmark. Some claim that the term means a cave, while others state that it means cavernous. The mountain was noted in a number of early surveys, land descriptions, and natural studies. Starting in the late 1800s, a series of health resorts and tourist hotels were established on the mountain due to the cooler temperatures and a series of natural springs. During the early 1960s, Senator Robert S. Kerr built a home on top of Cavanal Mountain for entertaining family and close friends. In 1963, President Kennedy spent a weekend there. Today, the hill is covered with communication towers, plus a public lookout and pavilion.

The actual railroad between Poteau and Witteville changed names more times than it had miles. The railroad was built about 1893 by the Cavanal Coal & Mining Company, which was bought by the Cavanal Coal, Coke & Railway on August 7, 1895. From the start, the railroad and the coal mines coordinated their activities, often under the same ownership. On November 8, 1899, the railroad became the Indianola Coal & Railway Company, which became the Fort Smith, Poteau & Western Railway two weeks later (November 21, 1899). Because the company records were never very good, other sources provide other dates on these sales. For example, the Interstate Commerce Commission stated that the Indianola Coal & Railway Company acquired the railroad sometime between July 21, 1898, and November 8, 1899.

The Fort Smith, Poteau & Western Railway was in financial trouble by 1915, and David J. Evans purchased it at a foreclosure sale on October 16, 1915. Evans controlled much of the coal mining and properties at Witteville, and had a vested interest in seeing the railroad stay in place. On January 10, 1916, the Fort Smith, Poteau & Western Railroad took over the railroad, which consisted of 3.415 miles of main track, 0.595 miles of yard track and sidings, one steam locomotive, and one passenger car. The Railroad Retirement Board later investigated the company and provided some interesting information about the railroad's operations. "In 1918 the coal traffic ceased because operation of the mines was suspended. After that date bricks in carload lots were handled by horsepower over that part of the line between the junction point with the Frisco and a brick yard, a distance of .75 miles." The Board determined that the railroad was a "carrier-employer" from December 24, 1915 to January 1, 1919.

Things became very unclear after 1919. The Fort Smith, Poteau & Western Railroad apparently sat unused until August 31, 1922, when it was again reportedly purchased by David J. Evans. Other reports state that it was sold at a receiver's sale on February 24, 1923. The new company was the Poteau & Cavanal Mountain Railroad. According to the Railroad Retirement Board, the "Poteau & Cavanal Mountain filed circulars with the Interstate Commerce Commission for the years 1923, 1924 and 1925, indicating that it owned 3.40 miles of road and that it was not in operation." From 1926 to 1930, the same information was reported by the ICC, but it stated that the information was from unofficial sources. In 1931, the ICC reported that the railroad had been dismantled. A final opinion from Railroad Retirement Board was that the Poteau & Cavanal Mountain was not an "employer" under the Railroad Retirement Act.

For those wanting to follow this old coal-hauling railroad, head north on Broadway and turn left on Smith Avenue/Mockingbird Lane. This street becomes Witteville Drive.

Heavener Sub Route Guide

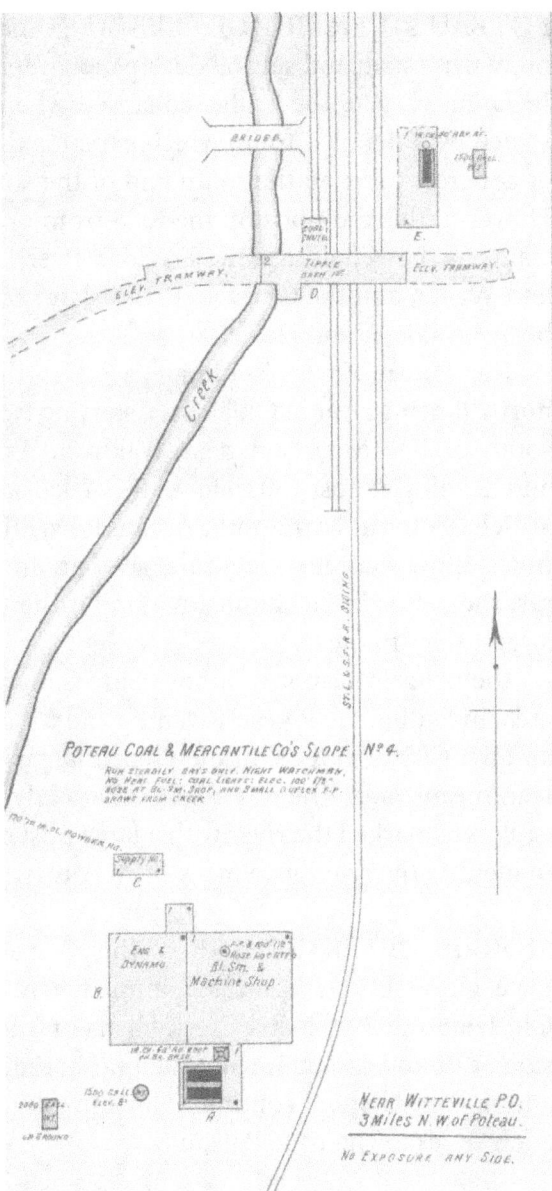

This Sanborn map shows the basic arrangement of the Poteau Coal tipple neat Witteville, Oklahoma. *Sanborn Fire Insurance Map from Poteau, Le Flore County, Oklahoma.* Sanborn Map Company, Oct, 1904. Map. Retrieved from the Library of Congress, https://www.loc.gov/item/sanborn07219_003/.

330.3 POTEAU RIVER BRIDGE – This bridge includes a pony truss span and several deck plate girder spans. In January 1976, the bridge collapsed when it was struck by a derailed train, which explains the newer concrete piers on the south end of the structure. However, this did not stop the KCS from operating trains as they could use the Frisco between Poteau and Wister, and the Chicago, Rock Island & Pacific between Wister and Howe.

The Poteau River is unique as it is the only north-flowing river in Oklahoma, starting two miles south of Bee Mountain near Waldron, Arkansas, and heading almost 150 miles to the Arkansas River at Belle Point in Fort Smith, Arkansas. While a few miles of the start and end of the river are in Arkansas, the rest is in Oklahoma, making it the seventh largest river in the state.

The name Poteau is used for many things in this area, including the Poteau River, Poteau Mountains, and the City of Poteau. In the French language, poteau means post. There is a belief that early French explorers marked the river with a large post or stake to identify the river or to mark the territory.

332.8 MORRIS CREEK BRIDGE – This 3-span deck plate girder bridge is located immediately east of Old Highway 59. Morris Creek forms on the south side of Round Mountain and then flows to the west and north to here. It continues flowing to the north a few miles to enter the Poteau River.

Heavener Sub Route Guide

Milepost 333 can be seen just north of the retired CRI&P Crossing at Howe, Oklahoma.

333.0 CRI&P CROSSING – This was once the Howe crossing between the Kansas City Southern and the Chicago, Rock Island & Pacific. By the 1930s, it was interlocked and there was a connection between the two railroads. Located at an elevation of 475 feet, this was one of the few places that the Rock Island and KCS actually touched each other. For a number of years, there was a joint passenger station, and in 1979 when the Rock Island was closing down, it was still an automatic interlocking. The Rock Island route was Subdivision 31 of the Southern Division, part of what was known as the Choctaw Route between Memphis, Tennessee, and Tucumcari, New Mexico.

Construction on the Rock Island track in western Arkansas and very eastern Oklahoma initially began at Wister, Oklahoma, and worked eastward. *Poor's Manual* (1899) reported that the Choctaw, Oklahoma & Gulf Railroad completed its track from Wister to Howe by September 6, 1898. The distance cited was 6.4 miles. The *Arkansas Gazette* (October 6, 1898) quoted the *Mena Democrat* by reporting "The Choctaw, Oklahoma & Gulf railroad has completed its tracks to Howe, a new station about four miles south of Poteau, and is now making direct connection with the K.C.P.&G. at the latter place, thus saving those going that route from a trip to Poteau and thence to Wister Junction. This will be a great benefit to Mena people, many of whom make frequent trips through Oklahoma, having interest there."

Construction began at both Howe and Little Rock "with great earnestness" on December 1, 1898. Various 1899 issues of *The Choctaw* covered this construction, stating that grading was to be done by July 1899. One issue stated that track laying began at Howe on April 20, 1899, and that construction materials were being brought to Howe and Mansfield. It went on to say that the parts for three steel bridges were at Howe and ready for assembly. There were also details about the construction. One such detail was that the construction for the "100 miles east from Howe was under contract to the Choctaw Construction Company, sub-let to McCabe & Steen, and the contract for 66 miles west from Little Rock was held by McCarthy & Reichardt, of Little Rock, who sub-let 43 miles to McCabe & Steen." The report also stated that McCabe & Steen was using a Roberts track-laying machine, getting as much as two miles a day of track built.

The Roberts track-laying machine was built by the Roberts Steam Track-Layer Company of Seattle, Washington. A track-laying machine included a pioneer (front) car with a conveyor belt that brought track materials to the point of construction. The Roberts machine featured a 20-horsepower steam engine on the lead car that drove the material conveyor belt to deliver the ties, and powered a derrick to pull the rails forward to the delivery booms. The steam engine was supplied steam from the locomotive through a series of pipes along the train. For those wanting more details, the July 1915 *Practical Track Work* issue of *Railway Engineering and Maintenance of Way* included a full article on the machine.

The October 1899 issue of *The Choctaw* showed that the line west of Howe was complete and being operated by the Choctaw, Oklahoma & Gulf (Howe to Wister completed in 1898), while the Little Rock to Howe track was still shown as being "now under construction." However, at 9:44am on October 13, 1899, the railroad was completed about 22 miles west of Little Rock.

For years, there was a joint depot in the northwest quadrant of the diamond at Howe, built square to fit along the tracks of the two railroads. The building featured an eight-sided windowed tower at the corner of the building, overlooking both railroad's tracks in all directions. In 1910, the Corporation Commission of the State of Oklahoma had several hearings at Howe on the issue of John Begley requesting a depot from both the Kansas City Southern and the Chicago, Rock Island & Pacific. About the same time, the Commission ordered both railroads to improve the depot at Howe.

Today, everything is gone except for a siding and a connection between the two rail lines in the southwest corner of the old diamond. The line to the west has been through a number of hands since the end of the Chicago, Rock Island & Pacific. The line at first sat unused, but in 1986, the State of Oklahoma purchased the line from near McAlester to Howe from L. B. Foster for $2,778,406. A contract was soon reached that had the Missouri-Kansas-Texas (MKT or Katy) operate the line, calling the track from Howe (MP 295.5) to the MKT at McAlester (MP 366.4) the Howe Subdivision. On August 12, 1988, Union Pacific (UP) acquired the Katy through its Missouri Pacific Railroad. UP took over operations of the line, but almost immediately began looking for someone to take over the railroad. On March 3, 1996, Union Pacific, with the approval of the State of Oklahoma, transferred all rights of the line to the Arkansas-Oklahoma Railroad Company (A-OK). Later, the A-OK Railroad also leased track in the McAlester, Oklahoma, area (August 1, 1997), as well as the track between Shawnee and Oklahoma City (July 7, 2000).

Heavener Sub Route Guide

The Choctaw Route of the Chicago, Rock Island & Pacific once crossed the Heavener Subdivision at Howe. Today, the KCS mainline still exists, but there is only a barricade and a stub track to the west.

The Arkansas-Oklahoma Railroad Company

The Arkansas-Oklahoma Railroad Company is a Class III shortline railroad. When created, the railroad operated seventy miles of track and served two customers. Within a decade, the company operated almost 120 miles of track, serving twenty rail shippers. The company handles products like coal, aggregate, decorative stone, wheat, corn, oats, frac sand and drilling fluid products, pipe, lumber, plastic resin pellets, automobiles, and various chemicals. The company has their own fleet of freight cars and also handles car storage for a number of companies. Besides direct on-line customers, the A-OK also has several transload facilities that allow shippers without tracks to use the railroad.

During April 2016, the Arkansas-Oklahoma Railroad Company bought the Howe to McAlester line from the State of Oklahoma. However, due to an error, the sale was never formally approved by the Surface Transportation Board. Therefore, a new application with the Board was made, and as of October 19, 2019, the line was officially sold. The notice published on September 24, 2019, stated that the Surface Transportation Board "is granting an exemption under 49 U.S.C. 10502 from the prior approval requirements of 49 U.S.C. 10902 for Arkansas-Oklahoma Railroad Company (AOK), a Class III carrier, to acquire from the State of Oklahoma and operate approximately 69.60 miles of rail line extending from milepost 295.36 in Howe, Okla., to milepost 364.96 in McAlester, Okla." The railroad is based in Wilburton, Oklahoma, and is known for its bright red and yellow locomotives painted to resemble those of the original Rock Island Railroad.

The interchange track between the Arkansas-Oklahoma Railroad and Kansas City Southern is shown just south of Control Point North Howe.

Heavener Sub Route Guide

333.5 NORTH END 1908 LINE DIVERSION – At this location just north of the Old Pike Road grade crossing, the railroad curves to the south. When originally built, the line headed to the southeast. The current route turns back to the southeast at Forest Hill and rejoins the original grade near the Industrial Road grade crossing at Milepost 336.7. The original railroad grade is now used as Old Pike Road.

The March 13, 1908, issue of *The Railroad Gazette* had a short notice about the work on the new Kansas City Southern grade between Howe and Heavener. "Building 3-mile cut-off south of Howe, Okla., to reduce grades. Some bridge work. Extensive surveys made last year for other similar work." During the early 1900s, Kansas City Southern management studied a number of track realignments to try to reduce the grades on the railroad. Few major realignments actually took place, but some earthwork was done all along the line to lower hills, raise low spots, and reduce grades.

333.8 HOWE (BX) – Milepost 333.8 is the location of Howe shown in recent KCS timetables, but earlier it was at Milepost 333.0 where the union depot once stood. Howe started as the small Choctaw Nation town of Klondike. The town was based upon farming and served as a post village for the Nation. When the Kansas City, Pittsburgh & Gulf Railroad (KCP&G) built through the area in early 1896, the residents renamed it for Dr. Herbert M. Howe, a director of the railroad. In 1898, a post office opened using that name, and the Choctaw, Oklahoma & Gulf was building east. In 1900, the KCP&G became the Kansas City Southern Railroad. That same year,

Howe had a population of 626, and business grew as coal was discovered.

The coal boom started in the late 1890s as several mines opened, and then the Mexican Gulf Coal and Transportation Company built one hundred coke ovens west of Howe. Soon the property was sold to the Degnan and McConnell Coal and Coke Company which only operated the coal mines. However, after World War I, the coke ovens were reopened by the Howe-McCurtain Coal and Coke Company. Farming was also still important, and 784 shipments of cotton were moved out from Howe in 1903-1904. All of this activity attracted a cotton gin, several general and grocery stores, a hotel, four doctors, four drugstores, and the *Howe Herald* newspaper.

A report by the Kansas City Southern in 1912 stated that "most of the business done in town is mercantile, the handling of cotton, live stock and the mining and transport of coal. The country surrounding Howe is open prairie limited in area by the Sugar Loaf Mountains. The lands in the vicinity are claimed to be of exceptional fertility, particularly so in the Horse Shoe Bend of Poteau River and the Sugar Loaf Valley." The report also mentioned that the Howe area was "underlaid with coal deposits of excellent quality and there are several large coal mines and a large coke plant in the immediate vicinity." The town was described as having a bank, "a large commodious hotel, a flour and grist mill, four cotton gins, a bottling works, a public school building, cost $12,000, telephone service, three or four churches and from ten to fifteen mercantile establishments."

Over the next several decades, the population went up and down based upon the activity at the coal mines. The Lincoln Coal Company was able to survive the Great Depression, but most other area mines closed, and by 1960, Howe was down to 390 residents. A contract to sell coal to Japanese steel mills starting in 1967 helped the Howe Coal Company and encouraged people to move back to Howe. Today, coal is no longer a force here, and agriculture is back to providing much of the purpose of Howe. Howe is also helped by having U.S. Highway 59 pass just to the east, where several gas stations and discount stores operate. The post office and the Howe School District are still here, and the town had a population of 802 in the 2010 census, the highest recorded in Howe's history.

Howe and the Kansas City Southern

By August 1896, the Kansas City, Pittsburg & Gulf had been extended through Howe. Within two years, the KCP&G was hauling track materials and supplies to Howe for the construction of the Choctaw, Oklahoma & Gulf, later the Chicago, Rock Island & Pacific. The two railroads also coordinated on building a union depot, and for a few decades, to promote the train connections available at Howe. For example, during early January 1901, the two railroads operated a through sleeper from Kansas City to Howe, and then on to the resort city of Hot Springs, Arkansas, via the Choctaw, Oklahoma & Gulf (Rock Island Railroad).

In 1936, the station was open 24-7 with a KCS agent-operator. The station was a scheduled passenger stop for all passenger trains, and regular freight interchange took place between the two railroads. A dispatcher telephone was at Howe, and also a yard and an 89-car siding. The continuous staffing continued until the end of passenger service in 1969, although the KCS passenger service did decline. Instead of being a scheduled stop for all passenger trains, trains were flagged at Howe by 1958. For the *Southern Belle,* Howe was a conditional flag stop – "Nos. 1 and 2 will stop on flag at Westville, Stilwell, Spiro, Poteau and Howe for revenue passengers to or from Neosho or beyond and for revenue passengers to or from Spiro or beyond." The only other major change was that the siding had been extended to 133 car lengths as part of the change in freight operations.

The conditions of the conditional flag stop for the *Southern Belle* had changed again by 1964, making it easier to understand – "Nos. 1 and 2 stop on flag at Westville, Stilwell, Spiro and Howe for revenue passengers to or from regular stops." The southbound *Belle* was scheduled to be here at 4:31pm. Another timetable change was that the siding was shown to be 150 cars long. The 1970 employee timetable showed the effects of the loss of passenger service with the agent changed to 8am-5pm Monday through Friday. Soon after, the siding was shown to be about 7670 feet.

During the early 2000s, the track layout on the north side of Heavener was changed to provide more capacity for crew changes and locomotive fueling. The railroad added a second main track as far north as Milepost 333.1, a location known as Control Point North Howe. Just to the south at Howe Storage North Switch, there is a small two-track yard to the west to allow interchange traffic between the KCS and the Arkansas-Oklahoma Railroad. The Howe Storage South Switch is located at Milepost 333.5, just south of Old Pike Road (E1425 Road).

Heavener Sub Route Guide

NORTH HOWE CONTROL POINT

The sign actually reads North Howe Control Point, not the typical Control Point North Howe. However, no matter the name, this is the north switch of the two main tracks from here to South Heavener.

Seen from the County Road E1425 grade crossing are two mainline tracks (to the right) and two storage tracks (to the left). Several interchange cars for the Arkansas-Oklahoma Railroad can be seen in the storage tracks.

Anyone who follows the Heavener Subdivision will find a few grade crossings with hoses down the middle of the tracks. These hoses are found where trains often have to stop for long periods of time. The hoses allow the train to uncouple and open the grade crossing, but keep the locomotive brake air on all of the cars. These hoses are found at the County Road E1425 grade crossing at Howe, Oklahoma.

Heavener Sub Route Guide

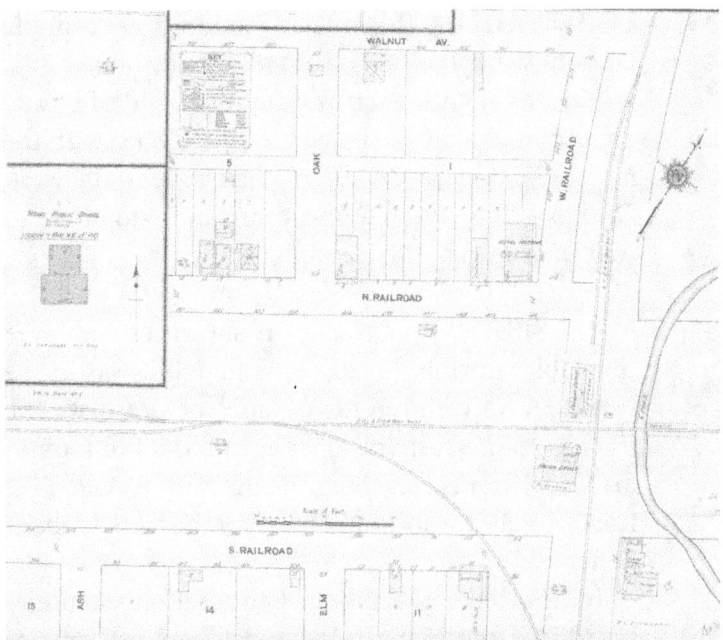

This map shows the diamond at Howe, as well as the union depot and freight house alongside the KCS tracks. While many of the plans had the town's center here, today it is further west, wrapped around the former Rock Island mainline. *Sanborn Fire Insurance Map from Howe, Le Flore County, Oklahoma*. Sanborn Map Company, Jan, 1911. Map. Retrieved from the Library of Congress, https://www.loc.gov/item/sanborn07131_002/.

334.7 SOUTH HOWE CONTROL POINT – This location is a full set of crossovers to allow trains to change tracks. Heading south, the first crossover takes a train from Main Track #2 (west track) to Main Track #1 (east track). The next crossover can take trains from Main Track #1 to Main Track #2.

To the east on Old Pike Road, there is an old bridge that features typical cut-stone headwalls. The headwalls are still used, but the roadway now uses a wooden deck.

335.2 FOREST HILL – This small community at the grade crossing with Forest Hill Road, County Road 172, was never a station on the railroad. Old Highway 59 is immediately to the west of the tracks, with the new U.S. Highway 59 about a half-mile to the west. On busy days, southbound trains may stop here to wait their turn at the Heavener fuel racks.

336.3 MINE SPUR – This track was shown in employee timetables during the 2000s, although it was in the Heavener yard limits for decades before that. The track is to the east and once featured a full loop to load coal trains, reaching all the way to Old Pike Road. Today, the loop and much of the track is abandoned.

In 1908, the Oklahoma Corporation Commission listed the Ingham Lumber Company Spur as being 3.1 miles south of Howe and 1.9 miles north of Heavener, placing it somewhere in this area. Ingham apparently moved their operations around the region, and also had sawmills at Poteau, and on the Waldron Branch at Bates, Arkansas.

336.7 SOUTH END 1908 LINE DIVERSION – Old Pike Road and the current KCS line come back together near the Industrial Road grade crossing at Milepost 336.7. This marks the south end of the new line built in 1908. To the northwest is Lost Mountain, which the new U.S. Highway 59 goes around on the west side, while the old Highway 59 and the railroad go around the east side. Also in this area are a number of facilities operated by OK Foods.

Milepost 336.7 is also the location of North Heavener, earlier located at Milepost 335.2. This is a Control Point that separates the fuel racks north of Industrial Road from those to the south. The signals allow trains that have stopped at the fuel racks to get a signal to depart and head north or south.

This street sign gives a hint that this is the south end of the 1908 line diversion. Old Pike Road to the north is actually the original grade for the Heavener Subdivision.

The Control Point North Heavener area is very busy, and it is clearly marked as private property with no trespassing allowed.

This control point sign can be found in the middle of the fueling racks on the north side of Heavener, Oklahoma. As long as you stay on the local roads and off of the railroad property, there are no problems with watching all of the action.

Heavener Sub Route Guide

This sign explains much of the activity at Control Point North Heavener. Essentially every train stops here for fueling and other services.

This sign greets all trains at Control Point North Heavener as they enter the yard complex.

The Heavener Sub: History Through the Miles

Any locomotive that can lead a train over the Heavener Subdivision can easily be photographed at the Heavener Fueling Facility. Here, KCS 4848 heads up a northbound freight on the east track, while BNSF 9242 is the trailing DPU (Distributed Power Unit) on a southbound freight on the west track.

This photo at the Heavener Fueling Facility from 2021 shows KCS 5020 next to Progress Rail (EMDX) 7234.

Heavener Sub Route Guide

338.0 HEAVENER (HV) – Heavener is a major, but somewhat small terminal on the Kansas City Southern. It is the south end of the Heavener Subdivision, and once the Third Subdivision and earlier the Third District. Until 1910, it wasn't even this, as Mena served as the division terminal. As the railroad was completed and train operations began to normalize, the railroad made improvements and adjusted its crew territories. At the north end of the Third District, the terminal moved from Gentry, Arkansas, to Stilwell, Oklahoma, and then to Watts, Oklahoma. These changes then encouraged changes at the south end of the district. A series of newspaper articles throughout 1910 reported on what were first rumors, and then confirmed plans to move the division point and railroad offices from Mena to Heavener. One of these was an interesting article in the *Arkansas Gazette* (October 4, 1910) which stated that the KCS trainmaster, his assistants, and the dispatchers moved from Mena to Heavener "between midnight Friday night and early Friday morning on September 30, 1910." It was pointed out that during the move, this part of the railroad was operated without dispatchers.

KCS didn't start Heavener, but it did help it to grow. Like many early communities in the area, Heavener was based upon Choctaw settlements after the tribe's forced removal to Indian Territory. The area was known for its good grass, perfect for livestock. The grass was also the source of some of the first names for the area, which included Prairie of the Tall Grass, Prairie View, Long Prairie, and Grand Prairie. Control by the Choctaw Nation also led to the name of Choctaw City. White settlement began in the mid-1870s using permits from the Choctaw

Nation. One of the first settlers was Joseph H. Heavener, who arrived in 1877. In 1880, the first store arrived when Zachary Taylor Ward and his Choctaw wife Tabitha Hickman Ward moved their general store from Skullyville to this area. Zachary Ward died in 1883 and Tabitha married Heavener, giving him actual land ownership. A church and a subscription school, a cotton gin and a gristmill, several other businesses, and a number of houses were here at what was becoming the town of Heavener by the mid-1880s.

During Summer 1896, the Kansas City, Pittsburg & Gulf built through this area. With the railroad approaching, the local residents had voted to make the name Heavener official for the community. With the unofficial organization of the community, a post office opened on May 12, 1896, initially using a boxcar as its home. At first, Heavener was just a station along the line, and the first depot was also housed in a boxcar. Heavener was able to incorporate in 1898 after the passage of *The Curtis Act*, which allowed municipalities in Indian Territory to organize and operate under certain federal guidelines. This led to the first population count in the 1900 census, which reported 234 residents. In 1901, Heavener was platted and streets and lots were officially designed and surveyed.

Heavener grew more when it became a railroad junction town in 1901 as the Arkansas Western Railroad built eastward into Arkansas. In 1904, *The Heavener Ledger* newspaper began publishing, as it still does weekly. In 1909, rumors began to circulate that Kansas City Southern was going to move its division point from the top of the grade at Mena, to the bottom of the grade at Heavener. An explanation for the possible move was that a new federal law mandated shorter working hours for train crews, so their territories needed to be shortened. As reported in February 1910, some 100 buildings had been erected in the town within the previous six months. The census showed a population of 780, and that fall the railroad moved its facilities to Heavener, creating another burst in economic activity. An interesting side issue with the move was that many employees owned a house in Mena, which they suddenly couldn't sell. The KCS agreed to purchase the residence of every company employee who wished to sell through its newly created Mena Land & Improvement Company. In 1919, Kansas City Southern sold the Mena Land & Improvement Company for $40,000.

A 1912 report by the Kansas City Southern Railway stated that Heavener was a division terminus, and a junction point with the Waldron Branch which ran "through an extensive coal belt and a fine fruit and truck country." The railroad had made a number of improvements, including "new round houses, repair shops, office buildings, depot, employes' hotel, and several miles of new yard trackage." Other new businesses at Heavener included the Pierce-McNeeley Grocery Company, the Heavener Supply Company, and the Grand Leader Dry Goods Company. The Heavener Smokeless Coal Company had just had a track built to it so that coal could be moved to market, and the Heavener Oil & Gas Company was making test borings near town. A final statement added that there were two substantial banks, two cotton gins, one hardwood mill, and numerous mercantile establishments. Because of all of this, Heavener's population jumped to 1850 in 1920.

Railroad billing reports from the 1920s show large movements of corn, cotton, Irish and sweet potatoes, oats, hay, radishes, blackberries, peaches and watermelons from Heavener. Coal was of course a local industry, with several mines to the north and south along the railroad. The population reached 2269 in the 1930 census. Timber from the nearby hills also was sold, and the Burnett Lumber Company opened a sawmill here in 1935. The loss of most of the coal mining led to a small decline in population, with 1891 residents in 1960.

While the railroad remained as the primary business in Heavener, other industries came and went. In 1960, the Heavener Charcoal Company began operations, but the Burnett Lumber sawmill burned in 1981. Like many towns across the region, poultry production grew and became important. In 1986, OK Foods established a poultry hatchery at Heavener, and then added a processing plant in 1992 and a feed mill in 1995.

During the 1970s, tourism also began to grow, especially with the creation of Heavener Runestone State Park, located a few miles to the east on the edge of Poteau Mountain. The 55-acre park includes trails, primitive and RV campsites, picnic areas, an amphitheater, event center and gift shop. The park protects a large stone with what appears to be eight runic markings. While a number of theories have been proposed, the most accepted is that they date between 600 and 800 AD and were made by Vikings. The eight runes translate best to gnomedal or glomedal, which is "Little Valley" or "Valley owned by Glome," making them a boundary marker or land claim. Since 2011, the park has been operated by a non-profit volunteer group and the City of Heavener. It is also the home of the Runestone Festival, a mix of Viking and Steampunk events each October.

This sign, located at the grade crossing of the Heavener fueling facility, points the way to the Heavener Runestone Park.

The current population of Heavener is about 3300. Kansas City Southern and OK Foods are the two largest employers. Heavener has a number of local and chain stores, plus restaurants and gas stations, most along U.S. Highway 59/270 just west of the tracks. Heavener also is the home of the Wolves, the mascot of the local school system. The railroad operates through the center of Heavener, and many of the businesses serve the local railroad employees.

The Kansas City Southern's Heavener

The Kansas City Southern Railway, which operates a major yard, crew base, and fueling facility in Heavener, has been the town's largest employer since the facilities were located here. During the first few decades of the twentieth century, a large roundhouse stood at the north end of Main Street, about where the shop building is located. To the north were servicing facilities, including coal, sand and water for the locomotives. An oil shed was nearby to provide lubricating oils, and kerosine for lamps. With the large number of coal mines in the area, a shop to repair freight cars was also built.

On the east side of Avenue B and West 1st Street was the Railroad Hotel, providing lodging for train crews and visitors to the community. The station was just to the south, and both were located on the west side of the tracks. At the time, the city blocks on the east side of the tracks were more developed, and a drive around town will show that this is probably still true today.

The Kansas City Southern station was once a two-story building with administrative offices on the second floor. The first floor featured a passenger section on the south end, and a baggage and freight section on the north end. Like all stations in Oklahoma at the time, there were separate White and Black waiting rooms. Train crews who were not based at Heavener used a dormitory-like railroad hotel that was located south of the station.

Heavener Sub Route Guide

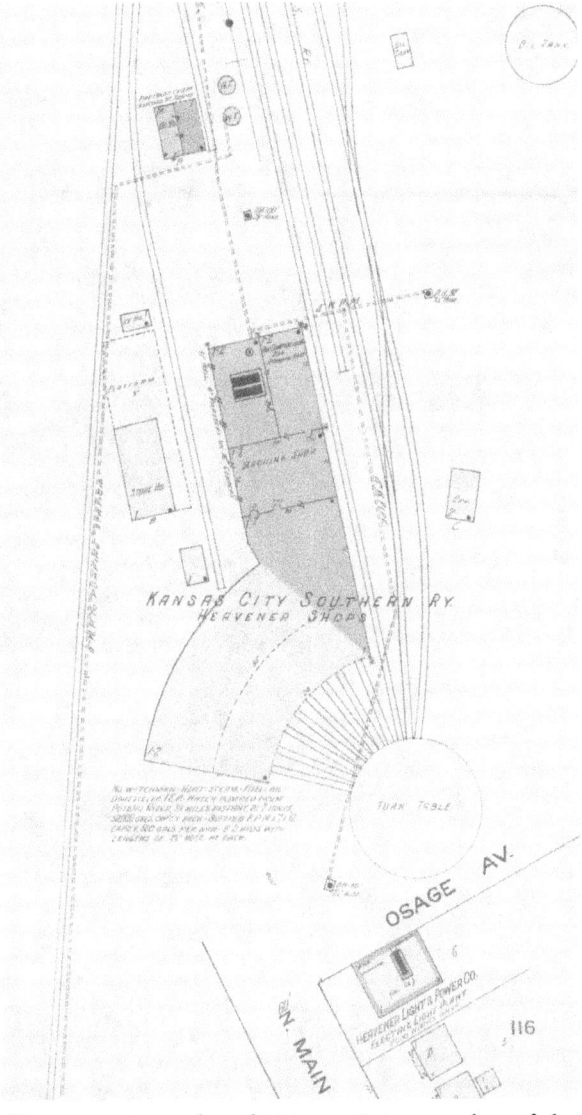

When Heavener was made a division point, a number of shops and facilities were built here. This roundhouse allowed locomotives to be removed from trains, serviced and inspected, and then placed back on a later train. *Sanborn Fire Insurance Map from Heavener, Le Flore County, Oklahoma.* Sanborn Map Company, August 1913. Map. Retrieved from the Library of Congress, https://www.loc.gov/item/sanborn07120_001/.

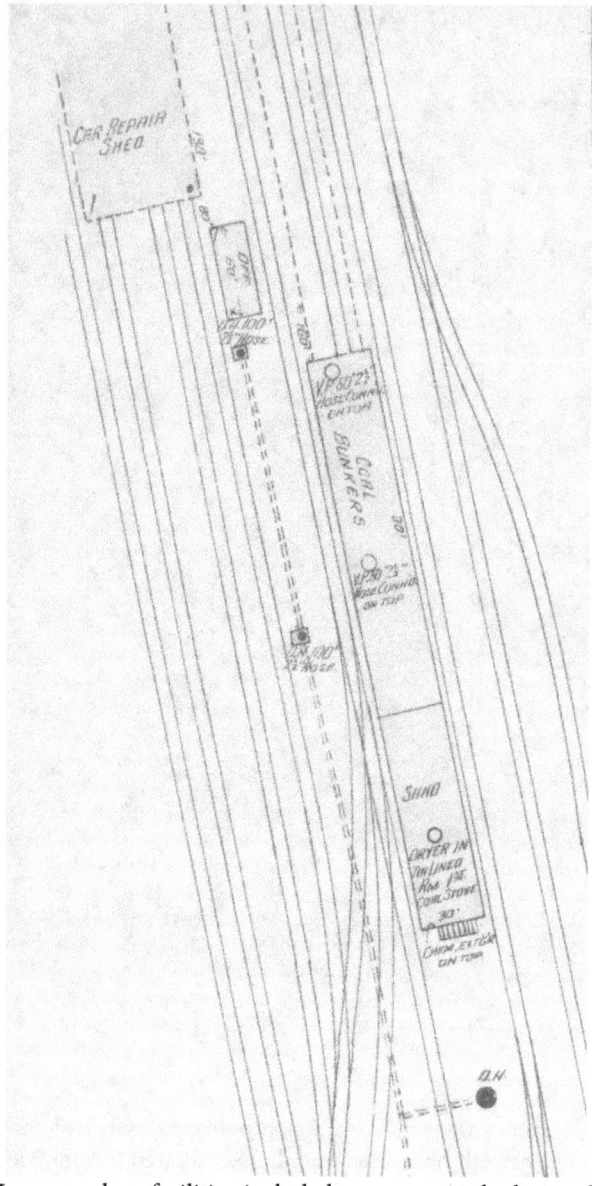

The Heavener shop facilities included a car repair shed, a coal bunker, and a sand facility. *Sanborn Fire Insurance Map from Heavener, Le Flore County, Oklahoma.* Sanborn Map Company, August 1913. Map. Retrieved from the Library of Congress, https://www.loc.gov/item/sanborn07120_001/.

Heavener Sub Route Guide

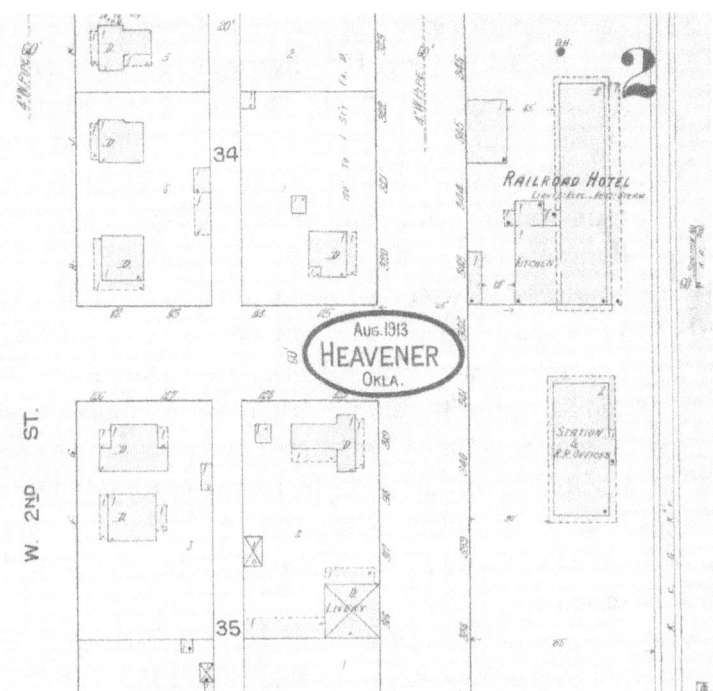

This Sanborn map from August 1913 shows the Kansas City Southern station and the adjacent Railroad Hotel, both on the west side of the tracks at Avenue B where the railroad office is still located. *Sanborn Fire Insurance Map from Heavener, Le Flore County, Oklahoma.* Sanborn Map Company, August 1913. Map. Retrieved from the Library of Congress, https://www.loc.gov/item/sanborn07120_001/.

The Kansas City Southern moved a great deal of fruit, berries and vegetables from the area. It also handled fish and other products from the Gulf Coast, citrus from Texas, and lots of other products that needed to be kept cool during the summer heat. Because of this, the railroad had a regular icing station at Heavener where many refrigerator cars were scheduled to be re-iced.

Despite the Great Depression, Heavener was still an important and busy terminal on the railroad. In 1936, the station was staffed continuously by agents and telegraph operators. All passenger trains stopped at Heavener for a five-minute crew change. The southbound No. 15 (*The Flying Crow*) stopped at Heavener daily 8:45-8:50am. Northbound No. 16 was here 9:35-9:40pm. The mixed second-class trains on the Waldron Branch (Arkansas Western Railway) also used the station at Heavener. Southbound No. 3 would depart at 10:30am on Monday, Wednesday and Friday. Northbound No. 4 would return to Heavener at 4:00pm on Tuesday, Thursday and Saturday. The station also included a dispatcher telephone, a train register, standard clock, and bulletin books (also found at the Heavener roundhouse). In the yard and at the shops were a wye and a turntable to turn equipment, coal, oil, water, and a track scale.

Some of the station functions, and the work of the dispatchers, began to change in 1954 when the railroad installed Centralized Traffic Control (CTC) signaling between Heavener, Oklahoma, and De Queen, Arkansas. This signal system allowed trains to be directed by signals alongside the track instead of paper orders obtained from station agents. The installation of the signals included track work, lengthening some sidings and removing others. Despite this, little actually changed at Heavener except that diesel fuel for locomotives was available instead of coal and oil for the now-retired steam locomotives. Other steam locomotive facilities were also retired. In 1960, CTC signals were installed from Heavener northward to Sallisaw.

In 1964, Heavener still featured a continuously staffed station, which handled all passenger trains (*The Flying Crow* and *Southern Belle*) for five to ten minutes. For example, *Southern Belle* No. 1 was

Heavener Sub Route Guide

scheduled to be at Heavener 4:40pm-4:45pm daily. As a crew change point, Heavener provided a number of services like a standard clock, register station, and general order books. The yard was still active and it featured a track scale to weigh freight cars for billing, water, diesel fuel, and a wye. Little changed by 1970 except for the end of passenger service, and this has held true to today, although much has been modernized.

The large two-story station at Heavener has been replaced by this more modern brick and glass structure.

North of town at the Industrial Road grade crossing is a relatively new center of activity at Heavener. Here, the Heavener Main Line Fueling Facility is located both north and south of the grade crossing. These two facilities allow locomotives to be fueled without blocking the grade crossing. The grade crossing is also officially Control Point North Heavener at Milepost 336.7 on both tracks. This allows the trains stopped at the fuel racks to have a signal to proceed.

The construction of the fueling facility was reported on in *Progressive Railroading* (July 12, 2004). It stated that each month the facility would handle more than 3.2 million gallons of fuel. About half of this amount would be loaded into tank cars and shipped to other fueling facilities, saving KCS about seven cents per gallon on diesel fuel. A new pipeline and tank farm was built by Magellan Pipeline Company as part of the facility.

Heading south from the fuel racks, the two main tracks cross Coal Creek and then reach the north switch to Heavener Yard. A series of complex track arrangements are to the south. At about Milepost 337.5, there are nine tracks to the west, including the mainlines. To the east are four tracks, the remains of a larger yard that is now used to store cars, track materials, and other railroad items. At the south end of the yard complex is a wye to the east and the old locomotive shop building.

In July 1988, the enginehouse at Heavener was almost surrounded by white KCS locomotives.

Heavener Sub Route Guide

By 1997, things look a little different at the Heavener enginehouse, especially the paint on KCS 4006.

At Milepost 338.0 is the current railroad office, a modern block building surrounded by parking lots full of cars owned by train crews and station employees, plus a number of KCS vehicles. Smaller buildings for maintenance-of-way and mechanical forces are also located nearby. At Milepost 338.1 is a grade crossing with West Avenue C. On either side of the crossing are crossovers that allow trains to enter or exit the Waldron Branch, which actually starts at the KCS office building. The east track through this area is the Waldron Branch, which curves to the east not far south of West Avenue F (Milepost 338.2). To the west of the tracks between Avenue C and Avenue F is Dale Elliott Deer Park, home of the Heavener farmers market. A number of shelters with picnic tables provide views of train operations in this area, plus a caboose (KCS 386) and a small deer herd. Just south of West Avenue I at Milepost 338.4 is South Heavener, where the railroad returns to a single main track. This is the south end of the Heavener complex, and is actually the north end of the Shreveport Subdivision.

Yes, the Dale Elliott Deer Park at Heavener does have deer, as shown in June 2021.

Heavener Sub Route Guide

Although the paint has faded, KCS caboose #386 sits on display at the north end of Dale Elliott Deer Park.

A popular rail attraction at Heavener, Oklahoma, is the Southern Belle Restaurant. The restaurant is located inside a former KCS passenger car, reportedly dating from 1905 and once numbered 108.

The Heavener Sub: History Through the Miles

Route Guide for the Fort Smith Branch

The history of this line is covered on Page 420 with the coverage of the Fort Smith Branch Junction at Milepost 325.5. As previously stated, Kansas City Southern began regularly using this track when a heavy flood washed out the Kansas City Southern Spiro-Fort Smith line in May 1943. The KCS then obtained temporary trackage rights over the St. Louis-San Francisco's Poteau to Fort Smith line. On December 12, 1944, the Interstate Commerce Commission granted authority to abandon the KCS line to Fort Smith and operate via trackage rights over 28.74 miles of the St. Louis-San Francisco from Poteau, Oklahoma, to South Fort Smith, Arkansas .

With Burlington Northern (BN) getting rid of the Monett, Missouri, to Paris, Texas, rail line, Kansas City Southern officially leased the Poteau-Fort Smith trackage from BN on February 9, 1985. During 1986, the Arkansas & Missouri Railroad completed a lease-purchase agreement on the line from Monett to South Fort Smith at Milepost 422.50. KCS obtained trackage rights over the A&M's Fort Smith trackage to reach its downtown terminal. On June 19, 1987, the Interstate Commerce Commission approved the sale of Burlington Northern track to Kansas City Southern between Milepost 453.14 at Wister, Oklahoma, to Milepost 422.50 near Fort Smith, Arkansas. The Wister-Poteau track was abandoned and from South Fort Smith to their terminal in Fort Smith, KCS still uses trackage rights over the Arkansas & Missouri Railroad.

The Fort Smith Branch is included as Kansas City Southern has traditionally listed the Fort Smith Branch as a part of their Heavener Subdivision. The mileposts shown are the new ones used by Kansas City Southern employees, but the former St. Louis-San Francisco mileposts are also included.

0.0F   FORT SMITH – Although it is in Arkansas, Fort Smith has a strong relationship with what was Indian Territory, and later Oklahoma. The end of the tracks of the Kansas City Southern are at the National Cemetery in Fort Smith, just north of the OK Foods feed mill. To the north of the cemetery is the Fort Smith National Historic Site, the location of the second U.S. Army Fort Smith and the home of Judge Parker and his court.

Fort Smith, as can be imagined, has an early military history. The first Fort Smith was established at the confluence of the Arkansas and Poteau rivers in 1817 at a place called Belle Point. It was the highest navigable point on the Arkansas River at the time the site was chosen by the U.S. Army. Soldiers arrived in 1817 and named the site Fort Smith after their commanding officer, Thomas A. Smith. The army abandoned the fort in 1824. Foundations from this original construction are visible to visitors today.

A second fort was built here in 1838, located a bit higher above the rivers. Major buildings included two officer's quarters, a barracks, commissary, and quartermaster storehouse, all enclosed by a stone wall. The former military barracks and the Commissary Storehouse, the oldest building still standing in Fort Smith, are part of the Fort Smith National Historic Site. General Zachary Taylor, later President Taylor, lived here 1846-1848 while he was Commander of the Western Military District. Remains of his home still exist.

Fort Smith Branch

For many people, the name Fort Smith might sound familiar. For anyone who has seen the movies, or read the book, Fort Smith is the base of action for the story of *True Grit*. It was here at the court of Judge Parker that Mattie Ross first heard of, and saw, Rooster Cogburn. While much of the story is fiction, Fort Smith was a base of the legal system for this area and into Indian Territory, now Oklahoma. While Rooster Cogburn wasn't real, there are enough stories about the real marshals to fill many books. One of the most famous was Bass Reeves, a Black U.S. marshal who worked under Judge Parker out of Fort Smith. He often rode into Indian Territory with his friend, an Indian policeman. Some have alleged that stories about Reeves could have been the inspiration for the *Lone Ranger* stories.

In 1872, the former military barracks were converted into the federal courthouse. While the military barracks were used as a courthouse the basement was turned into a jail. In 1888 a new jail wing was constructed. The federal courthouse, which originally was a 1½ story structure with full porches, was changed to its present appearance in 1890.

From 1873 through 1896, eighty-six men were executed on the gallows at Fort Smith. All the men executed were convicted of rape or murder. After the Civil War, there was a mandatory federal death sentence in cases of rape or murder. Of the 86 men executed here, 79 were sentenced to death by Judge Parker. During Judge Parker's 21 year tenure, a total of 160 death sentences were handed down. Of that number, 43 were commuted to life in prison or lesser terms; 2 were pardoned by the President; 31 had appeals that resulted in acquittals or convictions overturned; 2 were granted new trials and discharged;

1 was shot and killed while attempting to escape; and 2 died in jail while awaiting execution. During his years on the bench, Parker handled more than 13,000 cases with more than 9000 of the defendants being convicted or pleading guilty. A reproduction of the 1886 gallows stands on its original site and is a reminder of "the chaotic social conditions that existed in Indian Territory during Judge Parker's time."

The federal court for the Western District of Arkansas still exists today, holding court in the Judge Isaac C. Parker Federal Building, three blocks from the National Historic Site. Today the court has federal jurisdiction over the western counties of the State of Arkansas. The Indian Territory jurisdiction of the court came to an end on September 1, 1896, thus ending the unique nature of the court.

Today, Fort Smith is a part of the booming western and northwestern Arkansas area. It has a growing population of almost 90,000, with 300,000 in the metropolitan area. The town has a tourist-based downtown, and a busy industrial area to the south. Fort Smith has generally mild winters and hot, humid summers, often being the hottest place in Arkansas. If you need information about Fort Smith, stop by the Convention and Visitors Bureau in Miss Laura's Social Club. Miss Laura's is the first former house of prostitution placed on the National Register of Historic Places.

The KCS at Fort Smith

For most railroads in Fort Smith, their terminals often moved about to different locations, sometimes being shared with other carriers. The Kansas City, Pittsburg & Gulf began construction on their Fort

Fort Smith Branch

Smith line from Spiro on December 28, 1897, and there was a celebration of its completion on June 1, 1898. Discussion about a new passenger depot began by 1907 when it was announced that the KCS had acquired property at Wheeler Avenue and South Sixth Street and was going to build a three-story depot and dispatcher's office. In December 1909, there were reports that a dispute over the property had finally been solved, and that a 45' x 300' freight depot was going to be built next to the new passenger station. By 1911, the new KCS station, known as Union Station since the Frisco also used the building, was open at 700-10 Rogers Avenue, with the freight depot at 718 Rogers Avenue. The Frisco used the station off and on, and KCS passenger trains used it until 1949 when bus service replaced the trains. The station was demolished in 1966 and replaced by the Fort Smith Convention Center.

With the abandonment of the KCS Fort Smith-Spiro line in 1944, the tracks to the west were abandoned. During the following decades, many of the KCS tracks along the Poteau River were abandoned, leaving just the tracks in downtown south of the old Union Depot. Today, the tracks end near the Fort Smith National Cemetery north of B Street South, several blocks south of the old Union Station. The reason for the remaining track is the large OK Foods feed mill and a compressed gas facility. To handle this business, the railroad has a four-track yard and a wye south of the feed mill.

This view shows the small KCS yard in Fort Smith, as well as the OK Foods feed mill and its locally famous mural portraits of Fort Smith citizens.

This shows a better view of the OK Foods feed mill, the primary reason that KCS still serves Fort Smith.

Fort Smith Union Station

Once located at 700 Rogers Avenue, the Kansas City Southern Union Station was the largest and fanciest station built in Fort Smith, Arkansas. The station opened in 1911 and featured entrances off of Rogers Avenue and Seventh Street, plus through a parkway to the east. At the north end of the building along Rogers Avenue was a large waiting area. It also featured a small newsstand, telegraph office, and other facilities. A large passenger lobby was to the south, with the mail, express and baggage rooms to the east, and a "ladies retiring room" and "colored waiting room" to the west. At the south end of the lobby were the ticket offices and the passenger concourse to the tracks.

Fort Smith Union Station was designed by Daniel H. Burnham, a Chicago planner and architect. Burnham had been the Director of Works for the World's Columbian Exposition in Chicago and had been involved with the planning of a number of cities around the world. He had also led the design work on a number of buildings, including the Union Station in Washington D.C. Apparently Burnham was not afraid to borrow some design features as the Fort Smith Union Station was almost identical to the Southern Railway's Terminal Station that was built in New Orleans in 1907.

The entire complex cost a reported $130,000. This included $94,000 for construction of the complex, $28,000 for the tracks, and $8000 for the right-of-way. Union Station was an attempt to consolidate the many passenger stations in Fort Smith, but like other efforts, it didn't fully succeed. Initially, both the KCS and the Frisco used Union Station (sometimes called Union Depot). The station could be busy with the trains of the two railroads, with ten or more daily trains moving through the station. To reduce train conflicts, Passenger Station Tracks Nos. 1 and 2 were assigned to Frisco trains, while Passenger Station Tracks Nos. 3 and 4 were assigned to KCS trains. For several years during the late 1910s, the Midland Valley used the Union Station until they opened their own station in 1920.

However, by 1936, passenger train traffic at Union Station was down to six trains a day. The station's owner – Kansas City Southern – operated two roundtrip mixed trains from Fort Smith to the mainline at Spiro, Oklahoma. KCS No. 109 departed Fort Smith daily at 7:00am, and arrived at Spiro at 7:40am. There, it met southbound No. 15, *The Flying Crow*, which was scheduled to depart at 7:57am. It would then depart at 8:10am as No. 106, arriving back at Fort Smith at 9:00am. In the evening, KCS No. 115 departed Fort Smith daily at 9:20pm. It was scheduled to arrive at Spiro at 10:05pm. There, it met northbound No. 16 – *The Flying Crow* – which was scheduled to depart Spiro at 10:30pm. KCS No. 116 departed Spiro at 10:35pm, and arrived at Fort Smith at 11:25pm.

The Frisco was down to a single train in each direction by 1936, and their southbound No. 709 (*Texas Limited*) arrived at Fort Smith Union Station at 9:00am, and then departed at 9:20am. Northbound No. 710 (*St. Louis Limited*) arrived at Fort Smith at 5:45pm, and departed at 6:05pm.

KCS passenger service at Union Station ended on August 31, 1941, and bus service to Sallisaw handled the business. In 1948, the Frisco moved back into their own station at Fort Smith. The Union Station

Fort Smith Branch

building remainded for almost two more decades, used as office space, and then standing empty. In 1965, the KCS built a new modern passenger-freight office, using it as the bus station for service to Sallisaw. Union Station was torn down in July 1966, replaced by the Fort Smith Civic Auditorium and a hotel.

0.9F **FSR RRX** – This milepost is the one provided in current KCS employee timetables. This location, known as MP Crossing/KCS Crossing, was clearly identified in Frisco *Central Division Time Table No. 28*, dated May 17, 1936. Located at Frisco Milepost 416.9, this was where the Frisco crossed the Missouri Pacific Paris Branch, as well as the KCS Fort Smith District. For the KCS in 1936, this was S. F. Junction at Milepost A327.1, which included crossings with Missouri Pacific and the Frisco. Today, the Fort Smith Railroad crosses the Arkansas & Missouri Railroad and the Kansas City Southern's Fort Smith line here. Just to the south of the diamond, there is a turnout where the KCS connects with the A&M.

This area once was a puzzle of tracks, turnouts and diamonds. Two of these were included in Frisco employee timetables: S.F. Junction and KCS Diamond. According to Mike Condren (condrenrails.com), S.F. Junction (Frisco Milepost 417.0) was where the Frisco, Missouri Pacific, and Kansas City Southern crossed. Northbound Frisco passenger trains using Union Station left Frisco trackage here to return to their own track at GA Junction. A gate located on the MP diamond was normally against the Missouri Pacific. Later timetables showed this to be Union Pacific Diamond after Missouri Pacific was acquired by the western railroad. KCS Diamond (Frisco Milepost 417.1) was where the KCS Fort Smith District from the mainline at Spiro, Oklahoma, crossed the Frisco.

The KCS Fort Smith Dodger often has to pull out onto the Arkansas & Missouri mainline as they switch their small Fort Smith yard.

Missouri Pacific Paris Branch

The Paris Branch, today operated by the Fort Smith Railroad, was originally part of the St. Louis, Iron Mountain & Southern's line to Greenwood, Arkansas. About four miles south of Fort Smith, a line headed east, chartered by the Arkansas Central Railroad to build from Fort Smith to Paris, Arkansas. The idea of the railroad was to serve the coal fields in the area. The line was completed to Paris in 1900 after Jay Gould acquired the line.

The Arkansas Central Railroad, incorporated on April 29, 1897, was at least the fourth railroad that used the Arkansas Central name. Construction on the line began on August 5, 1897, and entered receivership in December 1898, after building as far as Charleston, Arkansas. Both the Frisco and the St. Louis, Iron Mountain & Southern attempted to acquire the railroad, but the Iron Mountain won the legal battle to operate it during January 1899. The railroad was reorganized on February 9, 1899, and work began on completing the line to Paris, Arkansas. The railroad again entered receivership during June 1899, but proposals were made to extend the line to both Little Rock and Hot Springs. By 1901, the Interstate Commerce Commission showed the Arkansas Central Railway to be a subsidiary of Missouri Pacific, and the name swapped back to the Arkansas Central Railroad. On March 1, 1922, the Arkansas Central was conveyed by deed to the Missouri Pacific Railroad and fully merged into the larger railroad.

On July 7, 1991, the Fort Smith Railroad Company, a wholly-owned subsidiary of Pioneer Railcorp, entered into a 20-year lease with Union Pacific Railroad to operate the line. After a few years, the east end of the line was abandoned after the Tyson feed mill at Paris was moved to the Union Pacific mainline near Russellville, Arkansas. Today, the Fort Smith Railroad, a part of Pioneer Lines, operates 18 miles of track from Fort Smith to Barling, Arkansas.

KCS Fort Smith District

Early plans had the KCS mainline pass through Fort Smith, but the mountains to the north changed the route and required a branch line to reach the city. Construction began on December 28, 1897, and there was a celebration of its completion on June 1, 1898. This didn't end the hopes of Fort Smith to be on the mainline as several surveys between 1906 and 1910 investigated moving the railroad to avoid the steep grades near the Arkansas-Missouri border.

Initially, a few passenger trains operated in and out of Fort Smith, but soon just connecting trains provided the service. In 1936, two mixed trains in each direction provided service each morning and late evening to connect with *The Flying Crow* at Spiro. Even this passenger service ended on August 31, 1941, and bus service to Sallisaw handled the business. Several local freight trains continued to operate over the line until May 1943 when heavy flooding washed out the Spiro to Fort Smith line. Temporary trackage rights over the St. Louis-San Francisco's Poteau to Fort Smith line were obtained. On December 12, 1944, the Interstate Commerce Commission granted authority to abandon the KCS line to Fort Smith and approved permanent trackage rights over the Frisco out of Poteau, Oklahoma.

The abandoned grade of the KCS Fort Smith District passes just south of the Riverside Furniture Corporation plant and crossed the Poteau River into Oklahoma. Further west, the grade of the Fort Smith District is often used today by U.S. Highway 271.

1.0F KANSAS CITY SOUTHERN DIAMOND – This location is actually Arkansas & Missouri Railroad Milepost 417.1. The KCS now reaches Fort Smith on their own Fort Smith Branch from Poteau (27.7 miles total), the former Frisco mainline south of town. The last few miles into town (KCS mileposts 0.0F to 6.0F) are via the Arkansas & Missouri Railroad, which bought the route in 2001. Note that while the KCS shows the distance to be six miles, older Frisco and current Arkansas & Missouri mileposts show it

Fort Smith Branch

to be 0.4 miles longer. Both sets of mileposts will be shown for the line.

KCS employee timetable #5, dated July 19, 2002, states **"FORT SMITH OPERATION VIA THE A&M RAILWAY**: From A&M MP 422.5 to A&M MP 417.0, Track Warrant Control is in effect. Trains must secure track warrants and track bulletins from the A&M Dispatcher. Yard limits are in effect between A&M MP 412.0 and A&M MP 417.0."

1.1F MILL CREEK BRIDGE – This bridge at A&M Milepost 417.2 is a 75-foot ballast deck frame trestle. The Mill Creek area was once considered as a separate community from Fort Smith. The point where Mill Creek flows into the Poteau River was important enough to be cited in a survey of the western boundary of Arkansas. For many years, ice was cut from the Poteau River near the mouth of Mill Creek. A native stone ice house was once located just west of the tracks.

The Fort Smith Dodger with KCS locomotives 2976 and 2819, shown crossing the Mill Creek Bridge, heads south and back to Heavener with their train on September 30, 2021.

Just south of Mill Creek was the large complex of the Fort Smith Wagon Works, in business here by 1908.

1.9F WARD – The Ward Furniture Manufacturing Company operated in this area. Identified in Frisco's *Central Division Time Table No. 28*, dated May 17, 1936, Ward (A&M/Frisco Milepost 418.0) was shown to be a 2-car-long spur track. During the early 1980s, there was still a short spur to the west at this location.

2.9F RUGE – Located at the grade crossing with Phoenix Street, Ruge (A&M/Frisco Milepost 419.1) was listed in Frisco's *Central Division Time Table No. 33C*, dated June 11, 1944. It was still listed as a small spur track in the early 1960s. Several industrial tracks were still here in the 1980s, but only one remains today. The border between Arkansas and Oklahoma is only one block to the west.

4.1F FENN – A large 113-car yard was listed as being at Frisco Milepost 420.4 from 1936 through the 1960s. A few tracks remained to the east of the mainline in the early 1980s.

As reported by the Interstate Commerce Commission (ICC), "Fenn is the name of the manufacturing plant of the Equitable Powder Manufacturing Company, located about 4.1 miles south of Fort Smith and connected by a spur track with the main line of the St Louis & San Francisco Railroad Company." The ICC also stated that the spur track was about 1 mile long and belonged to the railroad, and that no other industries were located at Fenn besides the powder works. The Equitable Powder Manufac-

Fort Smith Branch

turing Company plant was located to the east where the Norge facility was later located.

The Equitable Powder Manufacturing Company was founded in 1892 by Franklin Olin and several other investors. The company had two early plants, one at East Alton, Illinois, and the second one here. This plant was built to provide commercial explosives for area coal mining. The black powder mill used nitrate of soda in carloads imported from Chile through the ports at New Orleans, Louisiana, and Pensacola, Florida.

4.2F FORT SMITH INDUSTRIAL PARK – Back in passenger days, the Frisco 7am switch job would take the passenger equipment to the wye at the Frisco Industrial Park (Milepost 420.5) in south Fort Smith to turn the passenger train. The main business that the Frisco served in the industrial park was a Whirlpool appliance plant. Originally a Norge facility, the plant has been expanded several times and now features an adjacent warehouse, used by several companies. Whirlpool closed their part of the complex in 2012. A small yard, still known as Norge Yard, assists the A&M crews working this large complex. Car storage is a common use for many of the tracks throughout the facility.

4.8F BASHE – At A&M/Frisco Milepost 421.0, Bashe station was listed in the Frisco's *Central Division Time Table No. 28*, dated May 17, 1936. The track at the time had a 27-car capacity. In this area, the former Frisco line bends west into Oklahoma to avoid an east-west ridge that is an outlier of the Ouachita Mountains.

4.9F ARKANSAS-OKLAHOMA STATE LINE – At Frisco Milepost 421.1, the railroad crosses the border between Sebastian County, Arkansas (to the east), and Le Flore County, Oklahoma (to the west). The rail line crosses the state line five times over the next 8.2 miles. As reported by the St. Louis & San Francisco Railway Company in 1886, the line was located in Indian Territory for 3.38 miles, then in Arkansas for 2.67 miles, then back in Indian Territory for 1.81 miles, then again in Arkansas for 0.17 miles, then finally back to Indian Territory.

Sebastian County was created in 1851 and named after William K. Sebastian, a judge for the U.S. Circuit Court. The county seat was first located at Greenwood, then moved to the second-largest city in Arkansas, Fort Smith, before being relocated back to Greenwood in 1852. In 1861, it was decided that the county would have two seats of government: one at Fort Smith and the other at Greenwood.

The Territory of **Arkansas** was admitted to the Union as the 25th state on June 15, 1836. It is the 29th largest state, and the 34th most populated. The name Arkansas is a version of an Osage name for the Quapaw people who lived in this area. Little Rock, located near the center of Arkansas, is the capital and largest city in the state. However, most of the large cities in the state are found in a line along the former Frisco Railway between Bentonville and Fort Smith. Arkansas is the only state where diamonds are mined, and you can go mine them yourself at the Crater of Diamonds State Park. This explains the diamond shape found on the state flag. The former nickname of the state was the Land of Opportunity, but it now uses The Natural State.

Fort Smith Branch

To the west is **Oklahoma**, once known as Indian Territory (1834-1907), and later partly as Oklahoma Territory (1890-1907). Oklahoma means "red people" in the Choctaw language, and the name was decided during an 1866 meeting between federal officials and leaders of the five Indian nations who had been moved there. During the late 1800s, the western part of what became Oklahoma was the Oklahoma Territory, while the eastern part was Indian Territory. The two merged and became the 46th state on November 16, 1907. It is the 20th largest state and the 28th most populated, with about four million residents. About two-thirds of Oklahomans live in the Oklahoma City (the state capital) and Tulsa metropolitan areas. The state is known as "The Sooner State" due to the number of white settlers who staked their land claims out before the official opening date in the western Oklahoma Territory.

The Railroad Act of 1886 opened the way for railroad construction across Indian Territory. The builders of the various railroads took advantage of this Act to build across the state, in what was actually a relatively late burst of railroad activity.

LeFlore County was created at statehood from the major part of Recording District 14 in the old Choctaw Nation. The name LeFlore came from Greenwood Leflore, a Choctaw chief and a signer of the Treaty of 1830, in which the Choctaw Indians sold all their lands east of the Mississippi River. Interestingly enough, after the sale, many Choctaws migrated to present day Oklahoma, but Leflore stayed in Mississippi and became a politician and wealthy planter.

6.0F CONTROL POINT POCOLA – While historically known as South Fort Smith, this is now Control Point Pocola, the property line between the Arkansas & Missouri Railroad to the north, and the Kansas City Southern to the south. This location is essentially under the U.S. Highway 271 overpass.

According to KCS employee timetables, KCS 6.0 = A&M 422.5. South (westward for the KCS) of this location to Poteau, Oklahoma, the former Frisco line is now owned and operated by Kansas City Southern. KCS officially leased this trackage from Burlington Northern on February 9, 1985, then bought it on November 13, 1989.

CP Pocola is the home of a large number of railroad signs. This group of signs make it clear that this is Milepost 6.0F, the end of the KCS-owned trackage on the Fort Smith Branch.

Fort Smith Branch

These signs announce that the track north of CP Pocola is owned by the Arkansas & Missouri Railroad, and that there may be remote control locomotives operating in the area.

On September 30, 2021, KCS 2976 leads the Fort Smith Dodger on its way back to Heavener after a morning of switching at Fort Smith.

7.0F CEDARS – This station, at Frisco Milepost 423.5, was located in Oklahoma at the Hamon Avenue grade crossing. A 60-car siding was once at this location. At the south end of the siding, the track curved to the east and crossed back into Arkansas.

Cedars was a flag stop for passenger trains in 1936 when there were industry tracks with a capacity of 67 freight cars. Later, the industry track was turned into a siding.

Head-On Collision at Cedars

As reported by the Interstate Commerce Commission (ICC), on "December 30, 1952, there was a head-end collision between a freight train and a passenger train on the St. Louis-San Francisco Railway near Cedars, Okla., which resulted in the death of 1 train-service employee, and the injury of 18 passengers, 2 railway-mail clerks, 1 railway-express messenger and 7 train-service employees."

This head-on collision took place between a northbound Frisco passenger train and a southbound Kansas City Southern freight train. "No. 704, a north-bound first-class St.L.-S.F. passenger train, consisted of Diesel-electric unit 615, one baggage-mail car, one baggage car and one coach, in the order named. All cars were of conventional all-steel construction." The Kansas City Southern freight was an extra train, using trackage rights over the Frisco "between S.F. Junction, Ark., and Poteau, Okla, located, respectively, 1.6 miles and 29.1 miles south of Fort Smith." The ICC stated that "Extra KCS 1304 South, a south-bound K.C.S. freight train, consisted of Diesel-electric unit 1304, 10 cars and a caboose."

Fort Smith Branch

The report on the accident included a number of details about the railroad around Cedars.

> In the vicinity of the point of accident this is a single-track line, over which trains are operated by timetable and train orders. There is no block system in use. At Cedars, Okla., 8.1 miles south of Fort Smith, a siding 3,247 feet in length parallels the main track on the west. The accident occurred on the main track at a point 4,830 feet north of the north siding-switch at Cedars. From the north there are, in succession, a tangent 4,110 feet in length and a 4 degree curve to the left 744 feet to the point of accident and 451 feet southward. From the south there are, in succession, a tangent 2,124 feet in length, a 2 degree curve to the left 913 feet, a tangent 1,638 feet and the curve on which the accident occurred. At the point of accident the grade is 1.0 percent ascending southward. Immediately south of the point of accident the track is laid in a cut, the walls of which rise from about track level at the north end of the cut to a height of 16 feet above the level of the tops of the rails at a point 900 feet south of the point of collision.
>
> The maximum authorized speeds in the vicinity of the point of accident were 55 miles per hour for passenger trains and 45 miles per hour for freight trains.

According to the ICC, the cause of the accident was "copies of train order held by the crews of trains involved not reading alike." The crew of KCS Extra 1304 South received their copies of train order No. 56 from the KCS operator at Fort Smith about 4:35pm. Their order No. 56 stated "No. 704 Eng 615 run 30 mins late Hugo to Fort Smith." Passenger train No. 704 received their order No. 56 at Hugo, where they left at 1:58pm, 21 minutes late. The order they received stated "No. 704 Eng 615 run 20 mins late Hugo to Fort Smith." During the investigation it was discovered that the train order book showed that the order read that train No. 704 would run 20 minutes late from Hugo to Fort Smith. The order to Hugo was transmitted about 1:30pm by telephone by the first-trick dispatcher. The order to the KCS at Fort Smith was sent by the second-trick dispatcher at 4:30pm.

Just before the two trains collided, passenger train No. 704 passed Cedars 20 minutes late. Therefore, it was running on the schedule its train order established. However, KCS 1304 South was operating based upon No. 704 running 30 minutes late and planned to enter the siding at Cedars. During the investigation, each crew agreed what their order read, and the ICC could never determine where the mistake took place.

Fort Smith Branch

8.1F OKLAHOMA-ARKANSAS STATE LINE – In the middle of the curve to the southeast, the railroad crosses back into Arkansas at Frisco Milepost 424.6. This series of curves is required to pass between Gray Mountain to the west, and White Bluff Mountain to the east.

9.8F BONANZA – Located at Frisco Milepost 426.3, Bonanza was the site of a series of Central Coal & Coke Company coal mines. The town was incorporated on November 26, 1898. A large fire burned much of the town in 1904, but an even larger one in July 1909 caused $75,000 worth of damage to the business section. A report in the *Arkansas Gazette* stated that the "coal company's buildings were saved but most of the local businesses, built of wood, were destroyed."

The freight and passenger traffic during the coal boom had Bonanza listed as being a freight station and local ticket station in 1926. A small 20' x 42' wooden depot was built with two waiting rooms, an office, and a freight room. An 80-foot-long cinder platform was located between the depot and the mainline. In 1939, there was a 37-car siding, a house track with a seven car capacity, and a wye that led to the private tracks at the coal mines. At the time, Bonanza was a flag stop for passenger trains. Today, the town of Bonanza is to the east and consists of about 20 blocks, housing fewer than 600 residents.

The Heavener Sub: History Through the Miles

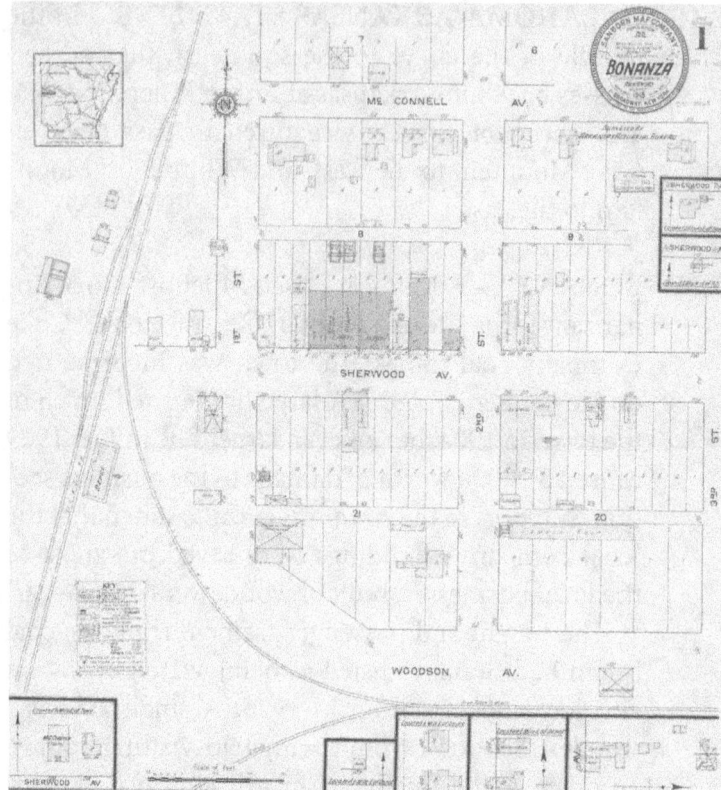

This Sanborn Map from 1913 shows the depot and wye area at Bonanza, Arkansas, near the peak of coal mining. *Sanborn Fire Insurance Map from Bonanza, Sebastian County, Arkansas.* Sanborn Map Company, Aug, 1913. Map. Retrieved from the Library of Congress, https://www.loc.gov/item/sanborn00206_001/.

Central Coal & Coke Company

Bonanza and the Central Coal & Coke Company have a complicated history that actually ties directly to the Kansas City Southern Railway. The Central Coal & Coke Company was incorporated in Missouri on May 1, 1893, from an earlier series of coal companies. The company owned and operated forty-five coal mines in Missouri, Arkansas, Kansas, Indian

Territory and Wyoming, several lumber companies, and a series of rail lines at its different operations. The firm was well-known, being the largest producer of semi-anthracite coal in western Arkansas, and actually across the Midwest.

The first connection to the Kansas City Southern Railway was that the founders of the company received financial support from Arthur E. Stilwell. Stilwell included them in his railroad construction plans and the coal company studied the territory for opportunities. Of the opportunities explored, Central Coal & Coke eventually invested in three locations in Arkansas: Hartford, Huntington, and Bonanza. At Hartford, one mine was located on the Choctaw, Oklahoma & Gulf (later Chicago, Rock Island & Pacific). Three mines were located on the Frisco's Mansfield branch at Huntington. Three more mines and a strip pit were located at Bonanza on the Frisco main line. These were shaft mine No. 10 (the first one opened with construction starting in late December of 1896), slope mine No. 12, slope mine No. 20 (the last slope mine opened at Bonanza, and the last one operating), and pit mine No. 13. All of these produced semi-anthracite coal that was considered to be the best available.

Now comes the second connection to the Kansas City Southern. With Stilwell's support, the company had access to his railroad as a market. As soon as the coal was available, the Kansas City, Pittsburg & Gulf (KCP&G) began buying the mine's output. Coal was moved over the Frisco line to Poteau, where it was handed off to the KCP&G, later Kansas City Southern. Until about 1920, the mines at Bonanza supplied all of the coal used on the southern half of the KCS.

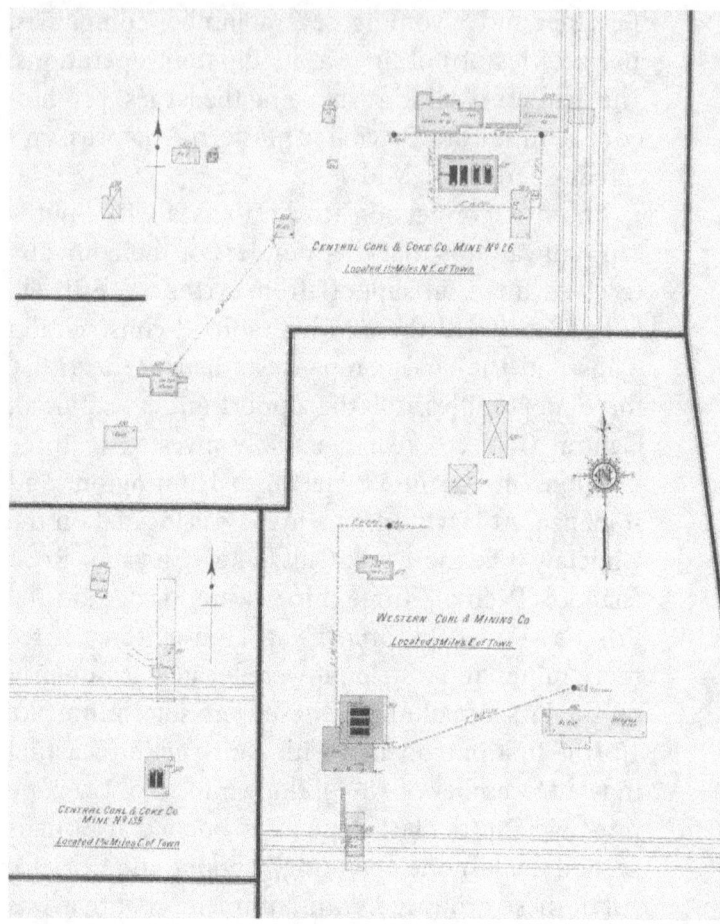

Sanborn maps from 1913 covered the Central Coal & Coke Company mines #26 and #135, as shown here. *Sanborn Fire Insurance Map from Bonanza, Sebastian County, Arkansas.* Sanborn Map Company, Aug, 1913. Map. Retrieved from the Library of Congress, https://www.loc.gov/item/sanborn00206_001/.

The Bonanza Railroads of the Central Coal & Coke Company

While the coal mines at Bonanza, and at their other locations, were fairly well documented, the same cannot be said for the railroads that operated to support the movement of the coal, and of the timber at its logging operations. The Central Coal & Coke Company's railroad at Bonanza played an important role for the company.

When coal production began in 1897, a means to move it to market was needed. The first step was to build a branch line off of the Frisco at Bonanza to connect to the coal mines. This line came off of a wye and headed east down Woodson Avenue to the mines. For the Frisco, their depot sat inside the north wye switch, at the west end of Sherwood Street. Now comes a third connection to the KCS as the wye and mine tracks at Bonanza actually were owned by the Kansas City, Pittsburg & Gulf, and later Kansas City Southern. These tracks were then used by the Arkansas & Choctaw Railway, which had been organized in Arkansas on August 31, 1895. Statements from the time indicated that the railroad would be operated by the Cincinnati Coal & Coke Company and that lines would be built west from Ashdown, Arkansas, throughout Indian Territory. The Cincinnati Coal & Coke Company reference was from an article in the *Arkansas Gazette*, but it may have been simply an error. Central Coal certainly used the Arkansas & Choctaw Railway as its operator over the mine trackage at Bonanza, and its trackage rights over the Frisco Central Division between Bonanza and Poteau.

The lines at Ashdown and Bonanza were not the only ones operated by the coal company. There were also lines at Bevier, Missouri, and at Neame, Louisiana. This got even more interesting when Central Coal organized the Arkansas & Choctaw Construction Company in 1901, and then gave it control of the Arkansas & Choctaw Railway. In 1902, the railroad became the Missouri & Louisiana Railroad Company, which owned about 100 miles of track, seven locomotives, 200 logging cars and 200 coal cars. The operations at Bonanza were known as the "Bonanza Branch" or "Bonanza District." The amount of track rented from the Kansas City Southern changed almost yearly as mines opened and closed. A statement in the 1905 KCS annual report covered the "Bonanza Spur Arkansas" which included 2.52 miles of mainline track and 3.96 miles of secondary track. The report stated that the track was operated under contract by Central Coal & Coke Company. The mainline mileage remained about 2.8 miles until its last listing in 1922. During most of those years, the railroad hauled almost two hundred loads of coal a week.

Central Coal & Coke closed most of its Bonanza operations by the late 1910s, but a series of mines continued to operate here until the 1950s. Among these were Mines No. 1 and No. 2 of the Fort Smith-Bonanza Coal Company. The Frisco began operating the coal branch at Bonanza about 1920, handling the coal as needed. The volumes were large enough that the branch, shown as the Mine 135 Track, stayed in place until at least the 1950s. The name Mine 135 Track came from Fort Smith-Bonanza Coal Company Mine No. 135, one of the last operating mines in the area. Today, all of these tracks are gone at Bo-

Fort Smith Branch

nanza, but a few grades and ruins of mines east of town show where the best semi-anthracite coal was once mined in Arkansas.

10.5F FIRE CHIEF – Located at Frisco Milepost 427.0, Fire Chief was simply a coal loading station on the railroad with no scheduled passenger service. There was a 70-car track with switches on both ends. This was the location of the Great Western Coal Company mine, and Fire Chief was the trade name of the coal that the company sold. The company was incorporated on September 3, 1935, and built a large underground coal mine that was in both Arkansas and Oklahoma. The "Firm and Smokeless" coal was loaded into rail cars using a steel, four-track tipple. Some records state that the mine operated until 1942.

10.7F ARKANSAS-OKLAHOMA STATE LINE – For the third time in about six miles, the Fort Smith Branch crosses the border between Arkansas and Oklahoma. Here, it is on the northwest corner of Wofford Lake at former Frisco Milepost 427.2. This reservoir is regularly stocked with channel catfish by the Arkansas Game and Fish Commission. Just to the south of the lake is Backbone Mountain.

11.6F JENSON TUNNEL – Shown as being at Frisco Milepost 428.1, this is the first and only railroad tunnel in the state of Oklahoma. It was built by the Fort Smith & Southern Railway in 1885-1886, and the line opened in 1887. Three workers were killed in two separate accidents while building the tunnel. On July 26, 1886, one man was killed and four seriously injured when some scaffolding fell on the workers. A worse disaster took place in December 1886 when workers were drilling holes and hit an old drill hole that held several sticks of unexploded dynamite.

Originally known as Backbone Tunnel by the railroad, for the Backbone Mountain that it passes through, it is 1180 feet long. The tunnel is a mix of stone with brick arch at each end (about 370 feet), timber posts and arches (about 180 feet), and unlined (about 630 feet). The details on these sections varies between sources, but many date back to the tunnel's construction. Each end features a tall stone portal with the date 1886 carved into a date stone. Jenson Tunnel was listed on the National Register of Historic Places on May 13, 1976.

Some reports state that the tunnel was built with military protection to prevent attacks by members of the Choctaw tribe. This was because when construction on the tunnel began some members of the tribe were upset by the work, what they considered to be an intrusion into their country. After about a week of attacks on railroad workers, militia from Fort Smith arrived to protect the workers until the tunnel and rail line were completed.

For many years, Jenson Tunnel was protected by automatic block signals (ABS) and specific slow orders. Employee timetables showed that the ABS system was less than a mile long and ran from Milepost 427, Pole 21, to Milepost 428, Pole 16.

12.7F OKLAHOMA-ARKANSAS STATE LINE – The railroad crosses back into Arkansas for the last time as it heads south to Poteau. The state line is located at the former Frisco Milepost 429.2.

13.1F JENSON – Jenson was a junction town on the Frisco that never amounted to much more than a few buildings and the Mansfield Branch that reached more coal mines to the south. Jenson was in a unique position, just a few feet east of the Arkansas-Oklahoma state line, making it the closest town to Indian Territory that sold alcohol. When created during the late 1800s, there were plans for a town of several dozen blocks, but some sources state that Jenson never was much more than a railroad depot, hotel, general store, saloon and brothel. Most of these buildings were located in Arkansas, and early maps incorrectly showed that the railroad depot was located on the west side of the mainline, about the center of the wye and a few feet inside Arkansas. Nothing remains today except for a few foundations, now located on private property.

The location of the depot and wye was shown as being at Frisco Milepost 429.3. The wye and the Mansfield Branch that it created went southeast between Spring Street and First Street, and opened in November 1887. The Mansfield Branch headed 18 miles to the southeast, reaching the Rock Island Railroad at Mansfield, Arkansas. For a time, both railroads had common ownership and the two coordinated their passenger and freight services. The Frisco owned a large amount of coal along the line, which it at first used in its own locomotives. Frisco subsidiaries Arkansas Coal and Mining Company (1881-1932), Arkansas Mining and Coal Company (1932-1955), and Clarkland, Inc. mined the coal, first using traditional shaft mines, and later using deep strip mines. The south end of the branch was abandoned in 1978, and in 1983 Burlington Northern abandoned the same track between Midland

and Mansfield. The rest of the line was abandoned in 1985. Some of the grade at Jenson is now used as farm roads.

The railroad facilities at Jenson were never significant, but they were essential for the operations of the mainline and the Mansfield Branch. The two-story depot measured 20 feet by 43 feet and featured "White" and "Colored" waiting rooms, separated by the ticket office, at the north end of the building. On the south end of the depot was the 16' x 19' freight room. The second story was reached by stairs in the ticket office, and featured a three-room living quarters for the station agent. Built in 1887, the station was located just inside the north wye switch on the east side of the mainline, with "chatt and cinder" platforms. A section house stood nearby, and there was also a water tower near the north switch of the wye. A 37-car siding was here for many years, with anywhere from 97 to 132 car lengths of other tracks. There was also a water tower that was used by steam locomotives to fill their tenders. Jenson was listed as being a freight station and local ticket station in 1926.

Fort Smith Branch

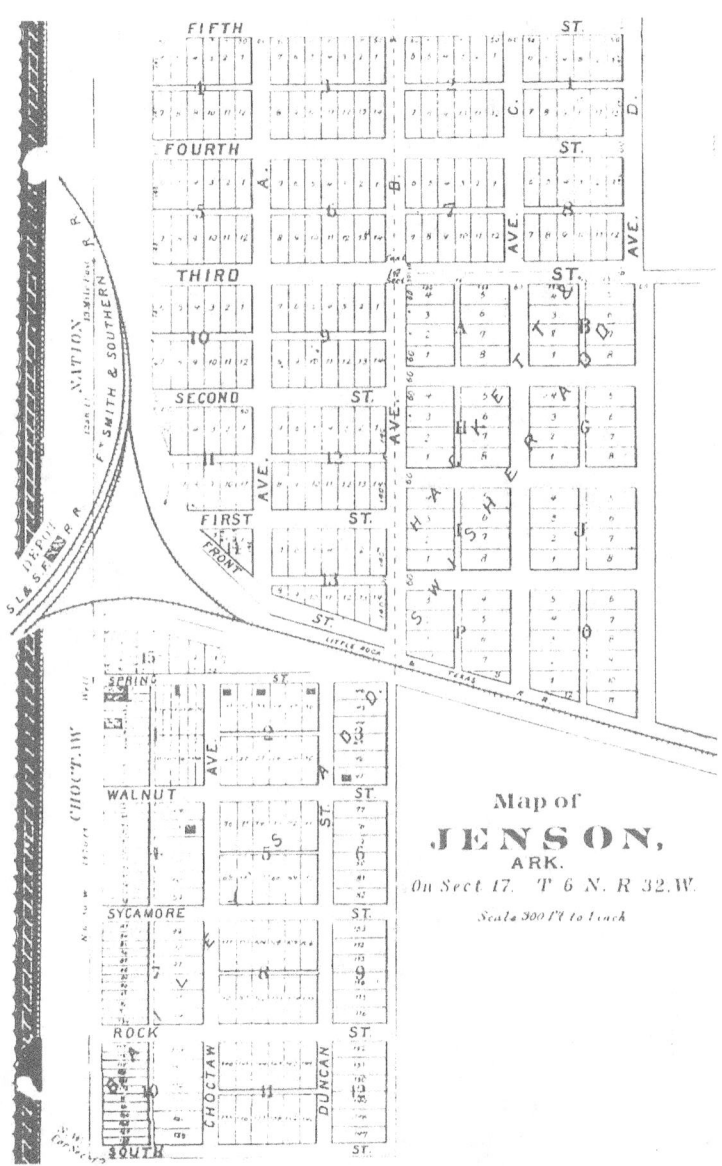

This map from the 1887 Sebastian County Atlas by E. L. Hayes & Co. shows the basic plan for Jenson, a plan that was never even remotely met. *Plat of Jenson – 1887*. Submitted by Curtis Hannah. From 1887 Sebastian County Atlas. Retrieved from Old Land Records for Sebastian County, Arkansas, on ARGenWeb.net, the Arkansas Geneological Resources Online website.

13.2F ARKANSAS-OKLAHOMA STATE LINE – At former Frisco Milepost 429.4, the railroad crosses the border between these two states for the fifth time since KCS Milepost 4.9. The border is located where Basinger Lane breaks off from Jenson Road and crosses the tracks.

The Fort Smith Dodger is shown heading towards Heavener, having passed through Jenson just a few minutes earlier, on November 11, 2021.

While the only train that regularly uses the Fort Smith Branch is the Fort Smith Dodger, KCS has continued to upgrade parts of the line. An example is this small deck plate girder span that had new concrete headwalls installed in 2020.

Fort Smith Branch

15.5F ROCK ISLAND – Rock Island was another town created when a railroad was built through the area. In 1886, the Fort Smith & Southern Railway built a railroad for the St. Louis & San Francisco Railroad as part of the line to Paris, Texas. The area was a simple collection of farms until the Midland Valley Railroad built their railroad between Excelsior, Arkansas, and Panama, Oklahoma, in 1904. Suddenly, a small community using the name Maney Junction was located here. The junction was an important one for the Midland Valley as they acquired trackage rights over 16 miles of the Frisco line to reach Fort Smith. The trackage rights agreement included charges for track rental, track maintenance and improvements, use of the Frisco station, and operating costs at the Frisco station. As many as six Midland Valley trains a day used these routes, and the cost was almost $20,000 in 1908.

In 1905, a post office opened at Maney Junction, but it was called Rock Island. There is no clear reason for either name – Maney or Rock Island – but some feel that the Rock Island name came from Rock Island, Illinois. The name Maney likely came from Manny Brothers of Chattanooga, Tennessee, which had some of the grading contracts for the Midland Valley. In 1910, the town had about 30 residents, a grocery store, a post office, and a railroad depot. There was some confusion about the name as the town used the name Rock Island, while the railroad station and junction still used the name Maney Junction. This situation lasted until the late 1910s or early 1920s.

Farming, ranching, and then coal mining, supported the community, which organized a school in 1918. A sorghum mill opened about the same time.

A slope coal mine opened in 1938 and closed during the 1950s, the same decade when Rock Island lost its school system, most of its stores, and its railroad passenger service. The post office closed in 1961. In 1968, the Midland Valley tracks between Panama and Excelsior were abandoned. In a effort to revive the community, Rock Island incorporated in 1989, claiming almost sixteen square miles. The population was 478 in 1990. One problem with the community's plans was that the Le Flore county commissioners did not approve the incorporation until 2004. Thanks to the growth of Fort Smith, Poteau, and a few other nearby cities, Rock Island is again growing. It has become a popular rural community with houses on large lots, and the population is about 700. Additionally, several stores have located along Oklahoma Highway 120 to the north. To the east of Rock Island, a large rock quarry (Green Country Stone) has developed where there was once coal mining.

The Railroads at Rock Island

Rock Island/Maney Junction was located at Frisco Milepost 431.7, as was M.V. Junction, named for the Midland Valley Railroad. The railroad crossing was protected by a gate that was normally lined against the Midland Valley. There was also an interchange track that allowed Midland Valley trains to use the Frisco tracks to reach Fort Smith. For example, in late 1929, the Midland Valley operated a pair of passenger motor trains (Nos. 1 and 2) daily between Fort Smith and Muskogee, and a pair of local freights (Nos. 41 and 42) daily except Sunday between Fort Smith and Shopton (east side of Musk-

Fort Smith Branch

ogee), Oklahoma. There was a small Midland Valley yard east of the Frisco tracks. The yard featured a wye track to the north that was used as the interchange track between the two railroads.

The railroad depot was in the northeast quadrant of the diamond that served both railroads and it was listed as a local ticket station by the Frisco. The Frisco had an industry track between the interchange track and the diamond that went west to serve a coal mine. In 1943, the mine was shown to be the Rock Island mine of the Kistler Coal Company. The Frisco stated that there was a capacity of 59 cars. Recent studies have looked at the former mine site as a possible source of coking coal. Today, the only track at Rock Island is the former Frisco mainline, now used by the Kansas City Southern as its Fort Smith Branch.

17.6F JAMES FORK BRIDGE – This bridge is located at former Frisco Milepost 433.8. The railroad crosses a small lake and then James Fork, a major tributary of the Poteau River. James Fork has been described as an upland stream in the central Arkansas River valley. A number of Caddoan cultural remains have been found along the stream, including several small farming villages and a number of smaller fishing and hunting encampments. All of these were abandoned by 1719.

The James Fork is considered to be part of the watershed of the Poteau River, which flows northward in Oklahoma, eventually entering the Arkansas River. The James Fork is about fifty miles long and forms on the northern slopes of Poteau Mountain, located in the Ouachita National Forest. As described by Goodspeed Publishing in 1889, in the book *History* of Benton, Washington, Carroll, Madison, Crawford, Franklin, and Sebastian Counties, Arkansas, "The James Fork of the latter [Poteau] river is formed by the conjunction of streams from the Poteau Mountains, and into it, from the extreme southwest portion of the county, flows West Creek, and from the valley north of Black Jack Ridge flows Prairie Creek. This fork then flows in a northwesterly direction, receiving the waters of many smaller streams, and finally leaves the county [Sebastian] near the center of its western boundary line."

Early reports about the James Fork almost always included statements about the coal found in the area, often calling it James Fork coal. A number of coal mines opened along the stream during the late 1800s and early 1900s. The James Fork was also a favorite route through the hills in this area, and settlements like Hartford, Midland, and Hackett (originally named James Fork) developed alongside it. Both the Frisco's Mansfield Branch, and the Midland Valley Railroad's route to Hartford, were built alongside the stream. Today, the James Fork is a major source of drinking water for southern Sebastian County and much of Scott County in Arkansas.

20.0F CONTROL POINT CAMERON – This location is at the private grade crossing at the north end (east end based upon the Kansas City Southern employee timetable) of Cameron. A control point functions to prevent trains from colliding, and is used as a reference point when giving a train crew authority to operate on a rail line. The switch for the Cameron house track is also located here.

Fort Smith Branch

To break up the Fort Smith Branch into two parts, CP Cameron is located at Milepost 20F.

20.5F CAMERON – Cameron is the only station listed in KCS employee timetables between the Arkansas & Missouri trackage at Fort Smith, and the KCS mainline at Poteau. There is still a short house track downtown. The frame depot built in 1887 was 20 feet wide and 70 feet long. By 1900, it was located on the north side of the tracks, with the two waiting rooms and a ticket office to the west, and the freight room to the east. The second floor had living quarters above the passenger section. A cotton platform, railroad stock yard, and a cotton seed warehouse were all on the south side of the tracks. For many years, there was a 38-car siding, plus other tracks with a capacity of 27 cars, all shown as being at Frisco Milepost 436.6. Cameron was listed as being a freight station and local ticket station in 1926.

The Heavener Sub: History Through the Miles

There are no current rail customers, and only this switch at Cameron, between CP Pocola and the mainline at Poteau.

The Community of Cameron

Cameron was a small settlement of about forty people by the 1870s. As with most such communities, the town featured a few stores and other services that supported nearby farming and ranching. Benjamin McBride, a member of the Choctaw tribe, ran a large farm that grew grain and cotton, and also raised livestock. Much of his farm was sold to the railroad and to a coal company which later mined and shipped out coal.

When the Fort Smith & Southern Railway (St. Louis & San Francisco Railway or Frisco) built through the area, the town grew further. On January 21, 1888, the Cameron post office opened. While nothing was documented at the time, there are two theories on the name of Cameron. One states that it was named after James Cameron, who was in the area in 1886 doing planning work to build the railroad. The second theory, and the one stated most often, is that it used the name of William Cameron. In 1882, William was the superintendent of coal-mining operations for the Missouri Pacific Railway Company, which owned the Osage Coal and Mining Company and the Atoka Coal and Mining Company. In 1885, William led a rescue crew after a mine explosion, and he later developed the long-wall system of coal mining. In 1901, he was appointed Indian Territory Mine Inspector.

Cameron became important enough that in 1895, it became one of the locations where Indian Territory's Central District conducted court hearings. In 1898, residents applied to incorporate, and the population peaked at 316 in the 1900 census when the town included a hotel, several retail stores, three doctors, three cotton gins, several lodge halls, two livery stables, and a blacksmith. In 1900, Congress decided to move the courthouse from Cameron to Poteau. The population began to decline, but the town added a bank, several general stores, and a drug store. Within a decade, Cameron was down to only one cotton gin as fruit and potatoes began to be more important to the local economy. Some coal mining was underway by the Williams Coal Company, and several natural gas wells were producing by the mid-1920s. A cotton oil company opened to handle the cotton seeds from the local gin, and the population hit its low with 203 residents in 1940. Several strip mines opened during the 1940s and 1950s, and the population began to grow, with there being 311 residents in 1970. A few businesses, poultry farms, and natural gas drilling operations are currently at Cameron. The town is also still the home of Cameron Public Schools.

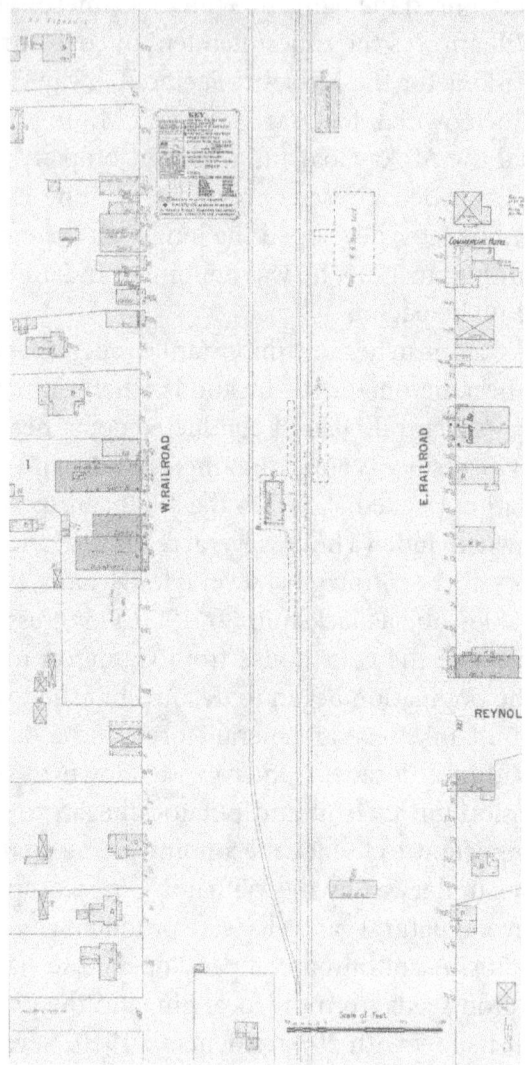

The railroad headed down the center of Railroad Street in 1901, an area that today is generally patches of woods. What was shown to be East and West Railroad Streets is today East and West First Streets. *Sanborn Fire Insurance Map from Cameron, Le Flore County, Oklahoma.* Sanborn Map Company, Jan, 1901. Map. Retrieved from the Library of Congress, https://www.loc.gov/item/sanborn07023_002/.

Fort Smith Branch

One of the most unique features of Cameron is Reynolds' Castle, also known as the Captain's Castle. The house, located on the east side of town off Castle Street, was built by James Reynolds, a former Confederate army officer who became a successful rancher, businessman, and coal land owner in Indian Territory. During the 1890s, he built the house from local natural stone for his wife Felicity Turnbull Reynolds, a descendant of the prominent Choctaw leader Greenwood LeFlore. The castle, which is still a private home, was listed on the National Register of Historic Places in 1977. The hill that Reynold's Castle nestles against is Cameron Mountain.

22.8F RIDDLE CREEK BRIDGE – Riddle Creek flows out of the mountains to the east, forming not far from Sugar Loaf Lake near Midland, Arkansas. It winds west from here and flows into Lost Poteau River. The Lost Poteau River is actually an old Poteau River channel that still collects water from a number of streams and then connects with the main channel northeast of Poteau, Oklahoma.

Riddle Creek was one of the streams that traditionally used several channels, and the Frisco had to work to keep it passing under this bridge. In 1912-1913, the railroad restored the Riddle Creek channel after it moved close to the mainline. In 1924, the deck plate girder bridge (Frisco Milepost 438.9) was rebuilt and strengthened, as was the wooden trestle that was part of the structure. Rebuilding bridges along the entire line was a part of the program to allow heavier trains to operate over the Frisco's Arthur Subdivision.

23.3F ROLLEN – Rollen was listed as a prepay freight station in the *Official List of Officers, Stations, Agents, Etc. of St. Louis-San Francisco Railway Co.* (May 1, 1926). Once located at Frisco Milepost 439.4, Rollen was gone by the May 17, 1936, employee timetable.

24.0F GAP CREEK BRIDGE – This is another stream that flows out of the mountains to the east, and then flows westward into Lost Poteau River. The railroad crosses it at former Frisco Milepost 440.1.

25.9F NEFF – Shown as Neff's on maps from the early 1900s, Neff was listed as a prepay freight station in the *Official List of Officers, Stations, Agents, Etc. of St. Louis-San Francisco Railway Co.* (May 1, 1926). Located at Frisco Milepost 442.0, it was listed as a 9-car spur track in 1936, but Neff was gone by the 1950s.

27.1F POTEAU RIVER BRIDGE – This through truss span, located at former Frisco Milepost 443.2, is easy to locate as it is immediately north of Old State Highway 112. The through truss span was installed in 1930 on concrete piers, with short deck plate girder spans off each end. From north to south, there are 16 timber pile bents, the original cut-stone piers for the original bridge span, the two concrete piers and then another cut-stone pier, and then 56 timber pile bents. Apparently, in 1930, a longer steel span was replaced with the current through truss span, designed to handle heavier trains.

Stories from the time of the railroad's construction state that Melvin Flener was in charge of the bridge's construction. He obtained the stone for the piers from a quarry on Town Creek, and the timber from nearby Cavanal Mountain. After the work was completed, Melvin Flener stayed in Poteau where he opened Flener's Hotel in 1886. The two-story hotel was a popular attraction as it often featured entertainment and dances on weekends and holidays

This area is known as "The Cutoff" because the river has two channels to the south and they merge back together here. The Poteau River is unique as it is the only north-flowing river in Oklahoma, starting two miles south of Bee Mountain near Waldron, Arkansas, and heading almost 150 miles to the Arkansas River at Belle Point in Fort Smith, Arkansas. While a few miles of the start and end of the river are in Arkansas, the rest is in Oklahoma, making it the seventh largest river in the state.

The name Poteau is used for many things in this area, including the Poteau River, Poteau Mountains, and the City of Poteau. In the French language, poteau means post. There is a belief that early French explorers marked the river with a large post or stake to identify the river or to mark the territory.

The Fort Smith Dodger crosses the Poteau River Bridge as it heads south to Heavener during the fall of 2021.

WPA's Poteau River Bridge

Immediately south of the former Frisco bridge is a new highway bridge that was built to replace an older Oklahoma Highway 112 bridge. The road is now known as Old State Highway 112, as a new Oklahoma Highway 112 route has been built to the north. To the south of the new highway bridge is the older WPA (Work Projects Administration) bridge, designed as a riveted Parker truss.

This WPA bridge opened in 1940 to replace an even older bridge that often washed out during heavy rains. The bridge was built by the Work Projects Administration, a New Deal organization created on May 6, 1935, as the Works Progress Administration. It was reorganized and renamed the Work Projects Administration in 1939. The WPA built a number of riveted Parker truss spans as they were lighter and used less material, but could also span longer distances than other designs. The WPA bridge closed in 1998, but still stands as an informal park area.

27.7F CONTROL POINT POTEAU – This is the junction between today's Kansas City Southern Fort Smith line and their mainline, and once the crossing between the KCS and Frisco. The Frisco listed this as being KCS Crossing, located at Milepost 443.6. The Frisco showed that this was an interlocker in 1936, and an interlocking in 1957. The Kansas City Southern showed that it was an automatic interlocking. The site of this crossing is easily visible from North Witte Street, also known as Old State Highway 112.

Located at the north end of Poteau, Oklahoma, the railroad curves to the south to enter the KCS mainline, and Dodger crews head through Poteau

Fort Smith Branch

and on to Heavener, the end of their territory assignment. Details about Poteau can be found on Page 425.

On a November day in 2021, the Fort Smith Dodger, with KCS 2819 leading, passes the Control Point Poteau sign as it enters the Heavener Subdivision to head on to Heavener, Oklahoma.

The Heavener Sub: History Through the Miles

Route Guide for the Waldron Branch

The Waldron Branch is included as Kansas City Southern has traditionally listed the line as a part of their Heavener Subdivision. The line was built by the Arkansas Western Railroad, which was incorporated in Arkansas on December 13, 1899. The original plan for the railroad was to build from Howe to Heavener, parallel to the Kansas City, Pittsburg & Gulf, and then east to Waldron, Arkansas. Newspaper reports from the time state that construction began at the Arkansas-Indian Territory line on January 8, 1900. By April, the grading contractor had 15 miles of right-of-way worked east from the border toward Waldron. There were reports that rail for the 32-mile line between Waldron and Heavener had been purchased, but other reports stated that purchasing rail for the extensions was on hold due to high steel prices. Meanwhile, changes in the route were being promoted, with a line from Waldron to Hot Springs in Arkansas, and Heavener to Wister Junction and Waggoner in Indian Territory.

Reports from the construction of the railroad indicate that there was a close relationship with the Santa Fe railroad. Apparently the used 48-pound rail (some sources state 80-pound rail), plus two steam locomotives, were all purchased from this larger railroad company. The Wear Coal Company reportedly provided most of the construction funding, receiving stock and credits on later shipments of coal over the line.

Building to Waldron was only the first part of the plan. On December 7, 1901, the Kansas City, Hot Springs & Southeastern Railroad Company was incorporated to extend the line from Waldron to Hot Springs and beyond, but no work was done and the company became defunct in June 1903.

The first nineteen miles of the railroad were completed from Heavener, Oklahoma, to Cauthron, Arkansas, by November 18, 1901, and then to Waldron by January 1, 1902, with full operations over the 32-mile line beginning on February 2, 1902. In 1902, a report about the condition of the new railroad was written by a consulting engineer. The report was not very generous about the railroad's condition and pointed out a number of problems. These included a large number of curves in deep cuts; ditches that were already filled with dirt; too many bridges (42 in total); the use of cull ties that were already rotted after only a year of use; used, heavily worn 48-pound rail from 1880 that was bought secondhand from the Santa Fe; two old 6-driver Santa Fe locomotives and only one freight and one passenger car; and a lack of revenue to cover all of the expenses.

After several years of operations, The Arkansas Western Railway Company was incorporated in Arkansas by the Kansas City Southern on May 13, 1904. The new firm was created to acquire the Arkansas Western Railroad and extend it on to Hot Springs. According to the Interstate Commerce Commission, the new railway began operations on June 1, 1904. In November, the KCS, through its Arkansas Western Railway, purchased $650,000 in first-mortgage bonds along with $649,100 in the stock of the Arkansas Western Railroad, taking control of the route.

The Sixth Annual Report of The Kansas City Southern Railway Company for the Fiscal Year Ending June 30, 1906 stated that The Arkansas Western Railway Company was controlled "by The Kansas City Southern Railway Company as the owner of all the Capital Stock and bonds of The Arkansas Western Railway Company." In that period of time, the Arkansas Western earned $58,529.29 in

Waldron Branch

freight revenue, $12,685.07 in passenger, $1367.36 in mail, $1407.86 in express, and $1255.48 in other revenues.

Initially, there were great plans for the line, and KCS operated two passenger trains in each direction to connect Waldron with mainline trains at Heavener. In 1908, train No. 1 would depart Waldron daily at 7:00am, pass through Heavener at 8:50am after a ten minute stop, and operate on to Spiro and Fort Smith, arriving at 10:40am. Train No. 2 would return later that evening to Heavener (6:20pm) and Waldron (7:50pm). Train No. 6 was the Monday-Saturday morning Heavener (9:20am) to Waldron (11:40am) train, and it returned after lunch as No. 5 (Waldron at 1:50pm and Heavener at 5:10pm). Train Nos. 4 and 3 covered the Sunday-only service, leaving Heavener as No. 4 at 1:40pm and arriving at Waldron at 3:10pm. No. 3 departed Waldron at 4:00pm and arrived back at Heavener at 5:35pm.

Information from the *Twenty-Second Annual Report on the Statistics of Railways in the United States for the Year Ending June 30, 1909*, showed that the Arkansas Western was being operated as a feeder railroad to its owner – Kansas City Southern. At the time, the average passenger rode 17.38 miles and paid $0.53286. The average number of passengers was only 10 on each train. The average number of tons of freight was only 56.85 per train, with the average amount received for each ton of freight being $0.79106. The average freight haul per ton was 21.65 miles.

In 1919, the Interstate Commerce Commission conducted a valuation hearing on The Arkansas Western Railway Company. The report from the hearing stated that the line included 32.348 miles of mainline between Heavener and Waldron, plus 4.566 miles of sidings and yard tracks. Of this, 9.659 miles of mainline and 0.529 miles of sidings were in Oklahoma, while 22.689 miles of mainline and 4.037 miles of yard tracks and sidings were in Arkansas. At the time, all stock and bonds were owned by Kansas City

Southern, which apparently had received no dividends in several years. KCS also provided all equipment, except for a single outfit box car (A.W. 01).

In 1928, there began to be talk again about extending the line east from Waldron. Timber was being harvested throughout the Ouachita Mountains, and large stands of timber were located east of Waldron with no good transportation to get the lumber to market. One of these loggers was the Caddo River Lumber Company, located near Webb, Arkansas. A town developed around the sawmill that used the name Forester, named for Charlie Edward Forrester, the person who handled the negotiations between the lumber company and railroad.

C. E. Forrester started business in Waldron long before the railroad arrived. He acquired his father's general store and created the Forrester-Goolsby Corporation. He expanded into cotton, lumber, groceries, dry goods, hardware, and many other business lines. He also partnered with Thomas Whitaker Rosborough of the Caddo River Lumber Company to create the town of Forrester (spelled Forester by the railroad and the post office). Forrester was a local philanthropist who donated to schools and to efforts to build new churches. The land that the town of Forester was built on was donated by Forrester. His house still stands in the Commercial Historic District in Waldron, and is listed on the National Register of Historic Places.

On April 23, 1929, the Interstate Commerce Commission approved the new line to Forester, and construction began on June 26, 1929. There was an interesting guarantee in the agreement that stated if the Caddo River Lumber Company didn't open and begin shipping within a year, they would pay 6 percent interest on the cost of the line until the mill was completed. If it wasn't open in two years, then the lumber company would be required to purchase the line from the railroad. On September 1, 1930, the line

Waldron Branch

extension was completed and rail operations began. Things ran steadily for the next several decades, even with the Dierks Lumber & Coal acquiring the town, mill and timber in 1948.

By the late 1930s, the Waldron Branch was essentially a freight line hauling lumber and coal out of the Ouachita Mountains. *The Fifty-Third Annual Report of the Statistics of Railways in the United States for the Year Ending December 31, 1939,* showed this in the ICC reporting. In that year, the Arkansas Western Railway earned $53,351 moving freight, but only $449 moving passengers. No mail was moved, and only $257 was earned by moving express shipments. Another thousand dollars came from "other rail line transportation revenues" and "incidental operating revenues," leading to a total of $55,014 for all of 1939.

The Waldron Branch, still known as The Arkansas Western Railway Company, was described in a National Railroad Adjustment Board hearing about a 1949 disagreement between one of the operating unions and the Kansas City Southern.

> *The Arkansas Western Railway Company is a subsidiary property of The Kansas City Southern Railway Company, with total trackage of 61.55 miles, of which 55.58 miles is its main line. It connects with the Kansas City Southern at Heavener, Oklahoma, and extends from Heavener, Oklahoma, to Forester, Arkansas. It owns no rolling stock equipment and has no employes of its own in train or engine service. All trains operated on the Arkansas Western are manned by Kansas City Southern employes. Coal mines, sawmills and several small towns*

are served by tri-weekly mixed train service: Train No. 3 departing from Heavener, Monday, Wednesday and Friday, and Train No. 4 departing from Forester, Tuesday, Thursday and Saturday, with an extra operated if and when required.

In 1952, the mill was closed as the last of the virgin timber was cut. After two years of inactivity, the railroad received permission to abandon the 20.8-mile-long line between Waldron and Forester on September 9, 1954. Thanks to the construction of a Waldron feed mill by Arkansas Valley Incorporated, the rest of the branch was saved from possible abandonment. Eventually, Tyson acquired the feed mill, and a related hatchery and processing plant. The line was rebuilt with federal and state grants during the mid-1980s, and the Arkansas Western Railway was finally merged into KCS on July 6, 1992. In 2005, the Waldron Branch between Milepost 4 and the end of the track at Waldron was leased to Watco Companies as their Arkansas Southern Railroad. The track between Heavener and Milepost 4 is now the Waldron Industrial Spur.

Traditionally, the Waldron Branch was considered to run north-south, with Heavener to the north and Waldron and Forester to the south. By 2002, KCS employee timetables showed the line to run east-west, with Heavener being the west end of the line. Because most of the line's history was spent using north-south as the terms, this is what will be used in this description. The line generally uses the valley of the Poteau River, and Oklahoma Highway 128 and Arkansas Highway 28 follow the line most of the way between Heavener and Waldron, and on to Forester.

Waldron Branch

THE ARK. WESTERN RY.

SOUTHWARD			NORTHWARD	
Capacity of Sidings.	Distance from Heavener.	TIME TABLE No. 2 Effective SUNDAY, JAN. 5, 1964 STATIONS		
9	0.0	......HEAVENER......		
		10.4		
12	10.4	......COALDALE......		
		3.1		
9	13.5	........BATES........	W A L D R O N	
		5.6		
....	19.1	......CAUTHRON......		
		2.1		
2	21.2	........OLIVER........		8A-5P Ex. Sat. Sun. & Hol.
		4.7		
6	25.8	..........HON..........		
		6.0		
24 Y 43	31.8	......WALDRON......		
		3.3		
	35.1	End of Line 35.1		

Tracks not shown on face of time table.

	Mile No.	Car Capcy.
Lee Taylor Coal Spur........	8	4
Royal Superior Coal Siding	9	7
Oronoga Mutual Mine Tracks	14	25

SPECIAL INSTRUCTIONS

The Operating Rules of the Kansas City Southern Lines, effective July 1, 1954, will govern on this railway.

Trains and engines run at restricted speed at all times not to exceed 20 MPH at any point. Rule 93 applies.

Trains handling wrecker or pile driver, must not exceed ten (10) MPH at any point.

The Waldron Branch was listed as the Arkansas Western Railway in the *Kansas City Southern Lines Time Table No. 2*, effective January 5, 1964. Employee timetable from the author's collection.

0.0 HEAVENER – The Waldron Branch starts at the KCS office in Heavener, located at an elevation of approximately 550 feet. Details on Heavener and the rail facilities there can be found on Page 457.

The Waldron Branch is the easternmost of three tracks through downtown Heavener. A crossover track located between Avenue C and Avenue F connects the Waldron Branch with the KCS mainline. Just south of Avenue F, the branchline starts to curve to the southeast and away from the mainline tracks.

The Heavener Sub: History Through the Miles

When trains are switching the OK Feed Mill, the locomotives are often just a short distance out of Heavener. KCS #4178 is seen through the front porch of a closed general store as it waits to switch and weigh more grain cars.

1.0   FARRELL COOPER – This coal tipple was served by trucks, and in 2002, had a 1400-foot spur track. The company had several coal leases in Le Flore County, overseen by the Bureau of Land Management. A few remains can still be found at the site.

The Ferrell-Cooper Mining Company was founded in 1974 and based in Fort Smith, Arkansas. The company mined coal near older strip mines north of Coaldale, Arkansas, during the early 2010s. The coal was trucked to here for loading onto the railroad.

1.3   MIDSOUTH WOOD YARD – Timetables from 1970 show a 10-car-long Reese Spur in this general location. In 2002, there was a 450-foot spur track here for Mid-South Wood Products. Nothing remains today.

Waldron Branch

A track scale is located just north of the site of the Farrell Cooper coal tipple. On April 26, 2022, a KCS grain train from the nearby OK Feed Mill is seen passing the track scale on its way to Heavener.

2.0 OK FEED MILL – The large feed mill is part of the OK Foods operation in the Heavener area. During the 1930s, Collier Wenderoth, Sr., founded OK Foods as a manufacturer of poultry and livestock. The firm slowly grew and built its large feed mill in downtown Fort Smith during the 1960s. Growth became faster during the 1980s and 1990s, and in 1995 this feed mill was opened. By the 2000s, OK Foods was one of the largest chicken producers in the United States. In November 2011, OK Foods was integrated into Industrias Bachoco, located in Celaya, Mexico.

This is a large feed mill, and various grains are delivered in unit-train shipments. To handle trains of this size, there is a five-track stub-ended yard east of the mill. To the west is a long lead track that starts south of the West Avenue I grade crossing. At Milepost 2 is the south switch to the feed mill.

The Heavener Sub: History Through the Miles

This photo shows the front of the large OK Foods feed mill located at Milepost 2 of the Waldron Branch.

For the railroad, this is the important side of the OK Foods feed mill, as it is where the railroad reaches the large grain silos with their inbound shipments.

Waldron Branch

On May 20, 2022, Watco #3845 led a westbound train from Waldron to Heavener. It is shown parked near the OK Feed Mill, waiting for the opportunity to interchange the traffic with Kansas City Southern.

4.0 BEGIN ARKANSAS SOUTHERN RAILROAD – From here southward to Waldron, the railroad is leased by Watco and used by their Arkansas Southern Railroad. The original lease was effective in 2005, and a new lease was agreed upon in 2016. Several amendments were made on July 20, 2020, that extended the lease to November 30, 2034.

5.8 LANK – Through the 1930s, there was a 17-car track here, located about where the private road crosses the tracks. The name Lank, or Lank City, was used for the location.

Just a short distance to the southwest was the unincorporated community of Forrester. This was a small town that grew due to coal mining, and then declined with it. A post office opened at Forrester on June 8, 1915, and then closed on February 14, 1922. Several government records clearly state that the location is named Forrester, "not Forester, Lank, Lank City." The Forrester Baptist Church still stands nearby.

Heading east, trains climb a steady 0.10% grade of almost five miles long, climbing from about 550 feet to about 675 feet above sea level.

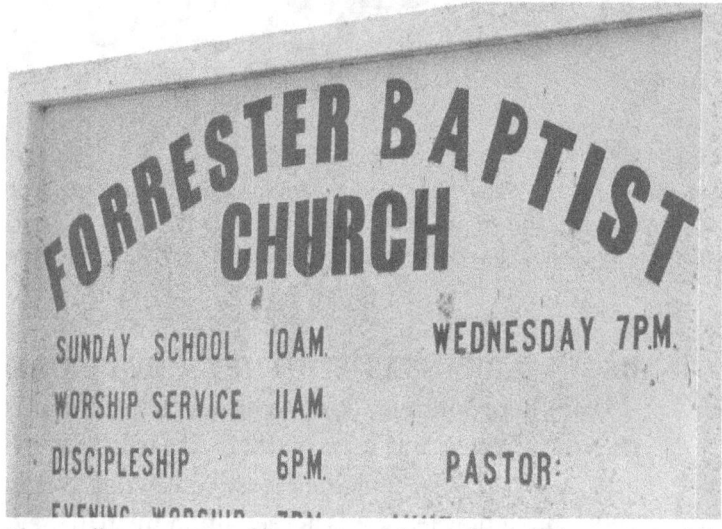

The small community of Forrester was located near Milepost 5.5, while the logging community of Forester was located at Milepost 55.9, both on the Waldron Branch. Little remains of each community, but the Forrester Baptist Church helps to locate the community in this area.

Waldron Branch

Unlike the mainline of the Heavener Subdivision, concrete posts don't mark the mileposts along the line. Instead, signs like this one are used along the Waldron Branch.

This sign at Milepost 7.1 of the Waldron Branch shows that coal isn't quite dead in the area. However, what coal that is mined goes out by truck, not rail.

8.5 LEE TAYLOR COAL SPUR – This was a small loading tipple for a truck mine in the hills to the north. This was known as Mine No. 1 of the Bell Taylor Coal Company in 1937. In 1940, the Oklahoma Department of Mines and Mining stated that the mine was "equipped with steam and worked on the room and pillar system. Coal is shot off the solid. Black powder is used. This mine was in good condition when last inspected." At the time, the mine, known as both the Sugar Creek Coal Company and the Lee Taylor Coal Company (Lee Taylor was Manager), had three workers and produced about seven tons of coal a day.

While the spur track used the coal company's name, this location was known as Hiawatha. In 1941, the Interstate Commerce Commission investigated coal rates from a number of places on the Kansas City Southern, including places along the Arkansas Western. Hiawatha was one of these origin points where coal was shipped from.

North of the railroad on some of the lower benches of Poteau Mountain was once a series of active strip mines, with the coal trucked to a number of different loading locations in the region. This track was short and held only four cars until it was removed between 1966 and 1968.

9.2 ROYAL SUPERIOR COAL SIDING – This was Mine No. 1 of the company. In 1937, it employed 15 men and produced 50 tons of coal per day. By 1940, it was down to 7 workers and 25 tons per day. The mine was described as being "equipped with steam and is worked on the room and pillar system. Coal is shot off the solid. Black powder is used. Average

Waldron Branch

height of coal is 6 feet." There was a seven-car spur track here, abandoned by 1968.

9.8 OKLAHOMA-ARKANSAS STATE LINE – The border is at the grade crossing with Paradise Road, shown as Coaldale Lane by the Federal Railroad Administration. To the west is Le Flore County, Oklahoma, while to the east is Scott County, Arkansas.

Look for the Coaldale Lane road sign as it marks the border between Oklahoma and Arkansas.

Oklahoma was once known as Indian Territory (1834-1907), and later partly as Oklahoma Territory (1890-1907). Oklahoma means "red people" in the Choctaw language, and the name was decided during an 1866 meeting between federal officials and leaders of the five Indian nations who had been moved there. During the late 1800s, the western part of Oklahoma was the Oklahoma Territory, while the eastern part was Indian Territory. The two merged and became the 46th state on November 16, 1907. It is the 20th largest state and the 28th most populated, with about four million residents About two-thirds of Oklahomans live in the Oklahoma City (the state capitol) and Tulsa metropolitan areas. The state is known as "The Sooner State" due to the number of white settlers who staked their land claims out before the official opening dates in the western Oklahoma Territory.

The land that makes up **Le Flore County**, Oklahoma, became owned by the Choctaw Nation after they ceded much of their homelands with the Treaty of Doak's Stand in 1820, and then the rest with the Treaty of Dancing Rabbit Creek in 1830. When this was Indian Territory, it was part of the Moshulatubbee and Apukshunnubbee districts of the Choctaw Nation. Coal and timber attracted settlers, industry and railroads to the region. The county has about 50,000 residents, and Poteau is the county seat.

The county is named for the LeFlore family, which dates back to Frenchman Louis LeFleur, who married the daughter of the renowned Choctaw warrior Pushmataha. LeFleur became a wealthy trader and fought with Andrew Jackson in the War of 1812. His son, Greenwood LeFlore, was a leader in education and Christianity for the Choctaws. He married Elizabeth Coodey, sister of Cherokee leader William Shorey Coodey and a niece of Chief John Ross. LeFlore later signed the Treaty of Dancing Rabbit Creek, thinking that moving west would enable the Choctaws to retain their sovereignty. The family continued to play a leading role in tribal matters, both in Indian Territory and in Mississippi.

The Territory of **Arkansas** was admitted to the Union as the 25th state on June 15, 1836. It is the

29th largest state, and the 34th most populated. The name Arkansas is a version of an Osage name for the Quapaw people who lived in this area. Little Rock, located near the center of Arkansas, is the capital and largest city in the state. However, most of the largest cities in the state are found in a line along the former Frisco Railway between Bentonville and Fort Smith. Arkansas is the only state where diamonds are mined, and you can go mine them yourself at the Crater of Diamonds State Park. This explains the diamond shape found on the state flag. The former nickname of the state was the "Land of Opportunity," but it now uses "The Natural State."

Scott County was created as Arkansas' 28th county from parts of Crawford, Pope, and Pulaski counties on November 5, 1833. The county was named for Arkansas Territory Supreme Court Justice Andrew Horatio Scott, appointed by President James Monroe. The Arkansas Territory was created on March 2, 1819, and Scott was the first territorial official to reach the capitol at Arkansas Post, arriving on July 4, 1819.

The initial county seat was the residence of Walter Cauthron, located near what is now Booneville. In 1836, the county seat was moved to Cauthron, which is also now in Logan County. In 1840, the county seat moved to Winfield, and then to Waldron in 1845. Some of these moves were made due to poor roads, while others were made to locate the county seat in the center of the county. A significant issue is that Yell (1840), Sebastian (1851), and Logan (1871) counties were all created from parts of Scott County. The county's population peaked at 14,302 in 1910 when coal mining, lumbering, and cotton production were at their peak. The population dropped to 7297 in the 1960 census, and then was back up to 11,233 in the 2010 census, but back down to 9836 in the 2020 census. Poultry production is currently the largest employer in the county, due to Tyson Foods and OK Foods.

In this area, the railroad peaks at 675 feet and the grade starts to drop at about 1.0% heading east through Coaldale. It then climbs a short distance and drops again into Bates.

10.0   COALDALE – Like many communities in the area, Coaldale started as a number of small farms in the 1830s. The area began to change when coal was discovered along Poteau Mountain, and the timber became valuable. An issue with many communities in Scott County came about when the courthouse burned in May 1882. Many records were lost, including those involving the school districts. In August 1882, an attempt was made to recreate the records for the fifty-six school districts, and the school district at Coaldale was named Hixon for 1840 settler Nathaniel Hixon. The school itself took the name Lisles School, for James N. Lisle, who began buying land here in 1879.

Another name began to be used for this area after the Arkansas Western Railroad was built. Charles C. Godman was president and a director of the new railroad, just one of several that he built, including the Arkansas Central Railroad Company east from Fort Smith into coal and timber areas in 1897. To honor Godman, the station built here was called Godman Depot.

The railroad was completed through Coaldale during late 1901. While the railroad built a number of tracks at Coaldale, a depot apparently was

Waldron Branch

not constructed. In late 1910, the Arkansas Railroad Commission investigated the petition of the town of Coaldale to require the Kansas City Southern to build a depot at that place. A platform was also located on the south side of the tracks.

The *Arkansas Gazette* reported in their November 28, 1901, issue that the Goldman Coal & Coke Company had opened a mine and the town of Goldman had been laid out, both obviously a misspelling. A post office opened at Godman in 1902, but its name was changed to Coaldale in 1903, the year the town was organized. The Coaldale School was created in 1903, but it merged with the Bates School in 1907.

KCS acquired the railroad in 1904, and by 1906, Godman's coal company had been sold to the Black Diamond Coal Company. About fifty men worked at the mine, enough to support a general store and a few other businesses. In 1921, the mine at Coaldale was shown to be the Liles Coal Company, and the town's population was 300. A study from the time stated that the coal was bituminous, and that the coal beds in the area consisted "of over 7 feet of coal divided by a parting of shale." Further to the east, the coal seams were broken up and were much thinner.

In 1922, the post office was closed and the service moved to Heavener, Oklahoma. Local farming suffered during the late 1920s as cotton prices dropped, and the Great Depression ended much of the coal mining. What mining that remained changed to strip mining using machinery instead of large numbers of miners. Mines closed during the late 1900s, but some reopened for a few years during the early 2000s.

The Ozark Mountain Region Of Missouri and Arkansas As it Appears Along the Line of the Kan-

sas City Southern Railway (1924) had a short listing about Coaldale, with a population of 150. It stated:

> A coal mining and lumber manufacturing point. The Hiawatha Smokeless Coal Co. has a coal mine and the Fogel Lumber Co. a sawmill in operation. The surplus products shipped from this station in 1910 amounted to 1,000 bales of cotton, 500 head of cattle, 50 head of horses and mules, 100 head of hogs and 5,000 railroad ties. There are in the town two general merchandise stores, a drug store, cotton gin and a public school. Coal deposits could be mined here and timber for sawmills available.

The railroad had several tracks at Coaldale, generally built to handle local coal and agricultural business. A short siding was located here, shown as being 14 cars long in 1936, and then 12 cars after that as freight equipment got larger. The siding was gone by the 1980s.

Today, Coaldale is an unincorporated community on the Oklahoma-Arkansas state line. A few houses are still there, as well as the remains of the Coaldale Store building, a two-story rock building that serves as a reminder of better times in the community. East of town at Milepost 10.8, the railroad crosses Arkansas Highway 28 at-grade.

The Coaldale Store building marks the location of what was once the coal-ming community of Coaldale. The Waldron Branch passes right behind the building, where there was once a siding.

This sign stands next to the Waldron Branch, marking the location of Coaldale, Arkansas.

The post for the old Coaldale station sign still stands next to the Waldron Branch. The base has the markings of "KCS 6-7-83", showing when it was installed.

13.5 BATES – Bates was another coal mining town that developed along the Arkansas Western Railroad. It too was originally a small agricultural community, dating from the 1820s and 1830s. The first noted settlers in the area included the family of Thompson G. Bates Sr., who established a farm along Jones Creek, south of present-day Bates. The family reportedly owned two slaves – Doc and Henry – who were later freed and given land about where Bates exists today.

The Arkansas Western Railroad was here by 1901, and in 1902 the Bates post office opened. In 1907, Bates was officially established and the Bates School District was created, then consolidated with the Coaldale School District later that year. The year 1907 was also when the Waldron Telephone Company installed a telephone line exchange at Bates. Soon there were several stores, a blacksmith, a sawmill, and about 500 residents. Commercial coal mining also began about the same time, and in 1921, there was the Bates Smokeless Coal Company, Harper Coal & Coke Company, and the Hodge Coal Company. The remains of many of these coal mines can be found along Strip Pit Road and Poteau Mountain Road, officially County Road 50.

The Ozark Mountain Region Of Missouri and Arkansas As it Appears Along the Line of the Kansas City Southern Railway (1924) had a short description of Bates, which had a population of 272.

> A lumber manufacturing and coal mining town. There are in operation here the yellow pine sawmill of the Ingham Lumber Co., capacity 50,000 feet per day; the I. R. Packard coal mine and the Bates Coal & Coke Company's mine. The town has five mercantile stocks, valued at $140,000; a hotel, church, public school and several minor commercial and industrial concerns. The surplus products shipped annually from Bates, exclusive of coal, amount to 800 bales of cotton, 50 carloads of railroad ties and 200 carloads of pine lumber.

Coal continued to be important around Bates into the 1930s. In 1937, the Bates Coal Mining Company and the Acme Semi-Anthracite Coal Company both mined the Lower Hartshorne coal seam in the area and showed their location as being at Bates. Over the next several decades, the names changed as coal production continued, but mining generally ended several decades after World War II.

WAMX 3842 is shown heading west across one of the few steel bridges on the Waldron Branch. Located just west of Bates, the train was spreading ballast after a few track maintenance projects during Spring 2022.

In 1974, the Bates Post Office closed and was replaced by the Bates Rural Station and service out of Waldron. The school had also been closed, used as a community and event center, and listed on the National Register of Historic Places. The other businesses in town have also closed, but a few churches and the Bates Volunteer Fire Department are still in the unincorporated community. The main part of the community includes several blocks squeezed between West Shadley and East Shadley creeks.

The railroad had a platform at Bates for many years, used by passengers riding the mixed trains over the line. While there were a number of coal spurs in the Coaldale and Bates area, there were not many tracks at Bates itself. A short 9-car siding was here until the early 1980s, and a 150-foot Bates Team Track was shown to be located at Milepost 14.9 in 2002. Another track near Bates was for the

Southwestern Wood Preserving Company, shown to be at Milepost 14.3. The company was incorporated on February 19, 1946, and bought timbers for pole and pile production. In 1970, the track was shown to have a capacity of three railcars.

As shown by this dog asleep on the tracks at Bates, train traffic on the Waldron Branch isn't very busy.

The Bates Coal Mining Company

The Bates Coal Mining Company was one of the largest employers around Bates for decades. Initially, this was one of a number of coal companies that had ties to the Kali-Inla Coal Company, a company controlled by the Choctaw, Oklahoma & Gulf (later Chicago, Rock Island & Pacific). The Choctaw controlled a major part of the coal industry in southeastern Oklahoma for almost half a century, with mines in 1900 listed as being at Hartshorne, Gowen,

Alderson, and Wilburton in Oklahoma, and at Hartford in Arkansas. There were communications between Bates Coal Mining and Kali-Inla about a railroad spur track at Bates that would be jointly owned.

The actual ownership of the operation near Bates was quite complex. For the Bates Coal Mining Company, the land was owned by Mrs. Waring of Joplin, Missouri. It was leased to the New Bates Smokeless Coal Company, which then subleased the operation to the Bates Coal Mining Company. From 1936 until 1940, there were three significant explosions at the mine. The first took place on November 27, 1936, and killed five miners. The second took place in May 1940, but no one was working in the mine when that explosion occurred. On August 27, 1940, a third explosion took place, killing ten miners who were working the night shift about 1700 feet below the surface. About this time, the mine was reportedly being subleased to the Scott County Development Company and being operated by Arthur L. Raines, although the lease wasn't completed until September 7, 1940. The investigation determined that the equipment used in the mine was not adequately maintained and that booster fans were improperly located to remove gas build up in the mine. Additionally, inspectors had found open switches with no enclosure to prevent arcs from igniting the gases. Today, the mines are closed, replaced by strip mines which have also closed.

The Oronogo Mutual Mining Company

For years, a series of other coal mines operated in the area. One of these was the National Coal & Coke Company, incorporated on December 8, 1906.

The firm was created by several residents of Bates with mining experience, and others involved in the industry. Articles from the time stated that the mine and plant would cost about $40,000, and that there would be a 400 horsepower power plant. Until sometime after 1936, a National Coal Spur was shown as being near Mile 14 on the Waldron Branch. The track had a capacity of 81 cars.

By the 1950s, the Oronogo Mutual Mine Tracks were shown at about the same location. In 1958, the tracks had a capacity of 60 cars, and then 26 cars in 1964. The tracks were not listed after that. The Oronogo Mutual Mining Company started with lead and zinc mining in the Oronogo mining district near Joplin, Missouri. The firm, founded in 1936, was owned by the Waring family, and mined lead and zinc at Joplin, and coal near Bates. The firm also leased land to other producers.

In 1946, the company operated the Oronogo Mutual Mining Company Strip Mine No. 2, also known as Bates Mine No. 2. The June 28, 1945, copy of the *Federal Register* stated that the coal was produced from the Upper and Lower Hartshorne Seams. The government report was part of a study that determined the quality and uses of various coal fields, and assigned the mines to various groupings for pricing purposes. "The Bates Mine of Oronogo Mutual Mining Company is hereby assigned Mine Index No. 1035 and its coals are classified in Production Group No. 9 of District No. 14."

The mining of coal continued until 1951, when the equipment used in the coal mining operation at Bates was put up for sale. On October 14, 1955, the rest of the assets were sold to Fenix and Scisson,

Inc., an Oklahoma corporation engaged in heavy construction and mineral exploration.

15.1 ARKANSAS HIGHWAY 28 – The railroad again has a grade crossing with Arkansas Highway 28, located east of Bates. Some sources state that there were several tracks in this area with names like Clark's Spur and Gipson.

The Community of Gipson

Gipson was actually a small community south of Bates. People began claiming land along the Poteau River by the late 1820s, with the Gipson family being among the first settlers. The Gipson Cemetery opened by 1875. During the 1880s, a town began to develop as several general stores opened. The largest was owned by James S. Gipson, who also established the Gipson post office in 1887. Gipson was murdered in February 1889 and his wife closed the store, with Albert S. Wood becoming the postmaster. At the time, Wood also owned what was described as a lucrative mercantile business in town. A school also operated at Gipson.

With the railroad building north of the community, and the new town of Bates being created, Gipson began to suffer. In May 1902, the post office at Gipson was moved to Bates. The Gipson School District closed in 1918 and consolidated with Bates. Today, the site of Gipson can be found where the Walker Mountain Road bridges the Poteau River.

Walker Mountain Road marks the location of the Bates railroad platform, as well as where the community of Gipson was once located to the south.

Wooden trestles like this one near Milepost 16 are a challenge for the railroad as it is clear that they haven't been modernized like those on the Heavener Subdivision.

The Heavener Sub: History Through the Miles

16.7 TYSON – This station existed during the 1930s and 1940s. The name of this small station causes a great deal of confusion. The station was here during the first half of the twentieth century, before the Tyson Foods Company was in the area. There was not a siding or depot here, but it was a train stop to receive and discharge traffic during the 1930s. The station was listed for years in copies of the *Official Guide*, but no location or milepost was ever provided.

It is not clear where the Tyson name came from, but there were several area families with the name Tyson. Additionally, Hans Tyson was the Kansas City Southern Roadmaster for the Arkansas Western and the mainline between Heavener and De Queen from 1910 until 1920. Hans Tyson was born in Denmark in 1852 and came to the United States in 1872. He soon became a track worker for Missouri Pacific and then a Division Roadmaster for the St. Louis & San Francisco. He managed a grain milling operation at Rolla, Missouri, before coming to the Kansas City Southern as Roadmaster. He retired in 1920.

19.1 CAUTHRON – The town of Cauthron was located on the Poteau River, just east of the coal fields, and was known more for its farming, ranching and timber. The community that formed here was at first known as Piney, but then began to be called Cauthron during the 1870s. The town was incorporated in 1876 by Asbury Tyler, who built a sawmill, grist mill, a blacksmith shop, a woodworking shop, plus several more stores. The name Cauthron apparently came from Judge Joe Cauthron of nearby Sebastian County.

The status of Cauthron appeared to change as a post office originally opened in 1871 and then closed in 1872. A high school opened at Cautheron about the same time, the first in Scott County. The post office reopened in 1878, and more stores moved to the town. Tyler continued to help Cauthron grow by donating lumber for a new schoolhouse and several churches.

The railroad was completed from Heavener to Cauthron by November 18, 1901, and a small wooden depot was built on the south side of the tracks. More stores moved to the depot area, and several sawmills were established alongside the railroad. J. G. Stout opened a cannery during the early 1900s to handle local farm products.

The Ozark Mountain Region Of Missouri and Arkansas As it Appears Along the Line of the Kansas City Southern Railway (1924) had information about Cauthron and its timber and farming businesses.

> *The surrounding country has an abundance of coal and timber and the latter is being manufactured by the B. R. Thaup sawmill, the product being yellow pine lumber. Cauthron ships annually from 375 to 450 bales of cotton, 3 to 10 carloads of live stock, 7 to 15 carloads of railroad ties and 40 to 50 carloads of pine lumber. During 1910 there were in cultivation in the immediate vicinity 600 acres in corn, 50 in oats, 1,450 in cotton and about 100 acres in fruit and truck. There are in Cauthron three general merchandise stores, two drug stores and a public school. Coal deposits that should be mined.*

The sawmills began to close as the timber was all cut by 1930. The town continued to shrink as residents moved elsewhere, and the school was consolidated with Waldron in 1940. In 1973, the post office closed. Today, Cauthron is an unincorporated community, located from the Poteau River and Arkansas Highway 28 northward to the railroad.

The railroad has nothing more than a mainline today passing through Cauthron. The railroad had a 10-car siding for the first few decades of the twentieth century, but it was gone by the 1950s. However, the station, located at the McDaniel Lane grade crossing, was shown in employee timetables through the 1970s.

Cauthron isn't marked by much on the railroad, but this sign identifies the location on the nearby highway.

Waldron Branch

Heading railroad-south towards Oliver, the tracks climb a grade of 1.2%. Much of the railroad was built to follow the natural profile of the land, leading to a series of climbs and falls as it crosses the many ridges and streams in the region.

Between Heavener and Waldron, the Waldron Branch was built with few large cuts and fills. Instead, as shown here, the grade simply climbed over the local ridges and then dropped back down to the streams that it crossed.

21.3 OLIVER – This is another small unincorporated community along the railroad and Poteau River that is not much more than a few farmhouses. The bottom lands along the river were some of the first settled, with farming immediately becoming important. Initially, this area was known as Harris for a local family. The Anthony family was another one of the early settlers, and their family cemetery (1859) became Oliver's Anthony Cemetery. The name of the community came from a third family, the Olivers, who settled several miles south of the Poteau River.

The mix of names caused some confusion, but the Oliver post office opened in 1903. The Arkansas Western Railway used the name Harris through late 1903, but was using Oliver by their July 1904 timetable. Oliver didn't grow much, and the post office closed in 1932 and the mail operations were moved to the Cauthron Post Office.

With the arrival of the Arkansas Western Railroad, several sawmills and lumber companies located in the area. According to newspaper reports, one of these was the Waldron Lumber Company, which in late 1901 planned to build a planing mill about two and a half miles east of Cauthron.

While the railroad through Harris opened in early 1902, no depot building was apparently built. During late 1914, there was a hearing by the Arkansas Railroad Commission to determine the need of a depot building at what was then known as Oliver. The request resulted in the construction of a "pagoda" which was abandoned in 1923, but a small platform remained on the north side of the tracks. The railroad kept a small four-car spur track at Oliver until the 1970s to handle the lumber business.

Dr. Florence Clyde Chandler was born in Oliver, Arkansas. So who is Dr. Chandler? Chandler was a plant geneticist with a broad background in tree-breeding and the induction of polyploidy (the quality of having one or more extra sets of chromosomes) in flowering plants. Using these skills, Dr.

Chandler helped develop a derivative for quinine, a malaria remedy, during World War II.

23.3 **BRYAN** – "Trains will stop at Tyson, Bryan and Anderson Crossing to receive and discharge traffic." This statement was in the 1936 employee timetable of KCS, when Bryan was shown as having no side tracks.

Bryan is an unincorporated community that was one of the stops along the railroad when it opened in 1901. Like much of western Arkansas, this area was settled starting in the 1820s, and by the Civil War, much of the region was made up of small farms. During the Civil War, the area was often patrolled by Union forces, but guerrilla actions also took place from supporters of both sides of the conflict. After the war, settlers moved back to the area as most of the towns and farms survived with little damage.

Two names were used for the area: Bryan and Center Point. The town that developed here seemed to be called Bryan, but the general area used the name Center Point for its location in Scott County. The Center Point School was established during the 1870s, and the Center Point Cemetery in the 1890s. When the railroad was built through the area, a team track was installed and the location became known as Bryan's Spur, or Bryan Spur. The Bryan Spur post office opened in May 1915, but closed in October of the same year, with all mail going to Hon. During the early 1950s, the Center Point schools were merged with the schools at Waldron, and almost everything else in the community basically went away or became part of other nearby communities. About all that marks the location is the Center Point Cemetery.

This sign points the way to the Centerpoint Cemetery, located at the former railroad station of Bates, Arkansas.

25.0 HON – Welcome to Valley Forge, then Poteau, and finally Hon. The history of the community states that Jackson Hon started a community here that was called Valley Forge. Jackson Hon and his family moved from Illinois to this area in 1836 and built a log cabin on the banks of the Poteau River, reportedly the first homestead in what would become Hon. In 1845, flooding forced the family to move away from the river, and then to a third home near Bull Creek.

As the town grew, especially after the Civil War, the name Poteau began to be used for the community since it was located on the bank of the river, between Poteau Mountain and Chalybeate Round Top. A post office using the name Poteau briefly opened in 1871, and then again in 1877. The town attracted a few businesses, and in 1880, the first church was established.

The construction of the Arkansas Western Railroad in late 1901 led to the establishment of a railroad depot at Poteau. In 1904, the railroad became part of Kansas City Southern, which already served a town named Poteau. That year, the railroad changed its station name to Hon, named after John Hon, the son of Jackson Hon. The name was used because some of the railroad route through the area was acquired from the Hon family, and John Hon was the postmaster. With the change in the railroad station name, the community and post office also changed their name.

One of the indications that you are at Hon, Arkansas, is this sign for the Hon Cemetery.

In 1907, it was reported that Hon had service from the Waldron Telephone Company, four stores, two churches, a cotton gin, a sawmill, and a school. By 1921, Lee Piles was operating a grist mill and a sawmill.

Like a number of towns along the Waldron Branch, *The Ozark Mountain Region Of Missouri and Arkansas As it Appears Along the Line of the Kansas City Southern Railway* (1924) had information about Hon, Arkansas.

> The village has two sawmills, manufacturing pine lumber, a cotton gin, grist mill, hotel, lodge hall, two churches and six general merchandise stores. The annual shipments of surplus products amount to 600 bales of cotton, about 4,000 to 5,000 pounds of poultry, 15 to 20 carloads of hardwood lumber, 5 to 10 carloads of railroad ties and 40 to 60 carloads of pine lumber.

Much of the farming was replaced by ranching and poultry by the 1970s, and the timber was gone several decades earlier. With the loss of population and businesses, the post office closed in 1973, with Ilene Syler serving as postmaster for the last thirty years. Today, Hon is an unincorporated community with the remains of a few businesses, and a scattering of houses over several blocks.

On August 20, 1989, KCS 788 was photographed pulling the Waldron Local through Hon. In front of the train is one of a number of cattle guards that once seemed to be everywhere on the line.

Waldron Branch

Until the late 1970s, Hon had a short siding shown to hold six cars. Not far east of town, the tracks cross several streams (Presley Branch and Bull Creek) and Arkansas Highway 28, and then turn to the southeast to reach Waldron.

27.2 POTEAU RIVER BRIDGE – The Poteau River is unique as it is the only north-flowing river in Oklahoma, starting two miles south of Bee Mountain near Waldron, Arkansas, and heading almost 150 miles to the Arkansas River at Belle Point in Fort Smith, Arkansas. While a few miles of the start and end of the river are in Arkansas, the rest is in Oklahoma, making it the seventh largest river in the state.

In the French language, poteau means post. There is a belief that early French explorers marked the river with a large post or stake to identify the river or to mark the territory.

This bridge is located in the middle of thick woods far from any roadway. It consists of several steel spans across the main channel, with timber trestles off each end. Here, the railroad is heading southeast towards Waldron.

29.8 ANDERSON – Anderson, named after a family who lived in this area, is located at the grade crossing with County Road 233, giving it the name Anderson Crossing in many documents. The Anderson family (Theodore and Sephronia Anderson, plus their five children) were actually relatively late settlers, not arriving here until the 1880s. The community never grew much due to being just a few miles from Waldron. While a short track was initially installed, it didn't last long. By 1936, the only services provided to Anderson by the railroad was stopping the mixed train "to receive and discharge traffic."

30.8 NEKOOSA WOOD YARD – Located just west of U.S. Highway 71 is a short spur track that was once used as a wood yard, where trucks could deliver cut timber for loading on rail cars for shipment to market. This track was listed in the 2002 KCS employee timetable and was shown to be 400 feet long. Nekoosa Papers operated a paper mill at Ashdown, Arkansas, for many years before being sold to Georgia Pacific. Pulpwood was loaded here for shipment to that mill.

On June 22, 2021, Watco 3842 and 3845 were parked on the west side of Waldron, waiting to pull the next westbound Arkansas Southern Railroad train.

31.1 TYSON FEED MILL – This feed mill supports poultry growers across western Arkansas and eastern Oklahoma. Arkansas Valley Incorporated began construction on the feed mill in 1960, and then added a processing plant and hatchery. The facility became Valmac Tasty Bird, and then Tyson Foods. The feed mill is the reason the Waldron Branch still exists, and Tyson is the largest employer in town. The 2002 KCS employee timetable showed that the Tyson Feed Mill track was 1150 feet long, but today almost every track in town is used to hold carloads of grain and other products for the company.

Tyson Foods is big, producing 20% of the chicken, beef, and pork in the United States. Tyson Foods started in 1931 when John W. Tyson moved to Springdale, Arkansas, and to feed his family, began buying chickens locally and selling them across the Midwest. The business grew rapidly during World War II as poultry was one of the few foods not rationed, and Tyson moved into chicken production. The company was incorporated in 1947 as Tyson Feed and Hatchery, Inc. During the late 1950s, the company built its first processing plant, meaning that it raised, processed and sold poultry, one of the first firms to control the entire process.

In 1963, Tyson's Foods went public, allowing it to continue to expand. The name became Tyson Foods in 1972, and other product lines were added throughout the 1980s. By 1990, Tyson Foods was the world's largest fully-integrated producer, processor, and marketer of poultry-based food products, and was quickly expanding its international market. Thanks to further expansion and several acquisitions, Tyson became the world's largest processor and marketer of chicken, beef, and pork by 2001. Since then, the company has continued to expand and the product names on the side of their trailers will surprise almost anyone.

This Tyson Foods feed mill is the reason that the Waldron Branch still exists.

For decades, this small 45-ton GE locomotive, carrying #205, has been at the Tyson Food's feed mill at Waldron. It was still there on a visit in June 2021.

31.3 WALDRON FURNITURE – This 300-foot spur track was listed in KCS employee timetables from at least 1970 until 2002. It was for the Waldron Furniture Manufacturing Corporation, a company that moved to Waldron from Fort Smith in 1953. One of the primary reasons cited for the move was to take advantage of the lower paid labor supply. However, within a few years, Waldron Furniture employed 400 workers who had the highest pay scale in town.

The company started as the Rush Manufacturing Company, incorporated in Fort Smith in 1946, and located at 101 North Fourth Street. Even after much of the manufacturing was moved to Waldron, many of the parts and supplies came from Fort Smith. In 1980, the furniture company was acquired by the Somers Corporation, which had been created in 1977 to acquire Mersman Tables, another large furniture manufacturer. The company and factory building are now gone at Waldron.

Downtown Waldron is just a few blocks south of the Main Street grade crossing at Milepost 31.4. Waldron is the largest community on the line, but only has about 3500 residents.

The Heavener Sub: History Through the Miles

A three-track yard remains at Waldron, surrounded by several former shippers, but it is seldom used by the railroad today.

31.8 WALDRON – Waldron was one of the key cities of the original plan for the Arkansas Western Railroad. The town was already a community of about 500 people when the railroad was built. The initial history involves the settlement of the Featherston family, and the fight between the Featherston brothers William Grandison (W. G.) and Edward. W. G. arrived at what would become Waldron in 1832, bringing his mother, wife, and four children with him. He built a store and tavern along a road that would become Main Street, and then became postmaster of the Poteau Valley post office in 1838. The community was located at an elevation of 665 feet on the South Fork of the Poteau River in the Ouachita Mountains.

Edward Featherstone settled to the northeast and created the community of Winfield. A battle over control of the post office soon took place, and Edward somehow had it moved to his town in 1843. Part of the reason the post office moved was the battle over the new county seat of Scott County. In 1840, the county seat moved to Winfield, and the post office was needed there. However, in 1845, W. G. Featherston donated ten acres of land for a new county seat, which he had surveyed and platted by engineer and surveyor W. P. Waldron. The county seat moved to the new town later that year, which was named after Waldron, who had designed the community. In 1846, the post office closed at Winfield and moved back to Poteau Valley, which was by then officially named Waldron. The first courthouse was the log barn of W. G. Featherston, and it wasn't replaced until 1859 when a new courthouse was built next door.

Waldron participated in the 1850 census, and reported a population of 90. With a growth in local businesses, Waldron was incorporated as a town on December 17, 1852. Most of the local business dealt with farming and timber. In particular, corn and cotton were traded in town, often through the grist mills and cotton gins that developed alongside the river. A road that connected Fort Smith and Texas passed through Waldron, and during the Civil War, Union forces attacked the town four times in 1863 trying to secure the route. Eventually the town was taken and parts of it were burned. After the war, a number of residents returned and the population was 162 by the 1870 census. During the 1870s, supporters of different political factions became violent, especially as part of the Brooks-Baxter War of 1874. This war was an open conflict between the supporters of two candidates for governor of Arkansas. More than 200 were killed statewide, with more than thirty around Waldron alone, and it took Federal action to stop the fighting. The end of fighting put a Democrat in office, ending what was essentially Republican rule and the era of Reconstruction. A new incorporation of Waldron took place in 1875.

During the late 1800s, Waldron grew slowly as the county seat attracted more businesses, especially those that did work with the county government. The twentieth century began with a population of 487, but the town began to boom when the Arkansas Western Railroad opened its line between Heavener and Waldron by January 1, 1902. By 1908, Waldron featured The Kansas Wholesale Lumber Company (northeast side of town), Ragon-Bates Lumber (south of the tracks and west of Main Street), Waldron Lumber Company (north of the tracks and west of Main Street), and the cotton gin and flour mill of R. A. Castleberry (alongside the Poteau River north of The Kansas Wholesale Lumber Company). Along Main Street for several blocks around the courthouse were the typical general stores, restaurants, hotels, banks, groceries, drug stores, and similar businesses. The railroad depot was located east of Main Street on the south side of the tracks.

By 1910, the population had grown by 85% to 900 residents. Within a few years, The Kansas Wholesale Lumber Company mill had been leased to the Scott County Land & Lumber Company, but it was noted as "plant is closed down temporarily" in 1913. Where the Waldron Lumber Company once stood was G. L. Bird's gin and saw mill. As the 1920s began, the town featured two newspapers (*Advance Reporter* and *Scott County Record*), a bank, telephones (Waldron Telephone Exchange), electricity and a cold storage plant (Waldron Light & Ice Co.), two lumber mills (Scott County Land & Lumber and the Waldron Planing Mill Company), a canning factory (J. T. Forrester), a flour mill, a brick factory, and a soda pop plant. The railroad also handled livestock with a one-pen stockyard.

The December 1927 issue of the *Port Arthur Route Agricultural and Industrial Bulletin* had a substantial article about the communities along the Kansas City Southern in Arkansas and Oklahoma. Among the cities covered was Waldron. The article stated that Waldron, located at an altitude of 700 feet above sea level and with a population of 1400, was an important business community along the Arkansas Western Railway line. Details about the community were included as follows.

> *The town is compact and substantially built, nearly all of the business buildings being brick and stone, most of them two-story structures. Waldron has seven attractive church buildings, a commodious eight room, two-story high school and numerous dwellings. Among the institutions of Waldron are five hotels, two lodge and assembly halls, a public library, two telephone companies, a planing mill, livery barn, electric light and ice plant, shingle mill, gas company, bottling works, flour mill, ice factory, several cotton gins, three grist mills, brickyard, county court house, and the "Advance Reporter" weekly newspaper.*

> *The shipments of surplus products in an ordinary year amount to about 4,177 bales of cotton, 125,000 pounds of poultry, 275 cases of eggs, one carload of horses, 27 of cattle, one of hogs. 21,000 gallons of cream, 5 carloads of potatoes, 370 carloads of lumber, 25 of railroad ties and several hundred crates of strawberries and cantaloupes.*

During the 1920s, a number of agricultural products were shipped by rail from Waldron, including watermelons, Irish potatoes, sweet potatoes, Elberta Peaches, green beans, cucumbers, Bermuda onions, and strawberries. Both the Waldron Truck Growers Association and the Scott County Truck Growers Association shipped many of these products to national markets. Additionally, lumber, farm supplies, merchandise for local stores, and other products moved in and out of Waldron. Waldron was also a regional center of banking with the First National Bank and the Bank of Waldron.

As with many rural towns in the region, much of the farming and timber industry went away by World War II, but Waldron benefitted from the concentration of stores and other business, which allowed its population to continue to grow. By the 1980s, the population was more than 2600, and several industries were located here. These included a large poultry feed mill and processing plant, a pulpwood yard, a furniture factory, a pole yard, and STI/Thermo Fisher Environmental Industries.

Waldron currently has a population of about 3500, with a number of restaurants and gas stations along U.S. Highway 71 on the west side of town.

Downtown, much of the old business district is active and now carries the title of Waldron Commercial Historic District, listed on the National Register of Historic Places. The Waldron schools are located on the very west side of town. Waldron also has a strong connection to music, including composer Anne Shannon Demarest, who was a noted concert pianist and teacher who also composed music for the Alfred Music Company. Another recent connection is Ashley McBryde, a country music singer and songwriter who was named New Artist of the Year during the 53rd Annual Country Music Association Awards in 2019.

The Railroad at Waldron

The railroad arrived at Waldon by January 1, 1902, and immediately impacted the community. Several lumber companies located here to handle the timber from the surrounding Ouachita Mountains. Farm products were shipped all along the line. To the north of Waldron were coal mines, while to the south were a number of lumber companies and sawmills. For most of the line's existence, Waldron has been the big town along the route.

While a depot had been built just east of Main Street, the agency was closed during much of the Great Depression, with the work handled at Heavener. In 1936, a dispatcher telephone was used with no telegraph service available. A wye track, 37-car siding, and other tracks with a total capacity of 29 cars were shown to be at Waldron. After World War II, the KCS agent-operator was back, working 8am-5pm Tuesday through Saturday in 1958. There was still a wye, a 24-car siding, and other tracks with a total of 43 cars of capacity. Throughout the 1960s and until the late 1970s, the agent-operator handled the business at the wooden depot 8am-5pm weekdays.

At the time, there were still a number of rail shippers at Waldron. The Southwestern Wood Preserving Company had a track where poles and piling was loaded. A pulp wood yard and chip mill, the Waldron Furniture Manufacturing Corporation, B&B Cedar, Citgo butane, and the feed mill provided business for the railroad. During the 1970s, trains operated three days a week and handled 40 to 50 freight cars a trip. As the feed mill grew, the local tracks were used more and more for their cars, especially as the other businesses closed.

In the 2002 KCS employee timetable, the feed mill and furniture factory tracks were shown separately, and Waldron was listed as having 950 feet of tracks. On October 9, 2005, the Arkansas Southern Railroad, owned by Watco, began operations over the line. The line was shown as the Waldron Industrial Complex by the Arkansas Southern, and it stated that the line extended from Milepost 3.0 to the end of track at Milepost 33.0, with permission to operate to Milepost 0 at Heavener. The track was shown to be excepted track, meaning no passenger trains, no more than five cars with hazardous materials on any train, and a maximum speed of ten miles per hour. For the KCS, the line is now the Waldron Industrial Spur (Mileposts 0.0-4.0). The company also states that the Arkansas Southern Railroad begins at Milepost 4.0.

Waldron Branch

32.3 END OF LINE – The end of the Waldron Branch is at the grade crossing with Arkansas Highway 248 – Greenridge Road, but records show that it is actually at Milepost 33.0. South of here was the Forester Extension, a line to the timber of the Caddo River Lumber Company. When the railroad between Heavener and Waldron was first planned, it was supposed to go further east to Hot Springs, so building to the southeast was not totally unplanned. However, the reason for the construction changed from reaching several railroads at the resort city of Hot Springs, to reaching the large sawmill that was to be built at what became Forester.

Planning for the line began in 1928 as the Caddo River Lumber Company was changing locations. A large sawmill was anticipated, and a railroad was needed to haul the finished lumber to market. Caddo River Lumber met with various railroad officials, including C. E. Forrester, a leading businessman at Waldron and a director of the Arkansas Western. Forrester was the primary driver behind the construction plans, and the lumber company named its new mill town after him, although with a small spelling change.

With an expected cost of $425,000, the railroad needed traffic guarantees, and Caddo River Lumber promised to ship at least 30 million board feet of lumber each year for a period of 15 years, or about 1500 carloads a year. With the promised traffic volumes, the Kansas City Southern bought the first mortgage bonds issued by the Arkansas Western. With cash in hand, contractor Williamson and Williams of Batesville, Arkansas, began construction on June 26, 1929, after the railroad received approval from the Interstate Commerce Commission on April 23, 1929.

As the grade was built, KCS crews installed the bridges and track. The new line was built with 85-pound rail on white oak ties. Because of the number of streams crossed, there were 24 bridges in the 23.2 miles of track. One of these bridges has been described as "a monstrous wooden trestle." The line was also very mountainous, with deep rock cuts and high fills, steep grades (2.5%), and sharp 10-degree curves. Leaving Waldron, the line climbed 360 feet to a summit at Milepost 37.8, and then another one at Milepost 41.1. The railroad then followed the Fourch La Fave River and Cedar Creek before reaching Forester at an elevation of 655 feet, just a ten foot difference from Waldron.

The railroad began service on September 1, 1930, but the mill at Forester wasn't yet in operation, and it was another year before the operation was in full production. The first regular schedule carried the date November 9, 1931, and thrice-weekly mixed train service began between Heavener and Forester on Monday, Wednesday and Friday, returning the following days. Switching was performed at Forester after the mixed train arrived.

The lumber was cut around Forester by the early 1950s, and the mill shut down on April 15, 1953. On April 24, 1954, the railroad applied to the Interstate Commerce Commission for permission to abandon the line south of Milepost 35.1. There was no opposition since Forester was basically abandoned, and permission was received on September 9, 1954. Later, the line was cut back to near here with approval from the Interstate Commerce Commission on July 17, 1975.

Waldron Branch

The current end of the Waldron Branch can be found at the grade crossing with Arkansas Highway 248 in Waldron.

37.7 ROSS MOUNTAIN – Heading south from Waldron, the railroad first followed the Poteau River, and then curved to the southwest and came alongside old U.S. Highway 71. Parts of this grade are now used by driveways and Park Avenue near the ball fields at Sodie Davidson Park. In this area was once a spur track that served several different shippers over the years. Just to the south, the railroad passed through a gap in Bohnstein Hill, alongside U.S. Business Highway 71.

The line then curved eastward on a grade now used by Mahaffey Lane, and continued a climb of 2.5% to the summit on Ross Mountain, a part of

Piney Mountain. The peak of the summit was found at Milepost 37.8, with an elevation of 1020 feet. A dispatcher telephone was located at Milepost 37.7. It was used by train crews to report their progress, and often the need to return down the hill to fetch the rest of their train up the steep hill.

For trains heading south towards Forester, the track began a series of drops and climbs as it headed towards the summit of Dutch Creek Mountain (1105 feet at Milepost 41.1). In this area, a short part of the grade is now used by Manorcrest Road and Primrose Lane. After crossing a large pasture, the old grade crosses Arkansas Highway 250 just west of Swift Bend. It then turns south and the grade is used by Scottsboro Road, which connects to Tram Road.

Several parts of the abandoned line between Waldron and Forester can be driven today, including this short stretch near the Sodie Davidson Park at Waldron.

Waldron Branch

40.8 CALLAHAN SPUR – Callahan Spur (940 feet of elevation), also known as Callahan Siding, was located near the top of grade on Dutch Creek Mountain (Milepost 41.1). In 1936, there was a seven-car spur track and a dispatcher telephone here. The spur track was sometimes used when the northbound train had to double the 2.0% grade due to the weight of the cars being pulled. The dispatcher telephone was used to communicate with the dispatcher about the train's progress.

Trains heading south to Forester would have soon passed through a deep cut at the summit of Dutch Creek Mountain, and then around a horseshoe curve as the tracks work back down Dutch Creek Mountain into the Hazel Creek valley. The railroad stays in the Dutch Creek Mountains until it passes between Gilbreath (to west) and Bill Hunt Mountain to east.

43.4 HORSESHOE CURVE – Heading south into the Hazel Creek valley, the railroad grade makes a series of large curves. The curves require a number of cuts and fills. Many of the fills were originally timber trestles, and culverts and lots of dirt have replaced them.

The horseshoe curve can easily be seen on maps, but is hard to recognize when driving the grade due to the deep cuts.

The Heavener Sub: History Through the Miles

The Horseshoe Curve at Milepost 43.4 on the Waldron Branch is almost impossible to see since much of it is in a series of deep cuts, as shown in this photograph.

44.2 HAZEL CREEK – There was a dispatcher telephone at Milepost 44.2, just north of the large Hazel Creek Trestle.

44.4 HAZEL CREEK BRIDGE – Hazel Creek forms on the south side of Dutch Creek Mountain, north of Hart Ridge and Salt Lake Mountain. The stream flows southwards less than ten miles before flowing into the Fourche La Fave. In this area, Hazel Creek has created a deep but narrow gorge.

To cross Hazel Creek, KCS bridge crews built a large wooden trestle, officially known as Trestle A-45. The bridge was 686 feet long and 58 feet high, and was considered to be the scenic highlight of the line. Much of the abandoned rail grade in the area is now used as Tram Road, or County Road 35. This road connects Arkansas Highway 28 at Parks with Arkansas Highway 250, a distance of about 8 miles.

When driving Tram Road, look for this low-water bridge. A short distance to the east is where the large Hazel Creek Bridge once stood.

To the east of Tram Road at Milepost 44.4 are the remains of the Hazel Creek Bridge, a large wooden trestle that was 58 feet high and 686 feet long. The two approach fills can be seen in the woods, and a large number of old piles can be found scattered through the area, such as these two located on the south approach.

Besides the large fills and many wooden piles, a few other bridge parts can be found such as this anchor bolt, once used to hold a wooden brace to a piling.

45.8 PARKS – For many years, Parks was an important station on the line south of Waldron as it was in a relatively flat location. There was a dispatcher telephone here, as well as a 15-car team track that was used for log loading. Being at the base of the northbound 2.0% grade, Parks was sometimes used to double the hill. Heading southeast, the railroad followed the Fourche La Fave river valley to Cedar Creek, which it followed uphill to Forester. A few traces of the line can be found along the north side of Highway 28.

The location of Parks can be confusing. Today, the town is alongside Arkansas Highway 28, where the post office, several churches, and the old school can be found. However, what was shown as Parks Railroad Station was actually 1.5 miles north of Highway 28 on Brush Creek Road, today just south of a series of chicken houses.

Parks is an old settlement, with the first farms established in the 1820s. Enough people had arrived that Cyrus Parks was elected Justice of the Peace for the area in 1836. The next year, the community of White Church was established around the new white Methodist church. In 1838, an application for a post office was approved and Cyrus Parks was named the first postmaster, thus the town changed its name to Parks. Being one of the first post offices in Scott County, it attracted several businesses such as a general store, blacksmith shop, grist mill, and sawmill. A postal road also connected Parks to surrounding towns and cities.

As with many communities in the region, the Civil War and Reconstruction negatively impacted Parks, and its post office closed from the late 1860s until 1870. Several cemeteries were also founded during the period, including the Parks Cemetery and the Hawkins Cemetery. A school district was created in 1882, known as White Church School. Although the name continued to be used for several generations, the white Methodist church burned down in 1891. A telephone connection with Waldron was built in 1907, connecting Parks further with the outside world.

The Great Depression hurt area farmers, but the construction of the railroad through Parks in 1929-1930 did open up new markets. A new school opened in 1940, a project of the Works Projects Administration (WPA). The school at Parks fully merged with Waldon in 1966 and was closed. The WPA-built school is now used as a community center and was placed on the National Register of Historic Places in 2002. A few stores and the post office remain around the Parks area, and hunting, fishing and other activities in the nearby Ouachita National Forest help keep the community busy.

The Parks schoolhouse, built by the Works Projects Administration in 1940 and listed on the National Register of Historic Places, still stands at Parks, Arkansas.

Driving Tram Road over Dutch Creek Mountain

Much of the old railroad grade over Dutch Creek Mountain is now used by a series of roads, with Tram Road covering the middle section. The route is a series of county roads, and while not paved, they are good roads that almost any type of motor vehicle can get over. Almost the entire route is wooded, passing through parts of the Ouachita National Forest, with a number of scenic views. Driving northward from Parks is recommended as this end is clearly marked, and it allows driving uphill almost the entire distance instead of using brakes for almost the entire eight miles.

At Parks, head north on Brush Creek Road – County Road 17. This road is just west of the old Parks schoolhouse. The road is paved for a short distance, and then becomes graded gravel. Look for Bellevue Road 0.3 miles from Highway 28. Turn east on Bellevue Road to find the old railroad grade where the road turns to the north. The grade heads east from here, staying on the north side of Schoolhouse Ridge. The railroad once headed across a series of fields and streams, and came beside Arkansas Highway 28 at the Fourche LaFave River. To the north, the railroad looped around a series of poultry houses and across several pastures before crossing Brush Creek Road at the location of the Parks Railroad Station. None of this route can be followed, so return to Brush Creek Road and turn north.

Heading north, the old railroad grade is to the east and on the other side of a low ridge. About 1.5 miles north of Arkansas Highway 28, the road comes alongside an old poultry house. This is where the Parks Railroad Station, as shown on various maps, was located. The old grade can barely be made out as it crosses the road. Head on north to the road junction, located 2.0 miles north of Arkansas Highway 28. Turn left and climb the low ridge.

If you look into the brush at KCS Milepost 45.3, about 2.3 miles north of Arkansas Highway 28, you might be able to find this old Tram Road sign. Even if you don't find the sign, the drive is definitely worth the time.

In 0.3 miles is another road junction, and Tram Road (County Road 35) is the route to the right. For years, a battered Tram Road sign has stood in the brush to the left. In the same area, the old railroad grade can be found as it comes in from the southeast. Heading north on Tram Road, you are now on the Forester Extension of the Arkansas Western. The stiff grade limited the number of loaded freight cars on each train. In 1.0 miles, look for the concrete low-water bridge. In the woods to the east is the site of the Hazel Creek Bridge, the largest wooden structure on the line.

Heading north, the large horseshoe curve is in less than a mile – look for the long curve to the left that is located in a series of deep cuts. Several more curves are also found in the area, as well as a series of deep cuts and large fills. The top of the grade is 3.5 miles north of the Hazel Creek Bridge. Note that the county road stays on top of the hill, while the old railroad grade is in a deep cut to the east. The final mile of the road to Arkansas Highway 250 passes by a number of houses and farms. This part of the road uses the name Scottsboro Road, County Road 333. Unfortunately, no sign carries its name at Highway 250 except for a campground sign for a local hunting club.

49.4 FOURCHE LA FAVE RIVER BRIDGE – This bridge included a 250-foot through truss span over the Fourche La Fave River. It was the only such structure on the line, and as trains got heavier, a few wooden pile bents were installed to strengthen it. Timber pile trestle spans were located off each end.

The Fourche La Fave River, often shown as Fourche LaFave River, starts in southern Scott County south of Waldron, Arkansas, and flows about 150 miles northeast to the Arkansas River. It drains much of the northern part of the Ouachita Mountains, historically flooding whenever a heavy rain fell in the mountains. To try to solve this flooding problem, Lake Nimrod was created in 1942 to hold back much of the river's water. This was not the first federal government involvement with the Fourche La Fave. On March 3, 1879, Congress passed an act to improve the river, and work began to make it navigable to Perryville. This work included the dynamiting of shoals along the stream, and the project was considered finished in 1889.

The name Fourche La Fave has created some argument over its origin. It is agreed that Fourche is a French word that means "fork," especially of a stream or road, thus a fork of the Arkansas River. However, different sources attribute La Fave to different families or people. *The Origin of Certain Place Names in the United States* by Henry Gannett (1905), for example, states that La Fave could refer to a family that once lived along the river or to early settler Peter La Fave. Other sources credit Peter La Fave with being the first to explore the river, and with giving it its name. During the early 1800s, the Dunban and Hunter exploration reported that a family named LeFevre lived on the river, while other explorers spelled the name LeFeve. The name probably came from some part of this family, but the spelling has certainly changed.

This sign marks the Arkansas Highway 28 crossing of the Fourche La Fave River. The former Arkansas Western bridge was once located nearby, and parts of the old grade can still be found in the area.

53.2 CEDAR CREEK – After crossing the Fourche La Fave River, the railroad continued to follow the valley to Cedar Creek, where it turned southward to follow Big Cedar Creek to Forester. Cedar Creek was a named location, but there were no side tracks by 1936.

The town of Cedar Creek was formed near the south bank of the Fourche La Fave, between Little Cedar Creek and Big Cedar Creek. Because many early farmers wanted to be along a stream, the community actually was spread along the two Cedar Creeks, covering several miles of territory. This eventually turned into a battle as each faction attempted to become the dominant location and the center of the town. Although actually formed in 1852, Little Cedar and Big Cedar competed to be the main Cedar Creek. A post office opened using the name Cedar Creek on November 16, 1852, as some mining of several exposed veins of lead and zinc took place.

The first school opened after the Civil War, using one of the first church buildings in the area. Located on the west bank of Little Cedar Creek, this school and a nearby store made the area the center of that part of the community. The Waldron Telephone Company built a line through Cedar Creek in 1907. By the middle 1910s, a few other businesses were also operating here, including the Will Clymer and George Crutchfield cotton gin, the Will Clymer sawmill, and the A. M. Abbott cotton gin. Two general stores also were open and doing business.

The battle between the two parts of Cedar Creek continued when the post office was moved from Little Cedar to Big Cedar in 1919. In 1929, the Big Cedar School District became the Forester School District to handle the demand from the families working at the new Caddo River Lumber Company sawmill. The Cedar Creek post office also moved to Forester in 1930. The post office came back to Cedar Creek in 1953 when the mill was shut down and sold off. With the loss of most of the business in the Cedar Creek Valley, the school was merged with Waldron and closed, and the post office closed in 1973. The area today is a scattering of farms, cattle, and lots of poultry houses.

This sign on Arkansas Highway 28 points the way to the former logging town of Forester, Arkansas.

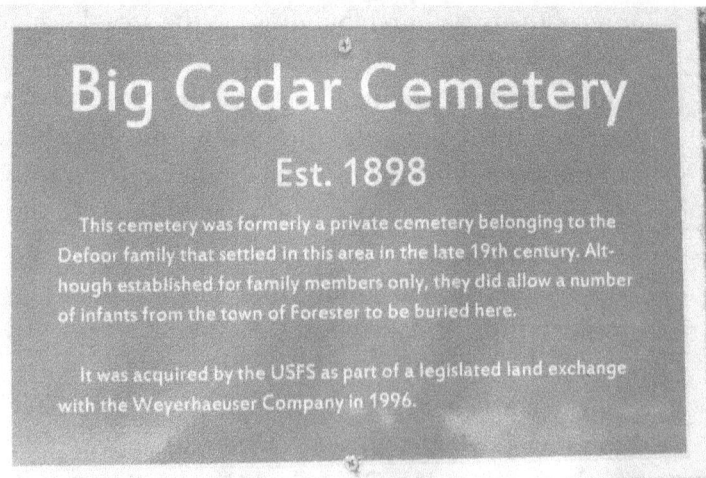

In 1996, the U.S. Forest Service acquired the land in the Forester area, including the Big Cedar Cemetery. This sign explains the history of the cemetery, and of the land acquisition.

55.9 FORESTER – Forester was THE reason for extending the railroad south from Waldron. Until 1929, this was just a spot in the woods at the junction of Big Cedar Creek and the West Fork of Big Cedar Creek. However, it was soon a town of 1300 people and the home of the Caddo River Lumber Company mill and town.

Thomas Whitaker Rosborough started his Caddo River Lumber Company in 1906 at Rosboro, in Pike County, Arkansas. After several dozen years of logging, he moved the company to Scott County to reach new timber. At the former location, the company operated miles of railroad tracks, both as private logging lines and as lines that were hoped to grow into common carrier operations. The company expanded and started operations at Glenwood (Pike County) and Mauldin (near Mount Ida in Montgomery County), making it the second largest timber firm in the Ouachita Mountains.

One major challenge for Rosborough was that he regularly employed black workers, often bringing them with him from other operations. Since the population of most towns in the Ouachita Mountains were all-white, several towns such as Waldron and Mount Ida rejected his application to locate sawmills there. Therefore, as timber was bought in Scott and Yell counties, the new company town of Forester and its mills were created to avoid many of the racial problems. The timing of Caddo River Lumber couldn't have been worse as large amounts of money were spent to build the new town and mill complex at Forester just as the Great Depression hit the economy. The sheds and planing mill at Glenwood burned in 1936, and the complex was shut down the next year. The company was out of timber elsewhere, so Forester became the center of logging for the firm.

Forester, named for C. E. Forrester who was associated with the railroad and business development in Waldron, was a true company town. It included 500 company houses, a company store, a large 28-room two-story hotel, drug store, service station, garage, theater, barber shop, beauty shop, churches and two schools. There was also a garage with car sales, a ballpark and stadium, a community hall/Masonic Lodge, a water system and power plant, and a company-paid doctor. The town was laid out in sections, with the main part of town known as Green Town, named for the green houses that white workers lived in. Other sections were called Angel Town (second largest section), Cannon Town, Water Tank Road, the Section Houses, and Happy Holler (the smallest section). While Rosborough hired black workers, he also gave them their own section (The Quarters, or Red Town for the color of their houses) which featured its own church, school and entertainment center. As the town was being completed in 1930, the Cedar Creek post office moved to Forester.

The mill grew to become the largest and most productive in Arkansas. It featured a 1000-foot-long by 80-foot-wide lumber shed that could store millions of board feet of kiln-dried, planed lumber. Some of the buildings were moved to Forester from Mauldin, while other parts of the complex were built new. When completed, the Forester mill had a nominal capacity of 40 million feet/year, with a total investment of more than $700,000.

The railroad was completed to Forester by September 1, 1930, and irregular service began almost immediately, bringing in materials, supplies and workers. It wasn't until the summer of 1931 that logging began, and then the mill started full production during the fall. Logging was conducted using two basic methods. The first was the old style of using mule teams and wagons, a practice of several contractors until about 1940 when they began using trucks. The second method was the more traditional practice of Caddo River Lumber – a standard gauge logging railroad. The logging firm had used logging railroads since it began, and some of the company's equipment had been brought to Forester over a temporary line from Mauldin, Arkansas. These logging lines grew to about 70 miles long, and the company operated as many as six steam locomotives from their Forester shops.

A fire at the Forester mill in 1938 did a great deal of damage, but it was quickly rebuilt. The town and mill at Forester stayed active through the Depression, but the Rosborough family seemed to be tiring of the Arkansas operations, and started a mill in Oregon by 1939. The Caddo River Lumber Company was soon sold to Hal Shaffer. By this time, the Arkansas operations were limited to the mill at Forester, plus timber cuttings in several places in the Ouachita Mountains.

The Caddo River Lumber Company boomed during World War II due to a number of military and government contracts, accelerating the use of the timber owned by the company. After the war, production dropped and the population of Forester declined to about 800. Paved roads were built close to town and trucks began to replace the logging railroads. This wasn't the first time that Caddo River Lumber used trucks, as the company acquired two log trucks in 1918. Another sign of the future plans for the logging company was that the cut-over land was generally being sold to the U.S. Forest Service, not being replanted for future cuttings.

On August 23, 1948 (some sources state July 17, 1945), the Caddo River Lumber Company was sold to Dierks Lumber & Coal, the only other major timber company operating in the Ouachita Mountains. In 1952, the timber was mostly cut and the sawmill cut its last company log on September 3, 1952, at 2:20pm. The planing mill kept operating into early the next year processing millions of feet of rough lumber from the storage sheds at Forester. With some clean-up work, the mill and planer were shut down for good on April 15, 1953. The town soon followed and everything was sold off by late 1953. The railroad was gone by the end of 1954. This was the end of a town that was for many years larger than the county seat of Waldron.

Today, little marks the location of Forester except a few foundations and other ruins in the woods. The largest collection of ruins is at the Forester Reunion Park, maintained by the Forester Historical Society. The park, founded in 1983, includes many of the old mill foundations and the mill pond, where logs were held before being moved into the sawmill. Located on Billy R. Wilson Road off Scott County Roads 25 and 26, the nine-acre reunion park includes camping facilities, memorials, a large sign at the pavilion with photos of Forester residents, and a 1½ mile-long interpretive trail.

If you want to read more about Forester, pick up the book *Sawmill* by Kenneth L. Smith. It has a full chapter about Forester, and many other pages about the work of the Caddo River Lumber Company. You can also visit the site of Forester and read all of the historic signs.

This sign welcomes you to Forester, Arkansas, a former sawmill town created by the Caddo River Lumber Company.

Many of the large concrete foundations of the sawmill at Forester still exist. This one stands next to the mill pond at the Forester Reunion Park.

The Heavener Sub: History Through the Miles

The 1.5-acre mill pond at Forester was the destination of many logging trains, and was still used when trucks took over much of the movement of logs from the surrounding hills.

Signs like this mark many of the features of the town of Forester. This one describes the lumber sheds, described as being "the largest in the South."

The Arkansas Western Railway at Forester

The rail line from Cedar Creek to Forester was rough, starting with a 1.25% grade with a final short stretch of 3.0%. Fortunately, most loads headed north to Waldron and on to Heavener.

The Arkansas Western was the rail connection required to allow the sawmill at Forester to prosper. Despite this, the service was never much more than a tri-weekly mixed train that handled both passengers and freight. At first, the local arrived at Forester at 12:30pm on Monday, Wednesday and Friday, and departed the next morning at 8:30am. In 1936, Second Class Mixed Train No. 3 was scheduled to arrive at 4:30pm on Monday, Wednesday and Friday. After unloading any passengers, the crew then switched the Caddo River Lumber complex before spending the night at the Forester Hotel, located near the yellow railroad depot. The crew and train were scheduled to depart the next morning at 10:00am as Second Class Mixed Train No. 4. These northbound trains were limited to 10-12 cars because of the 2% grade up Dutch Creek Mountain north of Parks.

During the first decade of the mill, Caddo River Lumber also switched the mill, using their fleet of steam locomotives that also headed into the woods to bring the timber back to Forester. After the Dierks Lumber & Coal Company acquired the Forester operation, they kept at least two steam locomotives at the mill, even after trucks took over almost all of the work hauling logs by 1950.

Being the end of the line and located at a private logging town, the Arkansas Western Railway didn't have a large number of facilities at Forester. There was a 20' x 60' frame depot at an elevation of 655 feet, but there was never a regular agent assigned to Forester. The depot did house a dispatcher telephone and a train register in 1936. Nearby was a water tank, a wye, yard tracks with a capacity of 24 freight cars, and a 24-car siding. There were also several section houses located north of the mill complex. At the Caddo River Lumber mill were several loading platforms that could accommodate 25 cars.

With the mill being shut down, only a few loads of pulpwood, logs, and machinery were moved by the railroad. Rail service was down to one train a week when the Arkansas Western filed an application to abandon the line from Walden to Forester on April 24, 1954. All of the railroad facilities were removed when the railroad was abandoned later that year.

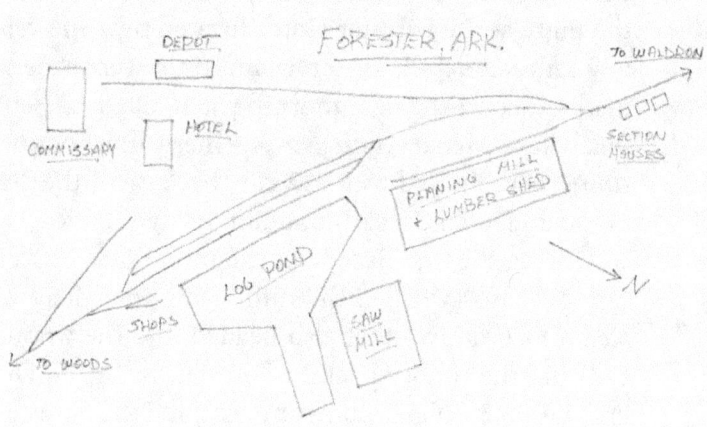

This sketch shows the basic railroad layout at Forester, Arkansas. The Arkansas Western (KCS) line headed down Williams Boulevard, the main road north to Arkansas Highway 28, to reach the depot. The tracks to the east alongside the log pond were used for interchange between the Arkansas Western and the logging railroad, and to dump logs into the log pond. A long spur track also served the planing mill and lumber sheds. While KCS had no shops here, the logging railroad of Caddo River Lumber did, located just south of the log pond and sawmill. Sketch by Barton Jennings.

About the Author

Barton Jennings grew up in Arkansas, spending years exploring the various railroad lines throughout the state. He has written numerous articles for magazines like *Trains*, *Railfan & Railroad*, and *Pacific Rail News*. Several of these articles covered the Kansas City Southern's Heavener Subdivision. He has also written books about area railroads such as the Arkansas & Missouri; the Missouri & North Arkansas; and the Rock Island's Choctaw Route.

Additionally, for almost three decades, Barton Jennings has been organizing charter passenger trains and writing the route descriptions, both for planning purposes and for the enjoyment of the passengers. These trips have been in all areas of the United States, often covering operations that haven't seen a passenger train in decades. He has also had the pleasure in riding the trips of other organizations, including a charter passenger train over the Heavener Subdivision, where some of the material for this book was collected.

His house has several rooms full of books, timetables and other documents about this and other railroads – important research items from a time long before today's internet. Today, Bart Jennings, after years working in the railroad industry, is a professor emeritus of supply chain management and teaches transportation operations. He also still teaches regulatory issues for the railroad industry, a way to stay in touch with the industry he loves.

The Heavener Sub: History Through the Miles

The author doing research for this book at Anderson, Missouri. Photo by Sarah Jennings.

www.ingramcontent.com/pod-product-compliance
Lightning Source LLC
Chambersburg PA
CBHW071946070526
44583CB00015B/1090